ISSUES OF THE SIXTIES

ISSUES

OF THE *SIXTIES*

EDITED BY *Leonard Freedman*
University Extension
University of California, Los Angeles

Cornelius P. Cotter
Stanford University

WADSWORTH PUBLISHING COMPANY, INC., BELMONT, CALIFORNIA

ISSUES OF THE SIXTIES
Leonard Freedman
Cornelius P. Cotter

FIRST PRINTING, AUGUST 1961
SECOND PRINTING, JUNE 1962
THIRD PRINTING, SEPTEMBER 1962

L.C. CAT. CARD NO.: 61-15837 9-17-82

PRINTED IN THE UNITED STATES OF AMERICA

087821

PREFACE

Challenging problems and great changes confront America in the decade ahead. The central theme of *Issues of the Sixties* is the impact of change—scientific and technological, social and political—upon our ideas, our aspirations, and our institutions. The major issues of this decade are, of course, redolent of those with which other generations of Americans have grappled. There are certain durable elements in the environments of successive generations, links that keep the future tied to the past. But if the vehicles of tomorrow travel on the roads of yesterday, they will nonetheless be significantly different; and if the emotions of man run the same gamut as they did in the age of Thackeray, their control, their significance, and their context will be vastly different in a space vehicle. Tomorrow will be similar to yesterday in the same way that a wheel on a jet airliner is basically the same as a wheel on an oxcart. And it will be different in the same degree that the opportunities available to people and the demands made upon them by the jet will be different from those imposed by the oxcart.

Only with clairvoyance could we be assured that this book provides an exhaustive list of the public-policy problems that will demand the attention of legislators, administrators, and the public during the sixties. We have, however, brought together what we regard to be significant and provocative material concerning key issues and problems that we believe will endure well into the sixties.

Chapter One of *Issues of the Sixties* reviews some contrasting interpretations of the 1950's, and suggests their significance for the next decade. Chapter Two deals directly with a problem that is implicit in many of the other sections: the social and political consequences of scientific and technological innovation. This is discussed here in relation to the questions of automation, space exploration, and the role of the scientist in the shaping of public policy. Chapter Three examines the thesis that we should shift our emphasis from consumer goods to public services, and relates it to the debate on economic growth. Chapter Four asks whether the public interest is best served by the interplay and self-regulation of private organizations, or whether government should intervene. The question is tested on three major issues: labor-management relations, health insurance, and television.

Chapter Five discusses the question of racial discrimination in its various aspects, and shows that it is a problem for the North and West as well as the South. Chapter Six examines the extent to which the Constitution and the governmental and political process provide an adequate policy-making framework in the sixties. It also asks whether decisions require a "national purpose" for their context, and examines the danger to individual liberties which the demands of national security present. Chapter Seven explores the effect of social and industrial changes on individual character, and inquires whether our society is producing the kind of individual who can deal effectively with the problems of the sixties.

Although these first seven chapters are primarily national in scope, the international implications of such questions as the state of the economy and civil rights are clear. Similarly, space exploration is very much a part of the world power competition; and most of the discussion of the decision-making process in Chapter Six relates to foreign and defense policy. Thus the world situation necessarily is considered at many points prior to the last three chapters, which deal specifically with the great international problems of our era. Chapter Eight presents the debate on the prospect for and desirability of coexistence with the Soviet Union and China; it also deals with Sino-Soviet relations. Chapter Nine is concerned with prospects for survival in the thermonuclear age and examines such questions as deterrence, limited war, testing, accidental war, disarmament, and arms control. Chapter Ten examines the complex problems of our relations with the underdeveloped countries, and presents the issues of foreign aid and trade which will be debated throughout the next decade.

Finally, a brief Epilogue sums up the central question of power and ethics which pervades these readings and which will confront us in acute form during the coming years.

The selections are drawn from important books, articles in periodicals and scholarly journals, government documents, testimony before Congressional and governmental committees, and public speeches. We have tried to illustrate the diversity of opinion that exists on most of the topics, for we are concerned with issues, and by definition an issue is susceptible of more than one valid resolution.

The task of excerpting is always difficult and often dangerous.

Wherever cuts were necessary, we have attempted not only to present the essence of the argument but also as far as possible to avoid undue disruption of the author's style and approach. Deletions are indicated by ellipses (. . .). Only obvious misprints have been corrected. Some liberty has been taken in eliminating a number of footnotes, renumbering those that remain. In some cases the original titles of the works from which the selections are drawn have been preserved. In other instances, however, we have presumed to use titles more appropriate to their place in this collection. Most of the headnotes at chapter openings are taken from the selections within the chapters.

Both editors have received many invaluable ideas and suggestions from various people in universities, in government, and in politics. Of special help to Leonard Freedman in discovering sources and in testing and discussing ideas was Mr. Martin Heisler, a graduate student in political science at U.C.L.A. Performing a similarly important function for Cornelius Cotter were Miss Katherine Huff and Mr. George Lewis. Our gratitude is also expressed to Mrs. Margaret Harris, who supervised the preparation of the manuscript, to Mrs. Gloria James, who provided a number of indispensable secretarial services in the development of this book, and to Miss Gloria Maistri, who provided cheerful and valued help in typing.

LEONARD FREEDMAN
CORNELIUS P. COTTER

CONTENTS

ix

4. PRIVATE GROUPS AND PUBLIC POLICY

7. THE CHANGING AMERICAN CHARACTER

8. COMMUNISM AND COEXISTENCE

9. NUCLEAR STRATEGY AND DISARMAMENT

ISSUES OF THE SIXTIES

PEOPLE OF THE STATES

1

INTRODUCTION:
THE LEGACY
OF THE FIFTIES

Leonard Freedman

The one incontrovertible statement that we can make about the 1960's is that they will be years of rapid change. On the face of it, this should not be a startling prospect to Americans. This is a country of personal mobility, of technological innovation, of the forced obsolescence of consumer goods almost as soon as they are produced.

Just the same, the sixties will be extraordinarily difficult years for us. For we are in a period not only of rapid change, but of a rapidly accelerating rate of change; it will become increasingly difficult for us to use past experience as a guide to action in the near future. Moreover, the forces of scientific and technological change will have a tremendous impact on our social, economic, and political institutions. And we have always been especially vulnerable to "cultural lag"—the delay that occurs before a basic new force is incorporated into our ideas and behavior. The urgency and magnitude of the problems of the sixties will be so great that any excessive delay in our understanding of what is happening to our world could be disastrous.

That we shall find it difficult to make sense of the future is evident from our perplexity over the events of the recent past. We are still bewildered by the fifties, and the quest for national goals by a Presidential commission and *Life* magazine in 1960 were indications of a loss of national confidence, of the fact that we were no longer sure of ourselves and where we were going.

So we shall begin by looking back at the experience of the fifties. Inevitably there were sharply differing interpretations, with cheerful optimism at one extreme and sharp criticism at the other. To listen to both sides was to become even more confused, for both were extraordinarily convincing.

The Evidence for Optimism

Most of the optimistic books of the time dated from the early years of the decade. Both Frederick Lewis Allen's *The Big Change* and David Lilienthal's *Big Business: A New Era* appeared in 1952. After that, one had to turn to *Fortune* magazine, which issued a hopeful forecast of *America in the Sixties* in 1958. And there were always the effusions of the advertisers and the public-relations agencies.

Yet there was substance even to the most ebullient of these effusions. All of the elements making for the realization of the American dream were present.

Scientific and technological change proceeded at an unprecedented pace. It was the atomic age, the space age, the age of jets, of automation, of television, of the rapid growth of cities, of great advances in medicine, biology, chemistry.

The population of the United States increased by over thirty million in ten years as the birth rate rose and the death rate fell. Educational facilities expanded enormously—and not only at the primary levels. No country in history had provided a college education for such a high proportion of its youth as did America in the fifties—and the proportion will rise still more in the sixties.

All of these trends foretold a privileged world for the American of the future. The population will be highly skilled and educated, as befits an era of automation and scientific advance. Living standards will continue to rise. The gross national product, which increased from around $350 billion in 1950 to a little over $500 billion in 1960, will very likely reach $750 billion by 1970. This should mean that perhaps twenty-five million families will have after-tax incomes of more than $7,500 in 1970.[1]

More leisure will be another aspect of the rising rewards for work. There was no significant reduction in the standard work week in the fifties, and President Kennedy, eager to see a rapid increase in output, has disparaged talk of a thirty-hour week. Yet automation will inevitably reduce working hours before long, and earlier retirement will be facilitated.

This combination of education, affluence, and leisure was already having its effect on American cultural life in the fifties, and the statistics on the sale of paperback books and attendance at concerts and art galleries were impressive.

The opportunities for the abundant life were not confined, as in previous societies, to a small aristocracy, but were open to the great majority of the people. National and religious minorities were no longer excluded. Upward social mobility was possible for people of German, Italian, Irish, and Polish origins. Catholics still comprised more than the average proportion of low-income families. But their chances for prosperity, status, and power were increasing rapidly, and were symbolized by the election to the Presidency of the wealthy grandson of an Irish Catholic immigrant. Negroes, Mexican-Americans, and Puerto Ricans continued to face barriers which had been removed from the upward path of other minority groups. Yet the Supreme Court decision on education in 1954 made it clear that, prolonged and obstinate though the opposition might be, color could not indefinitely remain a bar to the enjoyment of the complete range of opportunities in the coming age of abundance.

Nor were rising expectations peculiar to America. Europe recovered dramatically from the devastations of World War II; and the moves toward economic integration increased prospects of a standard of living similar to that of the U.S. And, as nation after nation established its independence from colonial rule, the underdeveloped areas of the world asserted their right to share in the opportunities provided by science and technology. For the first time in history, the demand for universal access to these opportunities has become an immediate political reality.

Finally, the optimist could point to the change in Soviet leadership from Stalin to Khrushchev, and the new emphasis on peaceful coexistence. Admittedly the Communists were still claiming that their ultimate triumph would be world-wide. But their attention now

---

[1] At 1960 prices.

had turned to the underdeveloped nations; and in a peaceful economic and political competition, it was said, why should we not be able to hold our own?

So cheerful predictions could still be made, and 1960 saw a spate of glossy brochures issued by large corporations depicting the impending marvels of life in America in the year 2000. According to these predictions, industry and communications will be transformed through such developments as electronic miniaturization and world-wide closed-circuit television systems. London will be less than one hour from New York. Automation and ultrasonic energy will free the housewife from most of her remaining chores. People will live in spacious, luxurious apartments overlooking graciously designed cities that extend over hundreds of miles. Liberated from drudgery, a highly educated populace will use its ample leisure to travel, engage in civic pursuits, and enjoy a golden age of the arts and the intellect.

The View of the Critics

The public-relations brochures were not, however, the most influential writings of the period. David Riesman's *The Lonely Crowd* appeared in 1950, and it raised some searching questions about the impact of technological and social change on American character Later in the decade came C. Wright Mills' *The Power Elite* and John Kenneth Galbraith's *The Affluent Society*. Other sociologists and economists disagreed with their analyses. Nonetheless, these were the books that touched the sensitive nerves of the 1950's, that reflected and helped shape the intellectual climate of the period. Together with such other widely read books as William H. Whyte's *The Organization Man* and *The Hidden Persuaders* of Vance Packard, they defined the arena for the key controversies of the age, and provided much of its terminology.

They looked at the same factors which, as we have seen, formed the basis for optimistic assessments of the trends of the fifties. But their interpretations were profoundly disturbing.

They are widely differing thinkers, of course. For example, Riesman's pluralistic view of American society is categorically opposed to Mills' thesis of a nation dominated by a relatively small group of men in the high places of power. Still, there are certain themes common to all of these books.

The spread of education, affluence, and leisure has not, they suggest, produced the Good Society, but the Mass Society. Affluence has led not to freedom from want, but to the incessant pursuit of frivolous and artificially created wants. Education has formed not the cultivated intellect, the independently thinking citizen, but the mind equipped only to respond to the manipulative symbols used to sell consumer goods and political candidates. Leisure is not seen widely as opportunity for creative activity, but as time to kill—all too often by watching television programs that reflect the prevailing mediocrity of the popular taste.

In the Mass Society, the individual has lost his identity. The values of the past have been undermined, but the urban, industrial community has developed no clear values of its own. Deprived of firm moral norms, the individual can model his life only on the behavior of his peers, his neighbors, his boss, his favorite TV programs. In a world too big, too complex for him to understand, his life shaped by forces far removed from his control, he sees no point in involvement in politics and withdraws into his conforming, "other-directed," anxiety-ridden, suburban existence.

This is the interpretation placed upon the decisive trends of the American society of the fifties by many of the most perceptive thinkers of the period. Only a limited number of people read their books, of course. But everyone could see such discouraging phenomena as growing juvenile delinquency, the television quiz-show scandals, the Teamsters' Union investigations, and the electrical industry price-rigging disclosures.

Nor did most people find cause for rejoicing in the international factors cited earlier. On the contrary, the world situation was widely viewed as a further dimension of the threat to the American system.

It was not easy, for example, for most Americans to see the new nations as a dynamic and hopeful new factor in world politics. For they had thought little about the question before the confused, violent melee of the Congo.

Perhaps science and technology would bring the underdeveloped areas of the world out of poverty and hunger and illiteracy. But there was also the fact that in those areas death rates were falling and birth rates were not. By 1960 the world's population was almost three billion, and was increasing at the rate of fifty million a year. By 1975 it would probably be four billion, and could reach six billion by the year 2000. This population explosion seemed likely to be a steadily increasing cause of instability and tension in the years ahead.

We have mentioned Khrushchev's reiterated insistence on the doctrine of peaceful coexistence. But—it could be argued—coexistence must involve bargaining, and bargaining must mean concessions by both sides. Neither of the power blocs appeared ready to make major concessions. And, even if Khrushchev were willing, would the Chinese go along with him?

Although the last decade revealed evidences of serious problems within the Communist world, on the whole these were years of growing strength for the Communist powers. Perhaps the most traumatic experience for America in the fifties was the launching of Sputnik I. This event did not put the Soviet Union ahead of the U.S. industrially. But it was an extraordinary triumph of technology and industry—the very fields in which American self-confidence has been nurtured. And the Soviet lead, built on the greater power of its booster rockets, was confirmed in 1961 by the fact that the first man in space was a Russian.

Finally, there was the Bomb—the megaton weapon a thousand times more destructive than the terrible instruments unleashed on Hiroshima and Nagasaki. Both sides could deliver it, so that a "balance of terror" existed. But it was a precarious balance; and with the strong possibility that several more powers would join the nuclear arms race in the sixties, the danger of a holocaust grew ever more threatening.

With all of these dangers looming over the American scene, optimism could hardly be unqualified. The very boons which we discussed earlier become, when looked at a little differently, nightmares. The revolution of rising expectations gives way to disappointed expectations. The roseate pictures of life in the year 2000 seem singularly unconvincing when our civilization may never get there. And from the vantage point of the sixties, Orwell's *1984* might not be so far away.

The Testimony of Philosophy and the Arts

Confronted with these conflicting interpretations of the meaning of the 1950's—one view optimistic, confident; the other doubting, alienated—philosophy and the arts reflected primarily the latter view.

Since we cannot here provide a complete survey of the state of philosophy during this period, we shall discuss only those systems of thought which were making significant inroads in America. Thus we shall say nothing about Pragmatism, since this philosophy was already well established.[2]

---

[2] Pragmatism was somewhat on the defensive during the fifties, for it was being blamed by some critics for many of the alleged shortcomings of our educational system.

Analytic Philosophy calls for mention, since it came to be the dominant school in a number of university philosophy departments. The significant fact about this school for our purposes is that it eschewed the traditional function of the philosopher of commenting on moral and ethical problems, and defined the task of philosophy as essentially methodological.

Existentialism, on the other hand, dealt centrally and specifically with the kinds of issues we have been discussing here. It was the characteristic European philosophy of the fifties, and it calls for special treatment here since its influence on American intellectual life began to be significant by the end of the decade, and seems to be increasing.

Existentialism *does* concern itself with contemporary moral problems; indeed, it is more an attitude about life and society than a philosophic system. It is not easy to say exactly what Existentialism is, or even who the Existentialists are.[3] Yet it is clear enough that the attitude of the Existentialists revolves around their view of life as essentially tragic. "The human condition" is one of "anguish." Man's life and accomplishments are inherently "absurd" in the sense that he can never escape the final reality of death.

However, anguish and mortality do not call for quietism and despair. Man's fate is not predetermined. He is confronted with the "terrible" fact of his freedom, and he must use it to establish his own "authentic" individuality. Existentialism thus claims to be a true humanism, a reaffirmation of the individual and his dignity and freedom against the forces of the past and the pressures for conformity. The individual must make a "commitment," he must be "involved" in life and human relationships.

There are two important aspects of this commitment that man is called upon to make. In the first place, it is not to the *status quo*, to the existing processes of compromising or avoiding problems. The implication of this is that we cannot have politics as usual, for the main problems of our time are too big and too urgent to be approached through conventional machinery. New ways must be found, and they can only be found if the individual develops his own values and then acts upon them.

Secondly, man's commitment must not be purely an intellectual one. Reason is not enough. Eighteenth-century rationalism appears naïve in the light of contemporary knowledge of the universe and of

---

[3] Of the three writers who are regarded as its key contemporary exponents—Jaspers, Heidegger, and Sartre—only Sartre is ready to have himself labeled as an Existentialist, and the other two question his right to the label.

man. Intuition, passion, character must all play their part in the total expression of a man's individuality.

Existentialism thus sees life in terms of dedication and effort on a heroic scale. But if the effort is inescapable, the triumph is never complete. To talk of glory is absurd in the face of the inevitability of death.

If this is not a despairing philosophy, neither is it comforting.[4] Nor could man find much more reassurance if he turned to the arts of the fifties. The American theater was replete with pathological characters and situations. Almost every sickness in the psychiatrist's case-book found its way into Tennessee Williams' plays during the decade. From Europe came Samuel Beckett's brilliant episodes depicting life as a great, sardonic abyss. The young American playwright Edward Albee fiercely attacked the conformism of the middle-class "square"; and his heroes, the outsiders, cried out against the failure of man to communicate with man.

In painting it was the decade of abstract expressionism, invented in New York, eagerly imitated all over the world. The prevailing view of Americans as being among the most extroverted and out-going of peoples finds no confirmation in this new American art. For Abstract Expressionism is essentially withdrawn, introverted. It turns away from subject matter, from the external world, and looks inward to the painter's psyche. This, it has been argued, is not simply an escape mechanism. Only by rejecting all external references can the artist make a statement about his own individuality. Reason, order, restraint are rejected in favor of intuition, spontaneity, accident; for it is in the act of creation itself that the individual can establish himself against the stultifying pressures for conformity.

This, of course, is not intended as a treatise on art criticism or philosophy. Such a highly simplified review can do no more than suggest the more significant testimony of philosophy and the arts on the mood of the sixties. And however favorable a view we may take of Existentialism, or Abstract Expressionism, or any of the other major philosophical and cultural movements of the decade, their implications are profoundly disturbing. First, there was the view of the human condition as tragic, tortured, anguished. Second, the place of

---

[4] One other philosophy—Zen Buddhism—should be noted here, since it did gain some American adherents in the fifties, and it was important in some schools of painting. It is difficult to see how an Oriental philosophy can be transplanted whole into the Western context. However, for some it provided a source of repose and serenity. Whatever its meaning in the East, in America its practice seemed to be consistent with a sense of detachment and a turning away from reason, which, as we show in this chapter, were symptomatic of this period.

reason at the summit of human values was challenged; and the irrational, the spontaneous, the intuitive were the new preoccupations. Third, there was the alienation of the individual from his society, and an attempt to find an expression of individuality outside the traditional framework.

Attitudes for the Sixties

Up to a point, each of the intellectual legacies which the fifties bequeathed to us—pessimism, anti-rationalism, alienation—has been good for us. We needed a measure of each as a corrective to our previous biases. But they will have to be tempered considerably if we are to cope effectively with the issues of the sixties.

Thus it was salutary for us to be confronted with the dark side of history, to become aware that world leadership cannot be taken for granted; to be told that the Mass Society does not necessarily pursue excellence; to see that, while change is inevitable, progress is not. The Positive Thinkers had to be challenged. *The Lonely Crowd*, the Bomb, Sputnik, and Existentialism have helped to do that. But while our earlier optimism may have been foolish, a reaction to a Spenglerian gloom is not justifiable. Life is, in a sense, anguish; but most people simply refuse to see it as unmitigated disaster. Freedom is a "terrible" responsibility; it is also an invigorating opportunity. The results of universal education have been disappointing; they are substantial, nonetheless. It is true that mediocrity is the prevailing standard of television; it is equally true that television has increased the general level of understanding of public and international affairs. We must, in other words, recognize the equal and opposite truths contained in each of the problems of the future. We shall have to live with paradoxes and contradictions, for the ability to do so is the test of a mature society, and we shall need maturity in the sixties.

Again, it was useful that so much was made in the fifties of the nonrational side of man's behavior. Our political and social thinking could no longer rest without modification on the assumptions of the Enlightenment. Yet, as Jacques Barzun has made clear, America's troubles have not been those of excessive intellectualism. We shall have need of more, not less, reason in this next decade. The function of the arts is not primarily to make political and social comment, and they will probably continue to express intuition and passion at the expense of the rational. But this approach will not do for the making of public policy.

Finally, we needed the challenges of those who have become alienated from our normal institutions and processes, who have protested our assumptions that business and politics could proceed as usual. We cannot go along at the old pace. The recognition of urgency is essential. We shall have to re-examine our procedures, every aspect of our structure and values, to see if they are appropriate to the immediacy and scale of the problems of the sixties.

The rational response to urgency, however, is not withdrawal. And the proposals of some critics are tantamount to withdrawal from our problems, for they disdain the only tools available to us—the tools of politics.

The Escape from Politics

Politics is not a high-status occupation in America. It has been widely regarded as a somewhat squalid business, in which decent people should not become involved; and this attitude has been combined with a distaste for the incessant compromises that blur the edge of principle and hinder the emergence of clear-cut alternatives. This general attitude is now being reinforced by the increasingly fashionable view among intellectuals that politics has become irrelevant.

The assumption is that the normal political process can handle only petty issues, not the real problems of our era.[5] The list of real problems is frequently limited to one—the Bomb. (Sometimes it is allowed that the world population explosion is sufficiently catastrophic in its implications to be added to the list.) The argument proceeds from there with the statement that we shall have to look outside the existing framework of institutions and beliefs to find the solution to problems of such cataclysmic dimensions. Some critics claim that politicians cannot handle the job, and that we shall have to place the task in the hands of dispassionate experts, scientists, intellectual leaders. Others say that we must start with the regeneration of the individual, who must discover new values within himself and then build the institutions which are necessary for survival.

Now, it would be difficult to deny that the thermonuclear arms race is the greatest danger that mankind has ever faced, and that the problem of survival looms over all of the other questions of our time. Still, in this book we think we are justified in dealing with several other issues. We shall not increase our chances for survival by refusing to bother about civil rights, or labor-management relations, or standards in television.

---

[5] We have already seen that this assumption is implicit in Existentialism. However, it is held by many in America who are not Existentialists.

Nor can the largest issues be handled in the sixties by any of the possible alternatives to politics. It may be that we should do better to turn to scientists and philosopher-kings to get us out of our dilemmas. But most scientists do not reveal more than average competence in dealing with large moral and social problems; and where are the philosopher-kings? No doubt we need a regeneration of the individual. But can we afford to wait until all of us are basically changed?

The Necessity for Politics

The fact is that we have no real alternative to politics. What, after all, is politics? It is *the process by which public policy is shaped out of a multiplicity of interests and values.*

There are two sides to this process. The first is *compromise, bargaining, the conciliation of conflicting viewpoints and interests.* This is indispensable, of course, to any decent and civilized means of ordering human relationships. As such it is accepted in most areas of life. Only with respect to politics is it regarded with distaste. For politicians are paid with public money; and we enjoy making them the scapegoats for reflecting our own prejudices and for doing in the public sphere what we must do in almost every kind of private activity.

Nonetheless, bargaining and conciliation alone cannot produce an adequate response to the issues of the sixties. There is a second aspect to politics beyond the process of compromising competing interests.

This is *the exercise of leadership*—that source of initiative which relates the various individual and group interests to larger concepts of the public interest. The American system has tended to place its emphasis on the conciliatory function of politics, rather than the leadership function. But leadership has been possible when the times required it. The system could not have survived otherwise. Once the crucial nature of the issues of our own times becomes clear to all, it is entirely feasible that politics will produce its response.

Even so—even if there is leadership and our national life takes on the necessary tone and pace—politics may not be able to do the job. The case of the skeptics is a cogent one. The odds against the solution of the major problems of our age may be increasing rapidly.

But since there is no alternative to politics, a general refusal to be involved, to be committed to the political process, will surely be disastrous. We need politics, and we need the involvement of both liberals and conservatives. Neither of these groups, however, can limit their thinking to what Galbraith has called their "conventional wisdom."

The liberals will have to break away from their self-pity, their belief that since the New Deal there have been no causes left to work for. They will have to be extraordinarily obtuse not to see that the sixties contain, in intensified and internationalized form, most of the great causes known to Western civilization. But once they have identified the new causes, they will have to recognize that there are no simple solutions, that each of the issues we face is immensely complicated. In this book we show repeatedly the very great difficulty of our problems, which becomes apparent as soon as we move from the ringing generalizations to the onerous but inescapable details.

The conservatives will, by definition, tend to be more cautious about causes. The sixties have not made caution obsolete. Moreover, the conservative's function of emphasizing traditional values will be an important one. Without some kind of value system we shall have no criteria by which to judge new developments, and we shall become prisoners of the random consequences of uncontrolled change. But if conservatives are to perform their function, they will have to face up to the fact of change, and to those forces—scientific, technological, social—which will make the pace of change an ever accelerating one.

So it is that liberals and conservatives—as well as those who do not fit into either category—must give their attention to the kinds of issues dealt with in this book. It will be seen that those issues have economic, social, cultural, military implications. Still, their resolution must be accomplished primarily in the realm of politics.

As a people, we have not acquired the habit of careful analysis and discussion of our political problems. It is probably not too late for us to do so, but we cannot postpone the task much longer. As C. P. Snow has pointed out, "The danger is, we have been brought up to think as though we had all the time in the world. We have very little time. So little that I dare not guess at it."[6]

---

[6] C. P. Snow, *The Two Cultures and the Scientific Revolution* (1959), p. 54. Reprinted by permission of Cambridge University Press.

2

THE IMPACT OF
SCIENCE
AND TECHNOLOGY

. . . the twenty-four-hour satellite . . . launched in such a way as to orbit at the same rate as the earth revolves. Thus it would appear to remain stationary over one spot. Here, truly, "Big Brother is watching you." * * * Intercontinental radio and television networks . . . World-wide telephone dialing . . . Message costs cut to perhaps one-tenth their present levels. * * * . . . an exciting and coherent picture of the earth's interplanetary environment, and of the mighty influences of a stormy sun in producing important effects on the earth. . . . unimagined advances in our knowledge of meteorology. * * * . . . the remote operation of automated machines . . . * * * . . . man being projected into a totally alien environment . . . the most exciting enterprise of our age.

* * *

. . . ordinary people feel helpless; some of them strive to maintain a mastery, not of things, but of their individual souls. They watch, with something like despair, the immeasurable powers of science

being used not for human welfare, but for the cold and essentially inhuman endeavour to reach planets on which men are never likely to live. The exploration of outer space may, I'm told, teach us to understand the weather. There is no doubt some arid consolation in the thought that in twenty years or so prodigious new discoveries about the nature of the universe will be made when we can shoot rockets to Mars or Venus. But this majestic triumph of the human intellect and skill will not buy as much as a single bowl of rice or improve the lot of one half-starved inhabitant of this globe.

In the words of J. Robert Oppenheimer, "new knowledge is useful," and "the getting of it is ennobling." We have also discovered that new knowledge can carry a threat in the shape of a mushroom cloud.

Let us put this threat aside for the moment. New knowledge—and its application—may lead to changed consumption habits, to the obsolescence of old products and of hard-won skills. The shift of consumption patterns from coal to natural gas and oil beggared entire regions of the United States and wiped out hundreds of thousands of jobs. As production and clerical tasks become more fully automated under the relentless pressures of technological development and the quest for lowered costs, we can expect that during each year of the sixties thousands upon thousands of jobs will be rendered as antique as harness-making and chimney-sweeping.

To the social visionary who has criticized the brutalizing effect that mass production has supposedly had upon the worker of the twentieth century, this is an ironic development. To the manager, driven by competition to reduce costs through automation, this must be depicted as progress of a sort which ultimately will enlarge job opportunities. To the temporarily dislocated worker it can be a tragedy of staggering dimensions, the more so if shared with thousands of fellow workers in neighboring communities. To union leaders, businessmen, and government officials, state and local, it is a challenge which must be met by co-operative action of all three, at all levels. Commenting upon the depressed condition of the railroads in 1958, one railroad president commented ruefully, "The culprit is a . . . thing called progress." It is easy to spin verbal rationalizations that progress in the form of scientific discovery and technological development should be the solution for the problems it creates—thus culprit and savior. The problem is to transform the generalization into action programs.

The discussion of problems of automation in this chapter draws upon statements presented to a Joint Congressional Subcommittee on Automation and Energy Resources in 1960. Each statement is a comment upon the meaning and nature of automation. The first, by the president of a corporation, approaches the problem from the point of view of management. The second, by the president of a labor union, places automation within the context of increased national productivity and maintenance of high levels of employment. The third, by the director of a school of industrial management, takes into account demographic projections, effects upon employment, and emotional impact upon workers.

The impact of the discovery of new knowledge is also illustrated by our programs for the exploration of space. But these programs present a further set of public-policy problems.

L. V. Berkner asks: "Are Space Probes Worth It?"; and he lists an impressive array of rewards for the huge expenditures involved. Other writers, however, have questioned whether the cost of space exploration is a proper allocation from the nation's resources. Advocates of rapid improvement in the protection of civil rights point out that the annual appropriation for the U.S. Commission on Civil Rights is less than the cost of production of a medium-sized rocket. At a time of tremendous interest in public health, medical researchers might properly question whether the program of research to eradicate such diseases as cancer is not just as deserving as a program aimed at putting a man in space. These are the kinds of questions asked here by Kingsley Martin.

Another problem is posed by Dr. William H. Pickering in his testimony before the House Committee on Science and Astronautics. Should the primary emphasis in the space program be on the potential military advantages or on the nonmilitary aspects of the cold war?

Consider, in this connection, the statement of Dr. Wernher von Braun to the same committee: "It boils down to this simple fact: If the value of American stock in the eyes of the world drops a billion dollars because the Russians publish a photograph of the far side of the Moon, and if we could have done it . . . it would have been a good investment to have done it ahead of the Russians. . . . It is . . . a question of national prestige in the eyes of the world."[1] The tone of this comment is quite different from Professor Oppenheimer's justification of the pursuit of basic scientific research. And here we

---

[1] *Review of the Space Program.* Hearings before the House Committee on Science and Astronautics, Part 1, 86th Congress, 2nd Session, January and February 1960, Government Printing Office, Washington, D.C., p. 420.

arrive at our final group of issues for this chapter. Should the space program be seen as a weapon (whether military or not) in the cold war, or as an opportunity for untrammeled scientific research? In more general terms, should we ask for rapid and specific returns on the resources we commit to basic research? And can these returns be best achieved within national boundaries?

These questions are discussed in the statement on "Science and Human Welfare," taken from the journal of the American Association for the Advancement of Science. The scientists who prepared this statement are confronted with the fact that the getting of new knowledge is expensive—so expensive as to require public support. The use of public funds is usually attended by application of the pragmatic yardstick of comparative utility. It is this kind of measurement that scientists traditionally have eschewed, and the statement excerpted in this chapter expresses anxiety over the inhibiting effect on scientific inquiry of the pressures of national purposes.

At the same time, the authors of the A.A.A.S. statement are fully aware that scientific innovation has profound social and political consequences, which pose a problem of responsibility not only for government, business, labor, and other groups, but also for the scientist himself. How the scientist can best exercise this public responsibility without undermining his function in the scientific enterprise is discussed in the statement. There is also, of course, the possibility that the scientists might take too much responsibility upon themselves. As Dwight D. Eisenhower warned in his last television appearance as President: "In holding scientific research and discovery in respect, as we should, we must also be alert to the equal and opposite danger that public policy could itself become the captive of a scientific-technological elite." This problem of the relationship between science and public policy is an intricate one, and it will grow in complexity and intensity as the pace of scientific and technological change accelerates throughout the sixties.

AUTOMATION

NEW VIEWS ON AUTOMATION*

Alan C. Mattison

. . . "Automation" as we understand it in the machine tool industry is a general term which covers only some of the most recent developments of the past half century with regard to the speed, productivity, accuracy, and power of machine tools. . . .

I am certain that this distinguished committee is fully aware of the nature and importance of automation as it has developed in the industrial history of the United States It is a concept and approach which, second only to democracy itself, is intimately identified with our country and its unprecedented growth to leadership of the free world. Millions of words have been written on the subject, and even the man on the street is conscious of the fact that the increasing availability and low price of the products which he buys stem directly from the production miracle brought about by increased automation.

Automation is the principal avenue leading to the establishment and maintenance of a consistent, high level of production of parts of maximum accuracy.

It avoids part damage due to careless manual handling. It provides increased flexibility essential to efficient production in an age where requirements may change overnight in the light of new tech-

---

* Alan C. Mattison, Walter P. Reuther, and Walter Buckingham; Statements to the Subcommittee on Automation and Energy Resources, Joint Economic Committee, 86th Congress, 2nd Session, 1960.

Mr. Mattison is President of the Mattison Machine Works, of Rockford, Illinois, and of the National Machine Tool Builders' Association.

nological changes in the chemical, physical, and engineering sciences. Automation makes it possible to squeeze the most out of a given work space—economizing not only on space but in movement of parts from operation to operation.

There is a very simple reason why the United States enjoys the highest standard of living of any nation in the world: production efficiency—more and better output per man-hour. And a very large measure of that efficiency is attributable to automation and related techniques.

This same efficiency has made it possible to pay the highest wages the world has ever known and yet maintain a price on the product produced which will still be within the consumer's reach and remain competitive with low-labor cost products from abroad.

If that efficiency is not maintained in relation to that of the other industrial facilities of the world, the only hope for competition and industrial survival would be lowered wages, a lower standard of living, and finally a reduction or at least stagnation of our basic productive capacity. . . .

The new machine tools are being built to perform operations in sequence, with loading and unloading—the shift of work from one operation to the next—completely automatic. Another development is the inclusion of automatic assembly as a part of the processing sequence. Accuracy in many cases is now assured by completely automatic checking and gaging at successive stations.

A further trend in machine tool automation is toward starting directly with a rough part rather than as in the past with one which has had to be preconditioned by another machine.

I think the advantages of these innovations are apparent. Amazing advances have been made possible in accuracy. Millionths-of-an-inch are now getting to be as common as ten-thousandths used to be. With today's controls, no longer are rate of output and accuracy of performance dependent upon the human operator. These factors are built into the machine itself. Quality of work becomes a known factor. Output per hour, in terms of work pieces machined, becomes a known factor. Costs are thereby accurately determinable. And last, but hardly least, output per man-hour is remarkably increased. . . .

. . . I have not yet come to the central problem of my industry or that of the industrial complex of the United States.

I think the problem can be stated quite simply. We are losing the race for productive efficiency. The fundamental basis for our high wages and high standard of living is beginning to erode and disappear. In short, our ability to compete in the world has been—and is being—seriously challenged; not only by our European friends but by those ideological enemies who have vowed the destruction of our economic and political system, who are determined to do away with our way of life.

I wish I could tell you that America's production efficiency still makes up for the disparity in wages which exists between this country and our European competitors. I wish I could tell you that American industry has kept pace with technological developments and that our productive capacity is maintained through constant improvement and the revamping or automation of our assembly lines.

In actual fact, I fear that the reverse is true. Due to a combination of factors—antiquated depreciation practices which discourage replacement, high taxes which discourage growth, and the specter of an inflationary wage-material cost spiral—our vital edge in production efficiency is shrinking, and shrinking more rapidly than I suspect many of us realize.

It is hard for us, with our assumption of American superiority in the industrial field, to realize that many of the metalworking plants of the United States are lagging behind those of various parts of the world in production efficiency. But bear in mind that a large number of the European plants have been built and equipped since World War II. By contrast, many of the machine tools still in use in American plants were built to designs crystallized for war production at the start of World War II.

Every 5 years, the *American Machinist*, a magazine regarded as authoritative, makes a survey of U.S. metalworking equipment. The last survey, made in 1958, showed that at that time 60 percent of the country's metal-cutting machines, and 62 percent of the country's metal-forming machines, were over 10 years old. New equipment buying since that time has not been sufficient to alter these ratios to any appreciable extent.

America builds the machine tools that could revitalize our efficiency and competitive position. We are capable of creating and producing the world's finest automated machines—if there is a demand for the product and the incentive to invest the enormous amount of money, talent, and time required to outpace our European and Sino-Soviet competitors. . . .

Nearly everyone realizes, including the Treasury, that we have to discard our outmoded depreciation and replacement practices in this country if we are to modernize our plants, reduce our costs and compete effectively. Many practical solutions have been suggested; none has been adopted. . . .

. . . Machine tool developments and automation innovations are coming so fast that forward-looking plant managers must plan on replacing many of their machines every 5 years and most of them in less than 10 years.

In the United States, writeoff periods for machine tools, for example, vary from 15 to 33½ years. It is now possible, by submitting specific proof to the Internal Revenue Service, to do better than that. But there are thousands of companies in this country still taking an annual 5 percent writeoff. This discourages capital expenditures. The period of capital recovery is extended too far into the future. Funds to replace obsolete equipment must come largely out of earnings after taxes, or borrowed money. . . .

Greater allowance should also be made in our tax structure for the high cost of the research and engineering work required for the development of the modern equipment which will keep our Nation competitive.

I would not like you to conclude from what I have said that U.S. manufacturers are always entirely blameless in this matter of modernization and automation. Some of them, for reasons best known to them, just do not take advantage of the long-range benefits to be derived from these new techniques. Again, very high corporate tax rates may act as a deterrent.

For some it may seem to be simply too late: costs have risen, efficiency is lowered or remains the same, and the market is flooded with low wage–low cost imports. What I am saying is that there may well be an educational job here which someone should undertake.

I have one last point I should like to make in urging this committee and Congress to take firm and early steps toward generating a favorable atmosphere for automation and the related techniques which result in increased production efficiency. I refer now to the Sino-Soviet bloc economic and military threat—the competition for survival.

With its directed economy, the Communists have been able to concentrate on those areas which seem to them to be critical on the path to economic superiority. Far from creating artificial barriers to modernization, they have gone all out to increase productive efficiency, irrespective of the cost. . . .

Finally, I wish to make clear that the ideas I have here expressed do not apply merely to machine tools. They apply as well to all types of cost-reducing equipment. . . . I am making a broad plea that American industry make—and in every way be encouraged to make— a determined effort to get costs down and maintain our world competitive position through the maximum use of every possible technological and automation advance. The program I urge can be summarized in just three words—"modernization for survival."

*Walter P. Reuther**

. . . .

Let me make our position clear. We welcome automation as a major force for growth in our economy, holding forth the promise of increasing abundance for all if we use it wisely and well. But it is necessary to look facts in the face if we ever hope to enjoy the benefits of automation without the cost of unnecessary hardship for those whose lives it dislocates. And when the combination of national policies which hamper economic growth and new technologies which accelerate man-hour productivity results in employment declines and displacement of hundreds of thousands of workers in major industries, it is clear that there is going to be hardship and suffering unless active measures are taken to prevent it. In fact, during the past 5 years there has been a tremendous amount of hardship and suffering affecting millions of American families which could have been prevented and was not because necessary measures were not taken. . . .

What can be done and what has been done to protect workers against either temporary or permanent severance from their jobs, or to cushion the impact of unemployment when it does occur? As I have said above, our union has long maintained the principle that protection of workers against such catastrophes should be considered one of the costs of doing business. Industry as a whole profits from technological advance and from the general dynamism of our economy, and one of the first charges against those profits should be the cost of reasonable protection for those workers to whom the change brings only loss of a job. . . .

Over the years we have been able to negotiate numerous provisions in our collective bargaining agreements which protect our members against dismissal in the event of job displacement. . . .

For the most part now employees who are permanently displaced from their jobs can exercise plantwide seniority in transferring to other jobs they can do. . . .

In areas such as Detroit, where one company may have several plants, our major agreements now provide that a plant which is hir-

---

* Mr. Reuther is President of the United Automobile, Aircraft and Agricultural Implement Workers of America, and President of the CIO Division of AFL-CIO.

ing must give preference to seniority employees of the company laid off from other plants. These employees can now carry with them to the new job the rights to such benefits as insurance, pensions, and supplemental unemployment benefits which they may have built up at another plant.

When jobs are transferred to a new plant, many of our agreements protect the right of workers to transfer with the job if they wish, carrying with them their seniority rights. In addition, some agreements provide that when a new plant is hiring it will give preference to laid-off employees from any other of the company's plants. . . .

An important protection for the older worker who may find it impossible to adjust to the demands imposed by automation has been the negotiation of flexible pension programs permitting retirement before the normal age. . . .

Among those features of our proposed collective bargaining program which relate closely to the needs created by automation, strengthening and extension of workers' transfer rights when jobs or plants are moved rank high. Workers displaced by a change in plant location should have the right to transfer to the new location whether or not the same job as they have been doing will be available, provided there is work at the new plant which they can do or can learn to do. This is now the practice under some of our agreements, but should be extended to many more.

Workers transferring to new locations because a company decision has displaced them from former jobs should be reimbursed by the employer for the costs involved in effecting such transfer, including allowances to defray the workers' unusual expenses connected with the move. Many corporations already recognize this principle as it applies to their executives. The principle behind this demand is the familiar one that the company will not make such a move unless it expects to profit by it, that the worker's moving and relocation costs are in fact part of the total cost of the company's decision, that the worker should not have to make a financial sacrifice in consequence of a decision from which his employer will profit, and that by reflecting such costs on the company's books, moves which in fact are not economically sound will be discouraged.

Workers who elect not to transfer should receive adequate separation pay without loss of seniority status. Under present agreements, a worker has to choose between forfeiting all future rights to be rehired if suitable work should become available, or forfeiting his claim to separation pay. We have proposed to the major corporations a formula by which the employee could receive separation pay and still retain his seniority status, while at the same time protecting the employer by provision for reduction of future separation payments by any amounts previously received. . . .

Areawide preferential hiring agreements should also be broadened to cover not merely plants of the same corporation, but other companies in the same industry and area. This would mean, for example, that when a plant is closed because one company cannot withstand competition, or even more importantly when a plant is closed or workers laid off because the major manufacturers have withdrawn contracts from a supplier firm, the employees in those plants would be given preference by other companies in the industry in that area when they are hiring new employees. . . .

The age of automation requires the establishment of programs under joint union-management control and direction, to train or retrain workers without loss of wages for jobs which will enable them to meet the requirements of technological change. Agreements should also protect against threatened dilution of skills and encroachments on standards of workmanship. . . .

While collective bargaining has an essential role to play in meeting the problems raised by automation, it cannot provide all the answers. Negotiated programs must function side by side with public programs. Negotiated retraining programs, for example, cannot meet the needs of all workers who require retraining, nor can negotiated relocation programs help the employees of a firm which has gone out of business. In addition, programs similar to those negotiated through collective bargaining will have to be provided for the millions of workers still unorganized. Such programs should include vocational training and retraining for workers in need of new skills; adequate unemployment compensation benefits extended over a sufficient time to enable displaced workers to prepare for and find suitable work without hardship to their families; travel and relocation allowances for those forced to move to new communities; pensions at a reduced age for displaced older workers who are unable to find suitable new jobs; and industrial development and rehabilitation of communities left stranded by the moving of plants. . . .

One of our primary needs is to be much better informed on a current, continuing basis as to the developments taking place every day which may open up new vistas and create new problems. . . . What is needed for that task is a permanent commission on technological change, with the resources and staff required to carry such a heavy responsibility.

Because technological change will continue to have a revolutionary impact on almost every sector of our economy, such a commission should be as broadly based as possible. Its membership should include representatives of Government, labor, and management. The Commission would have the duty and be given the authority to gather information on, and to keep under constant scrutiny, developments in such areas of technological advance as automation, major new developments in production processes and equipment, development of atomic and solar energy for industrial use, development of important new materials, and similar innovations, and to make appropriate recommendations to Congress and the President in order to insure that the social gains and the social costs of technological progress are fairly shared, and full employment achieved and maintained. . . .

Walter Buckingham*

The long-run record of technological growth has been one of increasing job opportunities. Case after case can be cited to show that total employment in firms and entire industries has increased following the introduction of mechanization or automation. The telephone industry offers a typical, though perhaps spectacular, example. Automatic dial equipment began to be introduced about 1920. Today 89 percent of telephone callers in the United States get their connections automatically. Since 1920, employment in the Bell System has increased from 200,000 to about 600,000. The oil industry also began to use continuous flow refining methods about 1920 and in this industry employment has since doubled. However, these particular industries have had a great overall economic expansion so the increase in employment cannot be attributed entirely to automation.

These cases, therefore, represent only one side of the picture. There are equally dramatic statistics to show declining employment in other industries. A million railroad jobs have disappeared in the last 20 years and the persistence of over 50 depressed areas where unemployment persists at 6 to 14 percent, even while inflation threatens, keeps the specter of hard times alive. Obviously automa-

* Walter Buckingham is Director of the School of Industrial Management, Georgia Institute of Technology. Mr. Buckingham's statement is drawn from his *Automation: Its Impact on Business and People,* Harper & Brothers, 1961. Reprinted by permission of the author.

tion is not the sole cause of this unemployment any more than it is responsible for the great expansion of jobs in other industries.

Stable full employment, even a labor shortage, could conceivably occur after 1980 but only if the most authoritative population forecasts turn out to be wrong. Remember there is about a 20-year time lag between birth and entrance into the labor force. Children already born practically insure no labor shortage for nearly two decades and current trends would have to reverse completely to remove the specter of unemployment. According to the latest prediction of the U.S. Department of Labor, the increase in workers entering the labor force in the 1960's will be by far the largest of any decade in history.[1] This is a 50 percent greater increase than the 1950's. . . .

In the last decade, which was characterized by the most rapid scientific development in history, output of all goods and services in the United States rose about 50 percent (in terms of constant 1954 prices), total employment increased 15 percent but employment of direct production workers remained about constant although population rose over 12 percent. The Bureau of Labor Statistics reports that in the last 10 years "nonproduction" workers in manufacturing have increased at about 15 times as fast as production workers. The *American Machinist* magazine recently reported about 40 percent of firms surveyed required more skilled maintenance men and 21 percent hired more engineers after automation. Managers, clerks, and professional, technical, and service workers are all growing rapidly as a percentage of the workforce; craftsmen and foremen are remaining about the same; and semiskilled and unskilled workers are falling slightly and farmers are declining drastically. . . .

In apparent contradiction to these overall industry statistics, the BLS automation studies revealed that few if any regular employees were laid off as a direct result of automation. . . .

There are two explanations for these discrepancies. First, in all of the BLS case studies automation was introduced during prosperity when there was expanding employment. Permanent reductions in the workforce due to technological changes are apparently sometimes postponed until a general downturn permits layoffs to be blamed on national or international conditions. Then, when recovery occurs, fewer are recalled than were laid off.[2] Since businessmen are sensitive about public relations effects of layoffs, some university research in-

---

[1] "Manpower: Challenge of the 1960's," U.S. Government Printing Office, Washington, D.C., 1960.

[2] Charles Killingworth, "Automation in Manufacturing," I.R.R.A., December 28, 1958.

vestigators have voiced the suspicion that they have had easier access to data in those firms where the introduction of automation coincided with increased employment.

This is why unemployment remained so high after the 1957–58 recession. There are about 160,000 unemployed in Detroit who will probably never go back to making automobiles, partly because the industry is past its peak of growth and partly because automation has taken their jobs. Steelworkers returning after the 1958 recession found the same work being done by 20 percent less men. Possibly half of the nation's 400,000 soft coal miners may have to leave the industry for good. . . .

The problem becomes not the worker who is fired but the worker who is not hired. The unions call this "silent firing." The major problem is a transfer one, displacement, not general unemployment. What do you do with a surplus of some kinds of labor and a shortage of other kinds at the same time, or a surplus in one location and a shortage in another? Jobs not upgraded in the short run may be in the long run. Whether people can be upgraded to fill them is a matter best considered as a problem of the absorption of displaced workers.

The often expressed fear that automation leads to unemployment is somewhat exaggerated for three reasons. First, even partial automation will probably be limited to industries which employ at the most a little less than half of the U.S. labor force. This is the manufacturing sector (which comprises 25 percent of all workers) and office clerks in large firms which account for another 15 percent. Yet manufacturing is the most highly union-organized sector. Second, automatic controls do not replace the labor force entirely, although in terms of labor hours there is a considerable saving. As routine clerical and operative jobs are abolished, new maintenance and technical jobs are created which go far toward offsetting the loss of former jobs. Third, extensive training and educational programs will be required as the labor force is upgraded and these will to some extent counteract unemployment by delaying entry into the labor market.

The impact of automation on the individuals affected should not be underestimated, however. Don Mitchell, chairman of the board and former Sylvania Electric Products Corp. president, said:

> It doesn't do much good to try to convince an individual worker that over a 25-year span there is no such thing as technological unemployment. He doesn't care whether there is or not. All he is worried about is that he lost a job.

Those who disparage fears of technological unemployment often assume the existence of a self-adjusting labor market. There is a real danger that imperfections in the labor market will seriously delay absorption of the displaced workers.

Neither automation nor technological growth in general have so far caused any lasting unemployment but there has been considerable labor displacement. Displacement is not the same as unemployment, of course, since displacement is an individual matter while unemployment is an aggregate. A displaced worker is counted as unemployed only when he cannot find another job within a reasonable time. . . .

A carefully conducted study of the Murray Body Co. showed that when 5,000 workers were released in the highly prosperous year 1954, 29 percent had still not found new jobs a year later. Many of the younger workers found new employment easily, and apparently some benefited by being forced out of dead end jobs and into better opportunities. But for three other classes of workers there was only tragedy. "Older" workers (over 45) were out of work at an average of 6 months (compared to 3 months for all workers together) and 82 percent used up all of their unemployment compensation before finding another job and had to retire into dependency on others or social security. All of the women exhausted their unemployment compensation benefits and only half ever found other jobs. Many of these were at lower skills and wages. Negroes also fared badly. While the average wage cut of all those workers who found new jobs was 9 cents an hour, Negroes on the average had a wage cut 60 percent greater than this.

Problems like this are not likely to ease as the percentages of older people and Negroes rise and the number of women seeking employment increases. The U.S. Department of Labor expects a 70-percent increase in people over the age of 70 by 1975 as against 17 percent increase in those of the 25–44 or "prime of life" group. Negro birth rates exceed whites and the percentage of women seeking employment is also rising. Already this problem is being felt. For example, the percentage of Negroes out of work to total unemployment in major industrial centers in mid-1959 was roughly double their percentage in the total population. It may be that "today's laborer is tomorrow's electronic engineer" but, as George Schultz says, "It is stretching language and compressing reality to say that semiskilled operators can easily become high skilled technicians." It is equally doubtful that the tremendous reduction in clerical jobs, held mostly by women, that office automation has caused will lead to expanding opportunities for women elsewhere. Nor will the displacement of unskilled Negroes necessarily ease the upward mobility of Negroes into skilled or professional jobs. Automation does not upgrade people, only their jobs. This vital distinction highlights the crucial transitional problem. . . .

What can be done for the worker who is displaced by automation? If he is young and energetic enough he can be trained for promotion to one of the new, high-skilled jobs created by advancing technology. If he is only moderately adaptable he may be trained or developed to keep pace with changing job requirements as his trade evolves. If he no longer has the zest, ability, or youth to learn higher or newer responsibilities he may be transferred laterally to another job with similar requirements to the one just abolished. In time this new position may disappear but time heals many wounds and in time this employee may not be replaced when he retires.

The barriers to labor mobility have always been great, but even in the face of increasing concentration of capital it is likely that labor is more mobile and flexible today then ever before. Cheap transportation, improved communication, and the disintegration of family and community ties, which specialization and industrialization have encouraged, all tend to make for labor flexibility among firms in the same industry or firms offering similar jobs. However, movement among occupations, particularly to more highly skilled jobs, entails great costs which individual workers cannot normally bear and this is exactly the kind of mobility which automation will require.

Rationality, self-interest, mobility, and flexibility, while highly desirable means of making industry more efficient and resource allocation more rational, are not ends in themselves. Too much of these make pirates of businessmen, gypsies out of workers and, in general, irresponsible citizens who do not own real property, vote, or assume civic responsibilities. On the other hand, too little of these qualities makes for narrow provincialism, ignorance, waste and a great loss of potential accomplishments.

It is not necessary that all workers be equally sensitive to changes in the demand for labor or differences in opportunities. A highly mobile minority in each occupational group will usually preserve the necessary flexibility of supply except where there are structural changes taking place such as automation may produce. The individual rewards for mobility, and penalties for immobility, seem likely to increase. This will favor young, aggressive workers with few family responsibilities and discriminate against older, more settled workers. It also may encourage the opportunists and the irresponsible as against the more stable elements in the work force.

There is no reason why labor should be more mobile, flexible, and willing to assume the enormous risks of economic dislocation than the other components of production—capital, management, and natural resources—which are to varying degrees organized, concentrated, and immobilized. The possible loss of an unrealized profit or, at most, the loss of a business investment may be a greater disadvantage to the growth of the economy but it is usually not as severe a personal hardship as the loss of a job is to a worker. . . .

In the past, undue unemployment has been prevented by general economic expansion, except for relatively short recessions like 1958, special problem areas like Detroit and parts of West Virginia, and of course, the great depression of the 1930's. Those workers no longer needed in manufacturing have been eventually absorbed in new industries, or in the service areas. How long this absorption takes is in large part up to the Government. Full employment and expanding markets are vital prerequisites to a rate of absorption of displaced workers that will avoid acute personal hardships and general injustice to workers. Full, stable employment is not only politically expedient and socially desirable. Automation makes it economically necessary for two reasons. First, the increased capital investment makes nearly continuous use of plant and equipment imperative. Idle capacity is too expensive to have for long. Second, the labor force, in general, is becoming more highly skilled. This means longer and more expensive training programs are needed and therefore labor turnover becomes less tolerable.

Displacement of labor is inevitable from automation as indeed it is from all technological change. The tractor displaced millions of horses; but workers can never again be treated like horses and displacement cannot be allowed to accumulate into pools of unemployment. Leaders of management and labor must jointly assume responsibility for relieving the hardships caused by automation. Relieving, of course, does not mean holding back technological progress. Workers will still have to move from place to place, change occupations and adopt new attitudes, but business firms and governments will need to pay a larger share of the cost. . . .

In view of the rapid growth of automation there may be an increased likelihood of abandonment of plants and the creation of depressed areas. There are several such areas already in Pennsylvania, Michigan, and West Virginia. If one large firm adopts automatic operations, other firms in the industry may have to scrap or sell undepreciated machinery and adopt similar techniques or be squeezed out of the industry by the lower costs of their automatized rivals. Entire communities could become ghost towns if this happens. Under these circumstances, older workers with accumulated seniority and higher skills are most affected. Although there should be no long run attempt to freeze existing industrial patterns, nevertheless, some kind of direct assistance may become necessary to mitigate the most acute hardships in these distressed areas.

Some considerable aid could result from requiring the firms that are seeking lower cost locations to bear a larger share of the social costs of their operations. . . .

. . . Displacement of labor and other productive elements are essential elements of automation as well as the older mechanization. Personal hardships caused by this displacement must be insured against but it is important to remember that the displacement itself must not be prevented. Free movement of workers, capital, and natural resources among alternative occupations and geographical areas are necessary for obtaining the benefits of technological progress. Without flexibility and mobility of productive resources of all kinds, our economy would stagnate and the rich harvest from economic progress would be lost. . . .

Automation improves working conditions in several ways. First, in nearly every case there is greater safety. This is due to mechanized materials handling, elimination of the most hazardous jobs, and the reduction of the number of people in direct production areas due to remote controls such as monitoring dangerous operations with electric eye or television equipment. Hernia, eye troubles, and foot accidents have virtually disappeared in the Ford Motor Co.'s automated Cleveland engine plant. . . .

The decline of physical risks could be partially offset by greater emotional hazards. The highest incidence of gastric ulcers in the hourly paid group is now among skilled machinists who exert less physical effort than most workers. Ulcers, although physical in result, are caused primarily by mental or emotional stress. It has also been reliably estimated that 20 percent of all employees in peacetime are borderline emotional cases. A recent medical study of heart diseases revealed that unskilled laborers are among the least likely to have heart attacks of all occupational groups while among those most susceptible are people working with computing machines.

Automation may increase workers' feelings of security because the continuous nature of automatic processes permits greater regularity of employment and hence more job security. On the other hand, this advantage could be partially offset if regularity of employment means regularity of nightwork, or if automation causes increased boredom or leads to a more rigorous industrial discipline from machines. Automation may reduce the interaction among workers both by reducing their numbers and increasing the distances among their workplaces. A study of workers' attitudes toward automation by Prof. W. A.

Faunce, of Michigan State University, showed that the main complaints of 125 workers were increased noise, need for closer attention to work, and most important, loneliness from being isolated from other workers. At least one British union has already asked for—"lonesome pay." . . .

Related to lonesomeness is boredom. This is not peculiar to automation, of course. It is perhaps more typical of old-style conventional mechanization than of automation but some operative jobs under automation may still be highly routine and boring. These jobs are usually the most likely to be mechanized or automated, however, since they are based on simple, repetitive tasks. In Coca-Cola bottling plants the old method of inspection was to put four bottles of finished product in front of a strong light and have an inspector watch for any foreign matter in the drink. Then someone initiated a conveyor system in which the bottles ran continuously. This was a much faster process, but the job was so boring that every now and then a Seven Up had to be run through to see if the inspector was alert.

People also become hostile if their personality is ignored. A good way to make an enemy is to ignore someone. Prof. William Faunce, of Michigan State, quotes a typical worker as commenting, "They (the supervisors) never say hello—they treat you like a machine. They used to be friendly. Now they seem under a strain." In general, however, automation reduces the number of workers under a foreman's jurisdiction and hence increases the opportunity for interaction between workers and supervisors. Likewise the greater integration of operations increases the foreman's contacts with other foremen and with his superiors. Man-machine relationships are also changed. A worker quoted by Faunce reflected this in saying, "On my old job I controlled the machine. On my present job the machine controls me." Still another worker expressed increased nervous tension saying, "I pushed the wrong button and stuff flew all over. I was lucky (not getting hurt) but it cost the company $13,000 to fix the machine."

Automation may stimulate the mental activity of workers with desirable or undesirable effects depending on the presence of constructive outlets and opportunities to utilize them. Prof. Charles Walker, director of the Yale technology project, quotes a worker as saying:

> On my old job my muscles got tired. I went home and rested a bit and my muscles were no longer tired. On this new automatic mill your muscles don't get tired but you keep on thinking even when you go home.[3]

---

[3] *Harvard Business Review*, February 1958, p. 112.

Professor Faunce also found workers' nervous tensions to be higher after automation but, significantly, 72 percent preferred their new jobs in automated departments over their previous factory work.

Automation clearly improves working conditions in general by permitting better "housekeeping" in the plant. Automated plants are cleaner, neater, and more pleasant to work in. There are automated grain mills that have eliminated all dust. There are foundry workers who never touch the molding sand except from curiosity and oil refinery workers who could wear dinner jackets and white gloves on the job and never get them soiled. Automation is not without its esthetic advantages. . . .

A sign on a backwoods Georgia road reads, "Choose your rut carefully. You'll be in it for a long time." Many people seem to get great satisfaction from burying themselves in routine activities. They strongly resist any threat of change because it strikes at their basic emotional security. Industrial workers are no exception. Often they believe that they are dependent for their livelihood on a unique combination of machines, plant organization and their own highly specialized skills. Sometimes they are right but, right or wrong, where this belief exists workers can be expected to resist automation in a thousand subtle ways. In some cases they are able to effectively sabotage automation even despite official acceptance by their union leadership. Serious obstacles to automation loom where management fails to foresee this attitude and forestall its consequences. Many employee attitudes will have to change, or be changed, through better planning, communication, consultation, and education. . . .

Studies at Harvard and MIT show that when employers treat a worker as a person possessing valuable skills and knowledge, and demonstrate it by asking his advice on how best to apply new technology, the results are usually full cooperation and many useful suggestions. Workers accept new technological and social conditions easily when consulted in advance and allowed to plan and participate in the changeover. But when merely told what is to happen, or what is happening or has already happened, workers often demonstrate their resentment to the changes in many overt ways ranging from lower productivity to sabotage. They may also exhibit a variety of unconsciously developed symptoms such as mistakes of all kinds, frequent accidents, and even severe and chronic illnesses bordering on occupational diseases. . . .

SPACE EXPLORATION

L. V. Berkner

ARE SPACE PROBES WORTH IT?*

. . . No month—and hardly a week—goes by without more news about man's trials and triumphs in the world of space.

In the five years since President Eisenhower's announcement of the United States space program on July 28, 1955, we have learned much, and not the least important fact is that space exploration will be expensive. In 1959, our space program cost us almost $500,-000,000, and in 1960 it is expected that military and civilian space activities will cost more than $1,150,000,000.

Are such huge expenditures worth while? Although it is true that we cannot yet predict the full returns to mankind that will come from thorough space exploration, we can already perceive very substantial rewards from our present program. Our space expenditures should be considered a capital investment, like the construction of a great factory from which will emerge profitable products in the future.

In many respects, the situation is parallel to the system of subsidy that was necessary for the aircraft industry thirty years ago. Such subsidies made possible the creation of a new industry which not only provided us with the benefits of fast transport between any points on earth, but created employment, new sources of tax revenue and new and challenging opportunities for business men. At the

* L. V. Berkner, "Are Space Probes Worth It?" *The New York Times Magazine,* August 28, 1960. Reprinted by permission of The New York Times and the author. Dr. Berkner is President of the Graduate Research Center, Inc., Dallas, Texas.

moment, many of us do not realize that a similar situation exists with respect to space.

The practical potentialities of space exploration are sharply punctuated by the development of our capability to recover space vehicles on earth. The success . . . of both the U.S. and the U.S.S.R. in returning space vehicles safely marks a major step toward ease in all aspects of space operations in the future. The ability to return vehicles with safety will increase the pay-offs to be anticipated from our space program in military, commercial and particularly in scientific applications of space activity.

Just what rewards can we expect from space? Each field of research has its hopes and has its attendant hazards. These are some of the pay-offs and problems:

Military

The most promising military application of space vehicles is the reconnaissance satellite. Already the first craft has been launched to develop this capability. A half-dozen such devices, in appropriate orbits about 300 miles above the surface, could scan during sunlight hours every point on the earth daily. If it was not considered necessary to cover the whole earth, a smaller number could do the job. The nation possessing them would have an immense defensive advantage.

Even with present techniques, it is reasonable to expect that surface objects about 100 feet across could be distinguished in the pictures sent back by a reconnaissance satellite. Radar would enable it to observe large movements, as of troops or airplanes, even through a cover of clouds.

It could also eavesdrop on communications carried on at such very high frequencies that they cannot be received over more than a limited surface distance. Indeed, the quantity of communications information that can be acquired in this way is so great that a special problem will arise in handling the data collected, so that only useful information will be sorted out.

A special application is the twenty-four-hour satellite. This is one launched in such a way as to orbit at the same rate as the earth revolves. Thus it would appear to remain stationary (or to swing very slowly in an arc) over one spot. Here, truly, "Big Brother is watching you." Such a satellite could be used not only for reconnaissance, but to broadcast television and radio programs into another nation's territory. Jamming such broadcasts would be difficult and could be accomplished only by another satellite.

Obviously, overflights by reconnaissance satellites will raise serious problems in international relations. We consider that space begins about 100 miles above the earth's surface, but how far do a nation's territorial rights extend? If a nation considers an overflying or hovering satellite inimical to its interests, it will be impelled to take countermeasures to reduce its effectiveness, or to destroy it. Thus the possibility of a space war arises, unless agreements among nations avoid the creation of friction in this way.

There is a more reassuring aspect to the use of reconnaissance satellites. By providing dependable data to show that a nation was *not* preparing an attack, they could conceivably quiet the nerves of a troubled world in a time of crisis, and so help to avert a war.

To reach these goals, however, costly development is required. Instruments are still primitive and great advances and repeated tests will be called for. Much experience will be required to evaluate and comprehend the information telemetered back to earth.

Industrial

Space activities promise to revolutionize communications—radio and television, telephone and teleprinter messages, wirephotos and radiophotos, and the like—to such an extent as to produce a whole new industry.

The number of radio channels suitable for long-distance communications by present methods is very limited. Cables can be used—across both land and oceans—but these also have limited capacity, and are very costly.

Communications by means of suitably oriented and instrumented satellites promise to change this situation entirely.

We have just seen the first such experiment, with the launching of an inflated, 100-foot metallic-coated balloon from which radio signals, sent from a highly directional antenna, can be reflected, or bounced to a distant receiver. The system will make very high frequencies—now normally confined to short-distance uses, such as television and car telephones—available for long-distance communications.

The simple reflecting sphere is but a beginning. A twenty-four-hour, or hovering, satellite, equipped with a solar or nuclear power supply and a relay transmitter, could increase the present communications capacity between two distant points a hundredfold. A hundred such satellites properly placed would increase our world-wide communications capability by a factor of 10,000.

Intercontinental radio and television networks are elementary examples of the applications of space communications that should be available in the next decade or so. World-wide telephone dialing will become possible. Message costs will be cut to perhaps one-tenth their present levels.

Whole new systems of international communications will doubtless appear. One can imagine a plant manager instantly ordering materials from anywhere in the world, with detailed specifications communicated automatically.

Indeed, the remote operation of automated machines in accordance with predetermined specifications seems entirely probable. Beyond lie applications in forms we cannot now even visualize, but we can be sure that they will bring peoples closer together and create enormous industrial opportunities.

Again, a heavy expenditure of effort will be needed. Component parts of electronic circuits must reach quite new levels of reliability to last for ten or twenty years in continuous operation on station. Even our largest present rockets could not place a heavy relay satellite in twenty-four-hour orbit, and we must await the Saturns and Novas that are now being developed.

To acquire this communications capability—with the industry and employment and other advantages that it can provide to mankind—will require the development of an intricate system of international agreements and controls.

For example, there must be agreement on the transmitters and receivers to be used. Frequencies must be allocated in detail to avoid interference among satellites or with the present short-range users of high frequencies. There must be controls to prevent commercial warfare in the form of jamming signals that would render satellites useless.

The International Telecommunications Union, an affiliated agency of the United Nations, provides a basis for such agreements. At its regular decennial meeting in Geneva last year, the I.T.U. called a special session on space communications for 1963. Already a work group of the agency has begun studies to see how the world can deal with these revolutionary problems. Within the United States, the Federal Communications Commission has announced hearings to review and evaluate the new problems that space communications impose.

Scientific

. . . Illustrative of [the immense advances in science brought about by space research] were the accomplishments of Pioneer V.

As it left the earth, Pioneer V found a third belt of electrification encompassing the earth 50,000 miles above its surface. Farther out, this great rocket found that interplanetary space was permeated by a small but significant magnetic field. Then, following an eruption on the sun, it encountered a dense cloud of ejected solar particles carrying with it a strong magnetic field. As this cloud reached the earth it caused a severe geomagnetic storm. This rocket showed that decreases in cosmic-ray intensity associated with geomagnetic storms occurred in distant space as well as at the earth, so that cosmic-ray decrease is an interplanetary and not a geocentric phenomenon.

From data like these observed in space, together with the I.G.Y. observations on earth, . . . scientists . . . pieced together an exciting and coherent picture of the earth's interplanetary environment, and of the mighty influences of a stormy sun in producing important effects on the earth. Where will this new knowledge from space lead us?

Let us consider, as an example, the benefits of space research in meteorology. At present, weather forecasts can be made with reasonable reliability only about forty-eight hours in advance. If we could extend our forecasts only a little, the monetary gain would be enormous.

A representative of the American Petroleum Institute recently remarked that a knowledge of climate only a few per cent more reliable than we have might save oil companies $100,000,000 a year, since they would know in advance where to ship their oil and could cut inventories elsewhere. In one way or another, almost every aspect of human activity is affected by the weather, affected in terms of actual costs of operation.

How can satellites increase the accuracy of our forecasts? One way is by observing and mapping variations in the earth's cloud cover. We know that clouds reflect back into space 10 to 12 per cent of the sun's heat which otherwise would reach the earth's surface. Since it is this heat that warms the atmosphere and powers the terrestrial heat engine that gives us winds and storms, variations in the cloud cover have a profound effect upon our weather. But we do not yet know how, when and to what extent these variations occur.

The primitive experiments now under way, such as the many cloud photographs taken by the satellite Tiros, indicate that we are on the threshold of unimagined advances in our knowledge of meteorology. In the long run, increased understanding of climatic trends may prove more important than improvements in day-to-day forecasting. Man's earthly environment changes constantly. After all,

New York was in the grip of an ice age probably not more than 20,000 years ago, hardly any time in geologic terms.

We do not yet know, although we should, what will be the ultimate effects on our environment of the simple activity of burning up the earth's fossil fuels—coal and oil—and discharging the resulting carbon dioxide into the atmosphere. Improved knowledge of meteorology has an enormous bearing on mankind's welfare in the future.

Astronomy offers another example of how space activity can pay off in terms of scientific research. Satellite-borne telescopes, outside the earth's atmosphere, will show the heavens with new clarity. From these studies, it seems likely, we shall learn not only much about the origin and character of the universe, but also new information about the basic physical processes of things about us.

Finally, space exploration will extend to the moon and planets. The first steps will be taken by placing a man in orbit around the earth and bringing him back—Project Mercury. A suborbital test flight is imminent, probably before the end of the year. Then will come visits to the moon made by unmanned craft equipped with instruments to study their targets as they circle them, and radio their findings back to earth. Next will come unmanned vehicles that can be landed, made to gather samples of the surface, and relaunched to return to earth; and, at length, manned vehicles.

No one can predict just what the material pay-off will be, but as John A. Johnson, general counsel of the National Aeronautics and Space Administration, has said:

"It is the thought of man being projected into a totally alien environment, whether in orbit about the earth, or standing for the first time on the moon, or preparing to land on another planet, that makes the whole business the most exciting enterprise of our age."

Certainly, landings of instruments on the moon to relay back information will be possible within three or four years. But to take man out, to give him protection, to equip him for useful work and to return him is a project that will require at least a decade.

The foreign-affairs problems in the scientific space field are fourfold. First, there is the need for international cooperation in tracking and communicating with space vehicles. Not only must there be observation stations in different countries around the globe but there must be agreements to clear specific radio channels for space use.

Second, there must be agreements for the exchange of data received from satellites, and of the codes whereby they can be "read." Clearly, scientists of a nation cooperating in the collection of data will want to share in their interpretation.

Third, scientists of non-launching nations must be given access to space. Agreements permitting them to use facilities aboard space vehicles for their own experiments are necessary if we are to avoid envy and hatred—and if we are to advance science by drawing upon the best men, regardless of nationality.

Fourth, international agreement on the biological decontamination of space vehicles is of the utmost importance. If there is life on other planets, even in the most elementary forms of viruses or bacteria, it is vital that it be identified without any confusion introduced by bringing earthly forms of microorganisms.

Fortunately, international scientific cooperation in space dates from the very beginnings of space activity, under the International Council of Scientific Unions, in the organization of the International Geophysical Year. It is being continued in the work of a worldwide group known as the Committee on Space Research (COSPAR). . . .

The United Nations, too, is working in this field through its Committee on the Peaceful Uses of Outer Space. The first U.N. International Conference on Outer Space is to be held sometime next year. Out of these discussions can come intelligent planning for the necessary steps toward international cooperation and agreement.

* * *

These are some of the pay-offs that we can expect from a solid program of space research. Without international controls on the use of space, however, the possibilities for good will become sources of serious international tensions—possibly even of space war.

For the moment, we have a period of respite while nations develop new and more sophisticated forms of space activity. We must hope that the nations use it for serious discussions leading to agreements that will enable space research to exploit its exciting opportunities and benefit all mankind to the full.

Kingsley Martin

REFLECTIONS ON OUTER SPACE*

I feel I ought to be excited about these dogs returning from outer space to eat mincemeat and lollies. Within a year or two there really will be a man on the moon and cosmic travellers will no doubt be writing in the popular press about what it feels like to have lost weight. These are indeed staggering, but no longer incredible, achievements. If civilised men survive to profit by them, their long-term effects on the human mind will be even greater than the discovery at the end of the Middle Ages that there were outer continents unknown to the Old World and that the earth was not the centre round which the spheres revolved. Nothing can so potently change thought as the discovery of limitless space beyond accepted horizons.

Science fiction has become science fact. When I try to realise what this means, I recall talks with H. G. Wells, the most engaging of the pioneers of science fiction. As a young man his imagination was caught by the potentialities of science; there seemed nothing that man could not do. Glory to Man in the Highest for Man is the Master of Things. He allowed himself to imagine a war of the worlds, great aircraft battling in the skies and biologists performing horrible experiments, transforming beasts into human shape. But these, like his story of men rocketing to the moon, were no more, he told me, than ingenious phantasies, not serious prophecies. What he did earnestly believe was that men would learn to use their knowledge for their happiness, and he wrote of utopias in which men were free from disease and poverty, lived in concord in a world state, co-operating in many-storeyed palaces, endlessly conversing together, their athletic bodies clothed in splendid robes of synthetic material, uncreasable and, presumably, requiring no ironing.

One often-made criticism troubled him. What would people do with themselves in these utopias? When all the world was a garden

* Reprinted by permission from the *New Statesman*, August 27, 1960, p. 265.
Mr. Martin is an editorial writer for the *New Statesman* of London.

and there was no longer pain or sin or shame, with what would the human mind have to grapple? He came nearest to facing this problem in the last of his serious books. In *The Shape of Things to Come* he imagined the nations destroying their civilisations in almost unending war; at last the air-men get together and end the strife with a 'peace-gas' and the world is reconstructed by the scientists according to their—and his—heart's desire. Disinterested lords of creation, they think of many wonderful things to do to make all the world beautiful as well as happy. Only then, when earthly problems are solved, do they decide to explore outer space: the book ends with a dialogue in which youth demands the right to adventure and to risk life by exploring the stars. It was after this book was published that I recall Wells bitterly denouncing Aldous Huxley, whose *Brave New World* was founded on the thesis that science would make, not an earthly paradise, but a new hell.

This is the clash of prophetic vision that haunts our present world. Is there any reason to believe that, either before or after a series of wars of unimaginable destruction, the scientific world will be one in which men will be happy and free? Today mankind is riven by warring ideologies and national disputes; it is also divided between those who possess and can manipulate the new inventions, while ordinary people feel helpless; some of them strive to maintain a mastery, not of things, but of their individual souls. They watch, with something like despair, the immeasurable powers of science being used not for human welfare, but for the cold and essentially inhuman endeavour to reach planets on which men are never likely to live. The exploration of outer space may, I'm told, teach us to understand the weather. There is no doubt some arid consolation in the thought that in twenty years or so prodigious new discoveries about the nature of the universe will be made when we can shoot rockets to Mars or Venus. But this majestic triumph of the human intellect and skill will not buy as much as a single bowl of rice or improve the lot of one half-starved inhabitant of this globe. Indeed it is likely further to impoverish mankind, since it will divert vast sums of money and an increasingly high proportion of the best brains and most skilful technicians from the task of making life more livable on our overpopulated world. Moreover, science is now being exploited so that one powerful section of the world may destroy another.

It is these mundane thoughts that make one angry rather than gloomy today. If we are to judge by most of the pronouncements of American physicists, their chief (though, I believe, not sole) anxiety is lest they should be behind the Russians in the ability to destroy the world. Soviet science, in its moment of triumph, speaks today with a more civilised voice; if we are to believe its spokesmen, they are, above all, moved by a passionate excitement to explore the solar system. Their present rocket achievements are not, so the scientists tell me, those that would have been undertaken if the object had been primarily military. They can, however, be readily switched if, like China, they decide Lenin was right after all and that a world war must be a prelude to a Communist utopia. The national pride of their cheering crowds can also be readily switched to militant chauvinism.

It is with such thoughts in mind that I approached the argument now proceeding in scientific and government circles about what part, if any, Britain should play in space projects. Clearly we cannot afford the huge sums devoted to this branch of science by Russia and America. It would be insane for Britain to devote any considerable part of her limited resources to such an adventure, while our people remain so largely uneducated, our slums so great a national disgrace and our contribution to the welfare of the undeveloped nations so miserably inadequate. Even in the scientific field we are far behind; large sums of money are urgently needed if we are not ourselves to become a backward area. There is, however, one possibility that might make it sensible for us to take part in space adventure. As things are now going, the probable upshot is that the new knowledge will be used to destroy this world in a war for possession of the moon. Governments faced with human annihilation might yet be persuaded to make joint space exploration a reason for a renewed Summit. They would have the backing of scientists who are angry at the perversion of their work. If space exploration becomes an International Project, Britain should take part in it, even if it means further impoverishing ourselves. Mankind would then have taken the first step towards world unity.

PRIORITIES IN SPACE EXPLORATION*

DR. PICKERING. Most of us concerned with space in 1955 would have dismissed as incredible the statement that in the 1960's the United States would be spending almost $1 billion on a space program. Let us remember that in 1955 the United States was everywhere the recognized world leader in technology, in know-how, in daring and imaginative engineering projects.

Now, in the short space of 5 years, we find the situation dramatically reversed. We do not debate the necessity for large expenditures in a space program, and the position of the United States as a technological leader in the world is seriously threatened, and perhaps overcome. . . .

Russia, quite frankly, attaches great weight to the propaganda value it can extract from its space program, and at least one major objective of this program is a well-planned campaign that can convince the world that Russia, and not the United States, is the technological leader of the world.

I think it is most important to recognize that Russian leadership in space technology is extrapolated by people everywhere to mean Russian leadership in all technology. I was interested in reading some time ago of a proposal to import small Russian cars to the United States for sale to the U.S. public. Five years ago, before Sputnik, the idea that a U.S. car-buying public would choose to buy a Russian automobile would have been regarded as absurd. But now, because of the Sputnik and Lunik shots, all Russian technology is suddenly invested with an aura of excellence.

While Russia has been skillfully exploiting these space successes in the past 2 years, what have we done in this country to compete? Actually, we have done a great deal, but much more remains to be done before we can say, in the words of the Space Act, that we are

---

* *Review of the Space Program.* Statement of Dr. William H. Pickering in the Hearings before the House Committee on Science and Astronautics, Part 3, 86th Congress, 2nd Session, February and March 1960, Government Printing Office, Washington, D.C., pp. 898–904.

Dr. Pickering is Director of the Jet Propulsion Laboratories, California Institute of Technology, Pasadena, California.

preserving the role of the United States as a leader in aeronautical and space science and technology.

The real problem results from our confusion and indecision as to what the exploration of space really means, and what is the motivation for the exploration of space. There have been statements, frequently conflicting, from Government sources, military sources, and experts in all fields, as to what the United States should do, and why. There has been confusion as to the relationship between the missile program and the space program—between the civilian space program and the military space programs. It seems to me that this is the heart of the problem. If we can really understand the motivation and the reasons for the space program, and agree upon this, then it is easy to establish the priorities and support necessary for the program.

I think that we should first understand the difference between the missile program and the space program of the country. It is true that the space program utilizes the large military missiles as booster vehicles, but beyond this there is very little relationship. Military missiles are being developed for a specific purpose as part of the military weapons systems, and as such, they must indeed have the very highest priority. I do not wish to comment about the so-called missile gap, but I have no hesitation in saying that I find it not only proper but necessary for the military to be developing accurate and reliable long-range ballistic missile weapon systems.

Our space program, and here I include both our military and our civilian space programs, is not in any way analogous to the ballistic missile weapon program. In a word, we can say that the missile program is developing a weapon to be used in war or to prevent war; and our space program is a cold-war weapon. It seems to me that if this key point could be accepted by the scientists on the one hand and the military on the other, then we as a Nation could establish a space program which would quickly reestablish our technological position in the world. At the same time, the scientists should be able to conduct the scientific exploration of space, and the military would be in a position to exploit possible military applications of space.

My concern with our present space program is that, as it is currently evolving, there is an increasing tendency for military applications to dominate the space picture. This, I believe to be unfortunate as far as our international position is concerned, and also as far as internal support of the total space program is concerned. Clearly, the military and civilian programs must compete for relatively scarce manpower and facilities as well as dollars, and because of the very high costs of this program, unnecessary duplication and competition should obviously be avoided. Therefore, it is essential that the program be kept in proper balance, consistent with our real national space objectives. . . .

MR. MC CORMACK. Doctor, in the world of today we have got to be very practical. We have to realize the question of self-preservation; is that right?

DR. PICKERING. Yes, sir.

MR. MC CORMACK. Not only of ourselves personally, but the way of life we believe in. And our way of life is being challenged, sharply so. While I recognize the importance of nonmilitary research and development—I was Chairman of the select committee out of which NASA came—we have to be practical in the world of today and realize not only the potential but actual danger that confronts our way of life, the way of life we believe in, democratic institutions of Government. The job we have to do, would you agree, is to try to create a harmonious relationship between the civilian agency and the military to make the maximum contributions to our national interest and our national preservation?

DR. PICKERING. Yes, sir.

MR. MC CORMACK. As a matter of fact, most of the developments in the field of research in the past conducted by the military have had tremendous peaceful results; is that right?

DR. PICKERING. Yes, sir.

MR. MC CORMACK. You don't advocate the elimination of research and development by the military in the world of today; do you?

DR. PICKERING. No, sir; I do not. I think the military is doing a fine job in supporting a great deal of fundamental research in many areas.

MR. MC CORMACK. You wouldn't—would you take the position that in the field of military research and development, and civilian, that the military should be subordinated in the world of today, to the civilian?

DR. PICKERING. Well, sir, if you are referring particularly to the area of space research then what I believe is that having established the NASA as an independent agency to conduct a space program, that this agency should, indeed, establish the national programs, part of which may very well be done by the military, but it should be done in a coordinated fashion with NASA taking the lead. . . .

MR. MC CORMACK. There should be a coordination, but I was try-ing to go beyond that to see what your thinking was on the question of priority—at this point in the world's history. I am not talking about a peaceful world. You can't deal with the Soviets on a moral plane; they have no moral origin, that is the institution as such. I am not talking about the people of Russia or many of them. I am talking about the regime in control. And if they have no moral origin you can't deal with them on the idealistic level. And therefore it is on the level of the law of self-preservation that we are forced to con-sider these questions.

DR. PICKERING. Yes, sir.

MR. MC CORMACK. Idealism is one of them and I am for it. I have ideals, but I try to be practical in the world of today.

DR. PICKERING. Well, sir, I think I am also trying to make a practical approach, which says namely that the military must devote its efforts and its support to the military-weapons systems and I would regard the intercontinental and long-range ballistic missiles as a very im-portant weapons system which the military must indeed be support-ing and be supporting with very high priority. I regard the space program as, indeed, another part of this struggle between two con-flicting ideologies, and that to much of the world the achievements of the United States in the space program are a very important factor in their attitude toward the United States. Therefore, I feel it is essential that the United States have significant and dramatic achievements in space.

The question it seems to me hinges around, How does the United States organize to accomplish this? It seems to me that having estab-lished the NASA, having set up a definite channel of scientific and general civilian achievement in space, that the United States should pursue this route with the military putting its research efforts in the field of missiles, as such, the NASA putting its efforts in the field of space.

MR. MC CORMACK. How about reconnaissance satellites, that could be used for both military and peaceful purposes, what would you say on that?

DR. PICKERING. Yes, sir; this reconnaissance satellite may indeed be a useful military weapon.

MR. MC CORMACK. There are various types of reconnaissance satellites.

DR. PICKERING. Yes, sir. I think the only question I would raise is whether or not one should at this time embark on a full-fledged reconnaissance satellite program or should one say to the NASA: "Move ahead as fast as you can in developing the technology appropriate to reconnaissance satellites."

For example, NASA is proposing to conduct some experiments with a meteorological satellite which will explore cloud cover and so forth. This surely is . . . the first step in looking at the Earth from a satellite, in transmitting back to the ground signals from the satellite which give you a picture of what the satellite sees.

As a result of this, then, it seems to me one moves ahead into the next step as to whether or not this is a military weapons system, rather than to say at this time, when nobody except the Russians have produced a picture which has been taken from a satellite, should we at this time conclude that we can indeed see our way clear to develop a reconnaissance satellite system. . . .

MR. ANFUSO. Dr. Pickering, you talked about a cold war. Isn't that really the thing that we are going to be most concerned with in the next few years, a cold war?

DR. PICKERING. Yes, sir; I certainly hope it is not a hot war.

MR. ANFUSO. And in a cold war you are fighting to capture men's minds all over the world. And the nation which convinces the rest of the world that what they are doing is for peaceful purposes will gain more friends; isn't that correct?

DR. PICKERING. Yes, sir.

MR. ANFUSO. Now, do you see a hope in the peaceful discoveries in outer space which someday can create an abundance and a sufficiency in this world to make all nations recognize the futility of war?

DR. PICKERING. Well, sir, it is difficult to predict exactly what will be the outcome of our ventures into space, but we can certainly say that at this time we have reached the stage in the development of mankind when mankind for the first time is able to look beyond our planet. We have explored our planet, we have mapped it, we have walked all over it and so forth and now we are beginning for the first time to go off the planet, and the ability to do this, it seems to me, is something which has fired the imagination of people all over the world and therefore achievements in this area are going to be looked upon by people all over the world as a very important index of the capability of a nation. . . .

THE SCIENTIST AND THE PUBLIC

SCIENCE AND HUMAN WELFARE*

. . . .

Four years ago, the report of the A.A.A.S. Interim Committee on the Social Aspects of Science stated: "We are now in the midst of a new and unprecedented scientific revolution which promises to bring about profound changes in the condition of human life. The forces and processes now coming under human control are beginning to match in size and intensity those of nature itself, and our total environment is now subject to human influence. In this situation it becomes imperative to determine that these new powers shall be used for the maximum human good, for, if the benefits to be derived from them are great, the possibility of harm is correspondingly serious." . . .

Now, as in 1956, our premises are these:

1. We are witnessing an unprecedented growth in the scale and intensity of scientific work.

2. This growth has been stimulated by an intense demand for the practical products of research, especially for military and industrial use.

3. The public interest in, and understanding of, science is not commensurate with the importance that science has attained in our social structure. It cannot be said that society provides good conditions for the proper growth of science.

4. For reasons such as those just cited, science is experiencing a period of rapid but rather unbalanced growth. Basic research, which is the ultimate source of the practical results so much in demand, is

---

* Prepared by the American Association for the Advancement of Science, Committee on Science in the Promotion of Human Welfare. Reprinted by permission of the A.A.A.S. from Science, July 8, 1960.

poorly supported and, in the view of some observers, lacks vigor and quality.

5. The growth of science and the great enhancement of the degree of control which we now exert over nature have given rise to new social practices, of great scope and influence, which make use of new scientific knowledge. While this advance of science has greatly improved the condition of human life, it has also generated new hazards of unprecedented magnitude.

Since 1956 this general pattern has taken on some new features which concern us at this time.

1. The conscious exploitation of science for military advantage continues at an accelerating rate. But in recent years this process has merged with another, equally important trend: science is being pressed into the service of international politics. Scientific accomplishment per se has become an accepted—and at present dominant—factor of prestige among nations. The philosophy of "getting ahead of the Russians" (or Americans), which once referred only to military matters, now includes scientific achievements as well. This rivalry has strongly motivated the recent intensification of government support for scientific research.

2. The rapid emergence of political independence among the "underdeveloped" nations of the world, and their natural desire to exploit modern technology, has added to the importance of international exchange of scientific knowledge and personnel. Perhaps one reason for the rivalry for scientific pre-eminence among the more advanced nations is the expectation of political advantage from this exchange.

3. Certain recent scientific advances add directly to the ease with which our knowledge of nature can be applied to the control of human beings and of social organization. Development of new psychotomimetic drugs and psychological techniques have suggested, to some, effective means for controlling the behavior of social groups. Progress in the science of cybernetics and the development of automation techniques result in new capabilities for direct control of social and economic processes.

4. Despite some recent effort toward improvement, there is no reason to alter the earlier conclusion that our present social environment does not favor the development of an understanding of science, or of science's aims and needs. The increasingly spectacular practical achievements of science have only accentuated misconceptions about the relative significance, for the growth of science, of practical results and the advancement of basic knowledge. To many people

physical science means nuclear energy and rockets. The public is sometimes led to expect that biological and medical research will conquer every human ailment—will overcome death. There is a tendency to equate scientific progress with a sum of money and a number of people. There is insufficient appreciation of the significance of basic research, or of the conditions in which it can flourish. . . .

. . . The military and political advantages, to a nation, of scientific progress within its own borders are self-evident. Yet, it is a truism—but nevertheless a vital one—that nature is the same everywhere, and that the study of nature is an activity of the whole human race. Any effort to divide science into fragments which are delimited by national boundaries, and dominated by a local social philosophy, will inevitably restrict the free discovery and communication of new knowledge that is the substance of scientific progress. A "nationalistic" science is an anachronism which cannot long continue without damage to science and eventually to the nation.

What, then, is the scientist's responsibility to his own nation's scientific effort? Clearly, we need to understand that what science contributes to the national purpose is measured by what it adds to the sum of human knowledge; science serves the nation by serving humanity.

A further examination of the effects of the present social uses of science on life inside the house of science itself leads to even more disturbing conclusions. There is some evidence that the integrity of science is beginning to erode under the abrasive pressure of its close partnership with economic, social, and political affairs.

In recent controversies about fallout and the detection of nuclear explosions, partisanship on the part of some scientists for a particular political approach to the problem has been so intense in some instances as to cloud—at least in the public mind—the identity between science and an objective regard for the facts.

The grim international competition for "supremacy" in scientific accomplishment also endangers the integrity of science. Unseemly claims of priority may be encouraged. Premature reports of new scientific discoveries, which will occur to some extent in any circumstances, may be permitted to acquire a semblance of credibility.

An illustration—as yet unrealized—is the matter of "the creation of life." Some scientists believe that the properties of life are inherent in the chemistry of nucleic acid, and would regard the artificial synthesis of a reproducible nucleic acid or nucleoprotein molecule—which may occur in the reasonably near future—as the "creation"

of life. Other scientists would disagree with this interpretation
because they believe that nucleic acid, nucleoprotein, or anything
less than a living cell is not "life," for the reason that it is not a self-
sufficient replicative agent.

Under ordinary circumstances this difference of opinion would be
occasionally debated among scientists and finally resolved when the
weight of evidence on one side or the other became sufficiently
strong, or when a new and more acceptable idea emerged. However,
in the present circumstances this matter may take another course.
There is some evidence that a claimed "creation of life" based on the
test-tube synthesis of an infectious molecule might be regarded by
a government as a scientific accomplishment of great political importance—a kind of "biological Sputnik." In this case, scientists may
be hard pressed to persuade government officials—and perhaps even
some of their colleagues—that the discovery should be given an
interpretation which is less dramatic but more in keeping with the
divided scientific opinion of its significance.

It is evident that the accelerating progress of science has evoked
a number of serious problems that affect both the social order and
the internal situation of our scientific establishment. Having become
a major instrument in political affairs, science is inseparably bound
up with many troublesome questions of public policy. That science
is valued more for these uses than for its fundamental purpose—the
free inquiry into nature—leads to pressures which have begun to
threaten the integrity of science itself. . . .

. . . The scientific community should accept the obligation to
determine how new advances in our understanding and control of
natural forces are likely to affect human welfare, to call these matters
to public attention, and to provide for the public and its social and
political agencies the objective statements of the facts and of the
consequences of alternative policies that are required as the basis for
informed decisions on the relative merits of proposed courses of
action.

At what point in the social process should the scientific community
enter as an agency of information? One view is that, since most
social decisions are executed by government, the scientist's function
is to inform and advise government departments and officials. The
government does, of course, need such advice, and a number of
useful methods of providing it have been evolved. In these instances,
scientists serve only by invitation. Inevitably, the general content of
the information that is provided and the tenor of the advice that is
offered are to some degree conditioned by the particular interests of

the requesting agency, which determines what questions are asked and who is given an opportunity to answer them.

Such a relationship does not wholly fulfill the scientist's social role, as we see it. In dealing with social issues, the scientific community must demonstrate its responsibility and its inherent regard for truth and objectivity and must zealously preserve the freedom of thought and communication that is essential to the pursuit of these goals. Accordingly, we believe that the scientific community ought to assume, on its own initiative, an *independent* and *active* informative role, whether or not other social agencies see any immediate advantage in hearing what the scientist has to say.

We believe, also, that what scientists have to say about the social implications of science should be addressed directly to the general public. Our traditional preference for democratic procedures requires that the citizen be sufficiently informed to decide for himself what is to be done about the issues that scientific progress has thrust upon us. Furthermore, our command over natural forces—for example, the destructive potential of nuclear war—is now so great as to create social and moral questions of such great moment that no social agency ought to intervene between the issue and the public.

In sum, we conclude that the scientific community should, on its own initiative, assume an obligation to call to public attention those issues of public policy which relate to science, and to provide for the general public the facts and estimates of the effects of alternative policies which the citizen must have if he is to participate intelligently in the solution of these problems. A citizenry thus informed is, we believe, the chief assurance that science will be devoted to the promotion of human welfare. . . .

3

GOVERNMENT AND THE AFFLUENT SOCIETY

> . . . I found the most extraordinary examples of what seems to me to be a deterioration in either our national sense of proportion or our national sense of humor. . . . I received for Christmas a small tool. . . . It had a rod that stuck out of the handle and a loop on the end of it, and a button. This was a drink stirrer, a portable drink stirrer. You carried it around with you and if you were so weak and debilitated a member of the public that you couldn't put your finger in your drink or otherwise agitate it, you would use this gadget.
>
> . . . If these things represent the amount of time and effort which I think any miniature product does, then I feel reasonably sure that there is excess engineering talent, time and productive capacity to do those things which have a greater importance to us nationally.

The great economic issues of the 1960's are centered around a national concern for the rate of economic growth. Should growth be an increase in production of consumer goods? Or are we already manufacturing and buying too many useless things? Should more of our labor force become involved in building schools and less in producing automobiles? What part is to be played in the 1960's by the federal government in the adjustment of the "social balance"?

It was John Kenneth Galbraith's *The Affluent Society*[1] which, more than any other single publication, defined the battleground for the great economic issues of the 1960's. The articles chosen for Chapter Three are thus set in a framework that was established to a very large extent by Galbraith.

Yet there is a paradox here. The titles for our selections reveal the preoccupation of the authors with the problem of economic growth. This was not the main theme of *The Affluent Society*. Galbraith, of course, favors growth, but he claims that we are too much concerned with work and output for their own sake. "I do not take seriously the ponderous cliché that economic growth is our major problem," he has said.[2] Galbraith was an influential member of the Democratic Advisory Council. But his statement has a ring to it very different from the Democratic campaign cry of 1960 for a much faster rate of economic growth.

In large measure the new mood of urgency is a response to the international situation—the Soviet challenge, the requirements of defense, aid to the underdeveloped countries. Galbraith does not ignore these factors, but W. W. Rostow and others argue nonetheless that Galbraith underestimates the scale of the challenge presented to us by international developments.

Why then, is *The Affluent Society* so frequently cited? It is because the major point of the book is that we must readjust the social balance in favor of public services as against consumer goods. And this has proved to be a potent argument on two grounds.

In the first place, the Galbraith thesis accords perfectly with the economic interventionism practiced by Democratic administrations during the New Deal and the Fair Deal. It requires vigorous federal action, and it entails an extension of the welfare state and of government planning. This is the main point of the article by A. A. Berle, which is the opening piece in this chapter.

Secondly, *The Affluent Society* articulates at a time of national soul-searching a widespread feeling that we have been preoccupied with frivolities. A number of recent writers have reiterated this

---

[1] Houghton Mifflin Co., Boston, 1958.
[2] J. K. Galbraith, in Symposium on "Problems of United States Economic Development," New York, Committee for Economic Development, 1958, p. 203.

opinion; and Robert Lovett's testimony before a Senate Committee (quoted above), which appears in this chapter, makes a similar point.

W. Allen Wallis reacts strongly against both of these arguments. He denies that we have been neglecting our public services and, while he favors a considerable degree of government influence over the economy, he resists the idea of an extension of central planning and a major increase in government spending.

It is also clear that there is a difference of degree between Berle and Wallis on the question of economic growth. Both of them want it; but, if they were to choose among the three alternative rates of growth projected by James W. Knowles in the last selection of this chapter, Berle would undoubtedly choose the highest rate, and Wallis would probably support a lower rate. Still, this is not the crux of their disagreement. Berle wants to change the social balance, so he favors more government spending and planning as the means of making the economy expand faster. Wallis thinks that the present social balance between public service and consumer goods is sound, so his primary means of promoting growth is to stimulate private business investment through the appropriate tax policies.

Leon Keyserling's view is an interesting variant of the Berle thesis. In a sense he is siding with Wallis in arguing, against Galbraith, that consumer spending has not been too high. Yet, like Berle, he is a strong advocate of rapid growth; and he has argued on many occasions for a considerable increase in the federal budget as one way to achieve it.

There are enormously complex economic problems behind all of these statements. How can we best promote economic growth, hold down inflation, prevent a recession from getting out of hand? Both liberals and conservatives can quote history and innumerable statistics to prove that the other side's policies will cause stagnation, or runaway inflation, or cataclysmic depression, or all of these.

Now the preponderance of expert opinion is that the choices before us are not between utopia and the abyss. If Knowles' estimates are correct, the economic-growth dispute will be over a matter of 1% more or less, which does not suggest catastrophe either way. Neither uncontrolled inflation nor full-scale depression seems likely in the 1960's.

Still there will be significant economic issues to be settled in the political arena. A difference of 1% in the growth rate is $5 billion a year based on the current G.N.P.; compounded over the next ten years it would amount to an impressive sum. The upward pressure on prices has been sustained over a considerable period, and a rapid increase in the rate of growth would intensify the danger of inflation. While no Great Depression looms, sharp recessions have not been abolished, and the unemployment rate of early 1961 was disturbingly high.[3] There is still poverty in the affluent society, especially among minority groups, the aged, and the populations of areas hit by technological change.

So the perennial disputes over government spending, welfare programs, tax policies, the rate of interest, and so on, will continue. But in the 1960's the terms in which such problems are debated will be those of economic growth and the social balance—the two closely interrelated concepts that are the subject of this chapter.

---

[3] There are already indications that the Knowles' projections on unemployment are underestimates. Some economists are now suggesting that it will be very difficult to keep unemployment below 4% or even 5% without a sharp rise in the price level. There are even predictions of unemployment ranging up to 10% by 1965—resulting largely from the increase in automation discussed in Chapter Two.

A. A. Berle, Jr.

WHY OUR ECONOMY
MUST GROW FASTER*

American production, it is said, is increasing too slowly. Annually the country's gross national product tops the previous year by about 3 per cent. Experts are now insisting that this is not good enough. A very impressive group of Americans, acting as a committee of the Rockefeller Brothers Fund, argued for a yearly increase of at least

---

* A. A. Berle, Jr., "Why Our Economy Must Grow Faster," *The New York Times Magazine,* February 7, 1960. Reprinted by permission of The New York Times and the author.

Mr. Berle, a writer on economic problems, has held a number of Administration positions and is currently working with the federal government on Latin-American affairs.

4 per cent, or preferably 5 per cent. Others have expressed the same view. Politicians, military experts, financiers and business men have entered the debate.

This discussion was touched off by two events. One was Premier Khrushchev's boast that the Soviet Union's production would equal that of the United States in 1967 (or thereabouts) and leave us far behind in the decade from 1970 to 1980. The other was our growing cost of defense and the fact that we are lagging in new types of armament.

To some, the Russian threat was reason enough for demanding acceleration of American economic effort. Others (myself included) are less worried about that. With a population thirty millions larger than the United States and the natural desire of her people to live in comfort, the Soviet Union ought to want to catch up. She may well be more comfortable to live with when she does. Just to keep ahead of her in the matter of productivity is not a good enough argument for straining ourselves.

The military reason is more serious. There is continuing need for adequate armaments, even though budget authorities question whether America can "afford" it. Defense, in a time like this, cannot be trifled with. But that is a grim, unhappy reason.

There are, however, stronger considerations for increased production than either of these, and they are quite unconnected with the cold war.

Some productive increase will be required merely to take care of population growth. Each new year sees about 3,500,000 more Americans added to our present roll of nearly 180 millions. (The annual population increase is approximately 1.8 per cent.) Production must increase that much merely to keep the American standard of living where it now is. In addition, Americans are accustomed to expect that each year they will live a little better than the last. This means a continuous production growth somewhat greater than population increase. It has been fulfilled by our annual 3 per cent increase. But, since the American standard of living is already far and away the highest in the world, do we really need to go faster than the 3-per-cent rate, and if so, why?

Some commentators doubt that we do. These promptly get down to cases. There is, for example, a moderate surplus of oil above ground and ample proven reserves in the earth. Why more productivity in oil? Aluminum plants with plenty of available raw material are capable of pouring out far more aluminum than the country now buys. Why more of that? Agricultural surpluses already constitute a prime economic and political headache. Surely not more of them!

As to steel, so long as the chiefs of the union and the companies compose their difficulties there is capacity sufficient to meet America's needs, with a moderate margin over. Slight but steady increase there will take care of the future.

Existing automobile plants can, without trouble, produce more than 9,000,000 cars a year, against a present firm predictable market for between six and seven millions. American textile mills regularly run below capacity. Clearly not much is gained by producing unmarketable surpluses of oil, aluminum, steel, wheat, automobiles or cloth. That might be "productivity," but it could not be called sense. Critics therefore suggest we relax and take ourselves less seriously.

Plowing below the surface, nevertheless, turns up another set of considerations. These are not disposed of quite so easily.

"Productivity," as economists use the term, is running now at about $500 billion a year. The figure is the value of the "gross national product." This includes two items. One is the value of tangible things—"goods"—produced in the year. Among these are the oil, steel, wheat, automobiles, new plants and so forth. The other item represents "services"—work done during the year by human beings for pay.

Last year's "services" include the pay of President Eisenhower and also of Jascha Heifetz, the salaries of school teachers and also of quiz-show performers, the compensation of doctors and also of circus clowns. All this was work for which Americans were willing to pay, valued at the price they actually did pay.

The figure for the "services" item may be open to some criticism. Economists make acid jokes about it. "If," they say, "the Congress wants to increase the 'productivity' figure, it can easily do so. Just raise the pay of every Congressman to half a billion a year. This will up the 'services' item, and up goes the productivity total by around $300 billion—that is, assuming the country would pay up." (Author's note: It wouldn't.)

But when not making jokes, your economist is apt to be a down-to-earth fellow. He reckons as services the amount Americans actually did pay for all these activities. He assumes the renderers of services were paid at about what their work was worth—at any rate, the pay represented what America thought it was worth strongly enough to pay for it. That measures their "productivity."

Just here begins one major argument of those who want an increase. For it is clear that in this service field there is not adequate "productivity," and everyone knows it. Bluntly, there are a great number of activities badly wanted—needed, if you choose—by the American public that it is not paying for and not getting.

Let us take a very few illustrations in a huge field. There is a dangerous shortage of nurses. Many hospitals in New York and elsewhere are dipping into capital endowment to cover expenses. There are not enough good doctors. There are far too few scientists. There is a crucial scarcity of engineers. In addition, great areas of existing services are badly underpaid. This is true of most school teachers outside the great urban areas; of all younger, and most older, men in college teaching; of many people in the administrative ranks of business.

We can get by for a while with present "productivity" in these and many other professions. But underpay means either that productivity in these occupations is inadequate now, or that the services will cease to be available a little later—if we are right in wanting them as we do.

Nor is there an overproduction of "goods"—if the United States fulfills some obvious tasks most Americans want done. A ride around any major American city—try Chicago or New York—will convince any sane person of that. Great areas of these and many other towns ought to be torn down and built over.

Cleaning out slums and blighted areas on an adequate ten-year plan would substantially increase demand for all kinds of very tangible goods. (Khrushchev, by the way, after looking at an American slum, is said to have made the comment: "We also have slums. But in ten years we will not, while you Americans will then have more slums than you do now.") From a downtown New York skyscraper window I can see about a billion dollars of badly wanted productivity. (The Narrows Bridge from Staten Island to Brooklyn alone will require around $300 million; a new Bellevue Hospital will call for $100 million more.)

Here we meet problems. It is not, apparently, a question of merely producing more goods, or more services. It is partly a matter of producing, in addition to what we do now, the particular goods and the particular services that will strengthen the American economy, American civilization and American defense.

We ought to be constructing a great deal more good housing, especially for middle and lower income brackets—which means more productivity in that line. Obviously, it would also increase productivity if we multiplied production of hula hoops or plastic balloons. But if we did, America would not be much better off.

We ought also to have more services, among them first-rate teaching, more scientific and technical personnel, adequate medical care, not to mention a country-wide system of drama and theatre, and so forth. These needs would not be satisfied by more "productivity" in the form of expanded quiz shows.

The professional economist at this point weighs in with a few tart remarks. You, he says, are talking about what America "ought" to have. Or about what it "needs," or about what will "strengthen" its civilization, and you conclude we should have more productivity. This, he rises to state, is all very well for a politician. But it is no business for economists. They measure not what people ought to want, or what they might want under different circumstances, or even what is needed or "adequate." Economics measures what they actually did want, judged by the goods they were able and willing to buy (and did).

True, he would add, if the country really wants to rebuild its cities as badly as it wanted to build its Army, Navy and Air Force in World War II, and if it is willing to pay for that either by taxation or by working harder, or by buying more, or otherwise, the production will be forthcoming. The labor and materials for it are all there.

But making a country want this sort of thing badly enough to pay the shot is not an economist's job. It is a job for preachers, professors, philosophers, politicians, editors and public-relations men. When their campaign is successful, the rest follows in course. Production, like all forms of economics, follows men's desires.

In fact, he will add (warming to the subject), if a country really wants things badly enough to sacrifice others, it can get many of them without increasing productivity beyond the annual increase in population.

Look over the shop windows on any Main Street. See how many are filled with stuff in the plastic-balloon class, and how many with goods that have enduring use. In wartime a country knows what it wants most so well that it accepts a rationing system. Then you cannot get plastic balloons or kiddie cars. Labor and materials used for that kind of production are channeled into steel, airplanes, guns, aluminum and solid stuff the country knows it needs.

Even in peacetime the annual American output of cars could be lower. With slight changes, all cars probably could be built to run for fifteen years instead of five or six. The country got along without cigarettes until World War I—it could do so again. By cutting out production of things people now want that don't amount to much, and by steering that production into goods or services considered more useful, this America of ours could strengthen itself a good bit and without substantial hardship.

But, he would add, this means that someone, somewhere, somehow, has made the country want something different from what, judged by results, it has wanted up to now. (Unless, of course, an economic dictatorship has been accepted, as in Russia, and then the

Government simply tells the public to take what it is given and like it.)

Thereupon the economist goes back to his statistics, leaving you and me with the problem, the Rockefeller report, a stack of other assorted material and a nice piece of homework.

We are pretty clear that Americans will, somehow, arrange to get both their important wants and their luxuries as well. We know that America will not accept an economic dictatorship. It will buy plastic balloons on some occasions, and it does like its cigarettes and its colorful feathers. We know, too, that it also wants its slums cleared away, its housing built, its cities made beautiful, its medical services available everywhere and better teaching than most of its children now receive.

An economy that will probably produce and pay for a half-trillion dollars' worth of "goods and services" in 1960 can "afford" all this and more, if it is willing. But there is a catch. It must be ready to steer part of this huge product toward the latter areas.

How to do that is a trick we are only just learning.

Possibly we have learned more than most of us realize. Factually, more than half of American production and the jobs and economic life based on it are "planned" now. The word "planned" is semantically bad. It conjures up visions of socialism. It jars the daylights out of most conventional politicians. But a glance at the record justifies the statement—and the still more surprising one that this "planning" has been demanded by the business community, the public and the community in general, without much regard to partisan politics. Let us take a look.

At the top we have the Federal Reserve Board. It controls the supply of money, and credit, and interest rates. This can more or less control, and to some extent does control, the amounts that can be borrowed by consumers to buy cars and television sets, or by business to manufacture sugar, steel or plastic balloons. Less directly, but still substantially, it affects the amount of money available to build houses and factories.

The Federal Reserve is trying to exercise that control now through its "tight money" policy. The system is complex and need not be explained here. In broad general lines, it works in terms of over-all quantity.

Next below that are control agencies for all the industries which render public service. Railroads have their Interstate Commerce Commission; electric power companies and natural gas have the Federal Power Commission; airlines have the Civil Aeronautics Board; broadcasting has the Federal Communications Commission.

Each of these has planning functions. Some planning is well done, some not so well done; but no one, it seems, wants it abandoned. President Eisenhower's Republican Administration initiated the vast system of federally planned highways that is now in construction.

Next comes the whole process of farm production. This is at present based on an elaborate system of price supports, farm credit and other arrangements aimed to keep farmers well off. It was begun in President Hoover's time. Problems have arisen, and many think the system could and should be handled better. But no one is prepared to scrap it.

Production and distribution of oil and gasoline are guided by an elaborate system headed up by the Bureau of Mines. It keeps oil production in rough equation to current American demand. This started in 1933 and has worked fairly well. A comparable system run by the Department of Agriculture governs the amount of sugar refined and sold in the United States.

Housing is perhaps the star example. Twenty-five years ago the Federal Housing Administration was organized to steer money into the home market. It made mortgage credit available on easy terms to anyone who would build certain kinds of housing. As you ride through the suburbs, most of the new houses you see were built according to this piece of planning.

A similar bit of planning got electricity into American farms and rural areas—a story by itself. Defense industries depend directly on the planning of the Pentagon. This accounts for most of the aviation industry, much of the electronics and chemical industries and a number of smaller operations. We have not exhausted the list.

Added up, it becomes clear that guiding American production of goods and services toward recognized ends is not unknown to us. Judging by out-turn results, and remembering the piecemeal way it has been done, the effect has been surprisingly good. The public image remains that of a "free" economy, in which anyone tries his hand at producing whatever he likes. In fact, much of it is run that way. But an amazingly large sector—I should estimate it included a majority of "goods" produced—is not.

This "planning" is not, to be sure, of the rigid, iron-clad variety Socialists and Communists advocate. Generally, it is accomplished by a minimum of regulation, accompanied by a handling of credit or other Government encouragement, so that business can do what it wants to do—but finds it profitable to do certain things the public very much desires.

Politically, socially and economically, business organization, as we have it, has thus been used to get some of the results the public wanted. Our problem is to find out what they are—and then to apply some of the techniques we seem to have discovered already in other connections.

Try to list the things you consider important. Your rough sketch would go something like this:

Adequate food, clothing and shelter. (Most of these America has now.)

Good health, which means adequate hospital and medical care and public health services. (We are doing fairly well, but could do a great deal better, especially in certain regions.)

Good teaching in schools at the elementary, high school, university and graduate levels. (We have a system now, but it could be far better.)

An adequate system of defenses, meaning men and armament sufficient to prevent the outbreak of a major war and to stamp out brush-fire wars. (Consensus is that it is not now good enough, or progressing fast enough.)

Adequate increase in quantity and technical quality—especially the latter—of our industrial plant. (This is a growing headache. Each new technical advance opens indefinite fields calling for more capital and plant.)

More and better organized cultural activities—universities, libraries, music, theatre, books, art, journalism, churches. (In many of these fields we are far behind the values we profess.)

. . . Let us not continue. Each individual will have different items and priorities. But the lists put together will show extremely wide areas of agreement. True, every item will stir some argument. What is "adequate"?

But the composite picture would give a very clear verdict. The American public has come to "want" a great deal more, of both goods and services, than it is now getting, although the resources, human and material, are here.

The new desires are wholly creditable. Something would be wrong indeed if we did not want a stronger, safer, better, more beautiful civilization.

Therefore we have to tackle the serious, troublesome problem of handling our affairs so that these wants shall be matched with the goals. This is likely to mean expanding and improving the techniques with which we have already experimented. This being America, we will ultimately satisfy our wants by increasing our product. We always have.

I think public opinion has reached a point (as it did in 1932) where it is asking for new leadership, recognition of a new priority list for

American development, and a proper handling of its economic system so that these wants shall be met. Awareness of that possibility brings the question of productivity into controversy, both in universities and in practical politics.

One school of economic thought fears any economic guidance system. Leading that school is Professor F. A. Hayek of the University of Chicago. His feelings are indicated by the title of his book, "The Road to Serfdom." Opposing him is a group headed by Professor Kenneth Galbraith of Harvard; his volume, "The Affluent Society," describes with force the gap between the present American economic system (he calls it the "conventional wisdom") and the requirements of a first-rate civilization. . . .

My view favors more productivity. I thought that when I signed the Rockefeller Report, with all its difficult implications. It will be necessary to steer the goods and services so that they accomplish the important goals of American life. In dealing with national defense or social evolution, international competition or unemployment, community development or daily necessities like parking space, the task is the same. A sane system of balancing and planning is a clear economic necessity.

Never mind the epithets and political torpedoes. They merely conceal the essential structure of our present economy. In its most essential areas it is, and has been, guided for many years. That is why it runs as well as it does and why it does not crack up every seven years or so as it used to do. If we had stayed as we were before Theodore Roosevelt began planning by tackling the transportation system, or before Woodrow Wilson carried it on by signing the Federal Reserve Act, we should never have arrived at our $500 billion production.

The present need is to pull together the numerous units now operating and make them work in harmony. Most of the requisite power is already in Washington, though I think we shall soon want a better arrangement of tax revenues to meet the growing needs of local government. A solid start toward over-all planning has been made by the Council of Economic Advisers, who brief the President on all these matters. The American system has grown up. It neither can, nor wants to, take economics like the weather—something about which nothing can be done.

A picture is emerging of a stronger, greater, more humane and more splendid America than we have yet seen. To achieve it demands more productivity and sane planning. Our democratic system is no less capable of doing this than the economic systems overseas—and it has more to work with. The quicker we get at it, the safer and better off we shall be.

Robert A. Lovett

FRILLS AND THE
AMERICAN ECONOMY*

. . . .

SENATOR JACKSON. Mr. Lovett, you mentioned frills in our society during the course of your comments here this morning. Would you care to comment a little more on that? Have you any illustrations? . . .

MR. LOVETT. Yes, sir.

I had found frills in the military departments which were objectionable in my time. I had in some fashion, perhaps unfairly, attributed such things very largely to government. But I do not think that they are.

When I returned to civilian life, and particularly more recently, I found the most extraordinary examples of what seems to me to be a deterioration in either our national sense of proportion or our national sense of humor.

For example, in December, as you all know, I think you receive catalogs through the mail that are usually addressed simply "Boxholder," or something like that, so you have no defense against them at all. They are just there in your mail. They come from stores scattered around the country and they have the most appalling list of suggested presents, ceramic things shaped like Buddha, and you put grass seed on it and it grows hair, or something.

I found in them what seemed to me most pertinent and devastating examples of what is happening to American civilization—perhaps a definite indication of the approach of sense-of-value decay. Although it was not necessary in my case, I received for Christmas a

---

* Statement of Robert A. Lovett in the Hearings before the Subcommittee on National Policy Machinery, Committee on Government Operations, U.S. Senate, 86th Congress, 2nd Session, Washington, D.C., February 1960.

Mr. Lovett has held high Cabinet posts in previous Administrations. Currently he is an attorney, and Chairman of the Executive Committee of Union Pacific Railroad Co.

small tool that was about the size, at its handle, of an electric flash-light battery. It had a rod that stuck out of the handle and a loop on the end of it, and a button. This was a drink stirrer, a portable drink stirrer. You carried it around with you and if you were so weak and debilitated a member of the public that you couldn't put your finger in your drink or otherwise agitate it, you would use this gadget.

That was one of three that I have added to my collection. I have two others. One is a foam rubber, electrically vibrated finger for use in massaging the gums. It is rather an attractive item. Its appeal lies in the fact that it looks extraordinarily like a finger. A good deal of time and effort went into the design, engineering and manufacture of that product.

The third I am not too proud of—I think the others are somewhat better. It is [a] motor driven, portable electric battery powered mani-cure burr with six attachments. You press the button and you can do practically anything you want to in the form of manicuring.

If these things represent the amount of time and effort which I think any miniature product does, then I feel reasonably sure that there is excess engineering talent, time and productive capacity to do those things which have a greater importance to us nationally.

SENATOR JACKSON. Perhaps it is an example of how soft we are getting in some ways, Mr. Lovett?

MR. LOVETT. That is what depresses me. . . .

W. *Allen Wallis*

ECONOMIC GROWTH
AND PRIVATE ENTERPRISE*

. . . .

Economic growth has been an important goal of our national policy since the founding of the Republic. It remains an important goal, in no way diminished by our remarkable progress. Indeed, economic growth has recently become a political rallying cry, accompanied sometimes by demands that the government revert to the mercantilist policies by which economic growth was sought in the 17th and 18th centuries.

The issue of economic growth has entered the arena of contemporary politics through a course which has characterized many issues in the past quarter of a century. That is that after we have gotten over the hill by private endeavors, and are on our way at a brisk pace, urgent demands arise that the government expedite and direct us.

Characteristically, individuals, private institutions, or general social forces break the paths and provide the initial momentum. Once the vision of an important goal gains currency, and once we are on our way toward attaining it, suddenly we become impatient for a magic carpet to put us there instantly. Our impatience is exploited by those promoting various political schemes. Some of these schemes have become as wilted and shabby as the proverbial saloon sandwich, as they are pushed decade after decade as means to reach whatever goals have most recently come over the horizon or are most rapidly being attained through private forces.

Much of the current emphasis on economic growth is of this character. All sorts of plans are put forth under the banner of growth,

---

* Address by the Honorable W. Allen Wallis at the Third Annual Loeb Awards Presentation Luncheon in Honor of Business and Financial Journalists, New York City, Wednesday, June 8, 1960. Mr. Wallis is Dean of the Graduate School of Business, University of Chicago, and was special assistant to President Eisenhower and Executive Vice Chairman of the Cabinet Committee on Price Stability for Economic Growth.

with little or no analysis of the way they might promote growth—except growth in Federal spending. The same spending plans, on the other hand, are often described as reasons for wanting growth. We could afford the spending, the argument runs, if we only had growth; and the implication is that those who paint these glowing pictures of what growth could do to expand Federal spending somehow have the key to growth.

The fact that too many of the considerations raised in discussions of growth cannot be taken seriously should not blind us to the fact that there are a number of important considerations that merit close examination.

The Soviet Threat is one of these.

The Soviet threat is real and has many points of thrust. It would be perilous to underestimate the danger. But how is it related to our own economic growth? Some people fear that the Russians will "catch up" to us someday and so fulfill the Khrushchev boast about burying us. Others fear that rapid Soviet growth will increase Russian military potential so greatly as to jeopardize the free world's defenses. Still others fear possible adverse "demonstration effects" of rapid Soviet development—that underdeveloped and uncommitted nations will turn to communism as a way of achieving national strength, politically and economically. All these fears merit sober consideration—more consideration than can be given to them here.

First, it should be pointed out that we have a commanding lead over Russia in terms of both total and per capita output. Even if Russian growth rates continue higher than ours, the absolute gap between us will continue to *increase* for some time to come.

Second, we don't know how large the gap really is—except that it is large. As was mentioned earlier, international comparisons, even if we had good data, are a difficult and unrewarding business. We don't know whether Russian GNP is one-half of ours or one-quarter of ours.

Third, international comparisons of rates of growth can be even more misleading than comparisons of levels of output. The Russians, starting from a lower economic base and in a period of post-war reconstruction, should be expected to have a fairly high percentage rate of expansion. Moreover, they are able to take over the accumulated technology already developed and exploited elsewhere. Furthermore, they are transferring masses of people out of low productivity employment in agriculture to industry with its more highly valued output per man hour. They still have approximately 50 per cent of their labor force in agriculture; we have only about 8 per cent. Our employment is expanding in services, where improvements in output per man hour are slow and limited. In other words, Russian growth is more rapid because they are still in the area where improvement is easy and the way has been shown, whereas we are more heavily involved in the difficult tasks of expanding productivity in medicine, journalism, education, engineering, and other services.

In short, there is no possibility that the Russian economy will overtake ours, at any time in the visible future—certainly not in this century. We should not begrudge the Russian people whatever rise they may achieve in their material levels of well-being in return for the privation and hardships they have suffered in the name of economic growth.

Even the "demonstration effects" of Russian economic expansion may be vastly overemphasized. While her 6 to 8 per cent annual rate of growth in total production in recent years may seem impressive, other countries not under communist domination have [done] and are doing better. The economic progress of West Germany, Japan, and Mexico, for example, is far more striking. As a matter of fact, Russia itself grew faster under the Czars during the decade before the First World War.

Unmet Social Needs is a slogan we hear these days as a call for accelerated growth. According to this argument, if we grow faster we will be better able to provide a greater variety of public services and to eliminate what we now regard as poverty.

One of the more pretentious versions of the "needs" argument is that we have shameful public squalor in the midst of vulgar private opulence. This argument has a strong authoritarian smell, an odor of desire to enforce the advocates' tastes on others through governmental machinery. It is reminiscent of groups abroad that used government power to burn other people's books, but our group wants to burn other people's tail fins. The argument about "public squalor" would be laughed out of court if confronted with the facts of the past decade on construction of schools, improvements in teachers' salaries, super-highways built, increases in the support of research, expansion in aid to the needy, diseases conquered, urban redevelopment, hospitals built, or indeed almost anything else. Growth in public services has been enormous in the past decade. The unmet-social-needers resort to pointing out plaintively that we don't yet have everything that they think we should want, and to lamenting that private opulence dulls interest in social revolution.

The public squalor argument is, in fact, simply this decade's battle-cry of socialism, which—intellectually bankrupt after more than a century of seeing one after another of its arguments for socializing the *means* of production demolished—now seeks to socialize the *results* of production.

Aiding the Economic Development of Other Nations is another reason often advanced for trying to accelerate our own rate of growth. This is a laudable and continuing goal of public policy. But it does not follow that increasing our own rate of growth and raising our own level of living will have much influence on the rate of economic progress elsewhere.

The problems of world economic development are formidable. The pressure of population on arable land, the extremes of ignorance in many underdeveloped countries, the diversity of languages, cultures, and political institutions—these and many other economic and social factors are far more important than the direct and indirect aid that we can give. This is not to underestimate the significant contribution that our foreign aid, investment, and technology can make to world development. But what we can achieve depends primarily upon how we allocate our resources to various ends, and on the kinds of international and domestic policies we pursue, rather than on variations in our own rate of growth. Our import and export policies, for example, are vastly more important to underdeveloped countries than whether our GNP grows at 2 per cent or 5 per cent per year.

The Real Growth Imperatives arise from the fact that a strong economy is a growing economy. An economy with a high per capita income such as ours generates a large volume of private saving which must flow into capital accumulation if the economy is to sustain itself. In other words, the continued vitality of the system requires growth.

But beyond such technical matters, we desire growth to promote our private ends and national purposes. It is that simple; we want growth because it enlarges the opportunities of our children, because it expands our capacities to pursue goals of our own choosing, because it increases the range of choices open to us, because it is a rewarding outlet for our creative energies and imagination, because achievement invigorates and stimulates. In short, through economic growth we lead richer and fuller lives.

Moreover, we desire growth for the preservation of our way of life. By continued growth we demonstrate to ourselves, and perhaps to the world, that our system of free enterprise and representative government is indeed strong and able to fulfill rising aspirations and to enhance the dignity of free men. We need to grow to demonstrate that our system is not headed for inevitable collapse, but will survive even in a world of oppression and hostility. . . .

For a variety of reasons there is general agreement that economic

growth is an important goal of economic policy. But there is disagreement over the relative importance of growth as compared with
other goals and even more disagreement over the means by which
growth should be pursued.

Growth is only one of several major goals of economic policy.
Economic freedom, stability of employment, stability of the general
price level, economic efficiency, and economic security all are important. Properly conceived and pursued, economic growth is compatible
with all these other goals; but it becomes incompatible when pursued
too ardently or by inappropriate means. Policies to promote growth
or any other goal must reflect a compromise among competing goals.

Growth entails certain costs, and attempts to achieve greatly accelerated statistical growth rates may be costly in terms of human
hardship. New machines may reduce prematurely not only the value
of old machines but also the value of human skills acquired through
long training and experience. New products may reduce the incomes of those producing old products. New industries in new locations may uproot homes and communities near old industries. Unless
the costs of economic growth are equitably distributed, it is only
reasonable to expect strong resistance to growth and its accompanying changes.

To get high rates of growth through more rapid capital accumulation means that people must save more, either voluntarily or by
compulsion. In the Soviet Union people are forced to sacrifice current
consumption and liberty to meet targets of capital formation imposed
by the authorities. As much as Americans want economic growth,
compulsions and depressed levels of consumption are costs which
they would not willingly pay except in dire emergency.

A great variety of recipes for growth are in current vogue. Most
of them are hackneyed antiques, spruced up a bit with new phrases
and served under new names. In the main, these recipes represent
two fundamentally different approaches: mercantilism and economic
liberalism.

In many ways the debate about economic growth today is similar
to the great debate two centuries ago over how best to promote the
wealth of nations. The mercantilist approach of the 17th and 18th
centuries was an engineering approach. The government by detailed
design and elaborate regulation of economic life attempted to impose
a coordinated plan of growth on society. Sumptuary laws to prevent
frippery and waste, public monopolies to channel investment wisely,
detailed regulation of labor and trade—all these were part of the
scheme of things. Mercantilism gave way to economic liberalism—

a biological approach to growth with the government cultivating growth, not imposing it.

The great success of the biological approach, especially in Great Britain and the United States, is a matter of historical record. It remains to be seen whether our basically liberal approach will give way to a rising tide of mercantilist reaction.

Today one school of thought, the modern mercantilists, say that the government should create growth by massive increases in the quantity and diversity of government services and activity—in short, that government should force growth on the economy. This approach also involves forcing people to save more either through taxes or through inflation, in order to divert resources into collective use.

The opposite school of thought, the supporters of an open society, hold that the kinds and levels of public services should be determined on the basis of what we really want government to produce, that each governmental activity should be justified either on cost-benefit principles or on sound grounds of social responsibility, and that government can best promote growth by policies which release and give effect to the creative energies of private citizens.

While the factors that determine percentage rates of growth over a span of years are not fully understood, the success of past growth efforts and accumulated economic knowledge do tell us a good deal about the conditions of economic progress and how the government can best cultivate growth.

The underlying forces that promote national economic growth are basically the same as those that account for the economic progress of individuals. An individual's desire for a higher and more secure standard of living for himself and for his family is the basic stimulus. To this end he studies, plans, works, saves, and invests. He searches out new ways of doing things, and develops new techniques and processes. Hence, one of the most effective means of stimulating economic growth—and at the same time one of our fundamental objectives in seeking economic growth—is to provide expanding opportunities for every individual to realize his own potentialities to the utmost and to open wider vistas for his children; to encourage initiative, independence, and integrity; to preserve and enlarge the moral worth of the individual; and to approach more closely to our ideals of personal freedom, justice and fair play, broad and equal opportunity, the rule of law, and mutual respect and charity.

Growth requires a flexible and adaptable economic system with freedom to experiment. New industries must spring up, and others must decline. New methods must be accepted and old ones discarded. Labor and capital must shift easily and cooperatively in response to economic rewards and penalties. The combination of an abundant flow of new ideas, a willingness to take risks, and the speedy adoption of successful new methods is a condition for a high rate of growth.

The translation of new ideas into practical processes is speeded by a high rate of saving, through which new equipment can be financed and put into use. Saving also contributes to growth even where new methods are not involved, since it makes possible a larger stock of plant and equipment, housing, and other physical capital, which add to our potential supply of goods and services. In this way, the prudence and responsible foresight of people in providing for future needs makes an essential contribution to our growth.

All of this requires an economic environment that can be brought about and maintained only by positive and progressive governmental actions. The government has a two-fold function in promoting growth. First, it must provide a legal and institutional climate conducive to private economic progress. Second, the government must provide various public services and facilities which, while valuable to the nation as a whole, do not offer sufficient rewards to induce private producers to provide them for sale, or do not offer sufficient direct benefits to induce private individuals to buy them.

Ten essentials of a positive government program for growth are as follows:

(1) *Orderly Government.* People must be free to pursue their private affairs—to work, save, invest, enter into contracts without fear of fraud, confiscation, or violence.

(2) *Equality of Opportunity.* Only when each individual has the opportunity to develop his potential to the fullest and to utilize his skills to the utmost will we obtain maximum growth. Public policy should be aimed at eliminating discrimination in education and employment, whether it results from color, religion, sex, birthplace, or social class. Our economy must be open to the ambitious and the able.

(3) *Price Level Stability.* Marked inflation or deflation destroys economic efficiency, distorts resource allocation, and retards growth. Monetary, budget, and debt policies should be conducted in such a manner as to promote reasonable stability of the general price level.

(4) *Stability of Employment and Income.* Occasional mild fluctuations in the level of economic activity are not yet avoidable, much as we all wish otherwise. In fact, the surest thing that can be said about our future growth rate is that it will fluctuate. But national policies must deal effectively with recessions so

as to assure continuity of maximum employment opportunities and to alleviate the consequences of such involuntary unemployment as may occur. To achieve maximum sustainable growth, national policies must also prevent speculative excesses in boom periods.

(5) *Taxes.* Tax policy must serve several masters, and economic growth should be one of them. Taxes which penalize thrift, risk-bearing, and innovation have no place in a good tax system. Punitive rates applied to too narrow a base, a great hodgepodge of exemptions and exclusions, and discriminatory levies distort resource use and impede healthy growth. Tax reform should be directed toward improving the quantity and quality of investment, releasing incentives to personal effort, improving the cyclical flexibility of the tax system as a whole, and treating equally people in equal economic circumstances.

(6) *Maintaining Competition.* Competition is the lifeblood of a free economy. To keep the system strong and growing the lines of entry into industry must be kept open, and monopolistic barriers to progress must be eliminated. A positive and vigorous anti-trust program is essential to growth. Restrictive labor practices, likewise, need to be eliminated. Regulatory activities of government should be aimed at protecting the consumer and should not be allowed to stifle competition and prevent innovation in the regulated industries.

(7) *International Trade.* International trade is a powerful ally of growth. By trade we can produce indirectly a greater quantity and variety of goods and services than by domestic production alone. The pressure of foreign competition also keeps our own industries more efficient. Continued efforts to reduce or eliminate trade barriers at home and abroad will pay large dividends in growth.

(8) *Governmental Blocks to Growth.* Although economic growth is an avowed goal of policy, many governmental programs and activities tend to block growth. Growth involves change. When the government protects the status quo or insulates particular groups of business, labor, or consumers from the causes or effects of change, it retards growth. Many pernicious and unwarranted obstacles to growth are to be found in our agricultural policies, business subsidies, natural resource policies, regulation of industry, foreign trade policies, and grants-in-aid. If we are really serious about accelerating our growth, one of our first orders of business should be an attack on the whole structure of inefficiencies and impediments to growth induced by governments at all levels.

(9) *Public Works.* Growth requires social as well as private investment. The government makes a genuine contribution to economic growth when it provides complementary public facilities and services desired by the community. But here strict cost-benefit principles should apply or growth will be retarded. Because public services are generally not valued in the market place, economic criteria are difficult to apply. Realism and restraint are, therefore, of crucial importance in the use of public funds.

(10) *Maintenance and Development of the System.* Certain kinds of governmental expenditures to promote science, technology, health, and education also promote growth. Here again strict criteria should be applied, at least insofar as economic growth is to be served. Governmental activities should not supplant private activities and should be restricted to those areas where substantial benefits from governmental action are clearly apparent.

We are in the midst of a great national debate over economic growth. But until we understand what growth is, why it is an important policy goal, and how it can be achieved within a framework of economic and political freedom, the debate will range over many false and confused issues.

True growth in economic welfare involves both material and nonmaterial benefits, widely diffused. True growth must conform to the values and aspirations of a free people. The "right" or optimum rate of growth is that rate which conforms to the voluntary choices of the people, rather than a rate obtained by coercion, compulsion, or excessive social costs. The rate of growth can be increased by improving the efficiency of the economic system and by pursuing wise public policies to create a favorable environment for growth.

The future chapters of our story of economic growth are still to be written. We can be confident that these chapters will be happy ones if we have the wit and wisdom to preserve and strengthen the forces of progress that have produced in America an abundant economy, a great nation, and a free people.

Leon H. Keyserling

LESS FOR PRIVATE SPENDING?*

It has become fashionable for liberals to say that we should cut back on the private consumption of luxuries and even *necessities* (principally by higher tax rates) in order to channel more resources into essential public programs. While the need for a vast expansion of these public programs is imperative, the current crusade against private consumption is, in my opinion, a highly erroneous one.

It is economically in error because, during the past seven years or longer, we have experienced a long-term and serious rise in unemployment of plant and manpower, resulting not only from deficiencies in public outlays, but also from deficiencies in private consumption and investment. Roughly speaking, during this period, a deficiency of about $205 billion in total national production, correlating with about 15 million man-years of unnecessary unemployment, has been compounded of deficiencies of about $130 billion in private consumption, about $51 billion in private investment, and about $24 billion in public outlays for "goods and services" at all levels of government. Due to the difference between "goods and services" outlays and conventional budget outlays, public budgetary outlays as usually expressed have been about $40–$50 billion too low.

Let us suppose that during the past seven years we had repressed considerably more than we actually did the rate of expansion of private consumption by still higher tax rates, and put the "gains" thus achieved into highly essential public programs, such as schools, medical care, defense, etc. In that event, more public spending, balanced by less private consumer spending, would still have left us, broadly speaking, with a $205 billion deficit in total national production and a deficit of 15 million man-years of employment opportunity. Higher

---

* Leon H. Keyserling, "Less for Private Spending?" *The New Republic*, May 23, 1960, pp. 15–16. Reprinted by permission.

Mr. Keyserling, former Chairman of the President's Council of Economic Advisers, is a consulting economist and attorney, and President of the Conference on Economic Progress.

tax rates, under conditions then pertaining, might have forced our total economic performance still lower, with still larger deficits. And, psychologically and politically, an American people suffering as they have been from rising unemployment, and in the case of millions, real deprivation, would not have supported much higher tax rates for higher public outlays—including outlays "to help furriners."

To be sure, federal investment in our public needs should have been much higher during the past seven years. But this should not have been accompanied by higher tax rates or other measures to repress private consumption *until* total private and public spending became high enough to exert undue pressure upon our productive output at reasonably full employment of manpower and plant. It is by now standard economics, certainly confirmed by all recent experience, that efforts to "balance the Budget" when unemployment of plant and manpower is high and rising is self-defeating from the viewpoint of the Budget and the national economy. The revenues resulting from higher economic growth would have come much closer to balancing public budgets despite much higher outlays.

The "anti-consumptionists" say that schools are needed more than tailfins, and so they are. But in 1955, we were producing about 9 million automobiles and trucks. Within two or three years thereafter, the production was cut back to only about one-half of 9 million, and in 1960 it is likely to be only about two-thirds of 9 million. In addition, we are witnessing a great shift from luxurious automobiles to compact cars. These changes have added to the progressive unemployment of plant and manpower, because they have been one aspect of a *deficiency in total consumer spending* rather than a mere shift away from automobiles and toward other consumer goods which some may think are intrinsically more worthwhile.

These comments are just as pertinent to the future as to the past. To use our productive resources reasonably fully, we must achieve about $350 billion *more* of total national product in the aggregate during the five-year period between now and the end of 1964 than we shall have if there is a repeat performance of the very low growth rate of the past seven years. To devote most of this immense difference to expanded public programs would require that the federal Budget be approximately *doubled* almost at once—a procedure bearing no relationship to the desirable speed-up of public programs. Instead, the racing new technology calls imperatively for a balanced expansion of *both* private consumption and public programs.

Of course, the new white Cadillac Eldorados which some people buy every year, and the new luxury hotels at Miami and Palm Springs, stand in vivid contrast to overcrowded classrooms and odoriferous cities. But they stand in equally vivid contrast to the magnificent public bridges and roads in some of our cities, and the private poverty in the slums in close proximity. And even some of our recently burgeoning public universities, with hundreds of millions in endowments, are building luxuriously wasteful eating halls and recreation centers, while the poor who live nearby can't send their children through high school.

Actually, there is little evidence that during the past quarter century our private economic progress has outrun our public progress. In absolute terms, we have made tremendous advances in schools and public hospitals and the other markers of public endeavor, just as we have made tremendous economic progress in private well-being. But measured against the technology of today, we are grossly delinquent on both fronts.

Specifically, more than 40 million Americans, including multiple-person families and individuals living alone, are now trying to make ends meet on incomes falling below the established requirements to support even minimum health and a decent standard of living. The incomes of perhaps half of these families do not come up to 50 percent of these requirements. Four out of every 10 of our families, where the family head is 65 or over, have total income below $2,000. Three farm-operator families in every 10 are grouped below $2,000.

More public services alone will not remedy this evil. The removal of poverty is basically a matter of private income improvement through industrial advances which provide more work opportunity for more people at better pay, social security expansion, improved minimum wage laws, public aid to help reduce the high cost to consumers of adequate housing and medical care, and so forth. It is curious that those who disparage the expansion of private consumption stress the liquidation of poverty. For poverty is insufficient income to *consume* enough (quantitatively or qualitatively or both) food, clothing, shelter, medical care, recreation and other things.

If American consumers, even while their total consumption is too low, are spending too much for "the wrong goods" and too little for "the right goods," the problem is educational, not economic. And if, with total consumer spending too low, some consumers can afford to spend too much for luxuries, while other consumers cannot afford to spend enough for necessities, the problem is to promote shifts in the distribution of total consumer income, not to reduce total consumer spending—and above all, not to reduce it regressively, which inadequate expansion of total consumption usually does.

If we maintain a full rate of economic growth, we can by 1964 expand private incomes and consumption enough to reduce the number of multiple-person families in America with incomes below $4,000 from about 12 million to about 1.5 million. We can reduce those below $2,000 from about 3.5 million to less than one-half million. And we can lift average American multiple-person family income from about $7,000 to about $9,000 a year.

Simultaneously, with full economic growth, we can (*at existing tax rates* and with public budgets in balance over the years) lift our total educational outlays, private and public, from somewhat above $22 billion in the school year 1958–59 to about $38 billion by the school year 1964–65; come close to doubling average social security payments to individuals by 1964; lift federal assistance to public-financed health services from less than $4.50 per capita (related to the entire US population) in fiscal 1960 to more than $17 per capita by calendar 1964; lift federal outlays to improve housing conditions from about $3 per capita to about $11.50 per capita over the same period; expand federal outlays for natural resources from less than $10 per capita to about $13; and lift our outlays for economic and technical development overseas from about $1.7 billion to close to $4 billion. And if the international situation so requires, we can increase national security expenditures by the amounts urged by those experts who are not tailoring our defense outlays to the public revenues yielded by a stagnating economy. With all of this, in a fully expanding economy, the federal Budget would by 1964 be a substantially lower percentage of our total national production than during recent years, thus leaving room for more private economic progress not only in absolute but even in relative terms.

The worldwide situation should warn us against insisting that we can serve one great purpose only by neglecting others. The determination of the Soviets to use their existing total output in accord with their relative priorities of need never for a moment blinds them to the fact that they must achieve a maximum rate of over-all economic growth, and therefore be able to sustain more and more varieties of advance. To date, as an underdeveloped country relative to ours, the Russians have given highest priority (aside from the military) to the industrial base, science and technology, and education, precisely because they know that this opens the avenue to higher living standards for their families in the long run. In the years ahead, they will improve these living standards at a rapid rate.

If we respond to this challenge correctly instead of being panicked by it, we shall use our intrinsically superior economic and political systems to keep ahead on all important fronts. We shall not neglect over-all economic growth, nor desirable public services. We shall not say that the battle cry for better wages, higher farm incomes, and improved distribution of national income in the private sectors of our economy represents old clichés unadjusted to new times. We shall not say that going beyond the New Deal and the Fair Deal calls for a return to the earlier concepts of 19th-Century socialism—based upon the redistribution of economic scarcity.

We shall go beyond the reforms of these earlier times to the abundance of the Sixties.

James W. Knowles

POTENTIAL GROWTH: PROSPECTS AND PROBLEMS*

. . . .

Three alternative projections of potential output and of its rate of growth to 1975 were prepared; high (labeled A), medium (B), and low (C). These projections reflect trends of population, participation in the labor force, unemployment, hours of work, changes in the capital stock, and the average level of prosperity. These projections, which, of course, are subject to some error, are designed to indicate a realistic range of potential growth rates that our economy might experience over the next decade. . . .

(1) *The A or high projection.*—Projection A assumes that our economic affairs are managed in both the private and public area to maintain a high level of prosperity. While occasionally minor recessions might occur, it is assumed that the Nation will not experience a deep and prolonged depression, such as interrupted growth

---

* James W. Knowles with the assistance of Charles B. Warden, Jr., *Study Paper No. 20: The Potential Economic Growth In The United States*, for the Joint Economic Committee, 86th Congress, 2nd Session, January 1960, Government Printing Office, Washington, D.C., pp. 38–44.

Mr. Knowles prepared this study as Special Economic Counsel to the Joint Economic Committee of the U.S. Congress.

during the decade of the 1930's. The precise combination of public and private economic policies this projection would require is left unspecified.

Unemployment is assumed to average about 3 percent by the mid-1970's. . . .

(2) *The B or medium projection.*—The medium projection (B) assumes somewhat more modest success in maintaining continuous maximum employment, but again assumes no deep, prolonged depression will occur.

Unemployment is assumed to average about 4 percent. . . .

(3) *The C or low projection.*—The low (C) projection assumes a continuation of public and private policies in such mixture that there will be fairly frequent interruptions to growth, inadequate mobility of capital and labor, and more slack on the average than in each of the other two projections.

Unemployment is expected to average somewhat higher than in the past best years or about 5 percent. . . .

. . . The lowest rate of growth (C) is expected to be about 3.5 percent, measured from the potential output calculated for 1959 or about 4.2 percent per year measured from the preliminary estimate of the actual output for 1959. This, the lowest of the three projected rates, is significantly higher than the 50-year average of about 3 percent per year.

The middle or B projection indicates a projected rate of growth of potential output of 4 percent per year, measured from the output potential for 1959 or 4.7 percent per year, measured from the preliminary estimate of actual output during 1959. The highest projection (A) indicates a possible rate of growth of 4.6 percent per year measured from 1959 potential output levels and about 5.2 percent measured from the preliminary estimate of actual output for 1959. Both the A and B projections indicate rates of growth that substantially exceed the average rate over the last 50 years. . . .

These projections have the following implications:

(1) Without changing our economic system in any fundamental way, that is, without instituting elaborate controls or having the Government impose a pattern of consumption, and without Government-imposed, forced high rates of capital accumulation, our economy can grow at a rate as high as 4.6 percent per year. On the other hand, it could prove extremely difficult to achieve rates substantially greater than this within our economic system.

(2) If we avoid stumbling into real depression, the rate of growth may be only as low as 3.5 percent per year, higher than the 50-year average of 3 percent per year which was achieved despite a pro-

longed interruption in the 1930's. Thus, there is a considerable range of possible growth rates, even within a range of assumptions which exclude depression and a forced-draft economy.

(3) There is a moderate inherent tendency for the rate of growth of the economy to rise in the coming decade if unemployment can be held on the average to about 4 percent, or less, of the civilian labor force. This is due to the increase in the rate of growth in the labor force and to the fact that the rate of increase in the capital stock and the decline in the average age of the capital stock would not be restricted as in the past by long periods of low investment such as occur in periods of prolonged depression. So long as recessions are neither too frequent nor deep, the rate of accumulation of capital can be quite favorable to growth.

(4) Our economic growth is within our own control. If the Government pursues growth-facilitating policies, the economy will expand near the upper limit of the range. If, on the other hand, the Government, as a matter of policy, sacrifices economic growth to the pursuit of other objectives, our economy will perform sluggishly, will add less to our capacity, and our potential growth will tend to be near the lower limit of the above range or even below.

(5) In recent years, including currently, the output of the economy has been well below its potential and probably would be in the 1970's under the assumptions of the C projection.

From the standpoint of public and private policy, this study and these projections imply that wide differences in the rate of growth can develop in the future, depending on the degree to which public and private policies contribute: (1) to increased mobility of labor and capital to meet the changing demands of our dynamic economy; (2) to a rapid rise in educational attainment to keep pace with requirements of the changing technology associated with higher rates of growth and the high mobility this technological change requires; (3) to a high and growing rate of research and development expenditures as a basis for a high rate of technological progress; and (4) to maintenance of such proportions between the growth in investment and in consumption as will not only provide for a high rate of growth of capital stocks and the achievement of a relatively low age of the stock, but also will produce a growth in final demand for private and public consumption sufficient to maintain operations of the continually growing capacity at rates of operation which will maintain private incentives for a high rate of investment and of technological progress.

4

PRIVATE GROUPS
AND
PUBLIC POLICY

. . . many [business men] who traditionally have wanted less Government control, not more, now say major strikes can do more harm than limited Government interference. [Others] believe in paying the full price of a free economy. . . . "Let capital and labor slug it out."

✱ ✱ ✱

The debate over health insurance, one may assume, will be exceptionally sharp. . . . Any state-sponsored system of prepaid medical care encounters the implacable opposition of the organized medical practitioners. This is based on a sharp (although disputed) identification of self-interest and long-standing conviction that the present organization of medical care will best advance the medical art.

✱ ✱ ✱

> Some of the criticism of broadcasting [seeks] to becloud the picture by citing certain advertising practices in broadcasting or elsewhere which seem at least to be undesirable. As we all know, such practices do exist, as indeed they do in all aspects of human life. Some of them are sufficiently reprehensible to justify government control. Others should be left to the corrective action of the market place.

David Riesman has said that "Power in America . . . [is] situational and mercurial; it resists attempts to locate it the way a molecule, under the Heisenberg principle, resists attempts simultaneously to locate it and time its velocity."[1] The existence of over a hundred thousand governmental units in the United States, the federal system, the congressional committee system with its seniority rule, the four thousand national and twelve thousand local organizations that seek to influence public policy—all combine to baffle the casual student of American politics as he seeks to pinpoint responsibility for policy-making, and to confirm the impression many foreign visitors bring with them that Americans prefer chaos to government. George Bernard Shaw probably had the United States in mind when he described democracy as "a defensive organization of the bourgeois against being governed at all."[2]

The fact is that in an age in which political leaders and newspaper columnists find it convenient to talk in terms of "national purpose," the United States retains a system of government in which policymaking is more responsive to the momentary pressures of shifting alliances of organized groups than it is to an integrative concept of public interest, comprehensive in scope and rational in the establishment of goal priorities. Studies of voting behavior in the Congress have amply demonstrated that constituency interest, above any other consideration, is the criterion that governs legislative decision-making.

This theme of the adequacy of American policy-making institutions to the needs of the sixties dominates Chapter Six. We raise it in this context merely to stress the point that American policy-making—adequate or inadequate as it may be to deal with international problems—*will* respond to domestic issues around which there have grown clusters of group pressures for change, for as little change as possible, or for the maintenance of the status quo. In the

---

[1] *The Lonely Crowd* (Doubleday & Co., 1950), p. 257.
[2] Quoted in Kingsley Martin, *Harold Laski*, p. 85.

age of the welfare state, change usually (though not always) means increasing reliance upon the federal government to promote, to regulate, or to provide security; and maintenance of the status quo usually means continuing to place maximum reliance upon voluntary private associations.

Three areas of domestic policy-making that may be expected to command Congressional attention during the coming decade are labor-management relations, health care for the aged, and television broadcasting.

In the first of these, we may expect to see the development of new concepts of unionism during the sixties. The struggle for survival has ended. Union leaders who once were social pariahs now play golf at the country club, direct United Giver's Fund campaigns, negotiate the loan of union funds to businessmen, and sit in the Cabinet. Unionism is respectable, and union members are relatively prosperous. School teachers now attempt to achieve wage scales equivalent to those enjoyed by union production workers. At the same time, membership in some of the strongest unions, such as the United Mine Workers, the United Automobile Workers, and the United Steelworkers, has fallen drastically as a result of changed consumer tastes and automation. And while strikes are no longer fought with machine guns, tear gas, and bayonets, as they were during the thirties, they are waged before a court of public opinion, which, whether pro-labor or pro-management in any given instance, increasingly is *anti*-strike where basic industries are concerned.

Labor unions, once held by the courts to be illegal conspiracies, achieved the ultimate in legal status in the United States with the Wagner Act of 1935. This Act gave formal recognition to the right of workers to organize to bargain collectively, and stated the legal obligation of management to bargain with unions. It also established the National Labor Relations Board, which had the function of conducting elections and certifying bargaining units, and of ordering management to desist from certain "unfair labor practices" defined in the Act. Since 1935, war needs, the desirability of "equalizing" the bargaining position of management, the dictates of internal security, and union corruption have been cited as reasons for enacting restrictive labor legislation.

The current concern is to fashion legal devices for avoiding strikes that cripple the national economy. The emergency strike provisions of the Taft-Hartley Act of 1947 have not proved efficacious. In one major steel strike—1951—the President preferred to avoid the cumbersome machinery of a Board of Inquiry, to be followed by an 80-

day court injunction, and possible resumption of the strike upon expiration of the injunction. In the second major steel strike in recent years—that of 1959—the President unsuccessfully invoked the Taft-Hartley emergency procedures, the strike finally being settled through the mediation of the Vice President and the Secretary of Labor. The tendency to stereotype certain groups and to assume that their positions are not only clear-cut and subscribed to by all group members, but are diametrically in conflict with those of supposed opposition groups, does not always lead to a sophisticated understanding of American policy-making. This certainly is true of labor and management insofar as the issue of compulsory arbitration of disputes is concerned. As Archibald Cox makes clear in his discussion of "Public Policy and Collective Bargaining," labor-management disputes can be the cause of national economic emergencies and as such make government intervention of some kind inevitable.

The question is: What should be the nature of such intervention? There is growing dissatisfaction with the emergency strike provisions of the Taft-Hartley Act. Compulsory arbitration might appear to some to be the logical solution to the problem. Archibald Cox argues against it. Joseph R. Marshall suggests that there is much business support for compulsory arbitration, though it is probably not the most influential section of the business community that backs the proposal. The view shared by most labor leaders on this question is argued by Robert R. France in "The Compulsory Arbitration Fallacy." Typically unions tend to advocate reliance on private groups for strike settlement, and sometimes they do so in terms which would have warmed the heart of a robber baron.[3]

It is the current vogue to proclaim that we live in a society of rising expectations. We also live in a society that is aging. Put the two together and they spell legislation. At the turn of the century, approximately 12% of the eligible voters were sixty or over; in 1960, approximately 20%; by 1970, it will be 25%. These "senior citizens" must live on small and fixed incomes in an age of rising expectations and rising living costs, and at a time of life when medical expenses can be catastrophic. Humanitarianism can be a potent force in a democratic society; so can potential votes. Bloc voting by oldsters has already proved its effectiveness in California, Colorado, and the state of Washington, where older persons enjoy favorable pension

---

[3] On the other hand, while he was still counsel for the AFL-CIO in 1960, Arthur J. Goldberg advocated the establishment of a National Council of Labor-Management Advisors. The Kennedy Administration has now acted on this proposal.

plans. Like labor and business and other groups that come to recognize a common denominator of interest, senior citizens are organizing to influence public policy. The Townsend movement, now in its third decade, claims a membership of 700,000 to 900,000. The California Institute of Social Welfare and the National Institute of Social Welfare press for improved state and federal programs of aid to the aged. The National Association of Retired Persons, with a membership of 500,000, presses for tax advantages and improved private medical-insurance programs. This smacks of "socialized medicine" to the American Medical Association and other groups representing conservative economic interests. Further, the A.M.A. contends that it is erroneous to assume that the aged either do not have sufficient public medical aid already available, or do not have the ability to finance their individual needs.

This is the pressure-group lineup on the health-insurance question at the outset of the sixties. As the decade advances, it is likely that the issue will broaden out from its current application to the aged. Thus, the conflicting views presented in this chapter by Rita R. and W. Glenn Campbell on one side, and Michael M. Davis and John Kenneth Galbraith on the other, deal with the problem of health insurance as such, and not simply in connection with the retired. In the context of this chapter the question they pose is this: Can health insurance be handled adequately by private associations and voluntary participation, or should there be a compulsory national program directly involving the federal government?

Some four decades have passed since station KDKA, Pittsburgh, broadcast the Harding-Cox election returns and introduced the nation to commercial radio broadcasting as an information and entertainment medium. By the end of the twenties a few broadcasting stations had begun to experiment with the transmission of images; and in 1941 the regulating body in the radio-television industry, the Federal Communications Commission (FCC), granted the first license for the operation of a commercial television station. Studies show that from 1950 to 1960 the average American watched television from twenty to twenty-four hours a week. The medium has become the dominant expense item on Presidential campaign ledgers, and the attention given to the Kennedy-Nixon television debates in the 1960 campaign—by the public, by the campaign staff, and by the candidates themselves—suggests the political significance of TV.

Just as the medium of television has proved expensive for political campaigning, it is becoming a more and more expensive vehicle for the presentation of privately sponsored programs. Spiraling costs are cutting down the quantity of program time that single sponsors can afford and, when taken together with the trend toward network programming, are resulting in the broadcasting of entertainment fare aimed at the mass audience. Many students of television regulations have come to the conclusion that cultural standards in programming can be raised only through subsidization. This might take the form of federal grants in support of cultural TV projects, or public ownership of broadcasting facilities. The former is not in immediate prospect, and the latter is so antithetical to the traditions that have been built up in the field of mass communications as to be unlikely indeed, even though such Western democracies as Great Britain, Canada, and Australia have demonstrated its feasibility. The principal reliance today, therefore, is upon reservation of certain channels for educational television stations, which are subsidized by public and private local groups.

This is not to say that Congress and the Communications Commission have no interest in, or proper concern for, television broadcasting standards. In the early days of broadcasting, before the establishment of the Federal Radio Commission in 1927 (later to become the FCC), the users of the air waves sometimes were guided by a kind of buccaneering spirit. Broadcasters indulged personal eccentricities, engaged in vendettas, and sometimes behaved as if they were running a medicine show. In Congress the temptation to censor the industry has existed side by side with the determination to regard it as protected by the free-speech-and-press provisions of the First Amendment. Under provisions of the Communications Act of 1934, the Commission is prohibited from censoring programs, but simultaneously it is enjoined to apply a broad public-interest criterion in licensing and renewing licenses—a criterion broad enough to enable it to establish standards of programming which, in theory at least, must be met if a station licensee wishes to avoid trauma at renewal time.

Recent revelations concerning the control of programming and the rigging of TV quiz shows caused Congressional inquiry and demands for FCC and legislative action to tighten programming standards. Whether the Commission already has adequate authority but has failed to exercise it, or whether new legislation would be a necessary precedent to Commission action is a matter of dispute. Also in dispute is the capacity of the industry to regulate itself. Varying views are presented in the Interim Report of the Subcommittee on Legislative Oversight, which investigated the TV industry, and in the testimony of Harold E. Fellows, President of the National Association of Broadcasters.

As with labor-management relations, the issue is how far private associations in our society can be relied upon to regulate themselves and to settle their differences with others. When this issue is considered in the abstract, people tend to take either of two positions: (1) as a matter of principle, we should have maximum reliance upon voluntary associations in a democratic society; or (2) as a rule, public regulation is more responsible than private regulation, and thus more in the public interest. Presented in a specific context, however, the conservatives do not always take the first position and the liberals the second. More intense and expanded government involvement in labor-management relations was outlined in the Taft-Hartley Act of 1947, a major product of the first postwar Republican Congress. Thoughtful liberals will have doubts about the advisability of federal programs verging upon censorship of television.

LABOR-MANAGEMENT RELATIONS

Archibald Cox

PUBLIC POLICY
AND COLLECTIVE BARGAINING*

The American system of industrial relations rests upon private enterprise in markets which, despite increasing government regulation, are still remarkably free. We believe in individual initiative, private decision-making, and personal responsibility not only as eco-

---

* Archibald Cox, "The Role of Public Policy in the Negotiation of Collective Bargaining." Excerpts are from the Fifth in the Monograph Series *Law and the National Labor Policy*, (c) 1960, The Regents of the University of California (Institute of Industrial Relations).

Dr. Cox is Royall Professor of Law at the Harvard Law School, and a noted authority on labor law.

nomic and political doctrine but also as moral philosophy, although our beliefs run beyond our practice in this respect as well as others. Organized labor is scarcely less committed to the existing system than other segments of the community. It attracts more idealists, reformers, and rebels, but most union officials, whether business agents or general presidents, have the same basic beliefs as their corporate counterparts. Specifically, they share the conviction that wages and conditions of employment must be fixed by private agreement.

Labor's acceptance of this postulate depends upon maintaining freedom to organize and bargain collectively, including the right to strike. Employees can influence negotiations in the labor market only by collective bargaining. One cannot negotiate without ability to reject the proffered terms. The only way in which employees can reject an employer's offer is to stop work. Consequently, collective bargaining can hardly exist without preserving the right to strike.

The role of labor relations law has been to provide a framework for this system. The Taft-Hartley Act prescribes a few procedural steps and the National Labor Relations Board has undertaken not only to judge the conduct of the negotiators but also to determine what subjects the negotiators must cover. These decisions contrast strangely with the utter lack of government policy upon such critical issues as wages and automation and with the want of machinery for making a policy felt. The full extent of our commitment to governmental inaction is evidenced by the Taft-Hartley prohibition against even recommendations by a Board of Inquiry appointed to investigate a dispute which endangers the national health or safety. The central issue of labor policy today is whether the country should chart a new course.

1. *Can we not devise a better method of adjusting conflicts of interest between employers and employees in essential industries where a cessation of operations may create an imminent threat to the national health and safety?* The steel crisis which ran from mid-July until early November, 1959, is the latest of a long series of critical disputes. In twelve years it has been thought necessary to invoke the emergency disputes provisions of the Taft-Hartley Act on sixteen occasions. Since 1945 there have been five major steel strikes. Two nationwide railroad strikes were averted by drastic presidential intervention after the machinery of the Railway Labor Act had been exhausted. A more serious dispute looms over the horizon. East coast shipping has been tied up five times during the same period.

Of course there are opposing considerations which should temper the demand for new legislation. The country has survived each apparent crisis without a catastrophe. The costs of great strikes are wildly exaggerated because the press never balances the production, sales, and wages lost during a strike against the greater production and higher sales and wage payments during the preceding and succeeding periods. There is good reason to believe that many strikes are only a substitute for layoffs or shortened workweeks. Furthermore, when we measure the net loss of a strike, we are counting the price of greater economic freedom. Yet these are only tempering forces; they should not block the search for a solution.

2. *In basic industries can we continue to rely upon private negotiations between management and labor without government participation to establish wage levels and terms and conditions of employment? If not, what are the alternatives?* In raising this question I am less concerned with 1960 or 1961 than with the long-run trend of the national labor policy. The strain which the next quarter century will put upon the economy is reason enough for inquiring into conceivable adaptations.

For the most part I shall discuss these questions separately, but it is convenient to consider them together in examining the thesis that it is the excessive power of labor unions that endangers the public interest because it enables them not only to shut down essential industries, thereby endangering the public health and safety, but also to secure excessive wage increases, thereby accelerating the spiral of inflation. The remedy, some say, is to deprive labor unions of the immunity from the antitrust laws which they gained as a result of Supreme Court decisions under the Norris-LaGuardia Act.

I

. . . There is nothing in experience to indicate how the Sherman Act can be used effectively to prevent the growth of excessive union power or to avoid the conditions giving rise to emergency disputes.

Indeed the basic theory and concepts of the antitrust laws are inapplicable to labor unions. The antitrust laws are designed to insure free markets by preserving and enforcing competition among a sufficient number of buyers and sellers of goods and services with sufficiently equal power to prevent anyone from controlling prices, supplies, or quality to the detriment of consumers. But labor unions do not compete against each other in the sale of labor. Can anyone imagine three or four unions of aircraft workers competing against each other for the privilege of supplying labor to Douglas, Lockheed, and North American? The only way in which competition can be restored among the sellers of labor is to destroy the labor unions so that individual workers will undersell each other, or at least to create a large enough pool of nonunion labor to be a threat to the bargaining power of unions. . . .

Even if such a program were theoretically sound, it is impractical. A program of breaking up labor organizations could not succeed unless it was accompanied by vigorous efforts to break up giant corporations. They will not be broken up. We cannot turn back the clock despite our nostalgia for a simpler economy. Although labor unions impose some restraints upon competition with which the law might deal, the antitrust laws provide no solution to national emergency disputes and no security for the public interest in the substantive terms of the settlements. . . .

II

Even in management circles there is wide agreement upon the inadequacy of the emergency dispute provisions of the Taft-Hartley Act. The Boards of Inquiry, which are charged with reporting the facts to the President before he seeks an injunction and again after sixty days, have sometimes engaged in useful mediation, but they can do no more. The injunction may forestall calamity by keeping the wheels of industry turning for an additional eighty days. It takes the leadership "off the hook" if management or union blunders into an unwanted strike, or if the rank-and-file employees compel union officials to sanction a strike against their better judgment. In the typical case, however, the injunction simply postpones the showdown at the price of relieving both employer and employees of the pressures which might have caused a settlement. . . .

As dissatisfaction with the Taft-Hartley solution spreads, so is there a growing body of opinion that the best hope for avoiding national emergency strikes, while preserving a large measure of freedom and private responsibility in the terms of the settlement, lies in legislation which opens the door to a wide choice of procedures. While this approach seems promising, in my judgment it should be combined with measures which impose upon each industry the primary responsibility for working out its own solution.

Standing Industry Procedures. Each industry in which a labor dispute might affect the national health or safety should be placed under a statutory admonition to create a standing procedure for resolving disputes which will not yield to the ordinary processes of negotiation. Among the possibilities are private mediation, fact-finding with or without recommendations, voluntary arbitration, or reference to a permanent bipartite industry board vested with power to decide by a stipulated majority. The essential points are (1) that it be a standing procedure which survives the termination of regular collective bargaining agreements; (2) that it come into play at an early stage in negotiations before positions have hardened; and (3) that it give *reasonable* assurance of avoiding an emergency. The Railway Labor Act already provides a standing procedure for the railroad and airline industries. . . .

The government cannot compel an industry to take these steps, but it can apply pressure and offer assistance. The statute should provide that upon request of an industry or a finding by the Secretary of Labor that an industry has failed to establish an industry procedure, the President should appoint a Board of Public Responsibility chosen from men of experience and high standing in the field of industrial relations who would remain private citizens but would serve as the occasion required. Such a board should have two duties: (1) to assist the industry in setting up its own procedure; and (2) to serve the functions of an industry procedure whenever there was none. Except for this and the normal work of the Federal Mediation and Conciliation Service, the government should not be brought into the first stage of the procedure. . . .

Presidential Intervention. Notwithstanding industry procedures, there will always be some critical disputes. The statute should therefore establish a National Emergency Disputes Board which the President would summon and consult whenever the Secretary of Labor certified the existence of an unresolved dispute which he had cause to believe was an imminent threat to the national health or safety. The Board should be composed of the Secretaries of Defense, Commerce, and Labor, and two eminent citizens, one with a background in management and the other from labor, but neither of them currently associated with parties to the controversy. . . .

The National Emergency Disputes Board should have three functions:

1. The National Emergency Disputes Board should arrange a settlement, if possible, or a method of obtaining a settlement without the cessation of normal operations.

2. The Board should make all possible arrangements for protecting the national interest in the event of a strike or lockout. If we are serious in our desire to preserve free collective bargaining, of which a few strikes are an inescapable part, we should spend more effort upon finding makeshift arrangements, however drastic, for ensuring the supply of truly essential goods and services during a strike.

3. The Board should hear the parties and advise the President

upon the single question whether a strike or lockout would do immediate harm to the national health or safety. . . .

If the President finds after studying the report of the Emergency Disputes Board that an emergency is imminent, he should have statutory authority to follow five courses of action, singly, consecutively, or concurrently:

1. He might appoint a fact-finding board with power to mediate and also to make public recommendations for the settlement of the dispute.

2. A Board of Inquiry might be appointed for the purpose of arranging voluntary arbitration, or, if this fails, reporting to the public the blame for imperiling the national health or safety rather than accepting an impartial decision. Fear of public indignation, properly focused, would probably lead to more acceptance of voluntary arbitration.

3. Since an injunction may be the only way to stop a strike, the statute should authorize the President to obtain an injunction for as long as he deems appropriate but not more than six months. The public health and safety are more important than the rights of either party.

4. The President should also have power to seize and operate the industrial property affected by the dispute. Such a step would be as distasteful to employers as injunctions are to unions, but the aim is to make presidential intervention objectionable to both. Since strikes would be forbidden during the period of government operation, the President should be authorized, but not required, to appoint a Wage Adjustment Board to recommend any changes in wages and conditions of employment for the period of government operation. The parties would be under heavy pressure to adopt these interim conditions as the terms of the final settlement in order to terminate the seizure, but the appearance of voluntarism and some of the reality would be preserved. The pressure is less than under compulsory arbitration, which I reject even as an available procedure upon the ground that it would too easily become the normal course. . . .

5. Finally, the President should be given his most important power in explicit terms—the power to do nothing. Sometimes the parties negotiate agreements very promptly after they are convinced that no one else will carry the burden.

In academic discourse it is easy to argue that the country has never faced a true emergency as a result of a peacetime strike, that the President would have ample constitutional authority to deal with a crisis, and that we can best preserve collective bargaining by repealing all legislation applicable to emergency disputes. In my opinion muddling through will not meet the challenges of the atomic age and space exploration. . . .

The flexibility of the choice-of-procedure approach is an important asset, but the chief advantage over other remedies lies in its capacity for preserving uncertainty as to the form and extent of government intervention. Any set course of procedure enters into the parties' calculations, with the result that their negotiations tend to run the full course before they buckle down to business. . . . Armed with a variety of weapons, the Chief Executive would probably be spared the use of any. . . .

III

Another moment's reflection is enough to demonstrate the public importance of the bargains struck between management and labor in basic industries. The current steel dispute affords two obvious examples: wages and work rules.

Although the economists closely associated with management exaggerate the inflationary tendency of collective bargaining while those close to labor argue that large wage increases are the best corrective, most independent scholars seem to agree that the continual increases in wages and fringe betterments contributed significantly to inflation because they pushed costs up to the point where further wage increases were requisite. . . . Wage levels are debated by the negotiators in basic industries largely in terms of broad policies which will affect the entire nation. It seems more than a little curious, therefore, that those charged with advancing the interests of special groups should be the only participants in the decision. The very same question would arise, of course, whenever the danger was deflation.

The work-rules issue in the 1959 steel dispute is also a useful example because there is less danger that the short-run interests of management and labor will coincide to the detriment of the public. One aspect of the question related to thousands of specific operations, but at bottom it was, how can industry make the most effective utilization of labor with due regard to human values? The other aspect was, how shall this decision be made—by management alone or by management and the union jointly? . . . It is no longer the process of periodic technological change which confronts us, affecting first one job and then another, but a revolution potentially involving the displacement of 20 or 25 per cent of the work force of entire industries. The pace of the transition, the retraining or other protection of displaced workers, the participation of union representatives to give employees assurance that their interests are protected, all have obvious public importance. . . .

If the argument up to this point seems to be a vague, theoretical plea for a greater degree of planning, let me hasten to emphasize the objections to detailed government determination of wages or other conditions of employment. Distrust of the cumbersome apparatus necessary for detailed control of the economy was one of the chief lessons learned by those who participated in the administration of wage and price controls during World War II and the Korean incident. Perhaps the worst feature is the rigidity of regulation even in the hands of imaginative and skilled administrators, rigidity in applying rules to remote situations whose variations and subtleties defy explanation at a distance and also rigidity in changing rules out of tune with events. But this objection and others such as the mediocrity of a permanent bureaucracy carry force only so long as one is speaking of widespread controls at all levels of the economy. The collective bargaining negotiations which raise important public issues are the pace-setters—the negotiations in basic industries which, because of psychological or economic forces, affect the entire economy. If the public interest were to make itself felt at this point, there would be no need for a bureaucracy, and flexibility and individual initiative could be preserved through thousands of ensuing private decisions.

Our dedication to free collective bargaining, as I remarked at the outset, also rests upon a moral philosophy. Private decision-making increases personal opportunity and responsibility. Reliance upon government lessens man's power of choice between good and evil; it makes him less a man. In a complex society of organized groups the individual's power to influence events is limited, his participation in decisions is vicarious, but so long as private decision-making prevails, a pluralistic society preserves power of choice and therefore the responsibility for the decision. But I wonder whether greater governmental participation would not preserve, or indeed increase, pluralism and opportunities for vicarious participation in the decision-making process in basic wage negotiations. Is it realistic to describe bargains struck between the president of the United Steelworkers and the chairman of the board of U.S. Steel Corporation as a democratic process in which those affected by a decision have the responsibility for making it? It is more democratic than if either made the decision alone, but the addition of a third chair at the bargaining table would further diffuse authority and further increase the vicarious participation of those affected. The general public is vitally affected, but currently its spokesman, the government, has not even the right to a hearing. . . .

Compulsion is not an inescapable ingredient of governmental participation. . . .

The most practicable starting point may be the regular annual or biennial conferences of senior government, labor, and management officials, suggested by Professor Dunlop,[1] for discussion of the public consequences of the decisions to be made in ensuing contract negotiations. The discussion should go far beyond general exhortation into detailed facts and figures. Although not a negotiation session and not aimed at formal agreements, there should be a genuine interchange of views upon the key issues.

Such a conference is only a first step. The forms through which government influence might be brought to bear more directly and with greater force remain to be devised, as do the techniques for ensuring that private decision-making in other segments of the economy would not undercut the policies followed in basic industries under governmental pressure. But we should welcome the fact-finding boards with power to make recommendations, Boards of Inquiry, and other special commissions mentioned in the discussion of national emergency disputes, as opportunities to add to our store of substantive concepts and methods of tripartite participation. . . .

---

[1] Testimony of John T. Dunlop at the Hearings before the Joint Committee upon the Economic Report of the President, 85th Congress, 1st Session, 1959.

Joseph R. Marshall

WHAT BUSINESS MEN THINK ABOUT COMPULSORY ARBITRATION*

Ever since labor became strong enough to strike, U.S. business men, legislators, union leaders, and experts have debated the merits of compulsory arbitration in peacetime.

Time and again, they have turned it down.

---

* Joseph R. Marshall, "Compulsory Arbitration? Business Votes 'Yes.'" Reprinted by permission from *Dun's Review and Modern Industry*, January 1960, pp. 40–41, (c) 1960, Dun & Bradstreet Publications Corp.

But today, in the aftermath of the nation's longest steel strike, most American business men have come to look with favor on compulsory arbitration of strikes that cripple the economy.

That, at any rate, is the finding of a big new survey conducted by DUN & BRADSTREET's field force among 1,423 business men running all types and sizes of companies in every corner of America. Reporters went into machine shops, meat packing plants, heavy equipment factories. They talked to business men who make clothing, food products, furniture, lubricants. They visited warehouses and wholesalers, and stopped in department stores, farm implement yards, and shoe shops.

They found that of 1,423, a startling 875, or more than 60 per cent, would favor compulsory arbitration of a situation like the recent steel strike.

Business men sometimes hedged their approval with qualifications. Sometimes they warned of political dangers.

But even the big-company men were split 50–50, and the smaller business man was resoundingly in favor of compulsory arbitration.

Putting the Question

Every business man was asked exactly the same question:

"In view of the effect of the recent steel strike on the national economy, would you favor compulsory arbitration of similar strikes in the future?"

Their reactions were sometimes explosive.

A large manufacturer in Columbus, Ohio, banged his hand down on his desk and said, "Compulsory arbitration represents one more step toward socialism!"

A business man at a Buffalo, N.Y., plant spoke thoughtfully. "I dislike the political implications," he said. "But compulsory arbitration appears to be the only means to settle these issues."

In Miami, the sun-tanned chief of a medium-size precision tool company said flatly, "I am against any kind of compulsion. It's undemocratic." Said a Cincinnati wholesaler, "I'd favor any measure to avoid crippling strikes." A manufacturer of belts and billfolds in Fort Worth, Texas, said, "I want no further Government intervention in any business."

But of the small business men who had an opinion, about 70 per cent took another point of view. It was summed up by a small retailer in Milwaukee, Wis.: "Strikes hurt small business too much."

In essence, the business man who gets hurt by a strike through no fault of his own—and who is least likely to come under compulsory arbitration—seems to be its strongest proponent.

Labor-management experts and leading legislators don't necessarily agree that compulsory arbitration would achieve greater labor-management peace. Most don't want compulsory arbitration, but many of them are aware of the growing feeling that something must be done to prevent collective bargaining breakdowns from crippling the economy.

Congress Views the Problem

Sen. Lister Hill (D., Ala.), chairman of the Senate Labor and Public Welfare Committee, told DUN'S REVIEW he favors an investigation by Congress to determine the wisest course of action in the steel strike or in any similar situation.

Congressman Graham A. Barden (D., N.C.), chairman of the House Education and Labor Committee, said the question of compulsory arbitration was being given "serious consideration." But he said it would be "a wide departure from our way of dealing with labor problems."

Organized labor has long opposed compulsory arbitration. Says David J. McDonald, president of the United Steelworkers, "Compulsory arbitration in the steel or any other great American industry would eventually permeate all phases of American life." . . .

Experts like Joseph S. Murphy, vice president of the American Arbitration Association, point out that compulsory arbitration is basically "not compatible with our free system." But, Murphy conceded in an interview with a DUN'S REVIEW editor, "In a grave industrial crisis, where the public might be injured, compulsory arbitration might be invoked as a last, desperate resort, assuming all other methods have been used."

A number of experts and national figures have spoken out in favor of compulsory arbitration in crippling strikes, including the late Harvard economist Sumner H. Slichter and Sen. Spessard Holland (D., Fla.). Sen. George A. Smathers (D., Fla.) has proposed a five-member supreme labor court.

American legislators have considered compulsory arbitration at various times in the past, but they have only approved it in wartime. Compulsory arbitration was proposed and rejected in setting up a Railroad Labor Board in 1920, and it was similarly proposed and rejected in the writing of the Taft-Hartley Law.

Compulsory arbitration has been used abroad by Great Britain, Sweden, Denmark, and particularly Australia, with varying degrees

of success. But its effectiveness, even in nations where labor constitutes a major political party, has been a matter for debate. Australia's strike rate, for instance, has been proportionately higher than
that of the United States.

Arguments against compulsory arbitration boil down to beliefs
that it would reduce the amount of good-faith bargaining by sending
many disputes to the final decision-making body, would be ineffective in the long run, would push labor fully into politics, and would
lead to Government control of profits and prices.

The Greater Danger

But business men in general appear more worried about the effects
of a crippling strike than about the potential dangers of Government-
enforced arbitration. And what seems to worry them most is a stoppage in the flow of goods from producers to consumers.

The manufacturers are more leery of Uncle Sam's policing hand
than either wholesalers or retailers. Wholesalers, standing midway
between the producers and the retailers, like the idea better. And
the retail merchants stand 65 per cent in favor.

The figures tell most of the story, but not all. For the business
men's opinions cover every shade of argument for and against policed
arbitration. Many blame unions for the situation. Some blame
Government. A very few even blame business. But most significant,
of course, is the fact that many who traditionally have wanted less
Government control, not more, now say major strikes can do more
harm than limited Government interference.

Still, there are many dissidents who believe in paying the full price
of a free economy. One of them summed it up in seven words:

"Let capital and labor slug it out."

Robert R. France

THE COMPULSORY
ARBITRATION FALLACY*

. . . .

Almost no serious student of labor relations in the United States, whether he be connected with management, labor, or the world of research and scholarship, advocates legislation providing for compulsory arbitration of labor disputes. Why is this so?

An explanation of this lack of enthusiasm for compulsory arbitration requires an understanding of collective bargaining and of the role the strike plays in that procedure.

Collective bargaining is the process by which management and the workers' representatives agree on the rate of pay and other conditions under which employees will be hired. It is essentially a private procedure, and it requires that both parties voluntarily accept the final agreement which is to govern the relations between the union and the employer.

Such agreements are reached by a great deal of discussion and persuasion. Facts and reasoning play a role in obtaining a solution acceptable to both sides. Because collective bargaining affects matters of vital interest to both parties, mere persuasion is sometimes not sufficient to bring about a meeting of minds. It is at this point that the strike plays an important role, for both parties know that unless agreement is reached they face the possibility of a strike.

The strike is usually looked upon as labor's weapon to force management to make concessions. In reality, the strike is a two-edged sword which inflicts penalties on both sides. True, the strike does shut down the employer's plant and thus causes him to lose profits he might otherwise have made. But, the strike also means that the workers lose their only source of income. From the standpoint of physical hardship and personal privation, in most cases the workers

---

* Robert R. France, "The Compulsory Arbitration Fallacy," *Industrial Union Department* (AFL-CIO) *Digest*, Fall 1959. Reprinted by permission.
Dr. France is Associate Professor of Economics, University of Rochester.

suffer more from the strike than management or the stockholders of the company involved.

It is this possibility of the large economic losses of a work stoppage that urges both sides to make compromises which persuasion and argumentation alone would never achieve. Thus the strike plays an important role in bringing about an agreement between the parties.

It is important to note that the mere *possibility* of the strike is all that is required in most cases to achieve agreement. As long as the parties know that a failure to reach agreement will result in the harsh reality of a work-stoppage, they are encouraged to make the necessary compromises. If the strike had to occur in order to perform its function, the frequent interruptions to production would become intolerable. However, it has been estimated that from 90 to 95 percent of collective bargaining negotiations achieve agreement without the use of a strike. . . .

Given this important function of the strike, what happens if compulsory arbitration legislation is enacted and work-stoppages are prohibited? Failure to reach agreement no longer results in the serious economic losses of the strike. Rather, a refusal to compromise only means that the parties must accept the risk that an impartial board will give it substantially less than could have been obtained voluntarily from the opposing side. This is a risk involving much less cost than a strike. Consequently, the collective bargaining process is weakened throughout the nation.

Situations in which agreement might have been forthcoming in an effort by both sides to avoid the strike will now result in stalemate because of the small cost of disagreeing. As a result, instead of management and workers' representatives working out their own agreements, a third party, the board of arbitration, will have to determine the terms and conditions of employment. . . .

. . . The genius of collective bargaining is that the parties work out their own agreement. Management and the workers' representatives know their own problems and are the best judge of what is feasible in their own industry or firm. . . .

The establishment of a compulsory arbitration law raises the difficult problem of enforcement. What is to be done if the workers strike in violation of the law? As John L. Lewis is reported to have said in a situation in which the coal miners were forbidden to strike: "You can't mine coal with the miners in jail."

Recent experience with compulsory arbitration on a limited scale in public utilities indicates that unless the laws are patently unfair in the minds of the workers, labor unions can be expected to observe them. Nevertheless, widespread use of the laws and the resulting deterioration of collective bargaining coupled with the reduction of our ability to deal effectively with industrial relations problems could easily create so much unrest and embitterment as to result in strikes in violation of compulsory arbitration legislation. . . .

The problems connected with compulsory arbitration are serious ones. It is necessary therefore to raise the question of whether the cure is worse than the disease. Although the economic losses connected with a strike are serious to the parties, the impact of work stoppages on the general public is rarely severe. Either other suppliers of the same or similar goods and services are available, or sufficient stocks are on hand to meet the public's needs while the strike continues.

The impact on total economic production is small. Man-days lost as a result of strikes are typically one-half of one percent of total man-days available. . . .

As compared to an unemployment rate of four to seven percent in recent years, the loss from strikes may not be considered as excessive cost for the advantages of free collective bargaining. Furthermore, in Australia, where compulsory arbitration is widespread, strikes have been as frequent as in such nations as Canada and Great Britain where free collective bargaining prevails. . . .

Since the parties to a labor dispute are much more seriously affected than the public, they must have strong misgivings about arbitrating the issues which they are unable to settle by discussion or persuasion. It is not that management and labor are unfamiliar with arbitration as such. Roughly 95 percent of labor contracts in existence in the United States provide for voluntary arbitration of disputes concerning the interpretation of existing agreements. Thousands of such arbitrations occur each year.

There is a great difference, however, between submitting a dispute involving the terms of an existing contract to a third party for a ruling on the meaning of the contract and permitting a third party to write a new agreement to cover the relations between the disputants. . . .

Although the over-all impact of strikes is not large when compared with total man-days available, strikes in essential industries might pose serious threats to the public health and safety. The problem of the so-called "emergency" strike is a difficult one for a democratic society. On the one hand the strike plays an important part in collective bargaining; on the other, the loss of certain goods and services would have a serious impact on society.

It is worth pointing out that the parties to labor disputes are well aware of the nature of their goods and services. Work stoppages in the gas, electric, and water utilities, for example, are very rare. Even when such strikes do occur, the police powers of the state or federal government are likely to be sufficient to prevent a complete loss of essential services.

If the public is unwilling to depend upon the emergency powers of the Chief Executive, it would not seem wise to rely upon compulsory arbitration alone. There are other methods of dealing with such strikes, such as temporary operation of the facilities by the state, public hearings and recommendations by impartial investigators, and special mediation panels.

Most students of the problem of emergency strikes feel that if any legislation should be enacted to deal with such disputes it should involve several alternatives open to the Chief Executive in order to avoid a situation in which the parties give up bargaining and concentrate on using a known procedure to their best advantage.

The strike involves undesirable economic losses and personal hardship for the firms and workers involved. Nevertheless, it plays a vital role in free collective bargaining. As the old New Englander said, "Before you begin tearing down a fence, you ought to find out why it was put up." Compulsory arbitration is not an appropriate solution to the problem of work stoppages in our society.

HEALTH INSURANCE

Rita R. Campbell and W. Glenn Campbell

VOLUNTARY HEALTH INSURANCE*

The growth of private health insurance in the United States has been spectacular. At the end of 1959 some 127 million persons, or 72 percent of the civilian population, were covered by some form of private health insurance—almost double the number covered a decade earlier and well over four times the number covered fifteen years earlier. Furthermore, health insurance coverage continues to expand rapidly.

There has also been a great increase in the kind and amount of medical expense covered by insurance. In addition to the more common types of hospitalization and surgical insurance providing either cash or service benefits, there are major medical expense plans, extended benefit plans, as well as the so-called comprehensive benefit plans. Over 100 million persons have two or more types of health insurance. At the end of 1959 some 21 million persons had major medical expense insurance, a form of insurance only in an experimental stage ten years ago. Depending on their desires and needs, individuals may purchase different combinations of these various plans.

Private health insurance in the United States is well on the way toward accomplishing what the "experts" in the field of social security stated on innumerable occasions was impossible, namely, near

---

* Rita R. and W. Glenn Campbell, *Voluntary Health Insurance In The United States,* American Enterprise Association, Washington, D.C., 1960, pp. 1–12. Reprinted by permission.

W. Glenn Campbell is Director of the Hoover Institution on War, Revolution, and Peace at Stanford University.

universal coverage of the whole population. It has demonstrated an adaptability to changing medical technology, a flexibility to varying individual needs as well as varying needs in different geographic areas, and an ability to devise new patterns of insurance care not equalled by any national health program.

The private health insurance record is a striking example of the unparalleled contributions that have been made to American life by voluntary and cooperative effort. It is an equally striking example of the extent to which the pessimists and the statists have been wrong as to the continuing productive achievements of private initiative and ingenuity.

For example, in 1948 Mr. Oscar R. Ewing, the then Federal Security Administrator, made an official report to the President (popularly known as the Ewing Report) which stated that "at a maximum, only about half of the families in the United States can afford even a moderately comprehensive health insurance plan on a voluntary basis."[1] We have already seen that within a decade this appraisal had been proven completely incorrect. . . .

There has been strong support for the adoption of a national health service in the United States during the past two decades. A national health insurance scheme was a perennial in President Truman's legislative recommendations. A steady series of bills has been introduced in Congress and extensive Congressional hearings have been held on a number of occasions. Dire predictions have been made as to the future health of the American people in the absence of a national health system. Innumerable statements have emanated from "experts" concerning the inability of private health insurance ever to "do the job."

. . . The greatest pressure currently comes from the proposal to provide a governmental program of health care for the beneficiaries of the Old-Age, Survivors, and Disability Insurance (OASDI) programs. Proponents of this proposal have adopted many of the arguments that have customarily been used to support a national system to provide medical care for all. Chief of these is that private health insurance cannot "do the job."

Many reasons could be advanced as to why a national health scheme has never been adopted. It has been strongly opposed by the medical profession and the insurance industry and by many leading statesmen, such as the late Senator Robert A. Taft, as well as by innumerable individuals and citizen groups who favor the preserva-

---

[1] *The Nation's Health: A Ten Year Program,* A Report to the President, Washington, D.C., Federal Security Agency, 1948, p. 85.

tion of a voluntary society and oppose the further extension of compulsion. Even more important, however, opponents of a national health service admitted the existence of a social problem and tried to solve it by voluntary cooperative methods. The proposed solutions which the medical profession and the insurance industry have supported may not always have been the wisest possible, but overall the record is an enviable and praiseworthy one. But for the development of private voluntary health insurance, the United States would unquestionably long since have adopted a compulsory governmental health service.

The general level of health in the United States although, as in all nations, not perfect, compares favorably with that of other advanced countries and it continues to improve. When national health services were being adopted by many countries, claims were made as to the many ways in which governmental provision of health care would prove superior to private provision. Such claims are seldom made today. Many proponents of the expansion of the welfare state, instead of extolling its achievements, are now devoting much of their time to pointing out that the situation under national health services is not really as bad as the critics said it would be. . . .

The 5.2 percent of gross national product spent on health in the United States is well above the 4 to 4.5 percent of GNP spent on health in Great Britain—a country with governmental provision of medical care for all. U.S. expenditures on health, therefore, do not support the social imbalance thesis[2] that has been so widely propagated recently. Rather, in the words of the U.S. Department of Health, Education, and Welfare:

> There has clearly been a significant stepping-up in the provision of medical care services.[3]

Today about two-thirds of the U.S. population see a doctor during the year compared to less than one-half the population some thirty years ago, and the number of visits per patient has risen.

In the governmental, welfare-oriented economy of Great Britain, on the other hand, the "social imbalance" appears to be much greater

---

[2] This refers to the school of thought which maintains that too large a share of our resources are being devoted to private consumption outlays for such commodities as automobiles with tail fins, alcoholic beverages, tobacco, and other "luxuries," and not enough of our resources are going for such welfare purposes as education, health, housing, etc. Thus an increase in public spending for these latter purposes is favored by this group. For a development of this thesis, see J. K. Galbraith, *The Affluent Society*, Houghton Mifflin Co., 1958.

[3] U.S. Department of Health, Education, and Welfare, Social Security Administration, *Research and Statistics Note No. 26*, September 17, 1959, p. 1.

with over £1 billion spent on tobacco, an amount greater than the £737 million spent on the National Health Service in 1958. In the U.S., expenditures on tobacco totaled $6 billion in 1957 which was not even one-third of expenditures on health. . . .

Health insurance plans are usually classified into three broad groups: service benefit plans as generally sold by Blue Shield and Blue Cross, cash indemnity plans sold by insurance companies, and plans sold or sponsored by various different groups, sometimes erroneously referred to as "comprehensive plans."

The Blue Shield and Blue Cross Plans, often referred to as the "Blues," provide, respectively, surgical and hospital benefits defined in terms of service rather than in terms of dollars. A Blue Shield contract may, however, not cover the complete surgical costs of higher-income subscribers since surgeons may charge these persons a fee above that paid by Blue Shield. In this respect, it departs from a pure, service-type contract.

Health insurance plans of insurance companies (cash indemnity plans) contract to pay a fixed dollar amount for a particular medical service—as a day of hospital care, a surgical operation—or for all medical costs taken together as in major medical insurance. . . .

The miscellaneous plans are much less important numerically. Although there is great variation among these plans, one type is often separated out, namely, plans that employ or are affiliated with a group of doctors since unlike the other purer insurance types, such plans generally restrict subscribers to doctors affiliated with the plan. In 1957 such plans, sometimes referred to as "closed panels," had enrolled about 3.4 million persons. All other plans, including many medical society plans differing from Blue Cross–Blue Shield in name only, had 8 to 9 million subscribers.

These numbers are small compared with the 55 million persons enrolled in Blue Cross at the end of 1958, the 46 million in Blue Shield, plus the 72 million in commercial insurance companies (corrected for duplication among insurance companies). These enrollments, of course, total well over the 127 million persons protected at the end of 1959, since many people carry more than one type of health insurance.

Few plans provide total medical care expenses in all instances. Those coming closest to this concept include some of the independents, comprehensive "major medical expense" plans sold by the insurance companies, and "extended benefit" plans of the Blues.

Many independent group-practice plans cover hospital, surgical, and physician's non-surgical care. Generally, they do not cover dental care, all nursing care or all drugs although some do. In addition,

some of the plans have cost control features such as a small charge—
one dollar—for a doctor's visit.

"Major medical plans" generally cover expenses in connection with
a more major medical condition such as surgery or a stay in an acute
illness hospital. These plans usually pay costs over a relatively small
deductible amount, such as $50 or $100, including medical and nursing care and drugs in the hospital and after dismissal from the hospital, on a percentage basis (co-insurance or corridor) such as 80
percent of costs, up to a maximum—$10,000 to $15,000 is common.

Extended benefit plans of the "Blues" vary greatly and are largely
in the experimental stage. Among costs outside of the hospital which
may be included are diagnostic examinations, nursing care in nursing
homes or the patient's home, drugs, etc. The Blues rely chiefly on
limits or maximum benefits, such as 60 or 120 days of hospital care,
as their form of cost control, but for extended benefit plans they also
employ deductibles and co-insurance.

It has been commented that with the great diversity of plans available, the purchaser of health insurance finds the shopping like that
in a Middle Eastern Bazaar. This, however, gives the individual a
wide range of choice in best meeting his own desires. Moreover, if
the purchaser does not like what any *single* contract makes available,
he can combine offerings of two or more. . . .

Prepayment of complete medical care, including dental, nursing,
and drugs is, however, largely unavailable. Even if an individual lives
in an area where the very few service-type plans which approach this
extreme are located, and he is willing to abide by their rules in
respect to choice of doctors and hospitals, he will be unable, except
in a few instances, to get *all* dental care, nursing, and drugs on a
completely prepaid basis.

If, as is frequently alleged, prepaid, group-practice plans are so
greatly desired, many more such plans would have developed—and
with more comprehensive coverage—despite the opposition of the
medical profession. Today fewer than 4 million persons are enrolled
in prepayment group-practice plans, which in many cases provide
less than comprehensive medical care. . . .

What of the future? . . . Can it reasonably be expected that 100
percent or even 95 percent of the U.S. civilian population eventually
will have some health insurance protection? The answer is "no."
Many uninsured persons do not want private health insurance as
they already have some form of government-paid health care protection. This group includes veterans, those in institutions, Indians,
merchant seamen, and dependents of military personnel. Others
have no means to pay premiums for health insurance. About five

million indigents and medical indigents receive medical care supported from tax funds. . . .

Some students of the subject further refine the numbers of potential purchasers of health insurance by eliminating those with relatively high incomes and large assets who prefer not to pay administrative expenses of insurance, but to meet medical bills from current incomes and/or private savings. . . .

Estimates as to what percent of the total civilian population can be expected at some time or other to purchase health insurance range from 75 percent to 90 percent. The latter figure, which gives some leeway for expansion and seems to be supported by the more recent data and studies, is undoubtedly closer to being the more accurate figure. . . .

The groups disproportionately underrepresented as of 1956–1957 were: non-whites, persons 65 years or over, rural people, the self-employed, those employed in small groups, and the unemployed. There is, of course, much overlapping among these groups, but any estimate of future trends has to consider whether health insurance can be successfully sold to these sectors of the population, particularly on a group basis.

Recent efforts to enroll, both on an individual and a group basis, members of these particular problem sectors have been successful. The "Blues" and insurance companies are selling through existing community organizations such as the Farm Bureau, the Grange, Golden Age Clubs, etc. The National Retired Teachers Association has enrolled well over 100,000 in their noncancellable group, hospitalization-surgical insurance program.

The group to which most attention is currently being given is the aged, those 65 years and over. Comprehensive data recent enough to reflect the very rapid increases in coverage of the aged during the last two years are unavailable, but the scattered data which are available indicate that concerted efforts of insuring agencies and of other groups have been very effective. . . .

Based on the extensive evidence examined in this study, it seems clear that a substantial majority of today's aged can afford to pay for health insurance and that in the future the percentage will be even higher. Certainly the four million persons over 65 who are either employed or wives of employed persons can pay for their own health care. In addition, the almost universal coverage of OASDI, the continuing and rapid expansion of private pension plans, and the steadily increasing real national income are signs pointing to the future when the great majority of the retired aged will be, if they are not already, out of the category of those unable to pay for their own health care.

Within the aged population, just as with other segments of the total population, there are indigent individuals who cannot afford to pay for the cost of medical care. There is, of course, a case for further government aid for this group to the extent that it can be demonstrated that existing public assistance programs and private charity do not provide adequate medical care.

The kind of program for which there is no case is Forand-type legislation which would provide government health benefits to millions of aged who can afford to pay for them on their own, and which would not provide benefits to the group which contains such a large percentage of those aged most in need of help, namely, the four to five million persons over 65 who are not eligible for OASDI. This program would be financed by tax money compulsorily collected from the rest of the population, many of whom are less well off than the proposed beneficiaries.

Such a program would inevitably become a political football as the numbers of present and future aged are too great to be ignored by any official wishing to be elected or re-elected. With each election year there inevitably would be pressures for further expansion of the program just as has occurred with OASDI benefits. The end result might well be National Government provision of medical care for all —the primary goal of many supporters of this legislation.

Michael M. Davis

NATIONAL HEALTH INSURANCE*

. . . .

Voluntary insurance plans have demonstrated to millions of Americans that meeting sickness costs through small regular payments while they are well is immensely better than having the burden of unpredictable fees which must be paid when they are sick. *But, after*

* Michael M. Davis, *National Health Insurance*, League for Industrial Democracy, New York, 1956, pp. 3–13. By permission from the publisher and the author.

Dr. Davis is chairman of the executive committee of the Committee for the Nation's Health.

20 years of effort, this voluntary insurance has left 60 million persons entirely unreached, and has provided only a few million persons with more than limited health services.

National Health Insurance is therefore proposed as the best way of enabling everyone to meet the costs of all basic medical services.

Such a plan . . . would make available to all employed and self-employed persons and their families, the services of family physicians of their choice. In addition, it would provide for care by specialists, for general hospital care, and for some other services. It would finance all these services through a national health insurance fund, collected with other Social Security payments.

The elements of National Health Insurance may be summed up in the following nine points:

(1) Payments would be required by law as with the rest of Social Security;

(2) Payments would be a percentage of earnings, divided equally between employer and employee, except when a different ratio might be established through collective bargaining agreements. . . .

(3) Comprehensive medical services by general physicians and specialists would be made available;

(4) Likewise care in general hospitals.

(5) The payments from earnings would be supplemented by appropriations made by Congress from general tax revenues for specified purposes, especially to bring needy persons into the health insurance system by paying their premiums into the national health fund (payments made as at present from state and local taxes for this purpose might be continued, thus reducing the federal charge);

(6) All persons would be free to choose and to change physicians or organized group of physicians;

(7) Physicians would be free to participate in the plan, or not, as they may desire;

(8) Voluntary funds that meet necessary standards would be free to participate.

(9) Collection of funds would be national, while administration of service would be on a local and State basis, by voluntary and governmental organizations. . . .

National health insurance will aid *to prevent disease.* People who belong to an insurance plan which covers the services of the family doctor, as has been before indicated, will have no financial reason for not going to their doctor to obtain a periodical medical check-up, whether one feels sick or well. A great many illnesses will be less serious if medical care for them is begun early in their course. In some cases, early examination by a doctor can detect a disease, like cancer, in a stage where it is curable, whereas later on there is little or no hope of cure. *Through national health insurance, these and other preventive medical services would be available to people from the physicians of their choice.* . . .

Under National Health Insurance, doctors are not employed by government. They remain independent practitioners, being paid by public or private organizations according to methods which they negotiate, similar to the ways in which thousands of doctors are paid by different types of health insurance plans today. The voluntary hospitals would not be taken over by government. The patient would be guaranteed by law the choice of his doctor. Contrary to the charge made in some of the opponents' literature, that "Your medical care would be dictated by a bureaucrat in Washington," the federal government would not enter into the administration of services at all. Administration would be by local or State bodies, governmental *or* voluntary. To call such a plan "Socialized Medicine" is to employ epithets and labels as substitutes for facts and logic. . . .

National Health Insurance is not new. There have been over 70 years of experience with it in other nations. Systems of national health insurance exist in various forms in some 40 countries. This experience, and the past years of discussion in the United States, show that the principle of National Health Insurance can be applied in different degrees of completeness in terms of the population covered and as to the benefits that are made available. As to coverage, the whole population may be included. Those without incomes, or for other reasons unable to contribute themselves, can be brought under health insurance by payment of their premiums from general tax funds. Thus we escape our present plans of "Poor man's medicine." Local, State and National governments might share in such payments, as they do now in paying for some of the medical care furnished to indigent persons.[1] . . .

---

[1] A National health insurance proposal might be confined to employed persons, or to industrial workers only. It might include persons of high income. Decisions on the extent of coverage might be based on administrative, political or economic considerations.

The scope of benefits might be hospitalization only, instead of physicians' services also. This narrow scope exists in the successfully operating plans in the Canadian provinces of Saskatchewan and British Columbia. The disadvantages of such restricted medical benefits have been already suggested. The legislation mostly discussed in our Congress provided for limited home nursing and for limited dental service, as well as for comprehensive physicians' services and hospitalization. There is a body of opinion that maintains that ordinary dental care should be excluded from health insurance, at least initially. Many, however, who voice this opinion approve of the growing policy in American communities of making provision under public health auspices for certain dental services to children. As to the payment for medicines under a national health insurance plan, that has usually been restricted to medicines prescribed by physicians, sometimes in other ways.

John Kenneth Galbraith

THE WELFARE STATE CONTROVERSY*

. . . .

. . . The case against any piece of welfare legislation must be based on hypothetical consequences—"assuming this legislation is passed this is what you may expect." For purposes of political suasion a bad hypothetical argument is usually as satisfactory as a good one, and it may be superior. The bad argument is no more susceptible to disproof than the good one, and it can, of course, be a great deal more dramatic. An impressive compilation of the grievous disasters which are expected to follow from the passage of the legislation will always attract more attention than something more moderate that makes sense. . . .

. . . For some time, the American Medical Association has been picturing the hypothetical consequences of adopting a system of national health insurance. These are grim. Physicians would become puppets in a political hierarchy. There would be a prompt and gross deterioration in the standards of medical care. There would be little

* John Kenneth Galbraith, *Economics and the Art of Controversy*, Vintage Books, Inc., 1959, pp. 81–86. Reprinted by arrangement with Rutgers University Press.

Dr. Galbraith was Professor of Economics at Harvard University before becoming U.S. Ambassador to India.

further progress in the art. Medical services would be monopolized
by hypochondriacs. People, as distinct from politicians, would
quickly come to excoriate the system, but would be caught helplessly
in its toils. Soon there would be a sharp increase in death rates. Those
left living would be unhealthy, unhappy, though (now) wise. As long
as the American Medical Association is able to stand off such health
insurance schemes, these dismal consequences will remain hypothetical and, hence, unrefuted. Should the country one day enact a
health insurance scheme, there is at least a chance that medical
catastrophe would not ensue. The reputation of the AMA as a
prophet would be sadly impaired. . . .

The debate over health insurance, one may assume, will be exceptionally sharp. Sickness, in a singular degree, renders the individual
incapable of looking after himself. It remains, perhaps, the most
serious of the uncertainties with which the average citizen must contend. At the same time, the opposition to health insurance stands on
a different footing from that to most other welfare measures. The
others—unemployment insurance, public assistance, old age and survivors' insurance, workmen's compensation, aid to dependent children and to the blind—were not viewed as deeply damaging to the
interests or welfare of any particular group. They were resisted on
grounds of general policy, in the belief that they could not be afforded, that they were deleterious to the moral fiber of the recipients,
that they reduced the will or disposition of people to work as they
should, or on some similar grounds. In this argument, those with a
specific interest in, say, old age pensions or unemployment compensation were pitted against those who had only their view of the general welfare (and perhaps some increase in their own taxes and book-
keeping) as their motivation to resistance. As frequently happens,
those with a specific and identifiable interest prevailed.

The argument over health insurance is very different. Any state-
sponsored system of prepaid medical care encounters the implacable
opposition of the organized medical practitioners. This is based on a
sharp (although disputed) identification of self-interest and long-
standing conviction that the present organization of medical care
will best advance the medical art.

Here, then, those who seek the benefits of a welfare measure face
a well-organized and determined opposition. So far in this argument,
moreover, it would appear that the medical profession has had its
own way. Few campaigns have been conducted with more superficial indications of total success than that of the doctors in recent
years against universal health insurance. It is one indication of the

extent of their victory that the office-seeker's standard disavowal of "socialized medicine" (the displacement of the term insurance by the term socialism was itself a workmanlike achievement in the technique of argument) is now only slightly less fulsome than his disavowal of communism.

Nevertheless, it cannot be assumed that this argument is over. While the supporters of a national health insurance scheme would seem to have met a decisive defeat, the problem of financing medical care for the ordinary family has remained. This need can any time serve as culture to a new argument. In addition, there is evidence that social innovation, having been checked on one medical front, is going ahead all the more rapidly on others. This is as one would expect. The difficulty of suppressing or resisting technical innovation, no matter how unsettling or uncomfortable, has long been recognized. Even if the invention is successfully bought up and buried, another is all but certain to appear somewhere else. Though the point is not commonly recognized, the situation with social innovation is much the same. Voluntary prepayment plans for medical and hospital care have been developed as a partial alternative to more comprehensive insurance. More striking, however, is the way in which the frontal resistance to health insurance seems to have brought organized and even wholly socialized medical schemes in at the back door. Private companies have started providing medical care for their employees as part of their compensation. More significant still, in a country where so many adult males and a growing number of women have seen service in the armed forces, are the rapidly expanding medical services of the Veterans Administration. While presumably intended for the veteran whose disability is connected with his service, there is inevitable elasticity in relating illness to military life. Moreover, care may be had for non-service-connected disability if hospital beds are available. This is not insurance but, in effect, fully socialized medical care. Yet veterans' organizations which defend it are notably invulnerable to the charge of social radicalism. . . .

TELEVISION

TELEVISION AND GOVERNMENT REGULATION*

. . . .

Function and Responsibility of the Regulated Individual Licensees

The airwaves used for radio and television broadcasting are part of the public domain held by the Government for the benefit of all the people. There is not enough space in the spectrum for everyone desiring to own and operate a station to do so.

Congress has provided in the Federal Communications Act of 1934, as amended, section 307, that grants of authority for a station license for a term not to exceed 3 years shall be made by the Commission when it finds that such grant is in the public interest. The licensee, who pays nothing for the license, is deemed a trustee of the use of the station license in the public interest. Under the terms of the statute and the regulations, the individual licensee bears the heavy burden of responsibility for control in the public interest of the content and balance of programs broadcast through his station. In spite of this heavy burden, Congress and the Commission have failed to give the licensee any guidelines by way of declaration of policy or otherwise. . . .

In his application, the licensee makes representations as to the type of service he proposes. He also makes certain pledges that time will be made available for civic, educational, agricultural, and other public service programs.

---

* *Investigation of Regulatory Commissions and Agencies,* Interim Report of the Subcommittee on Legislative Oversight, Committee on Interstate and Foreign Commerce, U.S. House of Representatives, 86th Congress, 2nd Session, Washington, D.C., 1960.

Section 307(d) of the Act provides that renewals of licenses may be granted upon application therefor "if the Commission finds that public interest, convenience, and necessity would be served thereby."

In 1952 section 307(d) was amended so that the Commission, in considering license renewal applications, would not have to take into account all the factors which it considers in granting an original license. Senate Committee Report 44, 82d Congress, 1st session, at page 7, states, however, that the Commission was nevertheless to review and consider the station's past programing performance when it applied for a renewal. The report states:

> It should be emphasized that while the recommended amendment does eliminate the necessity for the type of involved and searching examination which the Commission must make in granting an original license, it does not in any way impair the Commission's right and duty to consider, in the case of a station which has been in operation and is applying for renewal, the overall performance of that station against the broad standard of public interest, convenience, and necessity. This authority of the Commission is made explicit by specifying that such renewal grants are subject to findings by the Commission that the "public interest, convenience, or necessity would be served thereby."

In practice, however, as every licensee knows, not once during the past 25 years has the Commission revoked a license or denied the renewal of a license because of poor programing or failure to serve the public interest. . . .

The Act gives the Commission power of revocation. It specifically forbids FCC censorship of programs. Because of the drastic nature of the penalty of revocation it has seldom been invoked by the Commission.

Thus we have a situation where under the law and regulations the individual station licensee is made a trustee of the use of the airwaves in the public interest and left without any guidelines as to what standards he should employ. The statute gives him none. The Commission furnishes him with no explanation of policy. Yet, the law requires that his license be granted and renewed only upon proof that he is serving the public interest.

Almost every sizable television station is affiliated with a network. Without the advertising revenue from this source, few individual stations could survive. Under the terms of his affiliation agreement with the network, the licensee must, among other things, provide the prime viewing hours for broadcast of network programs.

Most of the popular programs originate with the networks, which transmit the package to the affiliated individual station licensee.

In the case of network quiz programs, such as "21" and "$64,000 Question," the individual station licensee had no knowledge or opportunity to acquire knowledge that, back in an originating studio thousands of miles away, TV tricksters had rigged the packaged programs dispensed to him by the networks. Our quiz show hearings demonstrated beyond dispute that imposition of legal responsibility upon the individual licensee for the quality and balance of program content and its freedom from deception has not worked and is not likely to work in the future.

The concept that the airwaves must be used in the public interest requires that definite responsibility should be imposed not only upon the individual licensee but upon the networks, advertisers, advertising agencies, and producers. Guidelines should be furnished by Congress. Unless this is done there is little likelihood that repetition of the quiz show fiasco will be prevented.

Function and Responsibility of Unregulated Networks (NBC, CBS, and ABC)

The Federal Communications Commission does not regulate the networks directly. It has power to regulate them indirectly through its authority over the individual stations owned by the networks. As we have seen from the discussion above, there is in fact little or no genuine regulation of individual licensees so far as program content and balance is concerned. There is no provision in law imposing upon the network as such any responsibility that its programs be in the public interest.

The networks perform a number of services: (1) They are the principal source of most popular programs; (2) they sell national broadcasting time and programs to advertisers; (3) they arrange for the interconnection of the affiliated stations by means of cable or microwave relays; (4) they help individual licensee station affiliates save the expense of producing their own programs; (5) they compensate the individual station for network commercial programs carried by the station; (6) they also help to secure a large audience for the non-network programs which precede or follow the network presentation; and (7) by attracting large audiences they help the individual station to sell more spot advertising time at a better price.

The network may produce its own program, may purchase the "package" from others, or may produce it jointly with others. . . .

Mr. Stanton testified concerning the network standards for program content, as follows:

> . . . Generally the standards of acceptability are in terms of taste and writing and content. It is not a thing that you can write down to the last decimal point, because taste is a difficult thing to define.
>
> But we think in terms of the broad audiences we are serving and say, "Is this the kind of product that we think would be of a standard that would satisfy the public?"

He also testified that with respect to responsibility and program content a network had two sources of responsibility. With respect to the individual stations owned by the network each such station is responsible to the FCC, but network responsibility flows from the corporate management which sets certain standards for what is wanted on the network.

Although the networks have no control over independent producers under their contracts with advertising agencies, they retain the right to refuse to broadcast the programs under certain conditions.

Function and Responsibility of the Unregulated Sponsors

The sponsor (or advertiser) contracts for network time generally through an advertising agency. He may contract directly or through the agency for the package of an independent program producer and for the master of ceremonies. The sponsor and its advertising agency originate and control "the commercials." The network interferes as little as possible, since, according to the testimony of CBS President Frank Stanton, the sponsor picks up the check. The cost to the sponsor for the time and package of a program such as "$64,000 Question" came to about $80,000 per week, of which about $15,000 was for prizes. All sponsors have control over program content, but some exercise more control over program content than others. Sponsors select material, properties, and casting. They also censor and change scripts or contents of programs. . . .

Function and Responsibility of the Unregulated Advertising Agencies

Advertising agencies represent the sponsor in making contracts with producers for shows and with networks for broadcast time. They prepare commercials and supervise the programs to see that the commercials are properly placed in the body of the show and that the program quality is adequate to hold an audience. Richard Pinkham, Vice President of Ted Bates & Co., advertising agency for

Colgate-Palmolive Co., testified that a program supervisor from his department attended every program they put on the air. Mr. Foreman[1] stated that because the sponsor has control of the program content, the role of the advertising agency is simply one of transmitting its point of view as to how the sponsor should exercise such control.

Function and Responsibility of the Unregulated Producers

The producers provide script, intellectual property, talent, and production. They generally sell the program package to advertising agencies who act on behalf of sponsors. The testimony of the producers who testified before the subcommittee was in substantial agreement that their function was to develop and present an entertaining and exciting show, one that by favoritism of popular contestants and by strings of consecutive tie "contests" would heighten tension and attract the largest possible number of viewers. Most producers admitted that manipulative practices were often essential to achieve those ends. Before knowledge of fixing and rigging became public, it appeared that the producers were able to suppress any moral qualms they may have felt in the interest of keeping the rating high. . . .

Response of the FCC to the Television Quiz Show Revelations

By far the greatest obstacle to any FCC regulation of program content under the present act was seen by Chairman Doerfer in the prohibition against exercise of the power of censorship contained in section 326 of the Communications Act and in the expansion by the courts of the scope of the right of freedom of speech guaranteed by the First Amendment to the Constitution. Under its power to grant applications for issuance and renewal of licenses if it finds that "public interest, convenience, and necessity would be served," the Commission admittedly has power to consider the overall programing of applicants. But it disclaims any power whatever over individual programs.

Throughout his testimony, Chairman Doerfer stressed his doubt that rules or standards could be formulated which would prevent deceptive practices like the rigging and fixing of quiz shows, yet not interfere with the accepted artifices involved in production of conventional dramatic, comedy, and variety shows. . . .

---

[1] Robert Foreman, of the advertising agency Batton, Barton, Durstine & Osborne, participated in the hearings. [Eds.]

*The Commission's Claims of Lack of Responsibility and Authority
    Are Unfounded*

While the FCC rightly maintains a hands-off attitude toward the free expression of ideas, it is reasonable to expect that it will exercise intelligent discrimination in determining the kinds of broadcast material entitled to protection and those not so entitled. It cannot use section 326 and the First Amendment to barricade itself from its responsibility to insure that the Nation's broadcasting facilities are used in the public interest.

The doubts of Chairman Doerfer as to the authority of his agency to do anything about the broadcasting practices disclosed in our hearings do not strike the subcommittee as being well taken. . . .

The First Amendment declares that "Congress shall make no law . . . abridging the freedom of speech, or of the press. . . ." While it is true that the right of free speech is guaranteed both by section 326 and by the First Amendment, and that this protection extends to entertainment as well as to other forms of broadcasting, it does not follow that the FCC is impotent to prevent deceptive broadcasting. The right of free speech is not absolute. Chairman Doerfer conceded that it does not apply to commercial advertising. . . .

A highly effective means of preventing deception in broadcasting is afforded by the short term of broadcast licenses. In passing on applications for renewal, as on original applications, the Federal Communications Commission must find that grant of the application will serve the public interest, convenience, and necessity. The obvious purpose of these short-term licenses is to permit frequent reconsideration of the use made of the public resource—the broadcasting frequency assigned to the licensee—to make sure it is employed for the benefit of the public. In making this determination, the Commission is entitled to consider all available evidence indicating what use the applicant may be expected to make in the future of the privilege sought. It cannot plausibly be maintained that deceptive broadcasting promotes the public interest. This is a factor which the Commission must consider in granting a license renewal.

The central fact which justifies licensing of radio stations—a control which the First Amendment forbids for other forms of expression—is the fact that the broadcast spectrum is too limited to accommodate all who wish to use it. While this does not mean that broadcasting enjoys no protection under the First Amendment, it does warrant governmental control to the extent necessary to insure that the limited broadcast frequencies are used for the public benefit. . . .

Denial of an application for renewal of a broadcast license to a broadcaster who knowingly engaged in deceptive broadcasting or who negligently permitted such broadcasts, would not be capricious, since such conduct must be considered by the Commission in determining the character and fitness of a licensee to operate in the public interest. It would not be based on the political, economic, or social views of the licensee. It would be a valid exercise of the Commission's discretion under the Communications Act of 1934 and would not contravene the First Amendment. . . .

Harold E. Fellows

THE TELEVISION INDUSTRY
CAN REGULATE ITSELF*

. . . .

Influences on Programming

ADVERTISING. Good advertising will always be to the benefit of broadcasting for it will enable broadcasting to constantly build and improve its facilities and its product for the American viewing and listening audiences. Advertisers, through their use of broadcast facilities, themselves are performing a public service by describing their merchandise, by increasing the sale of such merchandise and thus by creating and stabilizing employment.

Some of the criticism of broadcasting comes from those who are critical of advertising—from those who believe that all advertising is wasteful and lacking in significant social or economic purpose. Sincere as these people may be, they seem not to have studied the role of advertising in our economy. . . .

---

* Statement of Harold E. Fellows before the Federal Communications Commission, Washington, D.C., 1960.

Mr. Fellows is president and chairman of the board of the National Association of Broadcasters.

They will . . . seek to becloud the picture by citing certain advertising practices in broadcasting or elsewhere which seem at least to be undesirable. As we all know, such practices do exist, as indeed they do in all aspects of human life. Some of them are sufficiently reprehensible to justify government control. Others should be left to the corrective action of the market place. But whatever is done should be based on an understanding of the essential validity of the role of advertising in our economic life.

COMPETITION. . . . People unfamiliar with the structure of broadcasting often forget that broadcasting is a business. Also, they often have the impression that the industry is characterized by monopolistic conditions. Obviously, this is not so; yet the mis-impression persists, perhaps because radio and television stations are licensed by the Federal Government. Some may assume that a license indicates a monopoly, or at least guarantees a profit.

It is true that a limited spectrum does limit the number of stations in a particular market. From a public policy point of view, however, the fact of limitation alone is not significant. The extent of the limitation is. . . .

Scarcity of a public resource suggests regulation of its private use only where the scarcity is such as to encourage monopolistic practices which arise through a lack of workable competition. Where at least a reasonable degree of competition exists, the character of the product or service should be decided in the market place, not by directive from Washington.

Broadcasting at both the network and the station level is competitive. There is no guarantee of profit and in fact many broadcasters have lost, and are today losing, money. . . .

In television the limitations of spectrum space may impose restrictions on competition somewhat more stringent than those which would be imposed by economic limitations alone. In some markets, additional channels might be supported if they were available. I doubt, however, if the number of such potential stations is as large as some people suppose. The degree of competition in television today is partially reflected by the following facts.

1. In 1958, 164 of the 475 stations in operation for the full year operated on a loss basis.

2. On a market basis, 18% of the television markets containing three or more stations operated in the red on a market basis in 1958.

3. In the first 100 markets, which on a standard metropolitan market basis include approximately 92 million people, and in terms of

television coverage, probably include at least 125 million people, there is substantially more competition among TV stations than among newspapers. . . .

Because of the cost structure of the television business, TV networks and stations generally, although not exclusively, try to develop programming with maximum audience appeal, just as a newspaper or a major magazine tries to get maximum circulation or Ford tries to sell the most cars. By and large, television stations in the same market compete for the same potential audience, or the largest share of that audience. This is not only in their economic interest, but it is, in a very real sense, an excellent measure of the use of the facility.

Our critics sometimes forget that the production of goods and services to meet broad, popular demand is nothing new in this country. Nor is there need to apologize for it. Not only is our economy built on this foundation, but so is our public education and, even more important, so are our basic political institutions. All are based on the acceptance of the validity of the average response of the average person. Those who complain about the level of television programming are really complaining about the level of this average response. Television broadcasters have made, and will continue to make, significant contributions to raising the cultural level of this average response. Final responsibility is likely to remain where it always has been, that is, primarily with each of us as parents and, secondarily, with the schools.

Much is made of the fact that profits for some television stations have been substantial, but it is well to remember that the initial risk was also substantial. . . .

RATINGS—AUDIENCE MEASUREMENT. There is far too little public realization of the fact that we know more about current radio and television audiences today than we do about other current media audiences. Over and above a count of the numbers tuning in to radio and television, there is information supplied by the major broadcast research companies which show audience composition, characteristics of this audience and sponsor identification (a measure of the impression an advertising message makes). Other quality audience measurement studies of the radio and television audience are underway. We should know, soon, what people would like to see in television programs—not just what they think about the programs available today.

The question frequently has been asked—"Does not the overwhelming emphasis on program rating indicate a lack of responsibility on the part of the networks and the stations?" Those who ask the question usually have an affirmative answer pretty clearly in mind.

I think there is an answer, and a pretty good answer. In a word, it is "no." In my judgment, the reliance on program ratings does not indicate a lack of responsibility.

The purpose of ratings is to determine how many people are watching a program and broadly speaking, if properly handled, they do just this.

Here it would be well to realize that ratings are based upon a sampling of radio and television homes. The statements by un-knowledgeable people that a small sample cannot depict listening habits of large audiences is wholly without merit—if and when the sample has been carefully selected. Sampling techniques used by major research firms are based upon procedures and methodologies developed largely by experts in the Bureau of the Census, working with expert statisticians, employed by the research companies. It is obviously beyond the realm of practicality to attempt to measure every listener—there are not enough trained people to do the job, there is not enough equipment available, there isn't enough money for this purpose to pay for the work involved, and finally, it would be wholly impractical from the viewpoint of timeliness of reports.

In effect then, if the ratings are accurate, the viewing public is, through the mechanism of ratings, being given the programming choice. The broadcaster is continually searching to find the program-ming that will satisfy the popular taste. I think it can hardly be argued that this reliance on popular taste is an act of irresponsibility. In fact, the better argument is quite the other way. Anything less than this, at least on a substantial basis, might be well regarded as irresponsible. . . .

The essential point here is that ratings are used to determine popular approval of programs. They may be occasionally incorrect statistically and they may be occasionally misused managerially. Yet, the purpose behind the use, far from being irresponsible, seems to me to be both socially and economically sensible, as well as responsi-ble. Those who complain perhaps are not objecting to ratings; they may be objecting to popular taste. . . .

THE PUBLIC. As we have attempted to indicate, the final arbiter of this public interest is the public itself. No medium, perhaps no pro-fessional or business enterprise, goes to such expense to attempt to understand and evaluate the needs and the desires of the public.

Furthermore, nearly every national organization—The American Association of University Women, The Parent-Teachers Association, the General Federation of Women's Clubs, educational organizations and the like—has a radio and television committee. These committees constantly are engaged in the surveillance of broadcasting product and regularly issue reports of varying authenticity evaluating this product. These reports are examined by broadcasters and many of them, I would say most of them, influence the nature of programming in one way or another.

Thus, in sum, as we examine the history of broadcasting, we can see that its trends in programming have been, for the most part, ever-changing—cyclical—and to a certain extent until this time, unpredictable. Programming trends have been influenced by public reaction—both the reaction of the general public and the reaction of articulate minority groups within that general public; by the Government; by advertising; by competition; by program and audience measurements or ratings if you will; and by the critics. And, of course, there has been the influence induced by the sources of programming—the creative people who have given their inventive talent to developing new forms to capture and intrigue audiences.

In all of this, there have been incidents of error—of serious error, such as the reprehensible matters that have induced the instant hearings: the bad faith in the case of certain quiz programs and the evidences thus far adduced of the phenomenon called "payola" which is not new on the American scene. Here, however, we are not dealing with matters that indicate a calculated dishonesty on the part of an industry; we are dealing with the behavior of a relatively small number of individuals and the uncertainty or failure of self-regulation in a very limited area.

Steps have already been taken by the industry, through its self-promulgated systems of standards, to correct these evils. But as Woodrow Wilson once said: "When one overtakes a speeding auto, he arrests the driver, not the automobile." . . .

The Issues

The central issue that we are discussing in this hearing relates to what power, if any, has been granted to the Federal Communications Commission in the regulation or supervision of programming broadcast over radio and television stations. . . .

There have been notable examples in the past in which government officials have indicated that they would like to become, if not actual program censors, at least program directors. To some, apparently this temptation to impose their programming judgment upon that of several thousand licensees has been almost irresistible.

We believe the time has come when this temptation should be

removed, not only for the benefit of this Commission—which has shown admirable restraint in the matter—but for the benefit of those who will be our regulators in the future. Most of those who have spoken or written about this issue at the Judicial and Legislative levels have agreed that the First Amendment and the protection it offers to the American people in the area of free speech and free press relates directly to the activities of the Federal Communications Commission in its regulation of broadcasting. . . .

We believe the Commission should enunciate, once and for all, that no central governmental body should attempt to assume this basic responsibility of the licensee even if it could constitutionally be given the authority. How do we reconcile this belief with the Commission's sworn duty to administer the Communications Act in the public interest, convenience and necessity?

Well, first, the Commission must accept the premise that broadcasters are honest and conscientious citizens intent upon satisfying the wants and needs of the people to the best of their ability. Given this acceptance of the basic honesty and integrity of the licensee, implicit in the grant of the license to him in the first place, there follows the assumption that he is no more likely to undergo a change in this basic good character than the bank president is likely to embezzle. In both cases, as in all vocations, there are likely to be a few exceptions.

If we are to say that the licensee is the individual finally responsible for meeting the public interest, then we must presume that he has a better way of measuring it than the Commission or anyone else may have. I submit that by the very nature of his daily performance, he is the one best qualified. He or the executive responsible for the administration of his station plays an active part in the life of his community. He becomes acquainted with the wants and needs of his audience in the field of programming. He and his personnel participate in the actions of his community's government, civic, religious, business and social organizations. He is in continuing contact with the people he serves. He is aware of the competitive programming on other stations in his community, whether radio or television, of the service offered by the published media, the community's various educational institutions, the ethnic composition of his audience—and all of these factors play a part in his judgment of the fashion in which he shall satisfy the public interest through his facility.

He was not licensed originally to supplant the church or the parent in the home. He was not licensed as an educational institution. He was licensed to serve the public interest to the best of his ability.

There is only one real reason that he would fail to do this—and that would go directly to the question of his honesty or responsibility which I propounded earlier. If his actions are such that he demonstrates a continuing and feckless dishonesty or irresponsibility, then he shouldn't have a license anyway.

We believe, therefore, that the present requirement for a broadcaster to submit to the Commission a statistical breakdown of his programming activity is unrealistic and unnecessary. We believe it would be far more useful to the Commission and responsive to the public interest if the broadcaster, in applying for renewal, recited in narrative form the steps he had been taking in the preceding three years to determine the public interest, at the same time relating the changes that had taken place in his programming pattern and the local manifestations that impelled those changes.

This would not remove the obligation upon the applicant in the original instance, to tell the Commission what steps he has taken to determine the public interest requirements of the community he proposes to serve, but it would remove the implication that what he said at that time would be binding upon him forever more.

The Commission, therefore, would not consider individual programs in granting or denying a license other than those that clearly violate such existing laws as those dealing with lotteries, profanity and the like. The Commission thus would be judging a licensee on the basis of his responsible service to a responsible portion of his community—for it is possible to serve the public interest by scheduling only classical selections during musical periods and for that matter, also for scheduling only popular music.

If, in its review of such narrative reports, the Commission should find no evidence of a bona fide effort on the licensee's part to respond "to the wants of a responsible element of the community" or should find, for example, that deceptive advertisements were knowingly broadcast, then there would arise such question concerning the licensee's character that the Commission should investigate the matter further.

This procedure, we believe, gives meaning and substance to the phrase "public interest, convenience and necessity" without raising any question regarding free speech and censorship.

In this discourse, we have referred to the "wants" of responsible elements of the community. Obviously, broadcasters will continue to go beyond this in satisfying the needs of the community as they see them and this Association will constantly encourage them in this pursuit. Through editorializing, through the scheduling of discussions, through the deliberate effort to schedule at good times programs of cultural significance, they will be giving sum and substance to the narration of their efforts to determine and respond to the public interest. . . .

Conclusions

In effect, what we have said here is that we believe the Government should stay out of programming per se—that self-regulation by the broadcasting industry, even with its limited sanctions, is more in keeping with our democracy than government control, whether by lifted eyebrow or by lifted mace. . . .

The Television Code became the industry code of self-regulation on March 1, 1952. We believe it to be a remarkable and exemplary product and procedure both in draft, execution and adherence by a young and vigorous industry. . . .

We are formulating a plan in which we will endeavor to do a more effective job of promoting and publicizing the Code and the Standards in order that the public may know of their purpose. This plan, when adopted by the Board, will be publicly announced and, if it is the wish of this Commission, made a part of this record.

Generally, we will continue to enlarge our program of liaison with advertisers, advertising agencies, package producers and others whose product bears directly upon program performance.

We fully recognize that the confidence of the American public and of course of this Commission and the Congress and other interested parties in broadcasting will depend in no small part upon the success of our self-regulatory efforts.

Therefore, we propose to issue annually a published report that will summarize the activities emerging from these self-regulatory endeavors. This report will not reveal specific information that now is held in confidence with the subscribers but it will fully document the measures taken. The report will be made available to all interested parties, to the press and, we trust, to the public through the facilities of subscribing stations.

We believe that these actions, supported by the obvious revitalized interest of the broadcasters themselves, are sufficient to the purposes we are discussing in this hearing.

We respectfully submit that this places responsibility for broadcasting in the hands the Congress intended to bear such responsibility. . . .

5

CIVIL RIGHTS

. . . I noticed the streets where they vote, they were fixed; I noticed the roads where the people lived on where they vote, it was gravel; I noticed the people that vote, the officers of the law respected them and treated them different from the people that didn't vote, and after reading Negro newspapers, traveling quite a bit, I felt like that it was a responsibility . . . it always has been a burning zeal and desire in my heart, and I have never been able to tell my children the reason why that Negroes should be treated in such a way or be cast about. . . .

Constitutional guarantees to the individual against abuse by government fall into two categories. First there are those, like freedom of speech and press, the search and seizure clause, and the Fifth Amendment protection against compulsory self-incrimination, to which any American might have occasion to appeal. The second category is directed toward preventing governmental jurisdictions from singling out people on the basis of race or other demographic characteristics such as sex, and treating them differentially from the population in general. This second category includes, of course, the equal protection clause of the Fourteenth Amendment, the Fifteenth Amendment, and the Nineteenth Amendment—the latter two providing that race, color, or sex may not be the basis for denying individuals the privilege of voting.

Both categories, it may reasonably be argued, are essential to the maintenance of a democratic government and a free society. In the sixties, however, the dominant theme in the civil rights field will be the quest for equal treatment under the law by minority groups. People want not merely equal rights under the law—something of an abstraction for most—but substantial equality of opportunities for education, housing, and employment. They want effective social, political, and economic opportunities equal to those which are enjoyed by Americans generally.

The coming decade will not only witness the continued use of the courts to enforce constitutional rights, but it will see relentless pressure upon state and national legislatures for the imaginative and positive use of law to reduce if not erase discrimination based upon race. More than half of the states have established commissions to investigate civil rights problems and, in some cases, to enforce legislatively defined rights. In addition, twenty-eight states and the District of Columbia have laws prohibiting discrimination based upon race. These laws range over the fields of public accommodations, employment, housing, education, and health and welfare. New kinds of protection against discrimination are being demanded, and varying population groups other than racial minority groups are demanding such protection. A number of states, for example, are looking into the possibility of providing for the migratory worker, as a class, some of the protections which have been afforded racial minority groups; and New York State has enacted legislation prohibiting employment discrimination against individuals on the basis of age.

Since it is our purpose to anticipate the issues that will concern legislators and the American voting public during the sixties, the readings in this chapter are restricted to the problems faced by minority groups as they pursue the elusive goal of equal status in American society.

First we deal with the contention that it is futile, if not wrong, to pursue the goal of equality of opportunity through legislation, for law cannot perform the task. A variety of arguments are employed in support of this thesis. Federal legislation, we are told, would undermine state authority and endanger the federal system. Some forms of legislation at the national level would, it is alleged, be unconstitutional. It is suggested that the chief cause of any inequality which minority-group members may experience is the lack of either motivation or educational qualification. Finally, of course, we hear the aphorism that laws cannot change the hearts and minds of men.

Some, although not all, of these arguments were adduced by the Assistant Attorney General of the State of Florida, as he testified against the voting registration provisions of what was destined to become the Civil Rights Act of 1960. A defense of the efficacy of legislation in dealing with problems of racial discrimination is presented in a report of the California Commission on Race and Housing. This argument is not offered as direct rebuttal to that of the Florida official. The California report relates to state and local legislation. Many persons who would disapprove of civil rights legislation under the aegis of the federal government would at the same time defend the rights of individual states to enact such civil rights legislation as they choose. The report is, however, an answer to those who make the general assertion that legislation at any level cannot change attitudes and thus is an inadequate mechanism for lessening discrimination in American society.

The statement of the Assistant Attorney General of Florida is typical of the response to charges of deprivation of voting rights. On the other hand, the testimony of Reverend John Henry Scott, presented to the Commission on Civil Rights in New Orleans in 1960, makes poignantly clear the nature of the obstacles that are confronted by Negroes in some areas of the South.

The decision in *Brown* v. *Topeka*, 349 U.S. 294 (1954), in which the Supreme Court found that systems of pupil assignment based upon race violate the equal protection clause of the Fourteenth Amendment, has yet to find acceptance and observance on any significant scale in the elementary and high schools of the South. The statement of a superintendent of schools from a North Carolina community suggests the range of problems which promise to make the pace of integration deliberate indeed, even in areas that have officially accepted integration. And, of course, the history of Little Rock and of New Orleans suggests that local defiance can at times come close to nullifying federal intervention.

In the North and West, one is likely to encounter an attitude of smugness toward local problems of discrimination. This, together with a tendency to preach to the South, infuriates Southerners. Yet the fact is that anywhere in the United States, minority-group members find it difficult if not impossible to acquire housing of their choice in nonsegregated neighborhoods. It is an interesting irony that the white parents who refused to permit their children to attend school with Negroes in New Orleans in 1960 resided, for the most part, in integrated neighborhoods, while in many Northern cities, in which legal and mob sanctions for segregated schools are absent, schools tend to be overwhelmingly white or overwhelmingly Negro, due to "neighborhood" housing patterns. Minority-group members resident in ghettoes in the North and West frequently find life as segregated as they might in a Southern community. A study of segregation in New York City, prepared by Nathan Glazer, and testimony taken by the Commission on Civil Rights, in its San Francisco housing hearings in January 1960, suggest the magnitude and complexity of the problem.

FEDERAL LEGISLATION
WILL NOT DO THE JOB*

. . . .

MR. ODUM. At the outset, it must be made clear that we are not here to advocate racial discrimination in voting.

On January 28, 1960, Governor Collins made the following public statement emphasizing his—

> . . . own feeling that there can be no excuse anywhere in the United States of America for refusing the privilege of voting in any election because of race or creed. I do not condone any machinery or any attitude which has that as its purpose or effect. But I think it is the responsibility of the States to assure the freedom of our citizens to vote.

---

* Statement of Ralph E. Odum before the Committee on Rules and Administration, U.S. Senate, 86th Congress, 2nd Session, February 1960.
Mr. Odum is Assistant Attorney General of the State of Florida.

We believe that this statement sums up briefly and accurately the deep-seated convictions and attitudes of the overwhelming majority of the people of Florida.

We also believe that the record of Florida voting in recent years verifies and substantiates this position.

On January 29, 1960, Secretary of State R. A. Gray of Florida made the following statement:

> As the State official mainly concerned with the administration of election laws in this State, I do not know of any county or any supervisor of registration who has or would deny a Negro the right to register to vote.

On September 10, 1959, Governor Collins told a press conference that he had not received direct complaints or information to support a report by the Civil Rights Commission to the effect that in Gadsden County, Fla., Negroes are afraid to vote.

In this statement, Governor Collins made it clear that if there actually did exist instances of intimidation or other illegal interference with the right to vote, and such instances were reported to him, he would not hesitate to take corrective action.

He said:

> Specifically, the State government can call upon the people generally in those counties to adopt a different attitude and to improve that situation, and as Governor I don't hesitate to do that here and now. I hope that that can be accomplished there through their local processes. If, of course, there are specific acts that are brought to the attention of the local officials and if, that being done, there is not adequate redress provided at the local level, of course, that will be another matter in which I, as Governor, will be very interested.

To this date, no such complaints have been made to Governor Collins. . . .

We would like to respectfully call your attention to the fact that the problem of nonparticipation of Negro citizens in voting in Florida is rapidly taking care of itself through the efforts of our local people and officials. In 1947, Florida had 49,000 Negroes registered. In 1952 we had 120,000; in 1956 we had 148,703; in 1958 we had 144,810; in 1959 we had 152,675.

We think it is significant that between 1947 and 1959 Negro registration increased in Florida from 49,000 to 152,675, and this increase did not result from outside pressures either in the form of court orders or Federal commissions. It resulted, we believe, from local internal changes in the cultural and economic standards and civic responsibility of Negroes, our rapid increase in urbanization, and the voluntary acceptance of these changes on the part of their white neighbors.

We are fearful that if Congress should enact the bills you are considering here, the practical result will be a regressive trend in Negro registration. The reason for this is obvious: The exertion of outside pressure and coercion by the Central Government in local matters is regarded as a usurpation of authority which stimulates resentment rather than understanding, tolerance, and racial cooperation.

Patient understanding and tolerance in seeking voluntary improvement may be a longer road than some might like, but we believe it to be the best and most effective road leading to ultimate dignity, mutual respect, and equal opportunity for all our people.

Attorney General Rogers expressed the same concern in testifying before your congressional committees last year on other phases of civil rights legislation when he said:

> The image of the Federal Government trying to dominate the States could tend to harden resistance.

We think it self-evident that Attorney General Rogers' fears in this regard are being vindicated.

The four bills introduced by Senators Humphrey, Morse, and Javits do more than create an image of Federal domination. They constitute absolute and undisputed Federal control and domination in the exercise of the voting franchise, an area which by law and custom has been the undisputed responsibility and authority of State and local governments since the founding of this Republic.

All four of these bills are substantially the same. With minor differences, they provide that anyone who thinks he has been denied the right to register to vote in a Federal election because of his race, religion, color, or national origin may file a petition with the President requesting the appointment of a Federal registrar.

If the President receives as many as nine such petitions within 1 year from any voting district, he may cause an investigation to be made by the Civil Rights Commission. Upon recommendation of the Commission, he may appoint a Federal registrar in the voting district and all persons registered by the Federal registrar must be permitted to vote.

The effect of these bills would be to disregard normal judicial process and remedies both State and Federal in cases involving registration disputes and to place unrestricted power in the hands of a political appointee of whichever political party happened to be in authority at the moment. . . .

By the time of its report of April 1959 the Civil Rights Commission had only received 291 complaints regarding voting rights; 246 of these were sworn complaints and 45 were unsworn.

Of these, 12 sworn complaints and 2 unsworn were received from among the 844,000 Negroes living in Florida. We have been given no information as to the identity of the 14 people from Florida who complained or whether subsequent investigation indicated that these complaints were invalid. The local and State officials of Florida have not been called upon or given an opportunity to investigate and act upon any alleged racial voting complaints of any kind.

A special report of the Southern Regional Council released November 2, 1958, includes the following statement:

> In certain areas it undoubtedly has become more difficult for Negroes to register, because of new voting restrictions and stricter applications of the old requirements. In some sections where political leaders have fanned racial prejudices, Negroes are even more hesitant about attempting to register than they were 2 years ago. *But, in many parts of the South, lack of political consciousness remains the greatest barrier. Leaders of both races long have contended that if all bars to Negro voting were removed tomorrow, there would not be a great rush to the polls.*
>
> This is not expected until Negroes have been able to raise their economic and educational levels, their leadership has been broadened and they have reached a position where their political participation promises more tangible results. *Neither the new civil rights legislation nor the Federal agencies created by it promise any quick or dramatic improvement in Negro suffrage. Even where registration boards are cooperative, a gradual process of political education obviously will be required.*
>
> All this should not obscure the fact that the trend is upward and that the long-range prospect in the South is for a Negro registration comparable to the white. [Emphasis supplied.]

We think this statement provides the best clue as to why many of our Negro citizens do not vote. In Florida, it is indifference and apathy that keep most of them from the polls—not threats or intimidation. We have long since dispensed with the poll tax in Florida. We have in Florida no laws which either directly or indirectly discriminate against Negroes voting. Nor do we believe that our registration officers in administering their duties commit acts of intimidation against them.

If such has occurred, it has been the rare exception, not the rule. Certainly no problem has arisen which could not be handled properly by State and local officials. The denial of this opportunity by the enactment of these four bills we believe would create problems where none now exist and serve to fan fires of racial tension which we are doing our best to contain and ultimately extinguish. . . .

If fundamental rights of suffrage are abridged because of racial discrimination, the judicial forum is open for their enforcement without the necessity of Federal legislation invading this State traditional field of regulation.

In view of the gains which we have made in the area of racial relations and the other considerations which we have brought to your attention, we respectfully urge that the evolutionary trend not be prematurely disrupted by unnecessary, improvident, and provocative legislation. . . .

STATE AND MUNICIPAL LEGISLATION*

. . . .

The movement for racial equality during the past dozen years has relied heavily on legislation. Many states and municipalities have adopted laws prohibiting discrimination in employment, housing, public accommodations, education, and other areas. At the end of 1957, sixteen states and fifteen cities had legislated or officially resolved for equal rights in some aspect of housing. Almost all of this legislation applies to housing which is affected with some public character. The most comprehensive laws, with one exception, are those in force in six states—Connecticut, Massachusetts, New Jersey, New York, Oregon, and Washington—prohibiting discrimination in all publicly assisted housing including housing developments built with government mortgage insurance. The exception is New York City's law applying to all housing (public and private) in multiple-unit structures and to new sales housing in ten or more units. This is the first law aimed at prohibiting racial or ethnic discrimination in the housing market generally.

Many people doubt the possibility of promoting racial equality by

---

* *Where Shall We Live?* Report of the Commission on Race and Housing, University of California Press, Berkeley, California, 1958. Reprinted by permission.

law. It is often said that social customs cannot be changed by legislation, and also that law cannot change the attitudes that are the basis of the race problem. The failure of prohibition is cited, also the failure of the Federal civil rights laws enacted after the Civil War and the nonenforcement of state laws against discrimination in public accommodations adopted during the latter part of the last century. These legislative failures are enough to demonstrate that mere passage of a law is no infallible cure for a social evil, but they do not justify a conclusion that law is of no avail.

Most contemporary students of the subject hold that law *can be* a potent force for changing social habits and indirectly can modify attitudes. Laws against racial discrimination, even when running counter to customary practice, are consistent with the moral and political ideals held by most Americans and may expect public support for that reason. Moreover, it is essential to note that American laws in this field, as in others, do not require any persons to hold or change any attitudes but only to refrain from certain acts (discrimination). Although attitudes of race prejudice are undoubtedly basic factors in the situation, as previously pointed out, they do not control action in any simple or uniform way. Prejudiced persons do not always discriminate, and unprejudiced persons sometimes do discriminate. The situation in which a person finds himself is a major determinant of his behavior, and the situation can be changed by law.

A great deal of psychological research has demonstrated that a person's attitudes are largely shaped by experiences and factors in his environment. Attitudes of race prejudice, like other commonly held attitudes, are nourished and supported by environmental conditions. Law can weaken or sometimes remove the environmental supports and thereby lead to a change in attitudes. One of the major supports to race prejudice is discrimination itself and the results of discrimination. Hence action that prevents discrimination will lead to a reduction of racial prejudice.

Whether a law will be effective in preventing discrimination depends, obviously, upon its enforcement. Until recent years, state laws against discrimination (mainly the public accommodation statutes) made no feasible provision for enforcement and afforded no practical remedy for an aggrieved person. Lacking enforcement machinery, the older laws remained dead letters on the statute books. Recent antidiscrimination laws, in contrast, are not only broader than the older statutes, but they also incorporate a distinctive philosophy and method of enforcement.

The framers and the administrators of the modern equal rights legislation regard law and education not as alternative but as complementary methods of promoting equality. Together with the statutory restraints, an educational program is written into most, if not all, of the laws as a major reliance for securing public acceptance of the legislation and compliance with its provisions. Most of the laws in the different states have been modeled after those of New York and are, for this reason, quite similar, even to the point of much identical language. They have in common four essential features. First is administration by a special commission or agency. Experience has demonstrated that legal control of discrimination, to be effective, requires special administrative procedures. Second, when complaints of unlawful discrimination are received, the commission investigates the facts; if evidence of discrimination is found, it attempts by conference and conciliation to persuade the offender to comply with the law. These proceedings are informal and unpublicized. Third, if informal conciliation efforts fail, the commission invokes formal procedures, holds a public hearing, may issue a cease and desist order, and if the order is disregarded, apply to the courts for enforcement. Fourth is provision for a program of public information and education designed to create public understanding and acceptance of the law and to generate a public opinion favorable to compliance.

The formal sanctions provided by the laws have been very little used. The great majority of discrimination complaints have been settled by informal methods of investigation and conference. In essence, therefore, administrative commissions have relied upon voluntary compliance. Nevertheless, the existence of legal sanctions in the background is considered essential. The commissions are engaged mainly in a work of persuasion, yet it is not pure persuasion. The supporters of equal rights legislation are strongly convinced that the commissions, to be effective, must have authority and sanctions at their disposal, even if they use them sparingly.

The administrative procedures described were initially developed in relation to fair employment legislation. As other nondiscrimination laws have been enacted, they have been placed under the jurisdiction of the commissions and administered in the same way. The housing laws are the most recent legislation of this general kind; most of them were adopted only during the past two or three years.

It is difficult to evaluate the effects of modern antidiscrimination laws with any precision. In employment and use of public accommodations, a significant reduction of discrimination has occurred during the period in which the laws have been in effect. The laws, of course, have been only one of several factors operating to produce this result. The commissions can be credited with breaking through a number of barriers at strategic points, such as opening employment opportunities for minorities with some leading employers and in certain occupations formerly closed to them. The role of the commissions in opening opportunities will be particularly important in housing. The laws and commissions have afforded new opportunities and programs for community education which otherwise would not have existed. On the whole, it is the consensus of observers that the laws have played a significant, if not measurable, role in the decline of racial discrimination during the past decade or two.

The effects of the housing laws on racial residence patterns during the brief period of their existence do not afford a sufficient basis for firm judgment. Indications are that effects depend very much on the location and price of the housing developments affected. Except in the vicinity of existing areas of minority concentration, legal removal of discriminatory barriers seems to result in a rather thin scatter of minority families instead of new concentrations. In New York, several cooperative housing developments built under long-standing non-discriminatory law for this type of housing, but at a considerable distance from Harlem, have attracted only 5 to 10 percent of Negroes in their populations. Developments built on slum-cleared land in Manhattan have been more attractive to Negroes, but even here higher-priced developments have been occupied by Negroes only to the extent of around 25 percent. These experiences illustrate two central facts about minority housing demand as previously described: only a small proportion of minority families are able to pay for new, good quality dwellings at current prices; and, under existing conditions, comparatively few nonwhite families seem to be interested in moving far from the minority community. These conditions may change, of course, and the long-period prospect may well be quite different from the short run. For the present, however, nondiscrimination laws have not called forth a large demand from minorities for new development housing, and there seems to be no reason to expect it. When the demand which does exist is spread over a great number of projects and locations, the effect on any single location is obviously slight.

Fears expressed by some that nondiscrimination laws would disrupt the housing industry, causing lenders to withhold mortgage funds and discourage sales, have not been realized in the states which have adopted such legislation. No substantial complaints of economic loss have been made. In fact, real fears of destructive consequences have evidently not been widespread, since in several states the laws were enacted with little opposition. In the state of Washington, for example, a law very similar to that of New York, prohibiting discrimination in the marketing of FHA, VA, and other government-assisted housing, passed the lower house of the legislature without a dissenting vote and the state senate by an overwhelming majority. . . .

THE RIGHT TO VOTE*

REVEREND SCOTT. . . . The first time that I attempted to register, that is back in 1946. Another young man named Reverend Paul Taylor, we decided we would go and try. . . .

Well, we didn't know exactly where the registration office was, so finally we went upstairs, and we got to the door, and I said, "Paul, here is the door," and we went to the door, and the registrar of voters say, "Go to the next door." So we went to look for another door, and when we got back, the door was locked. So we didn't make any attempt to go in. We give up that time. . . .

The next time I tried to register must have been about two years later, around '47, the Reverend Mason and I went together. . . .

Went to the same place, the same registrar. She was very nice. She gave us the card to fill. When we filled it she looked at it and said, "Well, we wouldn't know where to find you all," or something, so we went out. . . . So I decided that probably trying to be a Democrat was making it difficult for me to register. . . .

So I decided to put on my next card "Republican." I didn't want to put "Communist" on there, and so when I put "Republican" on, the registrar of voters looked in the office, and she picked out a card, and she looked at it, and she said, "Well, on this card you said you were a Democrat. On this card you are saying you are a Republican." She said, "What are you?"

---

* Statement of Reverend John Henry Scott, in the Hearings before the U.S. Commission on Civil Rights, Louisiana, September 1960.
Reverend Scott is Baptist minister of East Carroll Parish.

I said, "Well, I am not anything until you register me."

So she said, "Well, don't you know you can't change your party that fast?"

So I had to go out.

So later on, about '50, somewhere about 1950, I believe, Reverend Mason and several others went in, decided to try again, and she gave us all a card, and we filled them out, and she told Reverend Mason that his was perfect, but he would have to get someone to vouch for him or sign, identify him. All of which he was successful, but that didn't work, either. . . .

. . . Recently they put . . . a new man in office after our present registrar resigned or went on retirement, and we thought we would try him, I believe last September, and several of us went. . . .

He asked us how long had we been living there. Most of us had been living there all of our life and he said, "Well"—he handed us a form, he said, "You will have to get two qualified electors from your ward and precinct to identify you." . . .

So he didn't register. So the lady that was with me, she said, "I can get two to identify me." I said, "Well, you think you can, but you can't." She said, "But I know I can," she said, "I have some white friends, and we are all Christians." I said, "But Christians and this registration business is different. Nobody's a Christian when it comes down to identifying you."

So she went and tried, . . . and she said, "Well, it is just like you said, they told me that they couldn't bother with it."

So we decided to go back, I believe, in July, possibly July 25.

VICE CHAIRMAN STOREY. What year?

REVEREND SCOTT. This year. A group of us went.

VICE CHAIRMAN STOREY. About how many?

REVEREND SCOTT. About 21. . . . So we went in. The registrar of voters asked us what did we want. We said we wanted to register. He said, "Do you have anybody to identify you?" I says, "We can identify each other." I said, "We identify folk at the bank and at the post office." I say, "We have come around and got folks out of jail and signed, went on their bond." I said, "We be here long enough to be known."

He said, "No, you can't do that. You will have to have two qualified electors from your ward and precinct, and you can't take these forms out for them to sign. You have to bring them to this office." So he asked us, he said, "Give me your names." One of the men that was with us, he said, "Oh, sure, we will give you our name," and I

said, "There is no use in giving you our name. You give us the card
to fill out, and we will sign our name to the card."

I said, "But we didn't come to sign up. We come to try to register."

So we could not register. It seemed to be, in my way of thinking—
and I am sorry to have to appear before this Commission, I am sorry
to be in New Orleans. I never did think that in America or that a
citizen would have to do all of this for an opportunity to vote.

VICE CHAIRMAN STOREY. Now, Reverend Scott, the last time you
went in July, what was the reason the registrar told you people that
you couldn't register? What reason did he give? Because you didn't
have these identifying persons?

REVEREND SCOTT. That's right.

VICE CHAIRMAN STOREY. Now, as I understand, the law as to identity reads this way: "If the registrar has good reason to believe that
he"—meaning the applicant—"is not the same person, he may require
the applicant to produce two creditable registered voters of his precinct to make oath to that effect."

Now, then, did you each time try to get some registered voter to
identify you?

REVEREND SCOTT. I did not because, Reverend Mason and Reverend
Henderson, the effort that they made, it was turned down, and I had
a white friend that was on the police jury at that time, and he told
me that it wouldn't be any use because it was strictly made up not
to register any Negroes.

VICE CHAIRMAN STOREY. Now, tell me how long have you lived in
this county? Since what date?

REVEREND SCOTT. Oh, I have been there since 1901. That is when
I was born.

VICE CHAIRMAN STOREY. Did you ever have any trouble being
identified at banks or the courthouse or any other place?

REVEREND SCOTT. No. My great grandfather lived there, my grandfather lived there; my grandfather was a minister, and I mean, we
are all very well known, . . . everybody knows everybody. You can't
—well, you just can't hide. When you walk down the street, everybody knows everybody.

VICE CHAIRMAN STOREY. Well, now, this other question. The records
show that there are no Negro registrants in your parish. . . . Why do
you want to vote?

REVEREND SCOTT. Well, I have always felt like that was a responsibility that belonged to the citizens, after reading—even Louisiana history and the Constitution of Louisiana and the United States, it say that that belong to the citizens, and another thing that I noticed, it always give recognition; I noticed the streets where they vote, they were fixed; I noticed the roads where the people lived on where they vote, it was gravel; I noticed the people that vote, the officers of the law respected them and treated them different from the people that didn't vote, and after reading Negro newspapers, traveling quite a bit, I felt like that it was a responsibility, and after my brothers— which I didn't go because I was a minister—went to the Army, and back there in World War I, when the President was talking about make the world safe for democracy, and everybody had the right and privilege to participate, it always has been a burning zeal and desire within my heart, and I have never been able to tell my children the reason why that Negroes should be treated in such a way or be cast about. . . .

SCHOOL INTEGRATION IN THE SOUTH*

. . . .

MR. SMITH. On July 23, 1957, the board of education of the Greensboro public schools, Greensboro, N.C., voluntarily accepted six Negro pupils for enrollment on September 3 in two previously all-white schools. One of those schools was both an elementary and junior high school. Also, one pupil in each grade, five to nine, at the Gillespie Park Elementary and Junior High School; and one in the 12th grade of the Greensboro Senior High School.

At the end of the year the elementary pupils were all promoted. The seventh grader was promoted. The eighth and ninth grade

---

* Statement of Ben L. Smith, in the Hearings before the U.S. Commission on Civil Rights, Nashville, Tennessee, 1960.
Mr. Smith is Superintendent of Schools, Emeritus, Greensboro, N.C.

pupils were retained in their respective grades. All the pupils were reassigned to the Gillespie School for the year 1958–59. The 12th grade pupil made the honor roll through the year, and having acquired the prescribed units of credit, was graduated with her class in June 1958.

Some things in connection with the experience were not unlike what took place in some other places. There were actions, procedures, and conditions which were, I think, peculiar to Greensboro and North Carolina. One: On May 18, 1954, the day after the announcement of the Supreme Court decision in the *Brown* case and at a regular monthly meeting, the Greensboro board of education passed a resolution taking cognizance of the Supreme Court decision; two, recognizing it as law and binding on the board; and three, instructing the superintendent of schools to begin making a study of the ways and means for complying with the Court decision.

After the May 31, 1955, announcement by the Supreme Court of the United States, and after two regular and special sessions of the North Carolina General Assembly, and the adoption of the constitutional amendment, Greensboro, Charlotte, and Winston-Salem held three joint Board meetings, advised with their attorneys and the representatives of the press in the three cities and reached conclusions that resulted in similar and simultaneous action. . . .

On May 21, 1957, the Greensboro board of education, in conformity with the U.S. Supreme Court decision and the laws of North Carolina, adopted resolutions as follows:

One, reassigned pupils either to the school they had been attending or to the schools to which pupils from that school had formerly been promoted, so they followed the traditional plan; second, provided the machinery for applying for and making a reassignment; and third, providing for pupils to be transferred in case pupils of another race than the previously enrolled should be accepted; fourth, on July 23, 1957, six Negro pupils were accepted for enrollment on September 3 in two different all-white schools; fifth, in August an injunction was sought to prevent the board from enrolling Negro pupils. The action of the board was sustained by the Superior Court of the State, and on appeal the decision of the Superior Court was upheld by the North Carolina Supreme Court.

All pupils were retained throughout the year; all school personnel stuck to their posts of duty. The biggest school bond issue ever floated in the county was carried.

There are three administrative units in the county. The vote in favor of the issue was as follows: rural Guilford, 5 to 1, and they had no desegregation in rural Guilford. In High Point, the city of

High Point, the vote was 2 to 1. They had no desegregation. In Greensboro the vote was 10 to 1 where there was the desegregation that had begun.

What made desegregation possible in Greensboro? Here are some of the reasons, I think, and I will enumerate them and then come back to speak of them briefly if there is time.

One, an enlightened and liberal-minded community. Two, an extraordinary school board and attorney. Three, school personnel who stuck to their posts of duty. Four, a favorable press. Five, an intelligent, alert, and courageous police force headed by a chief who believes in law and order.

Now, with respect to the community, Greensboro has a long history of devotion to public education and an excellent record of good race relations. There are six colleges located in the city or in the environment of the community. It has the oldest rated school system in North Carolina.

The Negro citizens had for some time served on the police force. A prominent Negro educator, Dr. David P. Johns, had for several years served as a member of the board of education and upon final illness had been succeeded by a prominent Negro physician. This Negro physician had formerly been elected a member of the city council, and he had led the ticket in the election at which he was offered as a candidate, and it is said that if all of the predominantly Negro ballot boxes had been thrown out, he still would have been elected by a majority of the citizens of Greensboro.

The Greensboro schools had operated the polio hospital school, which was administered on a desegregated basis or on a nonsegregated basis. When the disease struck the community, they had accepted any and all who were stricken, and we operated a school in this hospital that took care of the pupils as they were found in the hospital, which was desegregated, and we never had any adverse reaction from that whatsoever.

A recently established cerebral palsy school was being administered on an integrated basis. The Woman's College of the University of North Carolina had accepted some Negro pupils in their student body. A. & T. College had offered some courses to white pupils in that Negro college. The Catholic Parochial School had admitted pupils from other races than its predominant membership.

The city was influenced by the liberal views of the Friends who live in this community, I think, and by members of the Jewish element that numbers many of Greensboro's leading business and civic-minded citizens. Their attitude was quite liberal and favorable, and I think it helped the community greatly.

Greensboro has a cosmopolitan and highly enlightened population because of its location, balanced industries, and its many schools and colleges.

While a minority oppose vigorously the action of the board of education and many regretted the necessity, the majority felt that it was the best course that could be taken. Most felt that it was the least for the longest, that racial good will has been retained, and that the public education has been preserved. . . .

COMMISSIONER STOREY. Did you have any incidents in connection with your desegregation?

MR. SMITH. We had very little in connection with the schools. As was expected and as will always happen, the superintendent of schools, principal of the school where integration takes place, and the board of education bear the impact of the opposition.

There was a cross burned in my yard, and four times missiles were thrown through my front window. The police, although they had been giving assistance, after this final act placed a police guard and kept him there until the end of the year.

There was a little bit of picketing for a day or two at the Gillespie Park School. There was a little heckling, a little stir in connection with it. Mainly, though, it was a matter of anonymous letters, anonymous telephone calls, the sending out of products that hadn't been ordered, that sort of harassment, and these throwings of missiles. That was the biggest adverse reaction. It was never known but was suspected that the persons who committed the worst of these offenses were not people of the Greensboro school district at all, but were outsiders.

We did have Kasper to visit the community. We had organized in the community or there were members and leaders in the community of the Patriots' organization. Kasper organized a group which later apparently turned into a Ku Klux Klan group.

There were some four or five Ku Klux Klan meetings held in and about Greensboro, in the county, or around about Greensboro.

I think that was not actually within the city limits.

COMMISSIONER STOREY. You haven't had anything recently?

MR. SMITH. No; nothing at all, and there have been no—well, on the opening day of school the head of the Ku Klux Klan—the head of the Ku Klux Klan is not in the school district at all, but in the county— and a man from another city and two men from two different cities did a little picketing for a day or two at the Gillespie Park School and then were asked to withdraw and did so.

COMMISSIONER STOREY. Thank you, Mr. Smith.

CHAIRMAN HANNAH. Governor Carlton?

COMMISSIONER CARLTON. What was the attitude of the students toward one another?

MR. SMITH. There was very little adverse reaction. There was some slight tensions and some little, very small, incidents. . . .

COMMISSIONER HESBURGH. Mr. Smith, as you see it from living in this community, is there much chance that there will be more schools integrated? I notice there are 27 white schools that are not integrated at all. There are only 2 that are this year against 3 last year because of this graduation of 1 girl, and only 5 students out of 643 students integrated or going to white schools.

Is there any chance this very token number, now that the principle has been established by the good work you people have done, may increase?

MR. SMITH. The school board has taken the position that pupils should not be forced against their will into an inhospitable situation so that they have accepted only pupils who have made application.

Now, they didn't accept all of the pupils this year who applied, and there has recently been brought a case against the school board because they didn't do that. Actually the case has to do with the Gillespie Park School and the David Caldwell School where there is a Negro school and a white school on the same school site.

Now, just what will come from that remains to be seen. I was not present at the time that decision was made, but I am of the opinion that the school board felt that that was deliberate speed, that they should be entitled to take a little time, and that they shouldn't have so much pressure brought upon that particular school, and there shouldn't be integration just for that reason.

Now, the school population is pretty much centered with the residential population. In the section where the people are predominantly Negro, there are Negro schools to accommodate them, and I think that they would continue to be predominantly Negro.

Now, David Caldwell School and the Gillespie Park School are down the street between two other streets where there has been white population. It is an old section of the city, and it has been gradually receding. The population has been declining so far as the whites are concerned, and more and more Negroes are moving into the community, and I think, whether the decision of the Court had been made at all, that ultimately it would have gone over to predominantly Negro schools.

The churches, several churches, Presbyterian Church, a Friends church, and other conditions as well as families have moved out of the community, and they have sold to Negro population, to Negro membership.

COMMISSIONER HESBURGH. My problem basically is this, that it seems to me you folks have done a lot of planning and gone through a certain amount of turmoil. You have taken some embarrassment, especially your windows being broken 4 times, and if the total result of this is that 5 students out of 5,000 get into the school, it really is a lot of suffering without too much immediate proof, and supposing now these other 27 schools would have applications from some students to be transferred to them. What are the chances that they would get in the school?

MR. SMITH. I think the same decision would have been made by the board that was made in case of those particular students, and there are some Negro children in most of the areas of the schools, and I don't think that the board at all picked those particular schools. It was a question of their having applied and their approving it, and the same thing would have happened wherever the applications would have been received.

COMMISSIONER HESBURGH. Is there any chance there will be a lot more applications in the years to come, do you think?

MR. SMITH. Well, I don't think I can answer that question. I would hope that there would be a gradual changeover. . . . I certainly should not like to see Negro pupils forced against their will, the wills of their parents, into a situation that might prove to be inhospitable for them, definitely. . . .

CHAIRMAN HANNAH. Are there any questions the participants would like to raise?

DR. PULLEN. I should like to come back to the philosophical point, and I should like to address my question to Father. At this stage of the game is it more important that we have free acceptance of the idea by both races, or must we measure the success of it by numbers?

I am not trying to put you on the spot, but I think this is fundamental to the whole question as I see it.

COMMISSIONER HESBURGH. I quite agree. As the President told us when we were sworn in at the White House, that there is a problem of minds and hearts, and it is basically a problem of educating the minds and hearts of all Americans to give other Americans their due as citizens, equal opportunity in housing, education, voting, exercise of citizenship, and all the rest.

My only point is that I get confused at times by a lot of good intentions without much results. In my profession I sit and listen to the effects of this very often. We get in that box and hear a lot of good intentions and not much in the way of results, and you all know about the pavement and hell. But I think whereas numbers in themselves don't prove anything—we are not, as they say, in a numbers game here—the concrete results of good will have to gradually be shown, and while I wouldn't take it upon myself—I don't think any of the Commission here would—to try to define "all deliberate speed" or to try to define "inimical" in all areas because it will change from area to area, I think one does like to see there is some ray of hope for progress and that the condition does progress from year to year and that we don't merely have a static situation with much profession of good will without much evidence, and I think that the problem basically, as I see it and listen to it and read about it, is that on the one hand we have people that want results yesterday, and others that want them never, and somehow in between we have to work for progress.

I agree with you that the heart of that progress must be an acceptance on the part of all Americans of what it means to be an American citizen.

DR. PULLEN. I certainly shouldn't disagree with you, and being a minister's son, I know a lot about hell. Added to that is the fact that I am a school superintendent, which increases my knowledge.

I think this, and I cannot refrain from making this point, that the answer to the problem lies, as you say, in the hearts and minds of the people, and it is determined not in numbers, but in the relationship between the people, both races, and is determined by their feeling as to being treated properly, rights being preserved, and they, themselves, should be the judge of that, and I think in some cases you are going to have large numbers; in some cases, not so many, but we must look at this problem—I don't mean to make a speech—we must look at this problem a hundred years hence and not just one or two years.

Incidentally, for your benefit, we have accepted the decision of the courts. We are trying to work it out, but we are trying to work it out in that spirit.

MR. SMITH. May I say just a word? I think the fact that we have made a beginning and did it voluntarily, that an order of the court has been pleasing, greatly pleasing, to the Negro population, and there has been definite appreciation, and their leaders have said to us from time to time that they are not so much concerned about where we are now, but the direction in which we are going, and I think that the board of education in Greensboro having placed itself in a position of cooperation would like to see some other communities come up and the action be taken against somebody else rather than against them when they have tried to comply with the law and have moved in that direction.

COMMISSIONER HESBURGH. I don't want to be in a position of seeming to criticize you, Mr. Smith, because my windows haven't been broken, and I am in no position to criticize you because yours have. . . .

Nathan Glazer

IS "INTEGRATION" POSSIBLE
IN THE NEW YORK SCHOOLS?*

It is now more than six years since "integration" became an issue in the New York City school system; and, very likely, at the start of the new school term some of New York's Negro parents—for the third time in a row—will stage a "strike," and keep their children from attending the all-Negro (or nearly all-Negro) schools of their own neighborhoods on the ground that the education to be got there is inferior.

---

* Nathan Glazer, "Is 'Integration' Possible in the New York Schools?" from *Commentary*, September 1960, Copyright The American Jewish Committee, New York. Reprinted by permission.
Mr. Glazer is a noted sociologist.

One way or another, "integration" has become an important issue in every Northern and Western city in which there are large numbers of Negroes and (as in New York) Puerto Ricans or (in California and elsewhere) Mexicans. The constellation of forces and problems is in each situation different—and in describing what is happening in New York, I am not necessarily tracing any general pattern. What happens in New York is important enough by itself: here is the city with the largest population in the country, the largest number of Negroes, the largest number of Puerto Ricans. The New York school system had, at the beginning of the school year in 1959, 626 elementary schools, 127 junior high schools, 86 high schools. It comprises almost 1,000,000 students, has 45,000 employees, and spends $400,000,000 a year. Sixty new school buildings were opened in the three years 1957–1959.

I point all this out not to dazzle the reader with figures, but rather to show that there can be no comparison between New York's school problems and those of a community with, let us say, a half dozen schools, where citizens are in direct control of school planning through their power to elect school board officials, to approve or disapprove bond issues, and the like. In such a community, the citizen voting on a bond issue for a new school knows in advance just where the school will be, and what effect, if any, its location will have on segregating or integrating Negro students; such knowledge presumably plays a role in how the vote goes. So, for example, in Malverne, Long Island, when a school bond issue for a new school was voted down last March, the outcome was seen as a defeat for segregation—though conceivably other issues were involved.

There can be no such clear-cut victories and defeats in New York City. Perhaps in frustration, many people act as if New York were Malverne, and as if some single decision on zoning, or school building, or teacher placement would radically transform the educational system. The matter, unfortunately, is not so simple.

The story begins with the Supreme Court decision of May 17, 1954, outlawing segregation. What was involved, of course, was the formal and legal segregation of the Southern and Border states. However, a month later, Professor Kenneth Clark of City College, a psychologist whose studies on the development of Negro children in the South had played a role in the Supreme Court decision, asserted: "It would be a mistake to assume that the content and spirit of the . . . decision apply only to the Southern states that have laws which require segregation. As I understand the decision, the United States Supreme Court has clearly stated that segregation itself damages the personality of human beings. The court did not limit itself to the statement that only legal segregation is detrimental to the human personality. It was explicit . . . in stating that various forms of racial segregation are damaging to the human spirit. . . ."

There is of course no formal segregation in the New York City schools. But there are great numbers of Negroes and Puerto Ricans in certain areas—concentrations which partly exist because these groups meet discrimination in their efforts to rent or buy houses in many other sections of the city. For despite a city ordinance forbidding it, discrimination in housing is still widespread, and in any case the residential patterns created by it still persist. These concentrations have an equally important cause in the poverty of Negroes and Puerto Ricans, a fact which automatically eliminates the great majority of them from large sections of the city. Finally, the Negro and Puerto Rican concentrations have a happier, positive aspect, reflecting ties to family, friends, institutions—a community.

Professor Clark opened the integration issue in New York schools in the wake of the Supreme Court decision. He spoke of segregation in the North as well as in the South—and there is no question that there are 100 per cent Negro and 100 per cent white schools in the North, as in the South. But there is a decisive difference between the two situations. Because segregation is *legally* imposed in the South, and because the whole tendency of the American creed opposes legal distinctions made between human beings of different races and ethnic groups, it is necessary to strike down segregation in the Southern schools on moral and political grounds, independently of any effect such separation might have on education. Even if the Southern states had given superior education to Negroes in their separate schools (and in their frantic efforts to bring up the miserably poor quality of Negro schooling to avoid a negative Supreme Court ruling, many Southern states were beginning to spend a good deal more on Negro schools), it would still have been necessary to abolish this legal separation by public authority.

But in the North the concentration of Negroes and whites into separate schools was the effect of other social forces. There was no claim by Northern political bodies that they had any moral or political right to enforce such a separation. The situation was similar to the concentration of Jews in the schools of the Lower East Side in 1910, or of Italians in the schools of "Little Italy" around the same time. I emphasize this difference between the Northern and Southern states because I think the application of the term "segregation" to both introduces a radical confusion. In a word, the difference is: Southern segregation has to be abolished *independently* of its impact on education; Northern school concentration becomes a problem that demands action primarily *because* it may lead to inferior education for Negro children.

If the concentration of Negroes in certain Northern schools were not simply the product of their residential concentration, and if school zones were gerrymandered by political authorities so as to increase the separation of Negro and white children, then the situation would be comparable to that in the South. Indeed many observers believed this to be the case in New York City; it is certainly the case in other Northern places. But Professor Clark raised only the question of the quality of education that Negro children were getting or could get in Northern de facto "segregated" schools. And the day after Professor Clark's speech, the president of the Board of Education of New York City requested the Public Education Association to investigate the status of the education of Negro and Puerto Rican children in the city.

The report was submitted a year later. It compared schools with a high concentration of Negroes and Puerto Ricans with schools with a low concentration of Negroes and Puerto Ricans. . . . There were then 49 of these high-concentration schools—somewhat less than 10 per cent of the total number of schools in the city. . . . The comparison proved interesting.

It turned out that while slightly less was spent on the education of children in the high-concentration elementary schools than those in the other schools . . . , the situation was reversed in the junior high schools. . . . The professional staffs in the high-concentration schools were larger, indicating the need for, and the supply of, more special services. . . .

Two objective indices stamped the schools with high proportions of Negroes and Puerto Ricans as being inferior: they were on the average older. . . . And there were fewer regular teachers in the high-concentration schools, more substitute teachers.

On the crucial question of zoning, the report . . . asserted: "There is no significant evidence to indicate that ethnic separation is seriously considered in drawing school district boundary lines."

At this point, the Board of Education might well have said, well, that's that. We spend as much on the Negro and Puerto Rican children as we do on the others; we give them more services; if their schools are older, this is an unfortunate consequence of the fact that they live in older neighborhoods; and if they are inferior in academic achievement (as they were), this is owing to lower I.Q.'s, language difficulties, poor home environment, and the host of factors, known and unknown, that differentiate children of different backgrounds in academic achievement. Indeed, when one looks at this report, the only conceivable legitimate ground for complaint was to be found in the distribution of regular teachers. . . .

But we must separate the issue of "segregation" from that of education: regardless of what the study showed as to the *education* of Negro and Puerto Rican children, the fact remained that large numbers of them were in schools with very few continental white children—and this was, in terms of political impact, the real issue. The president of the Board of Education is a political appointee; even if he were not, the head of an enterprise of the size of the New York City schools would have to keep political realities continually in mind. . . .

The crux of the matter politically has always been, and still remains, zoning. The Board of Education, despairing over effecting any really satisfying changes through zoning, keeps on emphasizing programs to raise the level of education and services in schools that will have to remain largely Puerto Rican and Negro. But this does not get it off the political hook. It is caught in the dilemma of a political demand that is simple and clear—no all-Negro schools—but a demand which it cannot meet since the huge residential concentrations of Negroes and Puerto Ricans in effect must mean many largely Puerto Rican and Negro schools.

And despite laws against residential and occupational discrimination, which should serve to upgrade the economic level of Puerto Ricans and Negroes, and spread them more evenly through the city, the situation cannot undergo any great change. For—and this is the most striking and important fact in the report on the progress of integration—*three-quarters* of the school children of Manhattan are Negro and Puerto Rican; *two-fifths* of the school children of greater New York are Negro and Puerto Rican. If by an elaborate process of busing and pupil assignment it were possible to evenly distribute the Negro and Puerto Rican children throughout the city—taking the children of Brooklyn into Queens, the children from Manhattan into the Bronx, and then alternatively bringing the children of the Bronx and Queens into Brooklyn and Manhattan, etc., etc.—then Negro and Puerto Rican children would make up two-fifths of the total in every school in the city.

But even this theoretically perfect situation could not be maintained for long—the numbers of Negro and Puerto Rican children in the city are increasing rapidly. The Puerto Rican birth rate is much higher than the Negro birth rate, which is higher than the white birth rate. Migratory trends are harder to estimate, but it is certain that Negro and Puerto Rican increase through immigration, and white decrease through out-migration, will continue. In effect, the notion that much would be accomplished by the redistribution of a declining number of continental white school children is an illusion. . . .

Despite the absence of any data, the Board of Education has taken the position that an even mixture of groups is educationally desirable —that, to quote the resolution setting up the Commission on Integration, "racially homogeneous schools are undesirable." This means all-white as well as all-Negro schools. . . .

. . . If rezoning cannot accomplish much, a certain amount of redistributing of the school population can be done by busing. A thousand children from the heavily Negro Bedford-Stuyvesant area of Brooklyn are bused to schools in Queens and Brooklyn, and another 400 are bused from Harlem to Yorkville in Manhattan. . . .

The major problem is still: the poor educational results for Negroes and Puerto Ricans. And here is where the chief efforts of the Board of Education have been applied. One can only say, they are impressive in their scale.

The fact is that the needs of Negro and Puerto Rican children are enormous. Very large numbers come from homes in which they receive no care, are not fed properly, are perhaps abused physically and psychologically. The school may be a haven—but more likely it is another area in which a depressed and miserable existence is reflected in apathy, outrageous behavior, resistance. Obviously these are not problems peculiar to Negroes or Puerto Ricans—but equally obviously, the highest incidence of such problems occurs in that part of the city's population. All this is aside from special factors affecting the two groups that bear directly on the capacity to learn. In the Puerto Rican case, there is the serious language problem. In 1958, 62,000 children were considered "language handicapped." For this alone an army of special personnel is required. . . .

But the language difficulty may be the least of the factors affecting ability to learn—it does not seem to have been a great handicap for some other immigrant groups. Far more important apparently are aspects of home atmosphere, both as they bear directly on the general physical and psychological well-being of the child, and in setting up conditions of various kinds that aid learning. The absence of such conditions—parents who read, relatives who have professional jobs, home discussions of political events, exposure to cultural activities— probably counts for a great deal in the factors leading to poor educational results for Negro and Puerto Rican children. It is a tribute to American idealism, which seems to be convinced that every human problem is manageable, that even these defects in home environment are now the concern of the Board of Education, through its Demonstration Guidance Project and Higher Horizons Project. Under these projects, students who on the most generous interpretation seem to show prospects for doing good academic work are selected for special intensive efforts—testing, training, remedial work, guidance, and the like, including (in the case of Higher Horizons) trips to the opera and plays. Such investments of special effort have indeed been rewarding. They also mean an investment in the education of underprivileged children that is probably close to twice the cost of educating "other" children. . . .

[There are] Negro parents who will not send their children to all-Negro schools, regardless of what the Board of Education does for them, and regardless even of what the objective indices show. . . .

We can understand this Negro reaction to all-Negro schools. Negro parents cannot take the position that Irish or Jewish or Italian parents took before them—all this will change (or that perhaps some Jewish parents might well have taken in their paradoxical sense of superiority, "What do we need so many *goyim* for?"). Their history is different, their situation is different, their sense of self-confidence and self-worth is different.

Even so, all parents are very much the same: the Negro parents who don't want their children to go to all-Negro schools are very much like the white parents who also don't want their children to go to all-Negro schools, and it is equally difficult to say that either prejudice or self-hatred is the whole story. . . . It would be as wrong to say the motivation of the striking and distressed Negro parents is entirely to escape from their own kind as to say the motivation of the retreating white parents is entirely prejudice. In both cases there is a positive component; the desire to do the best one can for one's children.

But what is the Board of Education to do? It needs the few good children (more than a few) in each school—they are important for the morale of the principal and teachers, as well as of other students. . . .

. . . If one takes a long-range view one can think of possible solutions. Eventually the impact of a fairly good school system, nondiscriminatory renting, the movement of Negroes and Puerto Ricans into better jobs, will reduce the gap between Negro and Puerto Rican students and "other" students. In the meantime, the Board of Education, with the tacit consent of the people of the city, pours in heavy resources to make up for the disasters of history, trusting that in some way the injection of money and personnel at this end will overcome generations of misfortune. Even so, it is not likely to get much sympathy for its efforts from the victims of the misfortunes. But since when have victims been kind to anyone—to their persecutors, to those who tried to aid them, or to themselves?

SEGREGATION IN HOUSING*

. . . .

MR. WILLIAMS. Almost from its creation, California has wrestled with the problem of adjusting its community practices and governmental policies to the needs and desires of some racial minority, as well as to the racial antipathies of some of its majority citizens. Like our Federal Government, the main task of nullifying undemocratic acts has been assumed by our courts. From the late 1800's, the judicial condemnation of racism in its various forms has been fairly consistent. City ordinances restricting housing opportunities, alienland and other anti-oriental laws; prohibitions against racial intermarriage, restrictive covenants, segregated public schools and public housing; and even the practice of racial discrimination in the sale of publicly assisted housing have all been interdicted here by judicial mandate.

Until recently, however, we have not experienced a similar legislative concern for the protection or extension of civil rights. For over half a century the only civil rights statutes enacted in California were the codification of the common-law innkeeper rule, and provision for the recovery of damages by an aggrieved party against a place of public accommodation discriminating on the basis of race, creed, color, or national origin. This is most unusual when one considers the volume of statutory protections provided during that same period by other legislatures.

As you no doubt know, our State laws designed to insure equality of opportunity for all are not as broad as those existing in some States. Nevertheless, they are a long step in the right direction and foreshadow more effective legislation in the years immediately ahead.

Our broadest statute is the fair employment practices law, copies of which shall be provided you. Our FEPC and its highly qualified staff are already busy implementing the law's provisions with vigor and determination and with some early successes. There also has

---

* Statements of Franklin H. Williams and William T. Hogan, at the Hearings before the U.S. Commission on Civil Rights, California, 1960.

Mr. Williams is Assistant Attorney General, California Department of Justice. Mr. Hogan is First Vice President, San Francisco Real Estate Board.

been created within the department of education a commission specifically charged with the responsibility of working with local school districts toward the elimination of discrimination in the employment of teachers. Our newly enacted fair housing law is limited to publicly assisted facilities and provides for redress through civil suits for damages or injunction. Section 51 of our Civil Code, which I referred to earlier, has been amended to prohibit discrimination by all business establishments, and the minimum damages recoverable for violation thereof have been increased from $100 to $250. With the exception of the Fair Employment Practices Act and the innkeeper provisions of the Penal Code, all of these statutory protections provide for enforcement through civil suits for damages or, in some instances, injunction actions.

In an effort to implement our State's public policy wherever and whenever possible, Attorney General Stanley Mosk has established a constitutional rights section in the department of justice. He intends that the section do what it can within the limits of its authority and influence to assist in the protection of individuals from the wrongs of society.

While we are especially sensitive to the many problems resulting from the immigration of large numbers of Negro citizens from areas where they have for decades been deprived of equal economic and educational opportunities, we are also familiar and concerned with the barriers and difficulties faced by our many other minority-group citizens seeking to enjoy the blessings of California citizenship. . . .

Discrimination in housing is an almost universal pattern throughout our State. Its impact on some of our schools and on other community facilities has been substantial.

Discrimination in education has limited job opportunities, and the resultant demoralization of the discriminated group is apparent. While these experiences have been most heavily felt by the large Negro minority, most of whom, as I, have migrated here since 1940, it is by no means limited to this group. To some extent, the Mexican, Chinese, Japanese, and Filipino-American also suffers from this interrelationship, and even the native American Indian does not escape. Each of these groups has been at some time rigidly limited in its housing opportunities. To some degree, every segment of the housing industry—the governmental stimulators, the builders, lenders, selling agents, and property managers—has been guilty of enforcing racial exclusion or segregation.

While voluntary choice has influenced minorities to some degree in their home selection, our so-called Chinatowns, Little Tokyos, Harlems, Spanish towns, and other racially segregated neighborhoods have been primarily the products of enforced limitations. For example, here in San Francisco, the housing authority maintained a policy of racial segregation of its tenants upon the unconstitutional rationale of conforming to a neighborhood pattern of racial occupancy. While litigation enjoined the practice, this city's so-called Chinatown is officially recognized, if not encouraged, by the erection and maintenance of public housing facilities in the heart of the area complete with pseudo-Chinese architectural trappings and occupied solely by Chinese-Americans. Currently in several other communities, the local housing authorities have either created or are permitting racial separation as a pattern of occupancy of all or some of their units.

Few private builders, whether utilizing governmental guarantees or not, will sell on an open, nondiscriminatory basis. One notable exception is Joseph Eichler, a multiple-award winner, who has sold to Negro and other minority purchasers in each of his many tracts with, I understand, little or no criticism from white purchasers.

Much of this new tract housing will now be covered by our fair housing law, and our office is doing all possible to insure compliance with the law's provisions. We have communicated with each redevelopment agency in the State, requesting information as to the steps being taken to insure that contractors and builders will conduct the sale, rental and leasing of newly created facilities in compliance with the statutory requirement. We have announced our opinion that such agencies may not accept discriminatory listings nor in any other way permit racial or religious considerations to enter into their processes or procedures. . . .

One result of the closed housing market in this State has been the creation of a number of substantially segregated schools in our larger communities. We are concerned that every arm of government be aware of the trend in this direction and of the damage to the individual and to the community that inevitably follows. We are anxious that they act now, within the limits of their authority, to prevent or at least minimize the impact of this trend. Our office has requested the State Department of Education to adopt and promulgate a policy which will make race a factor in the determination of acceptable school sites, toward the end that so-called *de facto* segregation may be avoided or reduced.

Especially prominent in the creation and perpetuation of these minority neighborhood areas have been our real estate brokers and agents. Just last Tuesday one prominent broker told me that he and many others in the business were of the impression that their code of ethics still specifically prohibits their selling to minority families in all-white neighborhoods. Few of these people will admit to this practice, though I am sure you know how universal it is. While some real estate brokers or agents would like to break with the pattern, several have told us of their fear of being "blackballed" or otherwise ostracized if they practiced democracy in their business.

We have submitted herewith an opinion of Attorney General Mosk ... to the effect that real estate dealers are subject to the prohibitions of our Civil Code section 51. Unfortunately, if recent discussions with some of these men individually and at their organizational meetings is any indication, there seems to be a greater preoccupation with developing techniques for avoidance rather than with compliance. Recognizing this, we are requesting an opinion of the California commissioner of real estate as to the disciplinary action he will take against a licensee violating the law. Needless to say, an uncompromising policy requiring full and complete compliance under penalty of suspension or revocation of license would go a long way toward eliminating the practice.

At least one of our State departments has taken this forthright position. Recently, the director of the alcoholic beverage control department issued a policy statement which he is forwarding to all licensees and applicants for renewal or issuance which reads, in part, as follows:

> A licensee of the department of alcoholic beverage control who permits any discrimination, distinction, or restriction at the licensed premises on account of color, race, religion, ancestry, or national origin, contrary to the provisions of section 51, shall be subject to suspension or revocation of his license.

We are convinced that such action is squarely in line with the policies of our Governor, our State's public policy, and the proper implementation of our statutes.

We have received many communications setting forth examples of how these discriminations operate and affect the people. Excerpts from one such communication may suffice to prove their point:

> Dear Mr. Williams: The release, early this week, by the Attorney General to the effect that discriminatory practices by realty brokers and their sales personnel against ethnic minorities were illegal and punishable was, to me, extremely heartening. . . .
>
> I should like to emphasize emphatically that the "gentlemen's agreements" observed in my industry and officially condoned exist, in large measure, simply because the small minority, represented by the realty group, actually believe that ghettoization is desired by the dominant group for ethnic minorities. . . .

To prove my point, I am going to cite just a few of the situations wherein I functioned as a real estate salesman with clients who were either oriental, Negro, or colored. In all instances the opposing real estate man precipitated a problem where no problem existed.

Let me state now that every minority I sold a home, or rented a home or apartment to, has successfully integrated with the dominant group on his street and is accepted socially by his neighbors. In passing, there has been no depreciation of property values nor a single instance of "panic selling" because my client was a minority.

In 1957, I sold a home in Menlo Park to a very attractive Creole couple and devout Catholics. The owner of the home was a Mexican national. The next-door owner was also a Mexican. Both Mexicans were considerably darker than my clients. While the Negro family was sitting at my desk, one of the administrative officers of the firm noticed them and asked me, after their departure, where I had sold them a home. When I told him, he became panic-stricken and informed me he had just purchased a home nearby.

If you will refer to a map, you will note that these streets are some distances apart and are blocked off from each other. Propertywise, it is impossible for one to affect the other. For the next 3 days and nights I was besieged by telephone calls from anonymous callers, threatening dire results. In every case, where I could elicit the caller's address, it was nearby. When I appealed to the local Catholic church, they could find no opposition on that place. Although I had been profitable for my employer, very shortly thereafter I was summarily dismissed because my pipe smoking was offensive.

An American of Japanese descent in 1958 was a teacher in the San Mateo High School but could find no realtor in that area that would show him a home, and he related to me that he was told by a realty office there that he could not be shown a home in that area. I sold him a home in a Palo Alto area, completely unintegrated then, and he is still the only minority there. Property has risen in value consistently.

A Negro woman built a home on a small cul-de-sac just outside of Los Altos. A Menlo Park broker tried to panic the white owners, and the Palo Alto Chapter of the NAACP asked me to go down there and allay their fears. I did, and not one panic sale resulted. I have since, as a result, sold two homes there twice each, for valid reasons, and in each case to white buyers who knew the Negro family was there, and for more money each time. . . .

Several months ago a Negro man was referred to me by the Palo Alto Fair Play Council. He was a Los Angeles teacher and had taken a teaching assignment at an elementary school. The school superintendent personally telephoned me to insure my getting a home for him because "he is one of the finest demonstration teachers in the system I have ever seen." A demonstration teacher is a teacher's teacher. I sold them a home in Barron Park, and that very day a Palo Alto broker and past president of the local realty board telephoned my office to tell me that I was a "son of a _____" for having "spoiled" the neighborhood by selling to a _____ (uncomplimentary term for a Negro) after he had kept the area "clean" for 30 years. The neighbors seem very happy with the family, as well they should. . . .

Even now listings in my own board appear with the notation: "Not to be shown to minorities."

Your help is needed. . . .

Fortunately, here in California our racially segregated neighborhoods are not yet as large, as numerous, or as difficult to eliminate as those which exist in some eastern and midwestern jurisdictions. Unless we move rapidly to eliminate and guard against the causes of such community segregation, however, it will not be many years before we face similarly difficult situations.

This is a tremendous challenge. I am confident that our present State leadership is competent and anxious to meet it. With cooperation from the Federal Government we may yet insure all of our citizens, old and new, and of every race, creed, and color, an equal opportunity under law for life, liberty, and the pursuit of happiness. . . .

COMMISSIONER JOHNSON. Mr. Williams, you mentioned in your statement the problem which we have had called to our attention on many occasions: the *de facto* segregation in education resulting from residential segregation. I believe that you mentioned, also, that your office sought the cooperation of the State department of education to attempt to deal with the problem by way of site selection. What, if any, suggestion did you have?

MR. WILLIAMS. We have not, as yet, received a final policy determination from the department of education. We are currently participating in discussions leading toward such a statement. However, the chief of the bureau of school planning, in a memorandum to his superior, stated his view, in part, as follows:

In the department of education rules as now written, there is substantial room for judgment when weighing the factors which make up our standards of site selection. This kind of flexibility should be exercised to its fullest extent to meet the local conditions affecting the condition of a selection of a given site.

However, it would be indefensible to use this margin of flexibility as a tool to implement social policy. We feel that a school is not an instrument of social policy, but it is a community service provided equally to children and adults of all economic and social status or ethnic groups.

I am in vigorous disagreement with the view expressed by this statement, and we are hopeful that in our negotiations with his superior an affirmative policy on this question will be promulgated. . . .

* * *

MR. HOGAN. The San Francisco Real Estate Board is a 54-year-old organization incorporated under the laws of the State of California as a nonprofit corporation. It comprises over 2,400 members, including State-licensed real estate brokers and salesmen and, in addition, property owners, banks, title companies, et cetera. The board membership is integrated and it has been its policy not to exclude anyone on the basis of race, color, or creed. We have many members of the different minority groups of San Francisco. Our main qualifications for membership are integrity, business acumen, and the willingness to uphold the Code of Ethics of the National Association of Real Estate Boards.

The Unruh Civil Rights Act was passed at the last session of the California Legislature. On November 23, 1959, the attorney general of the State of California issued an opinion in which he holds that the Unruh Civil Rights Act includes real estate brokers and salesmen within the term "business" as used in that act. The California Real Estate Association, of which the San Francisco Real Estate Board is a member, is presently studying this opinion.

While we cannot speak for the individual members of our board, it is our understanding that our members will, as they have always done in the past, comply with all Federal and State laws and regulations. . . .

COMMISSIONER HESBURGH. Mr. Hogan, we have had housing hearings now in three cities, specifically on housing: New York, Chicago, and Atlanta. And we had a good deal on housing in Los Angeles in the last 2 days; some here today. And I must say that the normal reaction of one who sits and listens to all these things is that the real estate board is a target for a great deal of criticism. . . .

Does the real estate board, nationally, have some code of ethics that affords an equal opportunity in housing throughout the United States?

MR. HOGAN. Let me qualify myself. The firm that I operate is in Chinatown. It has been there for some 18 years. Previous to that, I worked for a firm that did a great deal of Chinese business.

At that particular time, the minority group of Chinese in the city of San Francisco, I believe, was in the same position that the minority group is here today—at least the one that we are talking mostly about.

As of today, and this is some 18 years later, we have absolutely no difficulty placing that particular minority group anywhere, and they have become a credit to San Francisco. They have the finest tourist section of any place in the United States.

I didn't like the criticism of the assistant attorney general—I believe he was—who criticized our housing project. I think it is beautiful. And as a matter of fact, I laid it out.

I don't know what the individual reactions of each member may be, but, as far as I know, the National Association of Real Estate Boards bars no one from securing housing for minority groups.

COMMISSIONER HESBURGH. Well, the reason I asked, I did not want to be contentious; I am just trying to develop information, which we have to do under our oath on this Commission. And the information seems to be everywhere that no real estate broker will say he discriminates. And yet, in fact, when you get down to the individual people—minority groups looking for houses—it turns out that practically every real estate broker they go to says, for some reason or other, "I can't get you a house except in this section of the town."

This is nothing new. It may be less a reality here than it is in many other parts of the country. My own part of the country, the city of Chicago—I think we all know it—was perhaps the most segregated city in the United States. And yet the real estate boards have not in the slightest indicated that there is any discrimination.

And would it not be good public relations for real estate boards, generally and nationally, to come to some statement of ethics on this, because I must say, in all frankness, they are under great fire in every single section of the country that we have gone to, and I know it would not be any different if we went to all the cities in this country.

I may assume again, and this may be ignorance on my part, that the real estate agents individually, who may act in this way, feel that they are acting in response to what is the desire on the part of the people they serve; their constituency; their customers. And I think perhaps they feel to act otherwise would make them persona non grata within their own community of real estate brokers, and that they almost have to act this way because this is the way people want them to act.

And somehow it has to be studied more deeply in its economic aspects. If we could somehow tear away a few of the myths, perhaps, and if we would only say one thing, and say it nationally and say it clearly and say it loudly: that any person of any race who has so qualified for good housing by, first of all, becoming educated; secondly, taking part in the political process in his own locality; thirdly, by qualifying for a position that enables him to buy decent housing and keep it up and raise a decent family; that this man should not be barred from a house where his desires and means permit. I think it would be tremendously effective if some forthright statement like this could come forth.

It may be wishful thinking on my part. I may be saying some things that I am somewhat ignorant of, but this is, offhand, the impression which I received, after listening to hours upon hours of testimony across the country. I don't say anything personal because I want to be friendly with you.

MR. HOGAN. I would like to take your statement back to the board. I believe it will be transcribed.

COMMISSIONER HESBURGH. I would be very happy to have you do that.

MR. HOGAN. Maybe this board can start something along that line.

COMMISSIONER HESBURGH. It would be a wonderful thing.

MR. HOGAN. I think the mayor of San Francisco practically answered a question for which the real estate broker is being condemned, as a general rule, and that is the fact that, although he may submit an offer from any group to the property owner, whether they be Irish, such as I am, or Chinese or Negro, the owner may have some reason or other why he doesn't want to sell it. And I don't know how the broker can force him to do it.

COMMISSIONER HESBURGH. Well, I think, if a man does not want to sell his house, no law is going to make him sell it.

MR. HOGAN. There is the same situation with rentals.

COMMISSIONER HESBURGH. But the point I was trying to make is that in many of these cities, individual brokers will say, "I would like to sell you the house. I know there is a house available, but if I were to sell it to you I would lose my position in an association and I am going to be in trouble."

MR. HOGAN. I don't know what the attitude of other boards is, but let me say that maybe San Francisco is a shining example of a non-prejudicial board. If anybody should have been criticized, I suppose it would have been myself. And yet I now have the honor of serving as first vice president of this board. And I didn't know anything about this suit that was forced on the board to take in a minority member. But, actually, I don't see why they would turn him down. . . . It is absolutely news to me.

COMMISSIONER HESBURGH. Mr. Hogan, this is the first real estate board we have met in the whole United States that has a minority member on it. As you know, there is a National Association of Realtors, but the Negro cannot be a "realtor"; he must be a "realtist." And I think this is the kind of semantics that we could well do without in the United States of America.

But we congratulate you on having members of a minority on your board. As far as the total program, I was merely pointing toward the possibility of leadership that might extricate the real estate boards, nationally, from the kind of contempt that certain segments of society seem to have for them today because they say one thing and, under all kinds of subterfuges, do something else.

And I think this is the constant burden of all the testimony we ever receive on housing, and we have received it from coast to coast. . . .

6

THE CONSTITUTION
AND THE
POLICY-MAKING PROCESS

*Just imagine, for example, how our automobiles have improved
over a short space of time. The other day I tried to go back and
drive a car with the old transmission instead of the automatic, and
I just felt in another world. That is happening, of course, in electronics and television, in aviation, in atomic energy, and so on. But in
government—no. Why is that?*[1]

Nearly two hundred years ago the Founding Fathers established
a government in which power was limited through the resort to
federalism and the separation of the central government into three
branches. At the turn of this century Henry Adams, one of the most
profound students of American government, termed the resultant

---

[1] Chief U.S. Circuit Court Judge Charles E. Clark, *Proceedings of the Attorney
General's Conference on Court Congestion and Delay in Litigation*, p. 127 (1958).

system "senile." Today many voices are raised questioning the ability of our decision-making process to cope with the scale and pace of the problems of the thermonuclear age.

For all this, the American Constitution has proved to be an extraordinarily durable document—because of a process of constitutional change embodied in historical precedent, changing court decisions, and formal amendment, which have combined to place more and more power in the federal government, and in the hands of the chief executive. Today, the question is: Has the process of change been rapid enough and aimed in the right direction?

The selection from the Brookings study in this chapter starts out by asking for "a bold adjustment of institutions" to deal with the new era. However, it later describes its specific recommendations for improving the relationship between President and Congress as "modest adjustments" rather than "drastic changes."[2]

Stephen K. Bailey expresses still sharper criticism of Congressional processes which, he says, lead to policy-making by "fits and starts"[3] and by "an infinitely intricate system of barter and legerdemain."[4] We shall not, says Bailey, be equipped to deal with the issues of our time until we build a bridge across the separation of powers by reorganizing and realigning our political parties. He points to the factors which, he believes, are already moving our parties in the desired direction.[5]

Richard Neustadt sees little likelihood that our institutions will be adjusted or our parties realigned significantly in the near future. In a book that is much admired by President Kennedy, Neustadt states his thesis that only by the full exercise of the powers which reside in the Presidency shall we get the leadership we must have. This means, says Neustadt, that the President has an obligation to use to the full the only methods available to him—those of politics.

Might there not be great danger in the resulting personalization of power? The power to make decisions there must be, but how shall its possible excesses be checked? It is traditional in democratic

---

[2] David B. Truman has suggested that the President, working with the Floor Leadership, now exercises a considerable degree of influence over Congress, so that we already have "integrated policy . . . without unnecessary sacrifice of a useful and perhaps inevitable diversity." *Proceedings of the American Philosophical Society,* vol. 103, no. 5, Oct. 1959, p. 692.

[3] Stephen K. Bailey, *The Condition of Our National Political Parties,* The Fund for the Republic, (c) 1959, p. 4.

[4] *Ibid.,* p. 5.

[5] The Democratic Advisory Council, which Bailey cites as evidence of his view that the parties are becoming nationalized and centralized, has now been disbanded.

theory to point to public opinion as both the ultimate source of authority and the most effective restraint upon it. But this theory is called into question by the statistics listed in "The American Voter," which appears in this section. A majority of the 1956 electorate, it appears, had only a rudimentary knowledge of most of the leading questions of public policy. How, then, could they be expected to make discerning judgments on the uses of power? With this in mind, some observers view the public as essentially an inert mass, ready material for manipulation. Such political scientists as Stanley Kelley have drawn attention to the increased role in our political life of advertisers and public-relations men, who use incessantly repeated slogans to distort the meaning of campaigns, to blur the issues, and to promote candidates with the same devices that sell movie stars or breakfast foods.

Now there is some evidence on the other side of this question. The second table in "The American Voter" shows that the more education a person has had, the more likely he is to be informed on public issues. Charles R. Nixon has suggested that the tremendous increase in our college population is one of the factors that will compel "the politician of the future . . . to pay more attention to the opinions of a large public than heretofore."[6]

And in the next chapter we shall see that in 1960 Gabriel Almond had revised upward his low 1950 estimate of the awareness and understanding of the American public in relation to foreign affairs. Thus, the opinion expressed in the Brookings study—that certain segments of the public should be more closely involved in the policy-making process—may have constantly increasing validity.

Nonetheless, there will be continued doubts about the efficacy of public opinion as an influence for responsibility and restraint in the making of public policy. Indeed, the approach of the Founding Fathers was the reverse of this. To them the majority will was itself among the forces to be restrained, and the system of checks and balances was designed largely for this purpose. Russell Kirk here reiterates the case for the principles of 1787, and he sees the trend toward the concentration of power in a relatively few hands as the great danger of our time.

Kirk is a conservative, and liberals will tend to discount his warnings of socialism or excessive executive discretion in foreign affairs. But liberals will not find it easy to dispose of the problem presented

---

[6] "The Coming Electorate: 1965–1970," *Western Political Quarterly,* Vol. XIII, No. 3, Sept. 1960, p. 635.

here by Smith and Cotter of preserving individual rights in the face of the growth of executive authority in the "amphibial state."[7]

C. Wright Mills, too, warns against excessive power concentrated in a few hands. But his assumptions are very different from those of Kirk. Mills claims that the kind of talk about Congress, political parties, and public opinion which is found in this chapter is largely irrelevant. The Congressional politicians and the pressure groups are not at the center of power, and the public is diverted from the real issues by the frivolity and distortions of the mass media. Power resides in the hands of an informal interlocking directorate of the top leadership of the great corporations, the military establishment, and the government. In *The Causes of World War III*, Mills argues that unless we take the decisions out of the hands of this "power elite," we shall drift inevitably into the thermonuclear holocaust.

A number of political scientists, and such sociologists as David Riesman, have argued against Mills; they maintain that ours is essentially a pluralistic society, and that power is widely distributed among a number of competing groups and organizations. A further aspect of this question is opened up in the conflicting views presented here on the question of national purpose. William Pickering is one of many who are proposing that decision-making in the sixties cannot be considered in merely institutional terms. The international challenges can be met, he claims, only if we are working in the context of clear national purposes. Against this view, William Chamberlin insists that a pluralistic society by definition cannot have a single statement of national goals, and that we must not be panicked by the Soviet challenge into changing our values and institutions.

---

[7] President Eisenhower, in his television speech of January 17, 1961, made a similar point: "We have been compelled to create a permanent armaments industry of vast proportions. . . . We recognize the imperative need for this development. Yet we must not fail to comprehend its grave implications. . . . In the councils of Government, we must guard against the acquisition of unwarranted influence, whether sought or unsought, by the military-industrial complex. The potential for the disastrous rise of misplaced power exists and will persist."

Richard E. Neustadt

PRESIDENTIAL POWER*

. . . .

. . . When it comes to power, nobody is expert but the President; if he, too, acts as layman, it goes hard with him.

Expertise in power terms is not a substitute for expertise in policy; it offers some protection, though, from errors and from bafflements in policy appraisal. From those a President needs all the guarding he can get. . . . And he, himself, the layman in most areas of policy, has no better protector than concern for his own power. . . .

The Presidency . . . is not a place for amateurs. That sort of expertise can hardly be acquired without deep experience in political office. The Presidency is a place for men of politics. But by no means is it a place for every politician. . . . Expertise in presidential power seems to be the province not of politicians as a class but of extraordinary politicians. . . .

If expertness in maximizing power for himself served purposes no larger than the man's own pride or pleasure, there would be no reason for the rest of us to care whether he were powerful or not. More precisely, there would be no reason except sentiment and partisanship. But a President's success in that endeavor serves objectives far beyond his own and far beyond his party's. . . . An expert search for presidential influence contributes to the energy of government and to the viability of public policy. Government is energized by a productive tension among its working parts. Policy is kept alive by a sustained transformation of intent into result. Energetic government and viable public policy are at a premium as we begin the

* Richard E. Neustadt, *Presidential Power*, John Wiley & Sons, Inc., 1960, pp. 149–193. Reprinted by permission.

Dr. Neustadt is Associate Professor of Government at Columbia University and head of the Government Department in Columbia College.

seventh decade of the twentieth century. Expertise in presidential power adds to both. A President's constituents, regardless of their party (or their country for that matter), have a great stake in his search for personal influence. . . .

The contributions that a President can make to government are indispensable. Assuming that he knows what power is and wants it, those contributions cannot help but be forthcoming in some measure as by-products of his search for personal influence. In a relative but real sense one can say of a President what Eisenhower's first Secretary of Defense once said of General Motors: what is good for the country is good for the President, and *vice versa.* There is no guarantee, of course, that every President will keep an eye on what is "good" for him; his sense of power and of purpose and the source of his self-confidence may turn his head away. If so, his "contributions" could be lethargy not energy, or policy that moves against, not with, the grain of history. The way he sees his influence and seeks it will affect the rest of us, no matter what becomes of him. . . .

What may the Sixties do to politics and policy and to the place of Presidents in our political system? The Sixties may destroy them as we know them; that goes without saying. But barring deep depression or unlimited war, a total transformation is the least of likelihoods. Without catastrophes of those dimensions nothing in our past experience suggests that we shall see either consensus of the sort available to F.D.R. in 1933 and 1942, or popular demand for institutional adjustments likely to assist a President. Lacking popular demand, the natural conservatism of established institutions will keep Congress and the party organizations quite resistant to reforms that could give him a clear advantage over them. Four-year terms for congressmen and senators might do it, if the new terms ran with his. What will occasion a demand for that? As for crisis consensus it is probably beyond the reach of the next President. We may have priced ourselves out of the market for "productive" crises on the pattern Roosevelt knew—productive in the sense of strengthening his chances for sustained support *within* the system. Judging from the Fifties, neither limited war nor limited depression is productive in those terms. Anything unlimited will probably break the system.

In the absence of productive crises, and assuming that we manage to avoid destructive ones, nothing now foreseeable suggests that our next President will have assured support from any quarter. There is no use expecting it from the bureaucracy unless it is displayed on Capitol Hill. Assured support will not be found in Congress unless contemplation of their own electorates keeps a majority of members constantly aligned with him. In the Sixties it is to be doubted—for reasons to be mentioned in a moment—that pressure from electorates will move the same majority of men in either House toward consistent backing for the President. Instead the chances are that he will gain majorities, when and if he does so, by *ad hoc* coalition-building, issue after issue. In that respect the Sixties will be reminiscent of the Fifties; indeed, a closer parallel may well be the late Forties. As for "party discipline" in English terms—the favorite cure-all of political scientists since Woodrow Wilson was a youth—the first preliminary is a party link between the White House and the leadership on both sides of the Capitol. But even this preliminary has been lacking in eight of the fifteen years since the Second World War. If ballot-splitting should continue through the Sixties it will soon be "un-American" for President and Congress to belong to the same party.

Even if the trend were now reversed, there is no short-run prospect that behind each party label we would find assembled a sufficiently like-minded bloc of voters, similarly aligned in states and districts all across the country, to negate the massive barriers our institutions and traditions have erected against "discipline" on anything like the British scale. . . .

Our parties are unlikely to be revolutionized as instruments of government because they are unlikely to be altered fundamentally as voter coalitions differently aligned for different offices in different places. The long awaited "nationalization" of our parties, breaking the old sectionalism, may be on its way despite the current setback in the South. But even if each party's voting base were nationalized tomorrow, the issues of the next few years hold out no prospect that the partisans in one place will stay put on the same terms as those in every other. In the next years we face a snarly sort of politics with party followings more likely to be brittle and unstable than secure and likely to shift differently in different locations. Nationalization may be coming, but if we find it with us in the Sixties we should not expect to find that it has brought us those clean cleavages so dear to advocates of "party realignment." Our history suggests that only sustained crises, striking deep into the private lives of voters everywhere, will produce *stable* partisan alignments; crises on the order of the Civil War and of the Great Depression. But a comparable crisis in our time would strike so deep that there might well be nothing left of our contemporary party system. . . .

The issues of the Sixties will be fought out in a system that keeps Presidents uniquely placed and gives them no assurance of sustained support. "Emergencies in policy with politics as usual" was my introductory characterization of the fifteen years just passed. Everything suggests that these mid-century conditions will persist into the new decade. But policy is likely to grow still more difficult, and politics is likely to grow hotter. Conditions will not be just what they were, they may be more so. It follows that our need will be the greater for a presidential expert in the Presidency. . . .

A President-as-expert is no cure-all. . . . Power cannot be his sole criterion for choice, nor will his choices be the only regulators of his influence. They are the only levers in *his* hands, but other hands hold other levers. And his influence, at most, is only one of many factors shaping what eventuates as governmental action; events and men beyond his personal control are much the greater shapers. One cannot look around the world in the late Fifties with any special confidence in men or in events throughout the Sixties. It is not easy, after such a look, to quarrel with those who think that science and technology have pushed our social competence too far. Yet it seems premature to write off the adaptability and the inventiveness of American public policy. Admitting that the future is not wholly in our hands, our policy responses may make a substantial difference. Despairing views could have been voiced—and were—in 1950, or in 1940, or in 1930. At a time and in a world where rates of change accelerate, the Sixties may be the decade that finally proves too much for us. But on the record of the past, the policy responses of our political system give us grounds for hope. (In the whole perspective of this century so far, our recent pause seems relatively brief; besides, it was a pause, not a regression.) We might as well enjoy the hope; there is no present prospect that we soon shall change the system. Nor is there any prospect that a change of system would eliminate our policy dilemmas.

An expert in the White House does not guarantee effective policy, but lacking such an expert every hope is placed in doubt. If past experience is reassuring, its assurances are conveyed with that caveat. The responses of our system remain markedly dependent on the person of the President. "As matters have stood," Edward Corwin writes, ". . . presidential power has been at times dangerously *personalized*," and with unerring instinct for an expertise in influence he distrusts Franklin Roosevelt only less than Abraham Lincoln. But if one wants effective policy from the American system, danger does not lie in our dependence on *a* man; it lies in our capacity to make ourselves depend upon a man who is inexpert. Any human judgment is worth fearing nowadays, but save for this the expert is a boon. His expertise assures a contribution to the system and it naturally commits him to proceed within the system. The system, after all, is what he knows. The danger lies in men who do not know it. . . .

PRESIDENT, CONGRESS, AND PUBLIC OPINION*

. . . .

The new era requires a bold adjustment of institutions as well as policies and, what is more fundamental, personal attitudes and skills so that the United States may be capable of orchestrating the growing range of talents and resources needed to support its international objectives. The outer edges of national societies are merging with one another ever more rapidly. This calls for turning the face of the U.S. Government more toward the outside world and, in support of this effort, to develop improved means of marshaling the many activities involved into a more effective program. . . .

Today most important policies bear on foreign affairs. This has affected the balance between the Congress and the Executive. Because the increasing involvement of the United States in world affairs requires constant and substantial legislative support, the Congress has become a more active participant in the foreign policy process, concerned not only with broad goals but with such vital elements as economic development, farm surpluses, shipping subsidies, and cultural contacts. At the same time, there are major obstacles that tend to frustrate the legislative role, including the growing volume and complexity of international transactions, the speed and flexibility with which many foreign policy matters must be handled, the limiting effect of having to work in harness with other countries, and the secrecy that conceals many of these activities. . . .

Division of Responsibilities Between the Branches

. . . How should the roles of the Congress and the Executive be defined? It is not easy to draw a clear boundary between the activities of the two branches for the simple reason that they overlap con-

---

* Reprinted from a study prepared by The Brookings Institution for the Committee on Foreign Relations, U.S. Senate, 86th Congress, 2nd Session, Washington, D.C., January 1960.

The study was directed by H. Field Haviland, Jr.

siderably. Nonetheless, it is both feasible and desirable to keep in mind certain general distinctions between their roles based upon differences in their constitutional mandates and the functions and structures that have grown out of those mandates.

The essential role of the Congress is to provide a forum in which the representatives of hundreds of local constituencies may scrutinize and pass judgment on matters of national policy requiring legislative action. The individual Member of Congress is not simply a passive transmitter of the "public will" but a creative leader and interpreter as well. His main concern is to make certain that the interests he feels he represents are adequately protected and promoted. When those interests are not involved or are more or less evenly balanced, the Member is freer to act in accordance with his personal views, which is often the case with foreign policy. The general functions he has a responsibility to perform are to participate in enacting necessary legislative authorizations and appropriations and to inquire into policy problems and governmental actions related to those functions. While the Congress does not have the authority, staff, or time to oversee all of the details of day-to-day formulation and execution of foreign policy, it is, and has a right to be, vitally interested in those details that affect its constituents' particular interests as well as broader policy objectives and programs.

The distinct nature of the Executive role flows from its basic responsibility to manage the multitudinous activities of the Federal Government within the limits of the laws and resources provided by the Congress. It follows that the Executive has no choice but to be concerned with all, rather than only some, of the details of daily policy. It must not only develop general directives into practical programs but, in turn, translate those programs into effective action. From these responsibilities flow the requirements for personnel and other resources that are capable of dealing with this vast range of affairs and at the same time are organized in such a way as to be responsible to a single, rather than multiple, source of authority representing the Nation as a whole.

Given this basic division of responsibilities, what specific functions should the Congress be expected to perform to carry out its role?

1. It has a responsibility to identify and inquire into problems that may call for legislative action.

2. It shares with the Executive the function of framing broad national objectives.

3. It can help to estimate the relative merits of alternative approaches to dealing with various problems.

4. It may give attention, on a selective basis, to questions of detail related to broader issues.

5. It has the exclusive responsibility for enacting authorization and appropriation legislation.

6. It can help, as part of its investigatory function, to evaluate the performance of the Executive, again on a selective basis. . . .

Cooperation in Relation to Public Opinion

A joint responsibility of the Congress and the Executive that deserves special emphasis is that of maintaining effective relations with the public which ultimately sets the limits of maneuver within which those who shape and execute policy must operate. The climate of opinion that emerges from the public is the product of many interacting factors—the impact of mass media, the activity of hundreds of interest groups, the initiatives of public leaders, the influence of foreign opinion, and the weighing of issues and individuals through the channels of party politics.

The anticipated course of future world developments promises to impose greater burdens than ever on the public in relation to foreign policy. At the same time, the obstacles to public understanding threaten to become even more severe. These include the secrecy that often shrouds official deliberations, the bewildering pace of change, and the intricacy of the issues. While this report cannot accommodate a detailed treatment of the role of public opinion, it is pertinent to consider briefly a few alternative approaches to thinking about the relationship between the Government, particularly the Congress, and the general public with respect to foreign policy.

One point of view would place minimal emphasis on governmental efforts to cultivate contacts with the public through informational activities. This attitude stems largely from the feeling that such efforts run the risk of putting the Government in the position of "selling" programs to the people, of manipulating them. There is also the concern that the general public cannot be expected to be well informed or active in relation to the daily flow of international affairs.

Another view is that the Congress and the executive branch should support a stronger foreign policy information program for the general public. The lives of all Americans are touched by the Nation's international policies; it is their survival which is at stake. The public's attitudes toward crucial foreign policies may be seriously distorted by the tendencies of some media toward sensationalism and superficiality.

A third view holds that a more systematic and energetic effort should be made to bring leaders of public opinion into closer touch with the officials and processes that shape U.S. foreign policy. These leaders are extremely important in informing and mobilizing the public and are most likely to make the best use of such an opportunity.

Many devices could be used to implement this third alternative. More high-level briefings might be conducted by the executive departments for selected groups. . . . More opportunities might be given to leading individuals to take part in the policy process as consultants, temporary staff members, delegates, or visitors abroad. Arrangements to provide information and other services for groups conducting programs in world affairs could be strengthened. The Congress could contribute by reinforcing its relations with special groups and the media that reach those groups. Hearings could be held in various parts of the country, and Members of the Congress might more frequently form bipartisan teams to explain aspects of foreign policy and to sample attitudes. A few Members have already performed valuable services in this regard and have developed effective means of discussing the essence of policy with community audiences.

Of these three broad alternatives, the second and third are the most promising. If the Government is to move in the direction of bringing the public into closer touch with governmental policy, it will be necessary to have more adequate continuing collaboration between the two branches regarding both substantive and procedural aspects of the effort. The Congress should provide broad directives for this purpose and the necessary authority and funds to give life to the directives.

The factor of secrecy is of vital importance here. Some secrecy is necessary, but it can be used as a shield against legitimate criticism. As more governments impose restrictions on the flow of information, the public becomes increasingly dependent upon governmental releases. This can lead to serious distortion of public attitudes. Because there will always be justification for some measure of secrecy, especially in relation to matters close to the heart of national security, the solution must be one of degree. The direction should generally be toward a more permissive balance between concealment and disclosure that will provide the public with the basic information it needs to fulfill its responsibilities with regard to fundamental issues. . . .

Organization of the Congress

The Congress is characterized by wide dispersal of power, leadership, and authority which makes it difficult to develop a unified strategy and reconcile conflicting policies. While both branches of government are troubled by the pressures of friction and diffusion, the Congress finds it particularly difficult to create structures and processes that will foster unity because of the inherent partisan conflict, the division between the two Chambers, and the traditional reluctance to accept centralized leadership.

Each house displays distinctive characteristics that condition its response to foreign policy. The Senate's exclusive power to consent to treaties and to major Presidential appointments, coupled with the tradition that the President should consult it about foreign policy generally, have enhanced the prestige and influence of the Senate.

In the past, the House of Representatives occasionally exerted strong influence in foreign affairs in response to public moods, but its concern was episodic. Now the House is involved almost as deeply as the Senate. The powers it shares with the Senate, and its special custodianship of the Nation's purse, are major sources of support for the conduct of the Nation's business overseas.

The committees are the key to congressional behavior. Their decisions, more often than not, become the decisions of each house. The most important committees on foreign policy are still the Senate Committee on Foreign Relations and the House Committee on Foreign Affairs. Both are looked to by their respective Chambers for leadership regarding general foreign policy developments. The Senate Committee on Foreign Relations enjoys an especially favorable position in this respect, partly because of the special constitutional powers of the Senate and its tradition built up since the early history of the Republic. A particularly close relationship of confidence usually prevails between a few committee members and officials of the executive branch. This relationship provides a means for consultation about delicate foreign policy developments which it is deemed unwise to publicize and aids in building a bridge of understanding and support between the branches. . . .

When the activities of the committees on appropriations are added to the activities of the substantive committees, it is evident that at least half of the standing committees of Congress directly affect foreign policy. Occasionally committees cooperate closely, or special committees are devised to work in overlapping policy areas. . . . But most of the committees and their staffs work quite independently of one another. Each carefully guards its jurisdiction. In some instances, subcommittees have become quite independent entities, pursuing inquiries and engaging in other activities over which the parent committees exercise only nominal control. The directing influence of legislative and executive leadership, personal ties among members and staffs, and the fact that a Member of the Senate serves on two major committees modify these barriers but still leave much to be desired in the way of communication among these units.

The behavior of all committees, and thus of each House, is affected by the practice of awarding committee chairmanships according to seniority. Some members who rise to these posts have exceptional capacity and experience; others do not. While the seniority rule has been modified in practice on rare occasions, it is normally enforced because most Members prefer not to risk the controversy that would be involved in a more selective process.

The top party leaders rarely exert their influence at the level of committee activity. They are careful to respect the prerogatives of the chairmen and the ranking members of the committees. On the floor they usually support the bipartisan coalition in charge of a measure. When either House threatens to engage in what they consider to be a major aberration, or when the achievement of agreement is difficult, they employ their leadership resources more rigorously. Seldom do party meetings discuss foreign policy issues and relate these to party policy or to the broader picture of general legislative policy. The leaders are commonly drawn into executive-legislative consultations regarding foreign affairs and in unpublicized ways work to promote responsible agreement regarding foreign policy issues both within the Congress and between the branches. The President maintains continuing contact with his party leaders.

Except in times of grave crisis, broad foreign policy issues must contend with heavy competition in the allocation of a Member's time, attention, and thought. This generalization is less true for the members of the foreign policy committees, but even they are often so overwhelmed by other burdens that they find it difficult to give extended attention to general international developments. Most Members of the Congress feel that it is necessary to concentrate primarily on domestic issues that preoccupy most of their constituents.

Despite these difficulties, some Members have been sufficiently concerned with the critical importance of international issues to devote a major portion of their energies to foreign policy and, in some cases, they have acquired extraordinary expertise. Despite the generally domestic orientation of the public, there has been a trend toward greater interest in international affairs, especially as the result of two World Wars. In response to these changes, each political party has been gradually reorienting its consideration of foreign affairs toward a concept of national interest that is broader than the particulars of sectional demands. . . .

. . . How can the Congress better coordinate its consideration of foreign policy?

The Congress should provide adequate means for its Members and staffs to acquire a broad understanding of the new dimensions of foreign policy. . . .

. . . Such briefing would not run counter to the primary representational function of a Member of Congress; it would reinforce that function. The Member would be in a better position to respond intelligently to public opinion and to provide stronger leadership. Such a program would seem best suited to the newer Members of Congress who labor under a handicap in acquiring the knowledge which others of long service have been able to absorb over the years. . . .

Another way of weaving the many strands of policy together more effectively is to look to the Senate Committee on Foreign Relations and the House Committee on Foreign Affairs as the primary centers of coordinating influence in their respective Chambers. It must be recognized, however, that their role will continue to be restricted by certain limitations. . . . To centralize all foreign policy matters in just two committees would not only be unfeasible but would place too much power in the hands of too few Members.

The principal foreign policy committees, nonetheless, lie closest to the heart of foreign policy, have the most extensive experience, and are best staffed to provide general guidance in the foreign policy field. . . .

The organization and behavior of political parties and their leadership condition the entire process of democratic government and the response of the United States to the rest of the world. The competition for nominations, campaigns, elections, and the quality of party leadership in and out of the Congress have a direct bearing on foreign affairs. Party leaders are logical channels for coordinating party, interparty, legislative, and executive attitudes at all stages of the legislative process and across broad policy areas.

The state of American political parties is being vigorously debated today, and many proposals for reform have been advanced. While the limitations of this report do not permit an extended discussion of the party system as it bears on foreign policy, it is relevant to say that the potential contribution of political parties has been only partly tapped. If strengthened, the political parties could provide more useful means than have yet been developed of marshaling the best resources of the Nation to deal with major foreign policy issues.

The present limitations on party leadership are well known. Yet, even in these circumstances, the leadership has on occasion been able to achieve admirable results, and could, within a sympathetic climate, provide even more effective direction in helping each House to achieve better coordination of its actions, to facilitate cooperation between the executive and legislative branches, and to aid in fostering bipartisan collaboration.

Another possible means of bringing the leadership together with the chairmen and ranking minority members of the principal committees concerned with international questions would be the creation of a select committee to study, review, and inquire in the broad field of national security policy. The experiment could be conducted on a joint basis or separately by each House. The Joint Economic Committee provides a possible model. . . .

There are, of course, many obstacles. The chief difficulty is the traditional independence of congressional committees which makes them extremely sensitive to any unifying effort. And, if the authority of the committee is to be purely advisory, rather than directly legislative, it may not evoke the best efforts of its members. Nonetheless, it could perform a useful function if the key foreign policy leaders were determined to make it work. Thus it seems worth trying. . . .

Another broad issue before the Congress as it prepares for the future is: How might the appropriation process be improved with respect to foreign affairs? Compelled to seek annual authorizations and appropriations, forced to obligate most of the funds appropriated in a single year, bound by complex limitations placed on the use of funds, many executive officials believe that the Congress should permit more flexibility in the administration of foreign policy. Others feel that the executive branch already has sufficient freedom. Still others argue that the Congress should control and instruct even more in the future than it has in the past. . . .

. . . Authorization for a substantial but limited period according to the special requirements of each program . . . would give a degree of permanence to foreign affairs programs and free the Foreign Affairs and Foreign Relations Committees from the automatic annual review procedure which imposes heavy demands on their energies and the energies of large numbers of persons in the executive branch. At the same time, the authorizations could always be altered at the will of Congress, and the substantive committees could review the programs even without altering the legislation.

A related problem concerns the period of time for which appropriations should be made available. The most traditional pattern is the 1-year cycle by which means the Congress—as well as the Bureau of the Budget and the President—can maintain especially close control over agency programs. . . .

In view of the need for more effective long-range programming, it seems essential to relax the present 1-year cycle to some extent, permitting somewhat longer periods, though seldom indefinite, according to the special exigencies of each activity. . . . It should also be understood that the Congress could review the program each year and could change the system at any time. . . .

In what ways might the Congress improve its internal procedures for handling the budget? . . .

The existing procedures still leave much to be desired. The Congress does not examine the budget as a whole and relate its actions on individual appropriation acts to the broad picture. Appropriations for foreign policy purposes are not viewed sufficiently in the perspective of a comprehensive national strategy and often suffer unduly amidst the competing pressures for domestic programs. Because the substantive and appropriations committees work in relative isolation from one another, there is duplication of effort, and the quality of the congressional performance suffers. . . .

. . . It would seem desirable to move further in the direction of relating individual appropriation acts to a broader policy perspective. While it has not proved feasible to formulate a "legislative budget," it should be possible to mobilize a clearer concept of general policy and budgetary guidelines that would help to coordinate the various appropriations subcommittees. . . .

A basic issue that each Member of the Congress faces is how he should distribute his time and energy. These individual allocations of resources have a direct and crucial bearing on the effectiveness of the Congress as a whole. The burdens of public service are enormous—far greater than the public realizes. Members of the Congress are generally overworked. As every Member knows, however, detached analysis would reveal that a large fraction of his energies is allocated to relatively peripheral activities which have accumulated from practices and habits of a simpler past when the issues were less crucial and complex.

In looking to the future, the Congress should reassess its role in the light of the vast changes that are taking place. The choice is up to the Congress. Basically, it is a question of reappraising priorities in relation to the interest of the Nation as a whole. Amendment of the Constitution and drastic changes in structure and procedures are not required. Modest adjustments, such as those suggested in this chapter, could mean substantial progress.

Stephen K. Bailey

CHANGES IN THE PARTY SYSTEM[*]

. . . .

For three quarters of a century America has heard warnings from a variety of distinguished political prophets about its governmental weaknesses. Whether their solution has been constitutional revision or political revision, they have all agreed about the limitations of our governing instruments. . . . Criticism has been directed at a single issue: the difficulties of achieving sustained and responsible political power adequate to contemporary necessities.

All seem to accept one proposition: such power can be achieved through a greater synthesis of presidential and congressional purposes. Some say the synthesis is impossible without broad constitutional revisions along the lines of the British parliamentary system, including provision for the executive dissolution of the legislature in case of loggerheads and provision for concurrent terms for President and Congress. Others believe that the catalytic effect of a reformed party system, together with certain changes in congressional organization and procedure, will make drastic constitutional reform as unnecessary as they believe it to be improbable. . . .

In 1950, a Committee on Political Parties of the American Political Science Association brought out a report which was in the direct line of this earlier prophetic writing. Called "Towards a More Responsible Two-Party System," the APSA report discounted the possibility of drastic constitutional change, but put forward a series of suggestions for political reform designed to create a party system capable of enabling the national government to cope effectively and responsibly with the great national and international issues of the twentieth century.

. . . A decade has elapsed since the publication of the Com-

---

[*] *The Condition of Our National Political Parties,* The Fund for the Republic, (c) 1959.

Dr. Bailey is William Church Osborn Professor of Public Affairs at Princeton University.

mittee's report. Nothing has happened in that time to suggest that the basic issues raised have dwindled in significance. . . .

. . . And inexorable forces, only dimly observable when the report was being written, are now clearly at work preparing the soil for a crop of politics far different from what we have known in the past century. . . .

The national parties have become what they are because of . . . historical conflicts which they have had to settle, hide, or gloss over. In some cases they have been the master brokers between rich and poor, country and city, butter and oleo, capital and labor, Italian and Irish, new and old. At other times, they have hidden certain conflicts in order to satisfy powerful economic interests which have stood to gain by exploiting conflict locally and disguising it nationally. Each party has been caught in the dilemma, on the one hand, of trying to forge an image of harmony in the interests of the majority in order to win the Presidency, and, on the other hand, of being unable to eradicate the very different kind of image which generations of conservative log-rolls and bipartisan "inner-clubism" in the Congress have created in the public eye.

But what happens when the conditions of conflict change? For they are changing, and rapidly, in the United States.

Take the struggle between the old and the new. We used to be able to tell the difference between old and new settlers by their accent, or dress, or occupational level. But we are fuller of hundred-per cent Americans every day and are rapidly reaching the time when nationality politics will be as anachronistic as the trolley car. Samuel Lubell has set the beginning of the end of this traditional conflict in the late Thirties, with the coming of age of those whose parents and grandparents had arrived in the great immigration surge at the turn of this century. With the acceptance of the stranger as a person has come acceptance of his ways and his beliefs. . . . Matters which once split us and made us fearful are now absorbed almost without question as our population becomes increasingly homogenized.

Or take sectional and class conflict. The heart has been cut out of sectionalism by vast changes in technology and communications which have dispersed industry and revolutionized agriculture. Where are the one-crop "Cotton Ed" Smiths of a few years back? The fact is that there are precious few one-crop areas left in America. And even where there are, as in some of the great agricultural regions of the Great Plains, technology is bringing a revolution of another kind. In the last five years almost four million people have left the farm. The forecast for reapportionment of congressional seats after the

1960 census suggests a dramatic decrease in rural representation in the United States Congress, and this trend will continue as the rise in population throws more and more people into metropolitan areas.

The movement in urban politics tends to be toward class rather than regional politics. But even class politics has changed. It is no longer a kind of rabble vs. gentry rivalry. Rather, among other things, it is national industry against highly bureaucratized and well-paid national labor. Senator Barry Goldwater of Arizona is not a regional figure. In the congressional elections of 1958, national giants contended in that sparsely populated desert state, and for national stakes.

What bothers the auto worker in Detroit bothers the auto worker in Los Angeles. What worries the businessman in Chicago worries his competitor in Boston. With transcontinental jet planes, the political or labor or industrial leader whose home is in San Francisco is almost more accessible to his counterpart in New York than is a train traveler from Boston; and, in any case, distance has been obliterated by electricity, electronics, and the direct-dial telephone.

And what is happening to the Negro issue? It, too, is becoming nationalized. Today there are more Negroes in New York than in New Orleans; more in Detroit than in Birmingham, Alabama; more in Pittsburgh than in Little Rock; more in Los Angeles than in Richmond; more in Chicago than in Atlanta. The Negroes' locust-like migration to northern metropolitan centers may have brought new problems to city governments, but it has aroused a critical competition between the two major parties in the North and West to capture the Negro vote. In heavily populated, evenly divided states, a bloc shift of a few votes can mean thirty or forty electoral college votes for a presidential candidate.

Perhaps more than any one other factor, the northern migration of the Negro is working tremendous transformations in our political life. The South no longer can exercise a veto in either presidential convention. . . . In more than sixty congressional districts in the North and West, the Negro holds the political balance of power if he decides to bloc-vote; and in the South his political power is likely to increase steadily despite the present tensions.

As for the clash of personal political ambitions in the United States, they are being completely submerged by the international and domestic concerns of the American public. War and peace, inflation and depression, are both personal and universal issues; tariffs, taxes, foreign aid, military spending, federal reserve policies, and hosts of other national policies affect local economic activities across the land. Politicians who wish to become statesmen must be able to talk intelligently about issues that concern people in *all* constituencies. The extraordinary social and economic changes now going on are absorbing and transcending the old conflicts of personal ambitions.

The shifts in the nature of the conflicts are reflected in the changes that are already taking place in our party system:

1) The number of one-party states and one-party congressional districts is dramatically declining.

In less than twenty years, the number of one-party delegations in Congress (in which the two Senators and all members of the House from a single state are of one party) has dropped more than 50 per cent. . . .

. . . From 1952 to 1956 . . . the total Republican vote in the South for members of the House rose from 1,872,000 in 1952 to 2,371,000 in 1956.

2) The permanent staffs of the national party committees and the variety of committee functions have grown greatly during the past decade. . . . Today both of them maintain year-round staffs of between seventy-five and a hundred people. In election years this number doubles or triples. The annual budget of each committee amounts to almost a million dollars—a figure which skyrockets during election years.

3) Both national committees are doing everything within their power to spread their financial base. The evolution has been from fat-cats and expensive fund-raising banquets to mass appeals and direct-mail solicitation.

4) Almost unnoticed, a revolution has occurred in the "nationalization" of off-year senatorial and congressional campaigns. . . . In 1958, both national committees sent out representatives to help develop party strength in various regions and to give services to local campaigns. The campaign committees on Capitol Hill also provided services to these campaigns as a matter of course and, in spite of occasional frictions, worked in closer cooperation with the national committees than in any previous off-year election in history.

5) Since 1937, the Presidents have met regularly with party leaders in the Congress on matters of legislative priority and strategy. . . .

6) The creation of the Democratic Advisory Council and the recent appearance of an embryonic Republican counterpart show a new concern in both parties for clarifying the party image. There is little doubt that, eventually, pronouncements of these "executive wings" of the parties will be more effective than similar attempts by congressional leaders or individual party spokesmen excepting the President.

This far from exhaustive list of the responses of our political system to nationalizing forces represents only the beginnings of adaptation and adjustment. Our basic political institutions, and their relationships to each other and to the public, are in a state of flux. If we want a political system designed to give full play to America's political energies and to hold them within bounds set by a popular majority, we are obligated to modify the system still further. . . .

Angus Campbell, Philip E. Converse,
Warren E. Miller, and Donald E. Stokes

THE AMERICAN VOTER*

. . . .

If an issue is to motivate a voter, he must be aware of its existence and must have an opinion about it. Although this statement is obvious, it draws our attention to the fact that many people know the existence of few if any of the major issues of policy. The teacher concerned with adult education, the member of a League of Women Voters engaged in civic education, the politician trying to drum up grass-roots support for a new campaign plank: these and others will testify that one of the greatest limitations on civic participation is imposed by sheer ignorance of the existence of major social and economic problems. . . .

In general, public officials and people involved in public relations tend to overestimate the impact that contemporary issues have on the public. They find it difficult to believe that the reams of newspaper copy and the hours of television and radio time could be

* Angus Campbell, Philip E. Converse, Warren E. Miller, and Donald E. Stokes, *The American Voter*, John Wiley & Sons, Inc., 1960, pp. 170–175. Reprinted by permission.

The authors are all on the staff of the Survey Research Center at the University of Michigan.

ignored by any normal person within the reach of those media. The fact seems to be, however, that the human perceptorium is highly selective, and unless it happens to be tuned to a particular wavelength, the message transmitted over that wavelength will be received only as noise. Increasing its amplitude does not always make the message more intelligible, nor does it impel the listener to pay closer attention rather than flicking the "off" switch. Like the homeostatic mechanisms that control the range of variation in body temperature, blood sugar, blood pressure and the like, this perceptual screening seems to protect the individual citizen from too strenuous an overload of incoming information. Some individuals have a much greater capacity than others of course, but it may be assumed that all of the content of politics encounters some resistance at the point of reception.

An example of public indifference to an issue that was given heavy emphasis by political leaders is provided by the role of the Taft-Hartley Act in the 1948 election. Following the rather swift and firm action of the Eightieth Congress in replacing the Wagner Act of the New Deal with the Taft-Hartley Act, the Democratic Party chose the latter act as a major point of attack in the 1948 campaign. Despite the prominence given to the problems of strikes, labor unrest, and labor legislation in the postwar period, and despite the fairly direct clash of the major parties over amendment and repeal of the Taft-Hartley Act, a full third of the public indicated in November of 1948 that they had not heard of the Taft-Hartley Act. An additional third did not have an opinion on this issue. Almost seven out of every ten adult Americans saw the curtain fall on the presidential election of 1948 without knowing whether Taft-Hartley was the name of a hero or a villain.

. . . To gather better information about public familiarity with issues of politics, a set of questions on public policy was posed for a cross section of the 1956 electorate. . . .

Our 1956 data illustrate the extent of variation in public familiarity with issues. About one fourth of the national population claimed familiarity with fewer than one out of every two issues presented to them. At the other extreme we find almost a third who claimed enough familiarity with the issues to give us statements of attitudes on at least 14 out of 16 issues posed for them. If these items were typical of all political issues, a more extensive listing would not have greatly changed our estimates of issue familiarity. It is likely, though, that our list included most of the better-known issues and could have been extended only by adding items familiar to fewer and fewer persons. If this is true, the previously given estimates may overstate the average level of familiarity with specific issues in 1956.

For many purposes of political analysis it is useful to introduce a further criterion in a discussion of public familiarity with issues. . . . whether the person had any notion of what the federal government was doing with respect to the policy in question. . . .

Familiarity . . . is intended to refer only to the existence of an opinion that is given some sort of political meaning by its possessor; it is not confined to the existence of "accurate" opinions that are "correctly" related to the "reality" of the political world.

Use of both criteria of familiarity over a variety of issues leads to the results summarized in Table 8–1. On the average, about one respondent out of every three failed to survive these two hurdles for any issue. There is some variation according to the nature of the issue. When the item involves some general posture that this nation might adopt, such as "being friendly with the other countries of the world," there appears to be more likelihood of an opinion being expressed and some perception of what the government is doing.

TABLE 8–1. Public Familiarity with Selected Issues, 1956

ISSUE	NO OPIN-ION	HOLD OPINION BUT DO NOT KNOW WHAT GOV'T IS DOING	HOLD OPINION KNOW WHAT GOV'T IS DOING	TOTAL
Foreign Policy				
Give aid to neutral countries	28%	19	53	100%
Send soldiers abroad	20%	13	67	100%
Economic aid to foreign countries	17%	16	67	100%
Act tough toward Russia, China	20%	11	69	100%
Avoid foreign involvement	14%	15	71	100%
Friendliness toward other nations	12%	10	78	100%
Domestic Policy				
Firing of suspected Communists	16%	39	45	100%
Leave electricity, housing to private industry	30%	19	51	100%
Segregation of schools	12%	34	54	100%
Influence of big business in government	28%	18	54	100%
Influence of unions in government	25%	20	55	100%
Insure medical care	12%	29	59	100%
Cutting taxes	19%	18	63	100%
Government guarantee of jobs	10%	23	67	100%
Racial equality in jobs and housing ...	14%	19	67	100%
Government aid to education	10%	23	67	100%

Where an item deals with more specific programs such as aid to neutrals, however, fewer perceptions emerge. It is clear that the level of specificity is not the only determinant of familiarity: relatively specific programs of social welfare that have been under debate for some time appear more familiar to the public. But it seems that the specificity with which the issue is formulated does play some role in responses, and this fact provides some warning about the relative nature of the results, as well as a substantive indication of the sorts of objects toward which the public can respond most freely. . . .

One of the functions of education is to acquaint a person with a wide range of information about social, psychological, economic, and political problems. A person with little or no education (where education includes both formal and informal gathering of knowledge) will not have opinions on many issues simply because he is not aware of the existence of the issue. If we use the number of years of formal schooling as a measure of the extent of a person's education, we can readily test this conclusion. As Table 8–2 shows, there is a direct relationship between increasing years of schooling and increasing familiarity with our selection of issues.

TABLE 8–2. *Relation of Education to Familiarity with Issues, 1956*

FAMILIARITY WITH ISSUES	FROM NO FORMAL SCHOOLING TO COMPLETION OF 8 GRADES	HIGH SCHOOL, SOME OR COMPLETION	COLLEGE, SOME OR DEGREE
High	21%	31%	50%
Medium	37	47	44
Low	42	22	6
	100%	100%	100%
Number of cases	543	890	331

. . . .

Russell Kirk

THE DANGERS OF
UNRESTRAINED POWER*

. . . .

Power, generally defined, is such an absence of external restriction and limitation that only the inward determination of the subject causes the subject to act or to refrain from action. Now the conservative of reflection always has been sedulous to seek out the precise meaning of words; for the ability to apprehend and employ words accurately is the chief instrument of true reason, and it is through the knowledge of words that we are able to link generation with generation, so that the minds of Aristotle and of Shakespeare are not alien to us. Well, power, in short, is freedom from restrictions and counterbalancing forces. Power over men is the ability to do as one likes, whether other men like that course of action or not. Intelligent conservatives, from Burke and Adams to our time, have looked upon power as a most dangerous thing; for though unchecked power means complete freedom for the powerful man, it means abject servitude for his neighbors; and where power is triumphant, justice cannot abide, since justice promises to each man the things that are his own.

Thus the conservative, reading the lessons of history, has sought to hedge about power with strong restrictions, and to divide authority among many groups and institutions, that concentrated power may reside nowhere. History convinces the conservative that wherever these walls and barriers to restrain power are cleared away in the interest of "efficiency" or "simplicity" or "modernization," power proceeds to make short work of all the elaborate structure of private and public rights which have been developed, through compromise and experience, in the course of history. . . .

---

* Russell Kirk, *A Program for Conservatives,* Henry Regnery Company, 1954, pp. 251–271. Reprinted by permission.
Mr. Kirk is a leading writer on conservatism.

The conservative . . . , now as formerly, knows the peril of power, and the practical means for restraining power. To John Adams and James Madison in the United States, to Burke and Disraeli in England, we can turn for guidance. The thinking conservative has consistently sought to keep power from the appetite of any man or any class, through respect for prescriptive constitutions, attention to state and local (as distinguished from central) government, checking and balancing of the executive and the legislative and the judicial divisions of political authority, and prudent confinement of the state's sphere of action to a few well-defined objects. Just this conservative policy of restraining power by constitutional arrangements has been the chief attainment of American political philosophy, from the colonial thinkers and the framers of the Constitution, through Calhoun and Webster, to our own day; and just this search after a just balance of authority has been the great practical success and lesson of the American political experiment, ensuring to us a high degree of freedom and right for three centuries. . . .

The system of checks and balances in government, the decentralization of authority, and the several other Constitutional devices to restrain power were designed, in short, by the leaders of both the Northern and the Southern states, to conserve the justice and the freedom which Americans had long enjoyed; and thinking conservatives have adhered to this system for hedging and confining power ever since then. . . .

In America . . . I do not think that there is much clear and present danger of our traditional society being overthrown by any concerted effort of fanatic zealots for the total state; even most of the people whose lust for power would be gratified under a new order do not yet recognize that vice in themselves, and would not yet tolerate it in others. What we have to dread is that our complex structure of sentiment and political institutions, which shelters justice and order and freedom, will be reduced piecemeal, gradually, often with the very best of intentions. Social planners, in colleges or out of them, are very fond just now of laughing at the late Senator Taft's phrase "creeping socialism." There is more than one sort of laughter; whether or not the damned cry, I am sure they laugh; and it is altogether possible that some of these humorists may laugh in a different key, thirty years from now. I certainly hope not, for people of my cast of thought would almost certainly have been exterminated by that time, in the course of events.

There *is* such a thing as "creeping socialism"; and the worst of it is that socialism never ceases to creep until it becomes totalitarianism, nor can it, in its nature. Though I do not agree with Herbert

Spencer in many things, he knew whereof he spoke when he wrote, "Socialism is slavery, and the slavery will not be mild." Most socialists today are gentle and benevolent people, with less than the normal share of the lust for power. But it is not men of this breed who manage the New Order, when it arrives in all its fullness: they are lucky, indeed, if they are merely ignored; ordinarily they are among the first to be marked out for elimination. . . .

This, therefore, is the process which is liable to make an end of American society as we know it, unless intelligent conservatives begin to oppose it effectually. Power will be released from its bonds by the decay of the old moral and institutional barriers to *pleonexia*. Religious faith, which through its inculcation of humility and resignation has made men ashamed of their appetite for power, may degenerate among us into mere humanitarianism, devoid of any spiritual sanction; and the pure humanitarian is no better than a man halfway down the road to pure egoism. Private property and ability may be so weakened by the fiscal requirements of the humanitarian state that the burden becomes unbearable, and the state has to assume control of the whole system of production. Constitutional provisions for the checking and balancing of political authority may be so nullified by judicial decisions and legislative infringements that we are left with a simple "plebiscitary democracy," in which the executive of a unitary state (preserving, it may be, some superficial vestiges of local governments and representative assemblies), elected nominally by the masses but actually brought to office and kept there by the publicist and the manipulator, is compelled to make all the decisions for everyone—and must, in the circumstances, make most decisions imprudently. . . .

And now a few words concerning power among the nations. It is ours already; and we have done with it what men always have done with pure power: we have employed it abominably. I do not say that the Nazis or the Japanese militarists would have employed it to better advantage, or that the Communists would use it mercifully; on the contrary, I am certain that, to the best of their ability, they would have striven to accomplish still greater mischief. But that does not excuse us. The learning of physical science, and the perfection of technology, instead of being put to the improvement of Reason, have been applied by modern man to achieve mastery over nature and humanity; and that mastery has been brutal. We Americans happened to be first in the race for the acquisition of the tools of mass-slaughter, and we used those tools as the Roman used his sword and his catapult against Carthage.

We might like to forget the circumstances of our triumph over

Japan, as doubtless there were Romans who, once the heat of the fight was past, would have preferred to forget the storm of the citadel. But in the history of nations, as in the lives of men, there are things done that cannot be forgot. Penance may be undertaken, and, by the grace of God, true contrition may be experienced; yet the recollection will not fade, and, though others may forgive us, we cannot forgive ourselves. The act *per se*, even the instant obliteration of great cities, though shocking enough, is not so unforgivable as the motive. What was our motive at Hiroshima and Nagasaki, in a country already pleading to surrender? We try to tell ourselves it was to "save American lives"; but in our hearts we know that if our primary concern really had been for American lives, we would not have prolonged the war in Germany by our insistence upon unconditional surrender; perhaps, after all, our primary concern ought not to be for our own lives, but for justice and mercy under God. If our primary concern had been for our own lives, we would not have gone to war at all.

In plain fact, our motives for destroying Hiroshima and Nagasaki were mixed, but chief among them seem to have been these three: a desire, based upon sheer expediency, to overawe the Russians; an unhallowed appetite for vengeance; and the ferocious intoxication of pure power. I say these things not out of any desire to revive dead grudges, but to emphasize that we Americans now are face to face with the problem of power; we are looking upon the stony countenance of Medusa. After all our humanitarian bragging, in the course of the war, we behaved precisely as we accused our enemies of behaving. I am afraid that we must confess, now, that Americans have no peculiar exemption from Sin, as a people, and that pure power, in our hands, is as dreadful as pure power in the hands of any other nation.

As to what can be done to hedge about this new form of power with restrictions, the conservatives cannot possibly offer any easy answers. We are not going to find ourselves led, of a sudden, by philosopher-kings, and I should not trust even Marcus Aurelius or Alfred the Great with pure power—they, indeed, would have been horrified at having such a trust forced upon them. What the conservative can do is to seek for means to prevent the employment of this power by any tight little circle of men who might judge it expedient to annihilate some obdurate opponents, the end justifying the means. A handful of individuals, some of them quite unused to moral responsibilities on such a scale, made it their business to extirpate the populations of Nagasaki and Hiroshima; we must make it our business to curtail the possibility of such snap decisions, taken simply on the assumptions of worldly wisdom. . . .

In working for a concert of the nations, the conservative in America ought to bear in mind the principles of liberty under law that are his own peculiar heritage, and the tactics of prudence which are his inherited method. He will look upon the United Nations Organization, for instance, as an opportunity for reasonable consultation and for applying some ethical standard to the conduct of international affairs; but he will not entertain extravagant hopes of a wisdom more than mundane issuing from the collective deliberations of that body. He will not be over-impressed by talk of a supranational authority administering impartial justice and establishing the terrestrial paradise; for he knows that the whole is no greater than the sum of its parts, and if no nation has yet achieved perfect justice and security and freedom within its boundaries, no new-born world state is going to do anything of the sort.

Improvement in nations, as in men, must come from within, for the greater part. He will not be led into fallacious comparisons of a projected world-federation with the federal union of the thirteen original states, for he knows that the American system was the product of a common history, common interests, common language, and common political and social institutions, not of sudden abstract inspiration. And he will take care not to sacrifice the present very real rights of Americans for some airily speculative future rights of Man, as expressed in that fantastic document called the Universal Declaration of Human Rights.

These latter observations naturally suggest the amendments of the Constitution proposed . . . by Senator Bricker and Senator George; and the projected amendments, in turn, suggest the sorry confusion which still envelops any discussion of the problem of power. Without going into the particular merits or failings of these proposals, still one may remark the rather disturbing nature of much of the opposition to them. These amendments were designed to reaffirm what clearly was the intention of the framers of the Constitution, that no treaty or agreement with a foreign power should override the Constitution itself or the will of Congress. The increased scope of executive agreements with foreign states, and the aspirations of the United Nations Organization, made urgent some such reaffirmation, which, indeed, had been needed ever since Justice Holmes' opinion in the Migratory Bird Case. But some very curious views were advanced by the opponents of these proposals.

One argument was that surely there could be no point in Constitutional restrictions here, if the Senate still retained the power to ratify or reject treaties—upon which premise, the whole Constitution might as well be abolished. Another argument, more generally advanced, was that such an amendment would be an unwarranted encroachment upon the rights of the executive branch of the government. Now there are times in the history of the American Republic when the executive branch has been genuinely threatened, as during Reconstruction; but to maintain that at present the executive power is menaced by the encroachments of Congress or the courts is an absurdity scarcely worth refutation. Executive authority is probably the only feature of our whole constitutional system *not* in any danger at present; the executive authority has been expanded, in recent years, until it is a burden nearly unbearable by any man. I do not propose to enter here upon the interesting complexities of this debate, but I refer to it by way of reminder that the placing of some rights beyond the scope of government, and the prudent division of authority among the several branches of government, are questions badly obscured in current political debate; and it is one of the conservatives' tasks to induce men to distinguish between the squabbles of the hour and certain enduring values in our political institutions.

It is Shakespeare who tells us that when order is dethroned, "then everything includes itself in power, power into will, will into appetite." The conservative, believing that not goodwill unaided can put a check upon power, defends that just order in society which puts laws above men and prescriptive rights above present expediency. At present, this problem of power is not merely a question of social well-being, but unmistakably a question of the survival of civilization, or even the survival of human life as a whole. The conservative, however oppressed by this responsibility, brings to it a cast of mind far better suited for the task than the disintegrating optimism of liberals and radicals.

J. *Malcolm Smith and Cornelius P. Cotter*

FREEDOM AND AUTHORITY
IN THE AMPHIBIAL STATE*

> For those who do not fit within the structure of the state there is but one alternative—to obey or die.[1]
> . . . criminal punishment after the act is, in time of great emergency, an insufficient protection against disclosures and destruction that may take a heavy toll in lives and defense facilities.[2]

It is [twenty] years since Harold Lasswell postulated the Garrison State, a hypothetical construct suggestive of the possible working out of political trends then observable in the United States. This was a state in which all organized social activity was governmentalized, and independent associations had disappeared. The judicial and legislative functions had atrophied, and the "specialists on violence" were supreme. In organization and process the Garrison State responded to the conditions of twentieth century total warfare. This had effaced the distinction between home-front and battle-front, had brought about "the socialization of danger," and the need to mobilize all the human energies of the nation in a total effort for survival—permitting to individuals the alternative of obedience or death.

The Garrison State has yet to be realized (Lasswell disclaimed any attempt at prediction). The social scientist cannot with certainty say that we are marching inexorably toward it or that we are on another road to serfdom. It is clear, however, that we live in an age of

---

* Reprinted from the *Midwest Journal of Political Science,* Vol. I, No. 1 (May, 1957), by permission of the Wayne State University Press.

J. Malcolm Smith is with the Governmental Research Bureau, State University of South Dakota. Cornelius P. Cotter is co-editor of this volume.

[1] Harold Lasswell, "The Garrison State and Specialists on Violence," *American Journal of Sociology*, XLVI (1941), 455–68; reprinted in Lasswell, *Analysis of Political Behavior* (New York, 1949), pp. 146 ff.

[2] Senator Paul Douglas, in debate on Kilgore substitute measure for McCarran Internal Security Bill, September 8, 1950. 81st Congress, 2nd Session.

political transition, and in a state which is different in some essentials from that which we knew fifteen, twenty, or thirty years ago. It is a state which is neither as free as some democrats think democracies should be, nor yet totalitarian in the Garrison State sense. Let us call it amphibial.[3]

The amphibial state is a state besieged. It is characterized not so much by the mobilization of human energies toward attainment of positive social goals as it is by the precautionary exclusion of individuals and groups from various occupations and activities in an effort to prevent breaches of national security. It is a state in which freedom of opportunity, of movement, and of expression increasingly are subjected to restraint based upon the application of political tests. War has facilitated transition to the amphibial state, and its essential features emerge from a description of governmental efforts to suppress disloyalty during the recurrent periods of military emergency in this century. It reflects a basic revision of the objective and mode for administering security controls, and of the tenable assumptions concerning the duration of war emergencies. . . .

Direct and harsh retribution was the goal sought and achieved in the enforcement of [World War I internal security] legislation; prevention was secondary and incidental, to be achieved insofar as the record of prosecution and conviction served to deter alleged disloyal activity by others. Since the program was retributive, there was no necessary logical relationship between the intensity and duration of controls exercised over individuals, and the objective need in security terms to immobilize them. Thus persons sentenced during the war for associations and utterances remained in prison well into the 'twenties.

In the Second World War the criminal process was employed with greater moderation. Local federal attorneys were not granted a free hand in seeking indictments for sedition. Suits were "undertaken only with the approval of the Attorney General, in order that a uniform policy may be enforced which will avoid use of the sedition laws to punish merely careless or unpopular utterance."[4] This is in part to be attributed to the fact that the lesson of 1917–1920—the danger of letting the nation see red—had been well learned. It is to

---

[3] The term "amphibial state" is borrowed from Joseph A. Schumpeter, "Capitalism in the Postwar World," in S. Harris, ed., *Postwar Economic Problems* (New York, 1943), pp. 113–26; reprinted in Schumpeter, *Essays* (Cambridge, Mass., 1951), pp. 170–83. Schumpeter used the term to depict a political economy beyond capitalism but falling short of a socialist revolution. Barring such a revolution he foresaw that the United States would be "an amphibial state for the calculable future."

[4] *Annual Report of the Attorney General*, 1944, p. 3.

be explained also by the fact that the 'thirties and early 'forties witnessed a shift in the objective of security legislation from retribution to prevention, with an accompanying transfer of emphasis from the judicial to the administrative process for enforcement.

Retribution and prevention are not clear-cut dichotomies. They are points on a continuum. Most legislation falls at intermediate points along the continuum. And while the most purely punitive legislation has an incidental deterring or preventive effect, the most purely preventive entails adverse consequences for individuals which have the impact, if not the purpose, of punishment.

Here lies a key to the distinction. The concepts of fault and punishment are absent from purely preventive legislation, which has the sole forward-looking objective of forestalling socially unacceptable occurrences. In his 1955 Godkin Lectures, John Lord O'Brian heralded the rise of "a new system of preventive law applicable to the field of ideas." He regarded it as "essentially different from traditionally American procedures." In fact, much of the administrative law of this century has been inspired by the perceived need to substitute prior restraint and prevention for the concept of guilt and *post hoc* retribution.

Emphasis upon prevention spells inevitable geometric increase in the incidence and variety of administrative control. The official scrutiny of government is extended from those who have committed proscribed acts to those who have the potential to do so. Not only is the administrative policeman's field of vision radically enlarged, but it is necessary to fashion and administer a myriad of novel deterrents to antisocial action.

Preventive law programs rest upon or embody certain assumptions concerning the predictability of human behavior. In formulating and administering a preventive program, whether in the sphere of economic or political controls, it is necessary, in two different dimensions, to identify "some of the antecedent characteristics which predispose to behavior" or to occurrences which it is the wish of society to avoid.[5] At the most general level of prediction it is necessary—unless the administrative officers are to be granted carte blanche—to delimit in the delegatory statute the general classes of persons to whom the program applies. What is involved here is an *actuarial prediction*.[6] In confining application of the program to specified

---

[5] Harold D. Lasswell and Gabriel Almond, "The Participant-Observer: A Study of Administrative Rules in Action," in Lasswell, *op. cit.*, p. 265.

[6] Adopting the analysis of John A. Clausen, in Samuel A. Stouffer *et al.*, *The American Soldier:* Vol. IV, *Measurement and Prediction* (Princeton, 1950), pp. 573 ff.

classes or groups of persons, the legislature is hypothesizing a high positive correlation between the "frequency of occurrence of specified behavioral characteristics" and the designated groups.

The probable future tendency of specific group members to commit the proscribed acts must now be measured, unless the entire group is to be subjected to the same kind and degree of inhibition. In theory this prediction can approach "unequivocal restraint," i.e., it may be an *absolute prediction*. The developing behavioral sciences contribute to solution of the problem of absolute prediction as they provide the administrator of political control programs with guiding models of "ideal (personality) types or coherent behavioral systems" tending toward patterned responses to varying social stimuli.[7]

The lineage of the present loyalty-security program can be traced to the Hatch Act of 1939, the first federal legislation "to promulgate standards for testing the loyalty of applicants or employees to their Government."[8] And what is it but a program for excluding persons from federal service on the basis of a prediction of the probable future likelihood that they will engage in acts inimical to the internal security of the United States? The Attorney General's list performs the function of actuarial prediction by specifying a high positive correlation between listed groups and subversion, and the hearings boards frame absolute predictions in individual cases. To say that individuals dismissed from government service under this program are not subjected to punitive action is not to suggest they do not suffer in property and in reputation. But if the program is administered in good faith, the hurt they experience is impersonal and unintended. . . .

. . . The Internal Security Act of 1950 blends administrative and criminal law techniques toward the preventive goals of barring members of "Communist-action" groups from federal or defense employment, and compelling members of "Communist-front" groups to reveal such membership in seeking employment with the federal government or with defense plants. In the first instance the Congress has framed both actuarial and absolute predictions, the latter extending to each member of the group, and in the second instance it has framed the actuarial prediction and sought to insure that employing officials would be alerted to the need to frame absolute predictions. . . .

---

[7] See Samuel A. Stouffer and Jackson Toby, "Role Conflict and Personality," *American Journal of Sociology*, LVIII (1951), 395–406.

[8] U.S. Senate, Subcommittee of the Committee on Post Office and Civil Service, *Administration of the Federal Employees' Security Program*, p. 17 (84th Congress, 2nd Session, Sen. Rept. No. 2750, 1956).

. . . The Emergency Detention Act of 1950, by now familiar to all, provides actuarial predictions to be applied by administrative officials in determining the need, in individual cases, to remove citizens to detention camps. The Attorney General may reduce the control to house arrest or something intermediate between that and detention, as he sees fit. This, of course, is preventive control, entirely lacking in punitive purpose. It ends with the end of the emergency giving rise to it. Thus the duration of the control exactly matches the duration of need, just as the duration of ineligibility for federal employment under the loyalty-security program exactly matches the period of justifying need. Both are of indefinite duration.

Publicity, as it intimidates the individual subjected to it, or forewarns those who are the object of his persuasive effort, has an immobilizing effect. It is a traditional and tried tool of preventive law. In the name of protecting national security, we have for nearly two decades required registration of "agents" of foreign countries. A list of such persons is available to the public. The Subversive Activities Control Board functions as much to focus public attention upon subversive groups as to identify them for the purpose of applying legal restraints to them. Once identified as subversive groups they must, like the foreign agent, identify on the envelope or wrapper the source ("a Communist organization") of any literature they disseminate through the mail, and they must similarly label television and radio broadcasts. Their printing equipment is subject to registration with the Attorney General.

The foregoing is not an exhaustive catalog of instances or types of preventive legislation. From one administration to the next and from Congress to successive Congress, the process of identifying new categories of subversive groups and new disabilities to be applied to the end of avoiding damage to our national security continues. The scope of security-affected activity steadily expands, the public realm continues to assimilate that of the private.

And we no longer have available to us the comforting illusion that the issuance of a proclamation of peace, or the signing of a treaty will reverse the process and a few years of normalcy efface memory of it. . . .

This does not mean that final degeneration of democratic institutions has set in. It would be premature to herald the Garrison State.

It remains possible to employ democratic institutions to influence the course of political development. But it is doubtful that we can radically check or redirect a process of governmentalization of human activity which is driven by pressures of the magnitude of those which play upon the United States today. Evidence of the pervasive and single-purposed nature of Communist infiltration of the Western democracies, and acquaintance with the destructive power of hydrogen weapons spur us to almost irrational efforts to protect the national security. . . .

. . . It is the continuing and inescapable problem of democratic government to strike a balance between individual freedom and social authority, between the right of the individual, relatively unrestricted by government, to define and pursue his own purposes and goals, and the right of society to stipulate and enforce superior social goals. So viewed, the task we confront in the age of preventive law and the amphibial state is generically identical to that which traditionally has been performed in democratic societies. Available to those who wish to participate in the process of striking a balance between freedom and authority, and insuring good faith and procedural regularity in the enforcement of security programs, are the courts, the vast array of private groups in American society, the press, and perhaps more important than all these, the Congress, acting in its capacity as author of such programs and agency for enforcing their responsible administration. . . .

We cannot be light-heartedly optimistic concerning the functioning of Congress as a conservator of freedom in the amphibial state; for the very body which must be the ultimate hope of curbing excesses has amassed a record of flagrant abuse of authority in pursuing internal security inquiries, and representatives of both major parties have engaged in naked efforts to exploit the real and existing security danger to their electoral advantage.

Yet the record is not so one-sided as might at first appear. Much dissatisfaction which should be directed to the need for an intricate and expanding program of national security legislation has been aimed at the legislature which, if disjointedly and unwisely at times, has attempted to respond adequately to the need. The egregious inquisitorial performances of a few members of Congress tend to blind us to the real accomplishments of others in casting light upon the nature of the national security problem, assessing alternative responses to it, and encouraging responsible administration of security programs. The investigating power was ably employed by Congress toward the end of insuring responsible administration of Second World War programs, and we have been given recent evidence of its suitability for the control of contemporary security programs. The joint "watch-dog" committee, which comes increasingly in vogue, could be employed advantageously to scrutinize, on a continuing basis, programs which are replete with novelty and danger. Other devices, such as the concurrent resolution used to secure to the Congress a veto power over administrative action, exist in abundance and need only be utilized.

The question which remains moot is not whether the facilities exist to conserve human values within the amphibial state, but whether individuals and groups will attempt astutely and resolutely to employ the American political process to pursue this objective.

C. Wright Mills

THE POWER ELITE*

. . . .

Among American spokesmen there is little doubt that the high and the mighty of the Soviet Union make history. The Red Dictators are regularly blamed for evil historical consequences thought to be directly traceable to their decisions and designs. But in the formal democracies—especially now that things are not going so well—it is claimed that no elite makes history or is in any position to do so. The omnipotence of evil tyrants abroad and the prevalence of virtuous but impotent leaders at home are widely assumed. For in America, after all, "the people" are magically sovereign.

As we examine the United States in the middle of the twentieth century, we come upon many such inherited images which confuse our attempt to confront its present reality. That is one reason why history is the shank of any social study; we must study it if only to rid ourselves of it. In the United States such images usually have to do with the first half of the nineteenth century. At that time economic facilities were very widely dispersed and subject to little or no central authority. The state watched in the night but was without decisive voice in the day. One man meant one rifle, and the militia

---

* From *The Causes of World War III*, pp. 20–30. Copyright (c) 1958 by C. Wright Mills. By permission of Simon and Schuster, Inc.

Dr. Mills is Professor of Sociology at Columbia University.

were without centralized orders. Such images are altogether historical.

Within the United States today three broad levels of power may now be distinguished: The top of modern America is increasingly unified and often seems willfully co-ordinated. At the top there has emerged an elite whose power probably exceeds that of any small group of men in world history, the Soviet elite possibly excepted. The middle levels are often a drifting set of stalemated forces; the middle does not link the bottom with the top. The bottom of this society is politically fragmented and, even as a passive fact, increasingly powerless; at the bottom there is emerging a mass society.

The power of decision is now seated in military, political, and economic institutions. Other institutions are increasingly shaped and used by these big three. By them the push, the drive, of a fabulous technology is now guided, even as it paces and shapes their own development. As each of the big three has assumed its modern shape, its effects upon the other two have become greater and the traffic among the three has increased. The U.S. power system is no longer composed of a self-contained economy and a self-contained political order, loosely incorporating local militia unimportant to politics and to money-making. This system is now a political economy intricately linked with a military order central to politics and crucial to money-making. The triangle of power formed by these three orders is now a structural fact, and it is the key to any understanding of the higher circles in America today. For as each of these domains has coincided with the others, as decisions in each have become broader, the leading men of each—the high military, the corporation executives, the political directorate—have tended to come together, to form the power elite of America.

I. The political order, once composed of several dozen states with a weak federal center, has become an executive apparatus which has taken unto itself many previously scattered powers, legislative and administrative. It now reaches into all parts of the social structure. Business and government have become more closely and explicitly connected; neither can now be seen clearly as a distinct world. Under American conditions the growth of executive government does not mean merely the "enlargement of government" as some kind of autonomous bureaucracy; it means the ascendancy of the corporation men into political eminence. Already during the New Deal such men had joined the political directorate; as of World War II they came to dominate it. Long involved with government, now they have moved into full direction of the economy of the war effort and of the postwar era.

II. The economy—once a great scatter of small productive units in somewhat autonomous balance—has become internally dominated by a few hundred corporations, administratively and politically interrelated, which together hold the keys to economic decision. This economy is at once a permanent war economy and a private corporation economy. Its most important relations to the state now rest on the coincidence between military and corporate interests, as defined by generals and businessmen and accepted by politicians and public. Within the elite as a whole, this coincidence of military domain and corporate realm strengthens both of them and further subordinates the merely political man. Not the party politician but the corporation executive is now more likely to sit with military men and answer the question, "What is to be done?"

III. The military order, once a meager establishment in a context of civilian distrust, has become the largest and most expensive feature of government. Behind smiling public relations, it has all the grim and clumsy efficiency of a great and sprawling bureaucracy. The seemingly permanent military threat places a premium upon high military personnel; virtually all political and economic actions are now judged in terms of military definitions of reality. The higher military, in short, have ascended to a firm position within the power elite of our time.

In considerable part, this power elite is the result of the historical fact, pivotal for the years since 1939, that attention has shifted from domestic problems centered on slump to international problems centered on war. Nowadays even slump (not to speak of poverty) must be seen, and is seen by knowledgeable higher-ups, in its international bearing. By long historical usage the government of the United States has been shaped by purely domestic clash and balance; it does not have suitable agencies and traditions for the democratic handling of international affairs. It is in this vacuum that the power elite has grown. . . .

The American system of power is usually interpreted as a moving balance of many competing interests. In the nineteenth century the balance was thought to occur among a great scatter of individuals and enterprises; in the twentieth century it is thought to occur among great interest blocs. In both views the politician is the key man of power because he is the broker of many conflicting powers.

The balance and the compromise in American society—the "countervailing powers" and the numerous associations, the "veto groups" and the "vested interests"—must now be seen as having mainly to do with the *middle* levels of power. . . .

The expanded, centralized, and interlocked hierarchies over which the power elite presides have encroached upon the old balances and relegated them to the middle level. This middle level, it seems to me, is better understood as an affair of entrenched and provincial demands than as a center of national decision.

Politics is not a forum in which the big decisions of national and international life are debated. Such debate is not carried on by nationally responsible parties representing and clarifying alternative policies. There are no such parties in the United States. More and more, fundamental issues never come to any point of decision before the Congress, much less before the electorate in party campaigns. In the case of the Quemoy incident, in the spring of 1955, the Congress abdicated all debate concerning events and decisions which surely bordered on war. The same is largely true of the 1958 crises in the Middle East and in the Far East. Such decisions now regularly bypass the Congress and are never clearly focused issues for public decision. . . .

The agrarian revolt of the nineties, the small-business revolt that has been more or less continuous since the eighties, the labor revolt of the thirties—each of these has failed as an independent movement which could "countervail" the powers that be. But each has succeeded, in varying degrees, as an interest vested in the expanded corporation and state; each has succeeded as a parochial interest seated in particular districts, in local divisions of the two parties, and in the Congress. What they have become, in short, are established elements of the *middle* levels of balancing power, in which we may now observe all those strata and interests which in the course of American history have been defeated in their bids for top power, or have never made such bids.

U.S. society is characterized by the increasing integration of real, and of potential, democratic forces into the expanded apparatus of the state. Much of what was once called "the invisible government" is now part of the quite visible government. The "governmentalization of the lobby" occurs in both the legislative and executive domains, as well as between them. Bureaucratic administration replaces electoral policies; the maneuvering of cliques replaces the open clash of parties. Corporation men move into the political directorate, and the decline of Congressional politicians to the middle levels of power is accelerated. The legislative function often becomes merely a balancing of sovereign localities and partial interests. A higher civil service that is a politically neutral, but politically relevant, depository of brain power and executive skill is virtually absent. Behind the increased official secrecy great decisions are made without benefit of public or even of Congressional debate.

In the U.S.S.R. and in modern totalitarianism in general the integration of autonomous forces is explicit; in the formal democracies it is much less so, and it is by no means a completed process. Yet it is well under way. Leaders of cliques, pressure groups, and associations maneuver within and between the organs of the democratic state and become a central part of that state. They discipline those whom they represent; their chief desire is to maintain their organizations, even if this requires them to lose sight of their ends in the effort to secure themselves as means, even if it results in their loss of independent action. They ensnare one another; such history as they make *is* history going on behind men's backs, including their own. The middle level of power in America is no moving balance; it is a semiorganized stalemate. . . .

William H. Pickering

WE MUST DEFINE
OUR NATIONAL GOALS[*]

. . . .

I am firmly convinced that this Nation is now involved in an all-out struggle whose outcome will determine whether the demo-

[*] Statement of William H. Pickering in the Hearings Before the Subcommittee on National Policy Machinery, Committee on Government Operations, U.S. Senate, 86th Congress, 2nd Session, Washington, D.C., February, 1960.

Dr. Pickering is Director of the Jet Propulsion Laboratory, California Institute of Technology.

cratic or the totalitarian concept of government will dominate in the future. We refer to this struggle as the cold war but in doing so, I believe that we are prone to occasionally forget that the real issues are ideas, basic principles and convictions, and fundamental doctrines. The more obvious conflicts that arise, for example, in debates over relative postures in economics or in science are, to me, merely the open manifestation of the basic struggle. . . .

These manifestations are important in that they represent the milestones whereby the progress of the opposing forces in this struggle are measured—and I happen to believe that the fruits of science and technology will, in the future, be used as one of the major signposts to measure the success of these opposing ideologies. It is in this sense that the so-called "race in space" assumes major and lasting international significance.

Something over a year ago I was invited to express my views to the House Committee on Space Exploration as to what the next 10 years in space might hold. I recall that in the process of pondering this question, I could not help but explore the related question of how these predicted events might materialize, and it seemed to me that the controlling factor might well be one of will and motivation as much as that of technical competency or funding.

I believe that this same thought pertains to the situation existing today. In short, the point I am making is that we must be concerned with defining our goals and making them known, as well as being concerned with funding, manpower, and organizational matters—or in other words, we must define the ends before trying to develop the means of getting there.

Whether a definition of national goals which relate to the specifics of the struggle we are in can best be accomplished through high-level committee action or by some other mechanism, I do not feel qualified to remark on; I am sure that there are others more skilled in organizational matters than myself who could evolve proposals in this area. I will only comment in passing that I feel much more needs to be done in the direction of developing dynamic national goals than the citizenry can comprehend and are willing to support. . . .

William Henry Chamberlin

AMERICA IS
MANY MILLION PURPOSES*

Defining America's national purpose has become a contagious fad. A considerable number of more or less distinguished persons have tried their hand at it in long articles; and it will be surprising if there is not, in due course, a spate of books on the subject. But somehow these attempts at definition, even when made by men with a scholarly knowledge of American history and above average awareness of contemporary American life, have not come off very successfully. What often comes out of these efforts is little more than a string of platitudes and a list of causes with which the writer is personally identified.

A vital point that is often over-looked is that in a nation like America, "conceived in liberty," as Lincoln said, there is no absolute authority, individual or collective, that can prescribe a set of national goals, binding on all citizens. National purpose in America is a synthesis of millions of individual purposes, sometimes conflicting, yet adding up to a very rich national total, spiritually, culturally, materially. The old-fashioned monarchies and aristocracies of Europe, against which the American Revolution was a political revolt and a philosophical protest, did have their ambitions, aims, and "purposes" directed, not toward the well-being of their peoples, but toward national aggrandizement by war and seizure of territory.

The Founding Fathers of the American Republic had a radically different idea. They proposed, first of all, to guarantee the freedom of the citizen and his unalienable rights to life, liberty, property, "the pursuit of happiness" (what cynical sneers that last ideal must have excited among European reactionaries who read the Declaration of

---

* William Henry Chamberlin, "America Is Many Million Purposes," *The Freeman*, Vol. 10, No. 10, October 1960, pp. 3–9. Reprinted by permission.
Mr. Chamberlin is an author on economic and political matters.

Independence) by a scientific balancing of power against power, so that no individual, no group, no instrument of government could wield unlimited authority.

This excluded, so far as was humanly possible, the exploitation of the people by any ruling group. It placed on the new republic an indelible stamp of voluntariness, of genuine consent of the governed. It eliminated the possibility that any group of Mr. Bigs, however sure they were right, however exalted their motives, could order and plan and push around and apply compulsion to their fellow-citizens. . . .

. . . In times of great stress and crisis there have been leadership and discipline. But it was leadership that was voluntarily accepted, not imposed by fear of a firing squad or a concentration camp. . . .

It is the glory of America that, at least up to the time when it became fashionable and popular to substitute state help for self-help, it has been a land of multiple purposes and unlimited individual opportunities. America is infinitely many purposes. It is the scientific inventor—like Morse or Alexander Graham Bell or Charles P. Steinmetz or Edison—working in his laboratory on some invention that will change the pattern of life.

It is Edgar Allan Poe, with his dark broodings, and Walt Whitman in his ecstatic jubilation, and Ralph Waldo Emerson working out a typical American philosophy of life, and the fruit of the imaginations of Hawthorne and Melville and the New England poets, with their more conventional messages. These and other similar figures were not, like writers in a totalitarian society, the hired propagandists of any particular order of things, political, economic, or social. They were following their own artistic impulses, expressing their own ideas, and thereby adding stone by stone to the edifice of American culture.

America offers, along with its big and often well-equipped state universities, a unique exhibit of private schools and private liberal arts colleges, often founded as an expression of religious faith or of devotion to a special educational or cultural ideal. And this strong concern with education, which has been marked since the early period of American life, has left its imprint, again on a basis of private initiative, in many foreign lands. One thinks of the colleges founded, with or without a missionary association, in China, Japan, India, Korea, Turkey, Lebanon. Some of these have been casualties of totalitarian suppression; others are still functioning. But here again is a unique example of private initiative in the cultural field, reaching out and probably winning more friends and exerting more constructive influence than all the expensive programs of government aid and "cultural exchange."

To suggest that America's greatness lies not in trying to frame national goals and purposes, but in making it possible for millions of individual Americans to realize *their* goals and purposes is not to intimate that America is devoid of ideals or lacking in the capacity for voluntary cooperation. Quite the contrary. The American pioneer, by his very way of life, was more self-reliant than the European peasant who was dependent for his livelihood on the local country squire in England, or nobleman in France.

But, in the case of an Indian raid, the lives of the pioneer and his family might depend on the willingness of his neighbors to come to his help. There was also cooperation in building cabins, in clearing woods, in husking corn. And this tradition of voluntary mutual aid finds expression in the very different conditions of modern life, in the service club that looks after handicapped children, in the alumni group of a small or medium-sized college that raises funds for scholarships for the students who have followed them and whom they wish to help.

As for ideals, it is doubtful whether any other nation came into existence in such a ferment of discussion of natural rights and natural laws and the nature of liberty and how liberty can be effectively implemented. In the literature of the American Revolution, from weighty essays on political theory like the Federalist Papers to resolutions of state assemblies and newspapers and periodicals, one finds constant emphasis on these five natural rights of free men: life, liberty, property, conscience, and happiness. These are regarded not as privileges which an arbitrary government can bestow or withdraw at will, but as unalienable rights derived from the Creator himself. . . .

There is no compatibility between respect for unalienable rights of man, based on natural law, and establishment of a "national purpose," binding on all citizens, or of compulsory economic planning. It is, of course, anyone's privilege to say what he thinks America's national goals should be, or how he would like to see our economy develop. The sticking point is the injection of compulsion into either of these processes.

It is sometimes argued that the challenge of communism makes it necessary to scrap or greatly modify the principles to which the signers of the Declaration of Independence "mutually pledged our Lives, our Fortunes, and our sacred Honor." . . .

. . . It would be a sorry and ridiculous paradox, in the name of fighting communism to take over, even unconsciously or subconsciously, some of the methods of communism, political or economic.

National ideals, Yes. We should become more familiar with them and live up to them better.

National purpose, as something set apart from the multiple purposes of millions of ambitious, devoted, capable American citizens, No.

7

THE CHANGING
AMERICAN
CHARACTER

Perhaps the greatest challenge of the metropolis will be whether it can effectively cope with the mushrooming autonomous political units to the end that there is a shared concern for urban totality. It seems singular that with all of our development of communications, the "togetherness" of family life, the return to the church, and group emphasis in education and living, we are becoming increasingly aware of a sense of alienation in the metropolitan man's innermost psyche. May this not be the inevitable consequences of life "sealed off" into socioeconomic and racial ghettos?

The system of government established by the framers of the American Constitution rested upon certain fundamental assumptions concerning national character, and the nature of its shaping environment in the United States. It is, by now, trite to emphasize that the institutions of American government described in the Constitution were adapted to the needs and ideals of an agrarian society. They were to be worked by a people characterized by a thirst for knowledge, a genius for social and technological inventiveness, and a sense of individual self-reliance and capacity to deal with one's environment if unhindered by government.

The hardy, individualist, scripture-reading, sober American tiller of the soil may always have been more fancy than fact. Certainly, however, this is a character-type and a way of life that does not predominate today. The phenomena discussed in other sections of this book—industrialization, big business and big labor, the welfare state, television, the hydrogen bomb—have had a profound effect on the values, the way of life, the fears, the anxieties, and the hopes of Americans, and thus have helped shape a new type of individual character. The basic question raised by this chapter is whether this new kind of individual will measure up to the complex and burdensome problems of the sixties and will be competent to make the political institutions of a free society work.

* * *

It has long been fashionable to point to the years 1890 and 1920 as marking, respectively, the settlement of the last frontier in the United States and the ascendancy of the city over the rural way of life. The rise of the city and of the mass industrial plant has fundamentally altered the nature of the influences which shape the character of Americans. In the first reading, "The Impact of Urbanization," Jean Gottmann speaks of the "new frontier." It is not necessarily sloganistic to employ such terms. As long as human beings inhabit the earth, they will be pursuing new frontiers. Where is the new social frontier of the sixties to be found? Will it be a rehabilitated core city offering a richness of cultural opportunity which can be achieved only in an urban context? Is it suburbia, exurbia, or some new pattern of grouping of human beings which would be dimly discernible to us now were we imaginative enough to identify its emerging outlines?

Dan Dodson, in his study of suburban living, takes a much less optimistic view than Gottmann of the impact of our changing patterns of community life on American character. According to Dodson, the suburb is the natural habitat of Riesman's "other-directed" character and Whyte's "organization man," and a bland conformity prevails.

In the third reading, Reuben Hill speaks of the "nuclear family," which—to employ a phrase current in industry—has "spun off" not only functions but also people. Hill suggests that the family still performs important functions for its members. Yet the general trend has been toward a steady constriction of social responsibilities performed by the family—which necessarily implies a steady increase of those which will be demanded of government. For someone must take care of the elderly maiden aunts and grandparents who a century ago might have found economic functions to perform within the self-contained family producing and consuming unit.

But, argues John Lord O'Brian, this is one more factor leading to the general undermining of individual responsibility, the quest for security through the large organization and especially through big government. This is an age, says O'Brian, of a deadening conformity in behavior and in ideas.

There is further cause for concern in Philip Jacob's chilling study of student attitudes. Today's student seems to be fairly tolerant of diversity in opinion and in ethnic origin; but, according to Jacob, it is a conforming kind of tolerance, unattached to deep individual convictions.

Seymour Lipset's analysis challenges the pessimism of Dodson, O'Brian, and Jacob. He does not deny the validity of the kind of approach advanced by Riesman and Whyte, but he thinks that they underestimate the desire for achievement which is still a powerful motivating force in Americans. He suggests that the influence of such writers of the fifties may help to correct the very developments which they are criticizing.

The themes of democracy and equality, conformity and individuality, which run through this chapter, are applied in the next three readings to the American educational system and the character-types it is producing. D. W. Brogan justifies much of what has happened in our educational system in historical terms, but goes on to question whether the present system will suffice for the future. The polemics of this question are set forth here in the selections by Dorothy Thompson and Harold Shane.

Finally, Gabriel Almond examines American values and character attributes as they relate to the kinds of foreign-policy questions discussed in the remaining chapters of this book. In 1950, the assessment he made of American character in this context was not a flattering one. By 1960—in a new Introduction to the book cited here —his estimate had been revised upward. Even so, he is far from saying that we now have the informed, independently thinking, mature citizenry needed to deal with the international challenges of the sixties.

Jean Gottmann

THE IMPACT OF URBANIZATION*

. . . .

Momentum and New Forms of Urbanization

Urban growth is no more a phenomenon affecting only a small fraction of the total population and several isolated spots over a vast country. In the United States the population in urban territory rose from 45.7 percent of the total in 1910 to 64 percent in 1950. The farm population meanwhile declined to 15.3 percent in 1950 and probably to 11.7 percent by April, 1956. Farming is now the occupation of less than 1 out of 10 Americans; more than 90 percent of the nation live from and by activities of an urban type. Similar percentages are being achieved or forecast for many countries in Western Europe advanced in industrialization. The trend is worldwide and appears irreversible: the progress of agricultural techniques and farm mechanization make it possible to produce more agricultural goods with less and less hands. Thus a migration from farm to city goes on and must be accelerated as large numbers come of age in farming areas.

For years the terms urban and rural have represented the major dichotomy in the division of human labor and in the classification of landscapes. On one hand the green countryside was the locale of agricultural production. On the other hand the built-up, crowded, urbanized areas were the sites of manufacturing, trade, government, worship, and recreation. The rural territory extended over almost the whole land and rural life was reputed simple, natural, and healthy. Cities occupied small parcels of land surrounded with walls or bou-

* Jean Gottmann, "The Impact of Urbanization," pp. 180–208. Reprinted from *The Nation's Children*, prepared for The Golden Anniversary White House Conference on Children and Youth, by permission of the National Committee for Children and Youth, copyright holders, and of the Columbia University Press.

Jean Gottmann is Research Director, Study of Megalopolis, Twentieth Century Fund, and Professor, Ecole des Hautes Etudes, University of Paris.

levards, isolated spots amid rural territory, and were usually criticized as offering an artificial, unhealthy, complicated way of life. These old contrasts still exist in underdeveloped parts of the world. They are a tale of bygone days in the more advanced countries and especially in the United States.

Since more than 90 percent of the population now live by pursuits other than farming, i.e., by activities within the categories of industry, trade, services, and government, usually located in cities, urban territory cannot be expected to remain limited to a few small spots on the map. Urbanization has taken on a size and a momentum that has reversed old concepts of simple contrasts between urban and rural. Cities have broken out of old bounds and scattered buildings of urban aspect and functions all over the countryside, thus coming to occupy vast regions. The U.S. Census has had a hard time trying to keep up with these trends. As suburbs mushroomed around the old urban centers defined as *cities*, the Census established first the notion of *urbanized areas*, which consisted mainly of densely built-up territory. Then, in 1940, there was introduced the *metropolitan area*, a wider concept encompassing entire counties whose economy appears tightly dependent on a central city. By 1950 the area of many of these standard metropolitan areas had to be extended and the population of the 174 areas in the continental United States totalled 85.5 million or 57 percent of the nation. In 1950 the majority of Americans lived in metropolitan regions; this does not mean they all lived in densely built-up districts, for a metropolitan area may well include green, rural looking sections, but its inhabitants engage in little agricultural activity and are primarily dependent for their livelihood on the connection with a central city of more than 50,000 people. . . .

. . . The rate of increase of metropolitan population is more than 50 percent faster than the nation's growth. Thus we see that modern urbanization takes on original forms which scatter the urban functions and population around the countryside. While the old migration from farms towards towns goes on, the towns spread out in irregular fashion back into the formerly rural countryside. . . .

The Revolution in Land Use

. . . .

Urbanization, in the modern sense, creates a growing dichotomy between daytime and nighttime populations in large cities. This is reinforced by the housing picture: as the trend of moving out to the periphery accelerates, the old urban core harbors age and decay. The houses emptied by middle-income occupants who prefer to move out to the suburbs or further are taken over by tenants in the lower-income brackets who cannot afford to commute far and who often cannot for reasons of social discrimination find lodging in the highly suburban communities. Negroes and Puerto Ricans are so crowded into the large central cities that some among them commute to jobs in the suburbs. The colored population is increasing faster than the total resident population in Manhattan and Brooklyn, Washington, D.C., Baltimore, Chicago, and Philadelphia. The same trend is notable in smaller cities, especially in the highly urbanized north-east, such as Trenton or Hartford. All these cities have active business districts; but the kinds of people who walk the central city streets in daytime are increasingly different from those who are abroad at night. As urban renewal proceeds in such cities contrasts may sharpen, for some of their central districts attract only affluent residents who can afford the higher costs. Even if they do not decay as residential areas, central cities become sites of great contrasts between opposite extremes of the income scale. This is especially and spectacularly so in New York City and Washington, D.C. In Washington, the urban renewal of Georgetown sharpened the contrast. These growing differences between residents and daytime population are not conducive to social happiness and relaxation of tension.

Another set of contrasting patterns has developed between the different parts of a metropolitan region: in addition to the differences between the population by night and by day and the range of income levels, the suburbs have a different set of economic activities (besides the dormitory function) and an age and educational level substantially at variance with the central cities. The suburban population today as a whole is better educated, and has better housing and more recreational facilities within easy reach than the population in the urban core. With the exception of a few very large cities, the downtown areas of old urban cores are losing a good deal of their special functions as the center of the retail and entertainment trades. The present revolution in land-use results from many factors, among which perfected automobile transportation, the rising standard of living for the average family, and constantly increasing specialization of labor are probably the three main agents. This revolution in land-use ought to bring much improvement to American modes of living, learning, working, and relaxing. Whether the progress of urbanization can be made to serve such improvement is a major responsibility of our time.

Children and Youth in Urbanized Environment

. . . .

. . . Children are being born and reared in the United States largely away from the main urban centers but increasingly not very far away. These statistics result partly from the inheritance of a traditional geographic distribution little related to modern urbanization trends, but partly also from the choice of the parents to move towards the metropolitan periphery. As the youngsters grow closer to coming of age they are increasingly drawn towards the urban centers not only by their work but also for residence. Finally, as the old urban cores have ratios of old and young people below the national average, they have a higher than average ratio of the adult and mature population (i.e., in the ages of twenty-five to sixty-four). This is true even of nighttime residents; the ratio is of course much higher for the daytime population as the commuters into the urban hubs are predominantly in these age brackets. Thus, although children today spend most of their time away from the cities (in the more crowded, densely occupied and built-up sense of the term "city"), they will usually spend at least part of their lives in a highly urbanized environment.

The whole evolution of the labor force indicates the growth of typically urban employment in nonagricultural and nonindustrial types of activities, or, according to a slightly different classification, the expansion of the white-collar labor force over the blue-collar. The vast majority of today's children will spend their later lives in urban or suburban work and residence. The education of most youngsters should therefore be definitely urban-oriented; it should also be more advanced for a larger proportion of the upcoming generation, as an increasing proportion of all jobs require more training, more skill, and involve more responsibility.

The isolated farm and the tightly knit and relatively isolated community of the small town in a truly rural region produce only a small minority of the younger generation. Does the present type of urban and suburban growth benefit the younger strata of the nation? For a long time it was traditionally held that boys from the farms or agricultural areas in general were a "better quality" of men, had more basic virtues—in brief were better prepared for life than city boys. This belief was not only American. It was also generally held in Europe. This writer grew up and went to school in the very crowded and large metropolis of Paris; he was taught, until he became a graduate student, that the farm population was the main strength, the backbone of France. However, he also knew, from everything he heard, that the leadership of the country, the policy makers in every field came from the schools located in the center of Paris to which he and his neighbors went. These two concepts did not seem to him contradictory but rather complementary: the countryside supplied the good solid rank and file; the leadership, predominantly urban, became strong through its rank and file following. But it seemed better taste not to insist on the latter proposition and simply to stress the virtues of rural education in which rural populations eagerly believed.

Systematic sociological studies of the early schooling and adult behavior of farm boys and city boys have exploded the old myth of the superiority of rural origin. A scholarly analysis of the records of the U.S. Armed Forces has recently shown in convincing fashion that the recruits from farming areas were on the whole less prepared for modern life than urban recruits.[1] The advantages of an urban environment for children and youth, especially in the industrialized nations of the West, were to be expected. The better organized and more strictly controlled system of supply of the large urban consuming markets has led to better nutrition. Even today in New York City it is difficult to find children (unless recently arrived there) with serious nutritional deficiencies. Water and milk have been made safer to drink in the large cities, precisely because of the dangers of infection and contamination inherent in the crowding in urban environment. Modern police forces are made necessary by the problems of crowded metropolises; and despite the merited outcry against criminality and juvenile delinquency, it ought to be recognized that people in the great urbanized areas of today are much safer by virtue of the policing and the legislation in force than their ancestors used to be in a rural environment.

The general progress of civilization has brought about improvements in nutrition, health, and security at the same time as it brought about urbanization. There is no direct relationship between, say, urban growth on one hand and better health conditions on the other. The latter could be achieved without the former and vice versa. It has happened at times. However it has been mankind's, and particularly America's experience that in the long run the two proceeded hand in hand. Similarly such modern trends as the rise of juvenile delinquency and of nervous disorders in modern society ought not to be associated too closely, as they often are, with urban growth.

---

[1] Eli Ginzberg *et al.*, *The Ineffective Soldier* (New York: Columbia University Press, 1959), 3 vols. See also to the same effect the results of an analysis of civilian statistics in Eleanor H. Bernert, *America's Children* (New York: Wiley, 1958).

The latter is, like the trends, a simultaneous product of the modern evolution of society; it does not determine them. The evil in society is of course concentrated wherever society itself is gathered. Crowding especially in its beginnings may cause the worst trends to intensify, but it also compensates this effect by working out legal and social antidotes. If it does not the people involved are at fault rather than the impersonal process. In the early nineteenth century, the first stages of the industrial revolution caused crowding of ill-paid industrial workers in slums in many cities. But social evolution has established today in American cities conditions of living and working for youngsters quite different from those denounced by Charles Dickens a century ago.

Today urban areas can confidently claim better organized health and educational services than rural areas. Charities, hospitals, welfare organizations can function better in a large community than in rural areas and the urban communities can afford these services more easily in terms of both adequate financing and competent personnel. If they are lacking, it is not because of the density of population or of the size of the community, but because of the spirit of the people. In India, as a noted sociologist observed, sacred cows flock into the large cities because they know they will find food and care more readily available there! Urbanization, properly managed, should benefit children and adolescents as well as other sections of the population needing help and care. Modern urbanization, however, with its differentiations between place of work and place of residence on one hand, between central city, suburbs, and outer suburbia on the other, requires that more thought and study be given to the new problems and opportunities it has helped to create.

Assets and Liabilities of Urban and Suburban Areas

As the central parts of cities continue to specialize in the functions traditionally concentrated in the "downtown" areas, children residing there may lose some of the advantages previously associated with cities of large size. The financial burden on the city government may become too great for it to maintain adequate services for residents who cannot offer a strong and expanding tax base. The city, having to provide adequate facilities for the noontime tide of business activities finds increasing difficulty in also meeting the welfare, health, educational, and recreation needs of a poorer resident population.

In the suburbs, meanwhile, because of the momentum of the metropolitan sprawl, local government is faced with such a rapid rise in the needs for facilities of all kinds that resources can seldom keep pace with the demand. Many suburban towns have trouble in providing adequate sewage for their rapidly expanding population. The schools are crowded and not always staffed with as qualified teaching personnel as the pupils' parents wish for.

The case of the schools is a constant issue because of the present trends of urbanization. Urban areas normally offer better schools and have a better educated population than the rural regions.

This latter proposition is true today of the suburban towns and of the daytime population of central cities rather than for the residents of old urban cores. . . .

As the many stages of production, agricultural as well as industrial, are being mechanized, employers are growing more insistent on higher educational levels for the average employee. "Completing high school or more" will soon be a prerequisite for most occupations. Cities have attracted so many people for decades because they offered greater economic opportunity; to take advantage of it, educational achievement daily becomes more essential—and an education that can seldom be replaced by early occupational experience. To provide the younger generation with adequate educational opportunity is an imperative necessity for a nation which wants to maintain national progress and the processes of democracy. The difficulties of the central cities and of the expanding suburbs in providing adequate programs for their schools now become disturbing concerns.

In a timely report on the high schools, Dr. James B. Conant stresses the great variety of these encountered throughout the United States. He speaks for a "comprehensive high school" whose programs would correspond to "the educational needs of *all* the youth of the community." But the survey shows that there are seldom entirely comprehensive high schools and the report prefers to speak of a "degree of comprehensiveness." In some cases high schools specialize in preparing their pupils for college and higher education. "High schools whose comprehensiveness is thus limited by the nature of the community are to be found particularly in suburban areas and in high income residential sections of large cities." There are suburban high schools which may not have the same problems in supplying an adequate degree of "comprehensiveness" as the large city high school. Selective academic high schools, designed for the academically talented youth, are found "in many of the Eastern cities of considerable size and in a few of the medium-sized cities." Such specialization of one or a few high schools among many more in that city seems to favor the comprehensiveness of the system as a whole. The

small high school presents more complicated problems: "The enrollment of many American public high schools is too small to allow a
diversified curriculum except at exorbitant expense. The prevalence
of such high schools—those with graduating classes of less than one
hundred students—constitutes one of the serious obstacles to good
secondary education throughout most of the United States."[2]

These remarks indicate that the long-range educational consequences of urbanization will be favorable. The report leaves aside
however the question of adequate financing in the forthcoming years,
when the number of high-school students in the medium-sized cities
and the suburbs will rapidly swell. The conclusions concerning the
small high schools make one wonder about the results of the par-
titioning of the mushrooming suburbs into smaller communities.
Will the less affluent suburban towns find the resources for adequately comprehensive high schools? Moreover, this suburban par-
titioning may affect the children's education in other ways and
before the high-school age.

Years ago, the variety of urban life and the city's activities, its
location at a crossroads, even its crowding, offered a picture of the
world's variety and of society's problems which was stimulating and
often provided the children with enriching experiences. Although it
is possible to spend a long life in a metropolis without seeing anything beyond a closed local circle, urban life offers many incentives
to learn how to feel the pulse of a wide, complicated, striving world.
This is an important aspect of educational opportunity at a time of
rapid change, of growing interregional and international exchanges
and interdependence. Here is an advantage available to youngsters
who fully profit from the urban environment. Some of them will of
course react negatively to the challenge and early build up an
attitude of blasé sophistication, hoping to thus protect themselves
from the on-rushing outside world. . . .

The New Frontier

It may well be claimed that urbanization has created for today and
for some time ahead a new frontier for the American people to
explore and to manage. This new frontier is not simply one of
civilization advancing against the wilderness, a struggle with an
environment of an unknown nature, but rather the reconstruction
and continuous improvement of the areas overrun by modern urban

---

2 James B. Conant, *The American High School Today: A First Report to Interested
Citizens* (New York: McGraw-Hill, 1959), pp. 77–95.

growth. It is the urban renewal in the heart of old cities, the revitalizing of the declining suburbs in the "gray zone," the building of new suburbs, the management of the green areas left in the vicinity of the metropolises. Cities age as they grow, and the task seems one of almost constantly rejuvenating the vast urban regions in which congregate most of the population. This is a frontier left by the past, which the present must not misuse; it is an essential modern aspect of the permanent struggle of mankind for a better and brighter world to live in. A nation engaged upon it can hardly stop on the way without serious prejudice to the next generation; the frontier must be pushed ahead with the needs of the younger section of the population in mind. The sooner the youth can be associated with this great task, the better it will be, for it is a consuming endeavor but one yielding great rewards.

In this great work of expanding and rejuvenating vast urban regions, the United States is today more advanced than any of the other countries in the world. All these countries, with the exception of very few backward lands, feel the impact of on-rushing urbanization. It is a major concern in the U.S.S.R. and Canada, in Britain and Germany, the Netherlands and France, Italy and Denmark, Mexico and Brazil—even the government of Southern Rhodesia has found it necessary to appoint a Commission on Urban Affairs. Many experts and authorities throughout the world are deeply interested in this new facet of the American experiment. They may well look at the impact urban growth will have on the children and youth of America, and especially those in the large metropolitan areas of the Northeast, as a laboratory from which to learn.

Although such attention will be, and is already focused on these areas it does not follow that local solutions or experiments will be easily copied or duplicated. Every student of urban affairs knows how different is every urban area in the practical handling of its problems, and in the possible attempts at solution. Within the United States alone these differences have already proven great. What is true of New York does not necessarily apply to Philadelphia, certainly not to Washington, and even less to Los Angeles. San Francisco and New Orleans are deeply different in almost every aspect of their urban and metropolitan problems, and so are Houston and Kansas City. Each can and must learn from the experience of the others but it must always put the knowledge thus acquired into the local or regional mold before any consequences can be deduced.

Just because urban growth multiplies along a street houses which look alike on the outside does not mean that it standardizes the people who live in them. Urbanization in fact probably brings more variety, movement, and turmoil to society than was ever expected. . . .

Dan W. Dodson

THE EFFECTS OF
SUBURBAN LIVING*

. . . .

The Cultural Dominance of Suburbanism

Since the war, urbanism as a way of life has been on the wane. It is rapidly being replaced by a new type of cultural dominance which can best be described as "suburbanism." In the past decades the urban place dominated its suburbs. Today the suburb dominates the city.

In contrast to the urban cultural values, those of the suburb may be characterized by "a home of one's own" in a development which is large enough to be self-contained; i.e., big enough to have an identified position in the status ordering among other such developments in adjoining sections of the area. The suburban population is extremely homogeneous both in economic status and ethnic background, and often in occupation as well.

The suburban value system is characterized by conformity to middle-class values, "togetherness" and familism in domestic life, and preoccupation with things: the arts of keeping the house painted, the heating system going, and the lawn green—the chores of husbandry. Autonomy is sacrificed to eternal concern with the man next door, who becomes the mirror in which one's life is appraised.

"Suburbanism" is what one authority recently called an "antiseptic" way of life; i.e., nice families segregated into nice homes away from the pollution of both industry and the heterogeneous masses of the inner city. "Suburbanism" has become the style pattern for the total society. That which is smart, chic, worthy of emulation, is suburban. The symbols are the station wagon, the "cook out," and a lawn mower which one can ride. . . .

---

* Dan W. Dodson, "The Effects of Suburban Living," pp. 13 ff. Reprinted from *Children and Youth in the 1960s* prepared for the Golden Anniversary White House Conference on Children and Youth, by permission of the National Committee for Children and Youth, copyright holders.

Dr. Dodson is an Educational Sociologist and Director of the Center for Human Relations and Community Studies, New York University.

The Social Setting of the Suburb

Some description of suburban living will suggest the kinds of impact which suburbanism has on children and youth.

THE SUBURBAN WAY OF LIFE IS A SEGREGATED ONE. Not only is it segregative insofar as racial and other ethnic differences are concerned, but also by socioeconomic status.

The extremes of these suburban types are the Levittowns of New York and Pennsylvania. They differ, however, only in their size and not in their quality from most others. In 1947, the school district which comprised the larger portion of Levittown, New York, had 36 children and 2 teachers in the middle of 6½ square miles of potato fields. In 1954, there were 15,000 homes, 12,500 children in school, and a larger number of preschool children. Residents were almost totally beginning families of an extremely narrow range of income, and not a single one would have been classified by the census as "non-white."

Next to Levittown is Bethpage, New York. Here the suburban expansion has brought more expensive houses—largely of the split-level type of architecture. They attracted those of greater affluence —many from Levittown who had now climbed up the socioeconomic ladder—and families whose children were slightly older.

One gets the impression that these suburban developments are designed for separate stages of the family cycle. Begin in the Levittowns (Cape Cod and small ranch type); as promotions, affluence, and more children come, move to the Bethpages (split levels); then as the children leave the home, move back to the city to small apartment-hotel type accommodations. . . .

THE SUBURB WIDENS THE GAP OF EDUCATIONAL OPPORTUNITIES. Each little political unit of the suburb must supplement the appropriations of the state government for schools and other services. There is a wide disparity of resources with which to meet this need. For instance, Levittown, New York, is a community without any industry. Except for a shopping center, the costs of community services must be provided by residential taxation. With land completely saturated with low-cost housing and such housing occupied by high-welfare-cost families—i.e., families with children to be educated and provided with other such services—the comparative opportunity for the resident of this community is unequal. At the peak of their school enrollment, Levittown will have less than $2,500 per child as a tax base from which to provide schools—this, in a state where the average child, in neighborhoods with comparable ratios of assessment to real value of real estate, has a tax base of $15,000 on which to draw for services. . . .

The opposite extreme from Levittown is the concentration of wealthy families in restricted neighborhoods with low welfare costs and highly assessed estate-type residences. One northern New Jersey community has a restricted estate zoning. The assessed value of the residences averages over $50,000. Here, people of high income provide public schools which vie with plush private schools. In situations where the income is in the higher bracket, a de luxe public school is an inexpensive luxury, for, did he not pay local taxes to support it, he would have to pay most of the cost in income taxes to the Federal Government.

This pattern of suburban inequality will undoubtedly grow in significance. The tendency is to zone for increasingly more expensive residences. The beginning family, started before the breadwinner is established, must then go to the Levittowns or the older slum sections of the community to find a house he can afford. Hence, in the years when the child and his parents need community assistance most, he tends to be relegated to areas which are solidly congested with others who share his plight. The alternative is a subsidy from the parents of the young couple in the beginning years. Either alternative is a "Hobson's Choice" which forebodes real challenges for suburban children in the decade ahead. . . .

Family life

In the suburb the parental roles undergo considerable alteration. The mother becomes the authority figure of the family, since the father is away for such extended periods of the day. . . . Life tends to be oriented around children. . . . The economy of family life centers on consumption rather than production and . . . it is optimistically oriented toward a future. All interests must give way to the efforts toward the child's "upward progress." This validation of upward status for the children is the prime family obligation. . . .

Mental health

While the suburbs provide the clean air, sunshine, and space that are imaged as good for health, there are no data to indicate that suburban children are in fact physically healthier than others. There are some data to indicate that suburbia produces untoward problems of mental health.

The one-class community does not provide the child with a realistic picture of the world around him. There has been observed a lack of spontaneity in play of young children. The child's school time is overorganized. The pressures on children to be popular, to be like all the others and yet maintain their individuality, create conflicts. There is general lack of accepted community standards for teenage behavior. The inexorable pressure to make good grades in order to get into the "right" colleges has frequently created hostilities toward academic curiosity. . . .

. . . Life in the suburbs is harder on boys than girls. It is believed that this is due to the absence of a significant male figure with which to identify, because of the father's excessive absence from home while commuting.

Conformity

One of the greatest criticisms lodged against the suburb is the pressure it engenders for conformity. Here again, the problem of separating out those factors which the suburb, per se, engenders, as against the pressures which are engendered by a mass culture, is difficult. Riesman[1] tends to assess the change in the national character from "inner directedness" to "other directedness" as the result of the emergence of a consumer economy. Whyte[2] assesses the change in character, the loss of the Protestant ethic, and the growth of emphasis on group structure in both child rearing and industrial organization. Both would seem to agree on the change in national character, and both seem to place the major responsibility for it on mass culture.

On the other hand, there is considerable indication that suburban living may play a significant role in such character change. At the peak of its youth population, Levittown, barring a mass exodus, will have close to 10,000 teenage youths of school age on the 6½ square miles of soil.

To serve this youth group there are only negligible institutional facilities. Resident families have comparable incomes and comparable social status. There are few relatives, such as uncles, aunts, and grandparents, to provide a link with other generations and older cultures. Inevitably, young people find themselves growing up in an environment where services tend to be on a mass basis.

---

[1] David Riesman, *The Lonely Crowd*, New Haven: Yale University Press, 1950; "The Suburban Dislocation," *The Annals of the American Academy of Political and Social Science*, Vol. 314, November 1957, pp. 123 ff.

[2] William H. Whyte, Jr., *The Organization Man*. New York: Simon and Schuster, Inc., 1956.

In such a circumstance one would expect the development of what some have called a "youth culture" which would revolt from the generation above them. Such, however, is not the case according to Westley and Elkin. They say:

> . . . the adolescents live in a protective environment; their lives are in full view of the adults; their world is relatively consistent and integrated, and they have little direct acquaintance with other patterns of thought and behavior. In this environment adolescents, by the age of 14 or 15, have already well internalized the ideals and values of the surrounding adult society. The adolescents appreciate the keen interest of the parents in their activity and feel that their parents are working in their behalf; they are in close agreement with their parents on general career and marriage goals and the manner in which these goals are to be achieved; they recognize the value of the parental attitudes toward financial matters and the training they receive in saving and handling allowances; they do not reject adult values or participate in an antiadult "youth culture"; and they tend to look at their distinctive adolescent activities from a relatively sophisticated and integrated point of view.[3]

Social class as a factor

There seems to be general agreement that social class is a factor in suburban living. The migration to the suburbs has largely been limited to those who could afford to buy a house and pay the commuting costs. Although communities vary from each other in socioeconomic level, each is nevertheless extremely homogeneous, with values oriented toward the middle class. The concentrations bring together, then, masses of people with aspirations and expectations which must be achieved in a social milieu of peers.

In Scarsdale, New York, an upper level income community, *the average IQ* of the top 20 percent of the Scarsdale student body is at the level of the top 2.5 percent of students of the entire nation. The upper half at Scarsdale is at the level of the top 8 percent in the nation. The lowest of the Scarsdale student body is at the level of the national average. Over 90 percent, and in some years as high as 95 percent, of the Scarsdale high school graduates go on to higher education. . . . The anxiety of parents to get their children into the "right" colleges means that there were pressures to "overplace" the student so that grades made and honors awarded in college were not in proportion to the seeming ability. . . .

---

[3] William Westley and Frederick Elkin, "The Protective Environment and Adolescent Socialization," *Social Forces*, 35, 1957, p. 249.

These citations are not to indicate that all the pressures to achieve, or all the anxieties about college placement are in the suburbs, nor is it to say that other segments of the population do not also have "great expectations" for their children. They do mean that when a class becomes segregated into homogeneous neighborhoods where roles must be validated by social class peers, the pressures are heightened, and the concerns mount.

Not infrequently, parental concern leads to bribes, what some youths are calling "academic payola," to get the children to work harder in school. One New York suburb reported recently that several parents had offered their children a vacation "on their own" in Florida at the semester break if they would work hard and achieve agreed-upon grades for the semester.

There is a growing concern for what this indicates about the values in such a society. It represents a seeking for grades as ends in themselves, or as status symbols, rather than a preoccupation with study for the sake of academic curiosity. It suggests a pressure from middle-class parents which strikes at the heart of more basic values. . . .

Suburbia in perspective

Most of the literature has tended to point to the limitations of suburban living. One gains an impression that there is a great need for research to fill the gap which would assess what are undoubtedly positive aspects of such a way of life. For example, the emphasis on family relationships is something most sociologists would have called "good" in other times and climates. In spite of the conflicts which erupt as people are delineating for themselves new status roles, there is a sense of community which must offer some inner resource to those who live in such places. . . .

Perhaps the greatest challenge of the metropolis will be whether it can effectively cope with the mushrooming autonomous political units to the end that there is a shared concern for urban totality. It seems singular that with all of our development of communications, the "togetherness" of family life, the return to the church, and group emphasis in education and living, we are becoming increasingly aware of a sense of alienation in the metropolitan man's innermost psyche. May this not be the inevitable consequence of life "sealed off" into socioeconomic and racial ghettos?

In the inner city, today, is left one of the few places in America where man can still make outreach to his fellow man across lines of race, nationality or creed. Symbolically, the inner city represents the whole—mainstream in a unique sense. One cannot leave it without sensing that he is leaving the "center of things." These heterogeneous populations represent for us all "the stranger" with which we must come to grips if we are to validate our sense of selfhood with the broad stream of human kind.

Whatever our protestations of faith and democratic ideals, our children learn what they are living. The suburb teaches not what we say, but what our behaviors indicate. How to preserve the advantages of the suburb and recapture our sense of community with the total metropolis is perhaps our greatest task ahead.

Reuben Hill

THE AMERICAN FAMILY TODAY*

. . . .

"What's Wrong with the Family?" A wide variety of writers have addressed themselves to this theme recently. . . . They point to the high divorce rate, to the changes in our sex morality, to juvenile delinquency, and to the rise in forced marriages of teenagers as proof of the breakdown of the family. . . .

I regard much of this hue and cry in the public press as useful and healthy, but I do not have too much confidence in the diagnoses advanced by America's self-styled family experts. . . . The social scientist studying the family takes the comparative approach and asks what troubles experienced by the American family are also reported for families in industrializing and urbanizing societies in other parts of the world. From this vantage point it is possible to conclude

---

* Reuben Hill, "The American Family Today," pp. 76–107. Reprinted from *The Nation's Children*, prepared for The Golden Anniversary White House Conference on Children and Youth, by permission of the National Committee for Children and Youth, copyright holders.

Mr. Hill is Director of the Minnesota Family Study Center and Professor of Sociology at the University of Minnesota.

that many of the disorders of the American family appear to be "growing pains," discomforts incident to adaptive change, normal symptoms of reorganization following adjustment to a new and baffling industrial urban society. . . .

One can recognize in [the] majority family pattern of the nineteenth century many characteristics which have survived into the twentieth century: freedom of mate selection, separate domicile for newlyweds (although one couple in five begins marriage even today in the home of one of the parental families), parental subsidy of marriage (although the support today may need to be more subtle and less openly admitted). In other respects there have been tremendous changes as America has industrialized and urbanized, changes which we identify as long-term trends: changed ways of making a living, decreased self-sufficiency of families, smaller households, increased mobility of families, changed authority patterns, and changed age and sex roles within the family, to mention only a few. Activities once centered in the home, such as production of food and clothing, family recreation, vocational apprenticing, and religious instruction, have been shifted to canneries, factories, recreation centers, vocational schools, and Sunday Schools.

From 1890 to 1960 the proportion of American families subsisting from farming changed from almost half to less than one-tenth. With this changed mode of making a living, the authoritarian, economically integrated, self-sufficient form of family which for centuries had been functionally adapted to rural living has become obsolete. As the family ceased to be a producer of goods and services, the need for an authoritarian foreman in the family disappeared. But as the family ceased to make its own living, and the father left the home to earn money to buy the goods the family once produced, the self-sufficiency of the family also disappeared. The rugged familism which extended the frontier and gave the tenor of individualism to America has disappeared except as it is found in isolated rural and mountain areas.

The family became dependent upon the availability of jobs, on continued prosperity, and on the productivity of the wage earner. Where the father's productivity was not great enough, mothers left the home to supplement the father's pay check. Children, once viewed as potential added hands who soon could earn their keep, have become in the industrial age mouths to feed, bodies to clothe, and minds to educate. Today children are financial liabilities from birth through their schooling. Conservative estimates place the cost of rearing a child to age eighteen at $20,000, and there is still his college education ahead of him.

In order to get ahead in the world young families have become mobile, migrating for added education, better jobs, and in response to the demands of military service. Compared with other countries of the world we are a people on wheels—1 family in 5 moves annually and 1 in 3 of these crosses county lines every year.

In the course of these long-term shifts in the economy and the larger society the family has given up many services it once provided its members: schooling, religious instruction, recreation, medical care, and job placement. Many see in these changes evidences of family decay and disorganization, but I find abundant proof that there is no repudiation of the basic business of families; namely, reproduction, housing, feeding, socializing, and guiding children from infancy to adulthood. Indeed, the family, is now more of a specialized agency concentrating on personality development of its members, providing warmth, love, and sanctuary from the anonymity of urban existence, services no other agency in society is prepared to offer. . . .

As a consequence of . . . younger age. at marriage, changes in child spacing, as well as changed ways of making a living and the changed emphasis on services performed in the family—the relationships between husband and wife and between children and parents have changed sharply with respect to the locus of power and in the division of duties and responsibilities in the family. Wives and children are becoming economic partners with the husband-father in spending as well as in earning the family income. The family is becoming democratized in the process.

Participation by wives in family decision making extends beyond financial matters and is concurrently being strengthened by their higher education, wider contact outside the home, exercise of responsibility in civic associations, activities in professional organizations, and by explicit encouragement by experts. Male pretensions to superior authority are widely ridiculed in contemporary comedy, cartoons, children's literature, and other forms of popular art. Moreover, when family decision making is viewed as a symbol of power the superiority of shared power in creating and maintaining warmth and affection becomes evident. It is easier to love a reasonable, companionable man, and harder to love an authoritarian husband and father today. . . .

Not only are parents professionalizing their marital and parental roles, they are undertaking once again training of the child for the job world, not by providing technical skills but by helping him in human relations. The child must learn the nuances of interpersonal relations to function in the large and complex organizations of industry, business, and government. The child must study his own relations to others and gain better control over himself and his associates. Parents in the professions today do have relevant, hard-bought skills to make the critical judgments of social situations that their children will need. . . . In sum, parents have learned that in the contemporary world, a parent is far better advised to endow his child with competence in interpersonal relations than to leave him with "a competence" in the old sense of the word. . . .

. . . Is the family any less important to its members and to American society than formerly?

It must be granted that the present-day family is not the giant in numbers and functions that it was a century ago. We no longer count as members of our families our kin out to third cousins on either side, and often forget both sets of grandparents and any great-grandparents when we reckon our family size. The modern family, shorn of kinship attachments and bearing two to four children, is smaller and less of an all-purpose organization—but is it therefore less important?

It would be a mistake to assume that because many families are free floating and geographically rootless, most urban families are separated from significant supportive relationships. Recent studies in London, Detroit, Cleveland, and Minneapolis attest to the perseverance of reciprocal relationships of gift giving, visiting, mutual aid, and advice seeking between grandparents and their married children, and between nuclear families and their kinfolk. In charting the social network of families they still tend to list relatives above friends and neighbors as the first place to turn when crisis strikes.

Yet there have also been social losses in the streamlining and specializing of the modern family. The modern nuclear family focuses primarily on the maintenance of the marriage and the provision of services to the immediate offspring of the marriage. In specializing, the family has not only given up *services* once provided by the traditional family but it has given up *people* who once could find a meaningful place there: maiden aunts, bachelor uncles, widowed and orphaned kin, and grandparents. As a consequence, many more individuals today live outside organized family groups in semi-isolation from the love and support families might give them.

American families are on the whole probably happier than they were in earlier times, yet so much is asked of marriage and the family today that many otherwise sound families experience relative deprivation. The standards of success today go beyond providing and getting ahead economically, beyond the maintenance of minimum goals of health and education for children, to include happiness and self-realization. Few families appear to measure up, yet every man regards a happy marriage as his right. The defects of the modern family develop primarily from the disabilities of the specific persons who marry and rear children. If greater stability of the family is ever to be assured, increasing the competence of young people in interpersonal relations and selecting people for marriage who are ready for parental responsibilities must be undertaken much more systematically.

Granting that marriages today are intrinsically less enduring, evidence can be brought to show that they are greatly improved in quality of performance and are more stimulating climates in which to rear children. In addition, the modern family has the virtue of fitting well the demands of our democratic and urban industrial society, something that would have been impossible to the larger, rooted, and authoritarian family of the past century. . . .

John Lord O'Brian

NATIONAL SECURITY AND INDIVIDUAL FREEDOM*

. . . .

It was not so many years ago that Professor Whitehead, with his urbane optimism and out of the wealth of his profound learning, assured us "that there is a freedom lying beyond circumstance de-

---

* Reprinted by permission of the publishers from John Lord O'Brian, *National Security and Individual Freedom,* The Godkin Lectures at Harvard, 1955, Cambridge, Mass.: Harvard University Press, Copyright, 1955, by The President and Fellows of Harvard College.

John Lord O'Brian is an attorney who has served in a number of Administrations, in various capacities.

rived from the direct intuition that life can be grounded upon its absorption in what is changeless amid change."[1] But since those words were spoken, the new and startling discoveries of science have raised a cloud of doubts which, we are told, will inevitably affect some of our oldest convictions on the nature of physical life, on man's relationship to the universe, and more particularly, on the problems of human destiny. As J. Robert Oppenheimer has told us, continuous change, accompanied by unaccountable variants, appears to be the only settled law of nature's processes, and the greatest of the changes that science has brought us is "the acuity of change." Dr. Oppenheimer has also warned us that our world is "a new world in which the unity of knowledge, the nature of human communities, the order of society, the order of ideas, the very notions of society and culture have changed and will not return to what they have been in the past."[2]

Although it is impossible to predict the ultimate result of these new conceptions, there is no doubt that for the time being they have had a most disturbing effect, have created problems presently insoluble, and have obscured our sense of values.

Other critical developments during the last generation have provided fresh emphasis for reconsideration of the status of the individual in today's society. Until recently we could rejoice in the statement of Mr. Justice Brandeis that "the right to be left alone by the Government is the most comprehensive of rights and the right most valued by civilized man."[3] But as far back as 1940 Professor McIlwain had sounded the warning that "never in recorded history has the individual been in greater danger from Government than now."[4] Even earlier John Dewey and others had warned that the fundamental beliefs and practices of democracy were being challenged as they never had been before. It is noteworthy that these considered statements were made before we entered upon the Second World War. To many serious-minded students today this warning seems even more impressive and minatory.

In the field of economics we have witnessed the emergence of a highly industrialized and interdependent society with its component elements of conflicting forces. The pressures from these develop-

---

[1] Alfred N. Whitehead, *Adventures of Ideas* (New York, 1933), p. 86.

[2] J. Robert Oppenheimer, "Transcience Is the Backdrop of the Play of Human Progress," *Science and the Common Understanding* (New York, 1954), p. 89; and Oppenheimer, in *Man's Right to Knowledge*, 2nd series, Columbia University (New York, 1954), p. 111.

[3] Olmstead v. U.S. (diss.), 277 U.S. 438, 478 (1928).

[4] Charles Howard McIlwain, *Constitutionalism, Ancient and Modern* (Ithaca, 1040).

ments are operating, as they have for some decades, in the direction of diminishing the freedom of the individual and decreasing his importance in contrast to what is thought to be the general welfare. Paradoxically the enactment of social legislation, much of it long overdue, has tended to intensify the desire of the citizen to obtain an even greater degree of economic security.

In fact, although objectives of the welfare state are certainly worthy objectives, we must admit that this great concept has to a substantial degree encouraged growth in the idea of the supremacy of the state over the status of the individual. The concentration of power and growth of centralized authority in different national industries, and even in the larger labor unions, everywhere tends to induce conformity and acquiescence.

The same pressures have long been apparent in the field of education, where interference by politicians, pressure groups, and intolerant busybodies is tragically frequent—and in some cases is injuriously effective. That the weight of mass opinion constantly tends to smother the individual's sense of initiative and independence is an elemental truth long since verified by experience. The processes of mass education and the use of mass media of communication, such as the continuous drum-fire of the radio announcers, are tending to make mediocrity the accepted standard and to reduce the intrinsic importance of the individual citizen. The current evolution in steadily expanding mechanization must inevitably have the same effect.[5]

It is an understatement to emphasize that one of the principal influences which threaten the very existence of democracy is the all-pervasive craving for security at any price. The two wars, the desperate experience of the great depression, and the threat of atomic warfare have all strengthened this desire. No doubt its growth has been fostered by national legislative policies in the field of economics, such as the various agricultural acts, the establishment of social security with its concomitants of old-age relief, unemployment compensation, pensions, guaranteed wages, and so on.

---

[5] "What menaces Democratic society in this age is not a simple collapse of order nor yet usurpation by a single powerful individual, but a tyranny of mediocrity, a standardization of mind and spirit and condition enforced by the Central Government" (Russell Kirk, The Conservative Mind (Chicago, 1953), p. 181).

In his recent book Walter Lippmann expresses grave anxiety over the mounting power acquired by mass opinion in the twentieth century, which, he asserts, has already shown itself to be a dangerous master of indecision when the stakes are life and death. He also emphasizes, as a surprising development, that the enfranchised masses have not been the ones who have most staunchly defended the institutions of freedom (The Public Philosophy, Boston, 1955, pp. 20, 40).

Another consideration of the greatest importance in affecting our sensitiveness to the rights of the individual and his freedom is the corrosive effect of the last war and the reëmergence of totalitarianism as an aggressive force during the last few decades. One of the most disturbing symptoms of our time is the casual way in which our people are already endeavoring to forget the events of that catastrophic period. Let us recall for a moment some of the happenings:

In that period millions and millions of innocent persons were deliberately murdered and unspeakable practices of torture were revived on a wholesale scale. Every primary value treasured by Western civilization was and still is under attack. Numberless innocent persons suffered depths of agony beyond belief. Macabre methods of devilish ingenuity were devised to debase the minds and spirits of human beings and even to destroy their personalities. Slave labor under the most abominable conditions was revived and practiced on a scale undreamed of heretofore. Perfidy has been erected into a principle of state policy.

These atrocities, this descent into brutality and bestiality, required the participation of hundreds of thousands of men, civilians as well as soldiers, and the brutalizing effect upon them, as well as their influence upon others, is something that only the future can measure. Looking at the distortion of values in Europe, no man today can prophesy how this vast quantum of human suffering, despair, and resentment will affect, as it is bound to do, the thinking of civilized man in the coming generations. The memory of these bitter and terrifying spectacles we deliberately seek to put aside; yet it is a platitude to say that no barriers can ever protect us from the imponderable and evil influences that must result from these tragedies. Already as a nation we are suffering from the impact of a disorganized external world and from the widespread challenges of "modern barbarism." But the effect of poisonous ideologies upon our internal affairs is only one aspect of the danger. The other aspect is the effect upon our nation's prestige and capacity for moral leadership in the outside world if we weaken in maintaining those principles of justice and fair play which in the past have given American civilization its distinctive quality.

I have mentioned the intellectual claims of the nuclear scientists, the shattering events of the war, the emergent totalitarianism, and the unprecedented power of the forces making for intolerance and conformity because throughout a great part of the civilized world these influences have all but obliterated any respect for the sanctity of the individual. The combination of these influences has produced, even in this country, a climate of opinion increasingly conducive to the depreciation of the rights of the individual by the exercise of governmental functions. The same forces also tend inevitably to weaken the individual's sense of responsibility for government. And here we approach a crucial threat to our society, for the oldest and most serious danger to the democratic state is the growth of complacency and indifference toward the processes of government and the difficulty of combating this danger.

It is generally agreed that at least one of the chief causes of the decline and disintegration of ancient society was the gradual withdrawal from the citizen of any real responsibility as well as any adequate opportunity to participate in functions of local government. Any influence, from whatever source, that tends to decrease the citizen's sense of personal responsibility for the integrity of his government is a source of danger to the democratic state. In the light of three centuries of political evolution, no historical fact is better settled than this. It is eternal struggle as well as eternal vigilance that is the price of liberty; for the problem of how to encourage and preserve the individual's sense of responsibility for his government is a new problem for every generation.

Since our recognition of the welfare state the problem has taken on new aspects. As described by the late Justice Jackson, the citizen is confronted with new temptations in appraising the essential values:

> It seems to me that these traditional freedoms are less in danger of any sudden overthrow than of being gradually bartered or traded for something else on which the people place a higher current value. In this anxiety-ridden time, many are ready to exchange some of their liberties for a real or fancied increase in security against external foes, internal betrayers or criminals. Others are eager to bargain away local controls for a federal subsidy. Many will give up individual rights for promise of collective advantages. The real question posed by the Fascist and Communist movements, which together have captivated a large part of the world's population, is whether today, liberty is regarded by the masses of men as their most precious possession. Certainly in the minds of many foreign peoples our type of individual liberty has been outvalued by promises of social welfare and economic security, which they want too passionately to be critical of the price. If this indifference to traditional values should spread to us, it would be the greatest threat to our own liberties.[6]

---

[6] Robert H. Jackson, "The Task of Maintaining Our Liberties: The Role of the Judiciary," *American Bar Association Journal,* XXXIX (November 1953).

Does not this go to the very heart of our overall problem?

Recently Chief Justice Warren expressed much the same anxiety in declaring that the times in which we are living are not normal times and that the interplay of hope and fear, belief and doubt, determination and frustration, are keeping the affairs of mankind and the minds of people in a state of turbulence—a turbulence that destroys perspective and clouds the vision. He also emphasizes that, entirely apart from the totalitarian menace, the emotional influence of the times, coupled with the latent suspicion and prejudice inherent in human nature, may prove a threat to the basic rights of everyone. . . .

Review of the policies established by the Congress and the Executive for the purpose of combating subversive activities and influences will demonstrate, I think, that in reality we have been establishing something like a new system of preventive law applicable to the field of ideas essentially and different from traditional American procedures. . . .

Officials frequently assert that these various procedures and practices do not amount to "thought control." Yet surely, disregarding semantics, it cannot be denied that they operate to promote conformity and standardization, as well as to constrain the freedom of thought and of association on the part of the individual. . . .

Philip E. Jacob

ATTITUDES OF COLLEGE STUDENTS*

. . . .

A dominant characteristic of students in the current generation is that they are *gloriously contented* both in regard to their present day-to-day activity and their outlook for the future. Few of them are worried—about their health, their prospective careers, their

* From *Changing Values in College* by Philip E. Jacob, pp. 1–5. Copyright (c) 1957, by Harper & Brothers. Reprinted by permission of the publishers.

Dr. Jacob is Professor of Political Science, University of Pennsylvania.

family relations, the state of national or international society or the likelihood of their enjoying secure and happy lives. They are supremely confident that their destinies lie within their own control rather than in the grip of external circumstances.

The great majority of students appear unabashedly *self-centered.* They aspire for material gratifications for themselves and their families. They intend to look out for themselves first and expect others to do likewise.

But this is not the individualistic self-centeredness of the pioneer. American students fully accept the conventions of the contemporary business society as the context within which they will realize their personal desires. They cheerfully expect to conform to the economic status quo and to receive ample rewards for dutiful and productive effort. They anticipate no die-hard struggle for survival of the fittest as each seeks to gratify his own desires, but rather an abundance for all as each one teams up with his fellow self-seekers in appointed places on the American assembly-line.

Social harmony with an *easy tolerance of diversity* pervades the student environment. Conformists themselves, the American students see little need to insist that each and every person be and behave just like themselves. They are for the most part (with some allowance for sectional difference) ready to live in a mobile society, without racial, ethnic or income barriers. But they do not intend to crusade for non-discrimination, merely to accept it as it comes, a necessary convention in a homogenized culture.

The traditional *moral virtues are valued* by almost all students. They respect sincerity, honesty, loyalty, as proper standards of conduct for decent people. But they are not inclined to censor those who choose to depart from these canons. Indeed they consider laxity a prevalent phenomenon, even more prevalent than the facts seem to warrant. Nor do they feel personally bound to unbending consistency in observing the code, especially when a lapse is socially sanctioned. For instance, standards are generally low in regard to academic honesty, systematic cheating being a common practice rather than the exception at many major institutions.

Students normally express a *need for religion* as a part of their lives and make time on most weekends for an hour in church. But there is a "ghostly quality" about the beliefs and practices of many of them, to quote a sensitive observer. Their religion does not carry over to guide and govern important decisions in the secular world. Students expect these to be socially determined. God has little to do with the behavior of men in society, if widespread student judgment be accepted. His place is in church and perhaps in the home, not in business or club or community. He is worshipped, dutifully and with propriety, but the campus is not permeated by a live sense of His presence.

American students are likewise *dutifully responsive towards government*. They expect to obey its laws, pay its taxes, serve in its armed forces—without complaint but without enthusiasm. They will discharge the obligations demanded of them though they will not voluntarily contribute to the public welfare. Nor do they particularly desire an influential voice in public policy. Except for the ritual of voting, they are content to abdicate the citizen's role in the political process and to leave to others the effective power of governmental decision. They are politically irresponsible, and often politically illiterate as well.

This disposition is reflected in *strangely contradictory attitudes towards international affairs*. Students predict another major war within a dozen years yet international problems are the least of the concerns to which they expect to give much personal attention during their immediate future. The optimism with which they view their prospects for a good long life belies the seriousness of their gloomy prophecy. They readily propose some form of supra-national government as a means of preventing war, but a very large number display only a limited knowledge of and confidence in the United Nations as an instrument of cooperative international action.

Turning to their immediate preoccupation, the pursuit of an education, students by and large *set great stock by college* in general and their own college in particular. The intensity of their devotion varies quite a little bit with the institution and sometimes with the nature of the students' educational goals. And the real point of the devotion is not the same for all. Only a minority seem to value their college education primarily in terms of its intellectual contribution, or its nurturing of personal character and the capacity for responsible human relationships. Vocational preparation, and skill and experience in social "adjustment" head the rewards which students crave from their higher education. . . .

Against the background of earlier generations, these values of today's students look different. The undergirding of the Puritan heritage on which the major value assumptions of American society have rested is inconspicuous, if it is present at all. Perhaps these students are the forerunners of a major cultural and ethical revolution, the unconscious ushers of an essentially secular (though nominally religious), self-oriented (though group-conforming) society. . . .

The values of the college graduate do differ in some respects from the rest of the society. He is more concerned with status, achievement and prestige. Proportionately more college graduates distrust "welfare economics" and "strong" government than in the country at large. Paradoxically they tend to be somewhat more tolerant and less repressive of "radical" ideas and unconventional people, also less prejudiced towards minority groups and alien cultures. They share few of the cold-war suspicions of the subversiveness of college faculties, nor do they support the popular stereotype of the colleges' godlessness. Religiously, they may be less superstitious or other-worldly than their fellow countrymen. The college man or woman thus tends to be more self-important—more conservative—more toler-ant—and less fearful of evil forces in this world and outside than those who have not been "higher-educated." . . .

Seymour M. Lipset

EQUALITY AND ACHIEVEMENT IN AMERICAN LIFE*

. . . Change in basic institutions can most fruitfully be interpreted if we assume that the interplay between the democratic equalitarian ideal and the strong achievement orientation in America has been a *continuing* theme throughout American history.

This thesis differs significantly from those interpretations of change in American society which have had most popular acceptance since 1930. The writers of the 1930's would have disagreed with the emphasis here on the continued strength of equalitarianism, and

---

* Seymour M. Lipset, "Trends in American Society." From *An Outline of Man's Knowledge of the Modern World* by Lyman Bryson, pp. 411–417. Copyright (c) 1960 by Catherine McGrattan Bryson, Executrix of the estate of Lyman Bryson. Reprinted by permission of Doubleday & Company, Inc. and published by McGraw-Hill Book Company, Inc.

Dr. Lipset is Professor of Sociology, University of California, Berkeley; Visiting Ford Research Professor of Political Science, Yale University, 1960–61.

analyses which have appeared in the 1950's suggest that the achievement norm has lost much of its significance. Men writing in the 1930's, like Robert S. Lynd, Harold Laski, and W. Lloyd Warner, all agreed that the equalitarian emphasis in American democracy was declining sharply under the impact of the growth of the large-scale corporation, monopoly capitalism, and economic competition. Twenty years later, these interpretations are rejected by almost everyone as wrong. Warner has implicitly acknowledged his error. In one of his most recent works he documents the increased opportunity as compared with the 1920's for men to rise into the top echelons of the largest corporations of the country.

In the 1950's David Riesman and William H. Whyte have suggested that the achievement motive and the Protestant ethic of hard work are dying and that society now values security, emotional stability, and getting along with others. Riesman's main thesis is that there has been a change in the American character structure, from the inner-directed individual oriented toward the fulfilling of powerful Protestant personal ideals to other-directed persons strongly concerned with securing direction from other people. Rather than changes in basic character structure, Whyte suggests that values as such have changed. He argues that the old Protestant ethic which he defines as "the pursuit of individual salvation through hard work, thrift, and competitive struggle" is vanishing to be replaced by "a belief in the group as the source of creativity; and a belief in the application of science to achieve the belongingness."

In large measure, this contrast between the men of the 1930's and those of the 1950's reflects the difference between observing a society in the middle of the greatest depression in history, and analyzing the same society during the longest and most prosperous economic boom which it has ever experienced. The Depression of the 1930's led men to view America through equalitarian eyes, and to see capitalism and achievement orientation as the source of "evils." Even conservatives such as Warner emphasized the growth of inequality and restrictions on opportunity. The prosperity of the 1950's, on the other hand, has involved giving legitimacy again to many basically conservative American institutions and values, and has spurred efforts to eliminate some of the innovations of the leftist 1930's. The social analyses of the 1950's usually involve at least a critique of the equalitarian excesses of the former period, if not a critique of equalitarian values themselves.

While Riesman and Whyte insist that they are simply analyzing changes, with both good and bad features, it seems fairly evident that, like the many conservative travelers of the nineteenth century, they dislike many of the dominant trends. Neither Riesman nor Whyte explicitly asserts that there is more conformity in contemporary America than in the past, for men have always conformed to the basic values of the day. But both argue that contemporary values and personality traits emphasize accommodating to others, while the declining Protestant ethic and inner-directed personalities stressed conformity not to others but to a basic set of behavior norms.

This reaction against the seeming decline in the Protestant ethic of achievement and hard work, which has emerged as a dominant theme among the intellectual middle-classes in the 1950's, should be viewed as the counterpart of the concern with the seeming decline of equality which moved comparable groups in the 1930's. The differences in the concerns of the two decades illustrate the important point that although the equalitarian ethos of the American Revolution and the achievement orientation associated with the Protestant ethic are mutually supportive, they also involve normative conflict. Complete commitment to equality requires rejection of some of the assumptions of achievement, and the opposite is true as well. When the values of equality which are associated with left or liberal political forces are dominant, there is a reaction against achievement. And when the values of achievement are dominant in a conservative political and economic atmosphere, men tend to deprecate some of the consequences of equality, such as the influence of the taste of the majority on culture.

The supremacy of equalitarian values and liberal politics in the 1930's was reflected in the school system in the triumph of progressive education, a movement always associated with left-of-center leaders and ideologies; in industry, by the introduction of the human relations approach as an attempt to resist the growing strength of unions by "keeping the worker happy"; and in the society at large, by efforts at a general redistribution of goods and services. Social scientists and others concerned with family structure criticized the supposed typical middle-class family as too authoritarian and rigid in its treatment of children, and suggested that this middle-class family (as contrasted with the more democratic and affectionate working-class family) bred "authoritarian" and "neurotic" personalities. Popular psychology saw the "competitive personality" of our time as the source of many personal and social evils. Historians pictured the creators of American industry as "robber barons" and irresponsible exploiters of American resources.

The strength of this liberal equalitarian ethos was perhaps most manifest in the school system, where educators stressed the goal of giving equal treatment to all, regardless of status or intellectual differences. Extra encouragement of the gifted child was rejected as "special privilege" and as a source of psychic punishment for the less gifted. Instead personality adjustment for *all* was the objective. Clearly, the underlying philosophy of the 1930's regarded competition as bad, and ideally favored a completely equalitarian society.

In the 1950's, these tendencies have been almost completely reversed. Big business and business careers are once more legitimated. . . . Although Keynesian economics remains official government policy, and is still supported by the bulk of economists, men have arisen to high status in that field who oppose almost all government intervention. Studies of the social structure of the family have reversed the findings of the 1930's, and suggest that the working-class family is more likely to be a source of "authoritarian" personality traits. Vulgarizations of the theses of Riesman and Whyte are now published in many magazines and are cited at P.T.A. meetings all over the country, where outraged middle-class parents demand a return to "old-fashioned" methods of teaching in which hard work and special support of the gifted are stressed.

To point out that these divergent interpretations of American social trends are to some extent associated with the political and economic cycle is not to suggest that they are simply ideological reflections of material conditions or of the dominant intellectual atmosphere. Both have pointed to genuine aspects of the culture and in so doing have improved our understanding of the functions of different institutions and values. Both the equalitarian and the achievement value strands in the United States remain strong, but changing conditions sometimes strengthen one at the expense of the other, or change the internal content of each. As the possibility of building up a major enterprise of one's own has declined, it has been replaced by the opportunity to move up the bureaucratic elite. The politics of liberalism and equality have fostered institutional changes, such as the constant spread of public education and training plans within corporations, which have increased opportunities for advancement.

Similarly, it may be argued that the work orientation has not declined. In the midst of the greatest prosperity in history, the U.S. Census reports that in the summer of 1957, three and a half million workers, 5.5 percent of the labor force, had two jobs, with the second job averaging 12 hours per week. In Akron, Ohio, where many workers in the rubber factories are on a six-hour day, six-day week, at relatively high pay and where a sizeable proportion of wives are employed, it is estimated that nearly 40 percent of the men engage in some sort of part-time outside work. Trade unions such as the

United Automobile Workers and the International Longshoremen and Warehousemen's Union have found that enforced retirement has deleterious effects on the social life and physical health of the mem-bers, who in fact prefer work to leisure, a phenomenon that is com-pletely incomprehensible to workers from many European and Latin American countries.

Whyte and Riesman have, of course, been primarily concerned with the work attitudes of the urban middle classes, particularly those employed in the white-collar and executive hierarchies of large organizations who are most exposed to the pressures to conform, to accommodating rather than work-oriented behavior. Again it seems hard to justify many of their conclusions about value change even among these groups. As Whyte brilliantly pointed out, in corpora-tions where the managers are not the owners, there is a strong em-phasis on group activities rather than individual responsibility. What-ever else the concern with group dynamics in industry may reflect, it may also be viewed as an excellent mechanism to motivate men to work hard for the company. Men do not work as hard as they are able when the rewards of their work seem to be going to others, whether in the eighteenth or twentieth century. No one works as hard as the head of an organization, or the self-employed, or the creative professional who is directly rewarded for his work. By en-larging the seeming structure of control to committees functioning at different levels of the corporation, by incorporating the ideology of democracy as a value for internal operation of bureaucracy, con-temporary American business society has in effect worked out a mechanism for co-opting a large number of people into the ranks of those who feel responsible for the whole organization. Thus, non-owners now feel responsible, and the group of hard-working "entre-preneurs" who never watch the clock and take work home with them has enlarged enormously. And competition remains part of the sys-tem, for the best are supposed to move up the bureaucratic hier-archy. Thus, hard work and competition remain strong elements in the American structure at both the working-class and executive level.

The same trend, the growth of the large corporation and other big organizations, has also been seen by some as reducing the area of freedom and increasing conformist trends in American life, because "organization men" must conform to succeed. However, the growth of large organizations may also give rise to trends in the opposite direction. Bureaucratization, the term that describes the process which develops as an organization increases in size, means, among other things, a decline of the arbitrary power of those in authority. By establishing norms of fair and equal treatment, and by reducing

the unlimited power possessed by the leaders of many nonbureau-
cratic organizations, bureaucracy has meant less rather than greater
need to conform to superiors. In spite of the emergence of loyalty
and security tests, there is little doubt that men are much less likely
to be fired from their jobs for their opinions and behavior today than
they were fifty or even twenty-five years ago. Anyone who compares
the position of a worker or even an executive in a family-owned
corporation, such as the Ford Motor Company when its founder was
running it, with that of comparably placed people in General Motors
or today's Ford Motor Company can hardly argue that bureaucratization has meant greater pressure to conform on any level of industry.
Trade unions accurately reflect their members' desires when they
move in the direction of greater bureaucratization by winning, for
example, seniority rules in hiring, firing, and promotion, or a stable
three-year contract with detailed provisions for grievance procedures. Unionization, both of manual and white-collar workers, is
maximized under conditions of large-scale organization and serves
to free the worker or employee from subjection to relatively uncontrolled power. But whether unionized or not, bureaucratization,
another word for increased emphasis on rules which are applied
equally to all with formal due process, necessarily carries with it
limitations on arbitrary power.

There can be no doubt that many of the changes that men like
Riesman and Whyte have called attention to are occurring; although
there may be some disagreement as to the extent and causes of the
changes. In large measure, with the growth in education, rising income, and greater power in the market place among the working
class, growth in trade-union strength, regained power of a liberal
Democratic party, and the growth of "cosmopolitan" metropolises as
the centers of population, has come a greater accommodation to the
values of equalitarian democracy. Inherent in such a democracy (as
Tocqueville and many other Europeans pointed out) are greater
similarities among the classes, greater conformity to popular taste
and opinion, greater emphasis on the interests of the average rather
than the exceptional. . . .

The question at issue is whether social trends will continue in the
direction of greater equality, a more encompassing "social ethic"
and increasing numbers of "other-directed" persons; or whether, as
in the case of the decline in the birth rate, these tendencies will be
reversed or stabilized—just as the strength of the factors operating
to undermine equal opportunity and equalitarian social relations has
waxed and waned from one period to another.

One significant indication of such a change in direction is the considerable influence achieved by Riesman's *The Lonely Crowd* and Whyte's *The Organization Man.* Both have made publishing histories in setting records for sales of serious nonfiction. Though they are written as analyses and not as tracts, they have been adopted by many throughout the country as basic political manifestoes of the struggle against the corruption of taste, education, and creativity.

The key institutions to watch in this contest are the school system and the family. The reaction against symbols of other-directedness in the school system has grown greatly and changes are beginning to be made. As parents demand changes inside the school, greater efforts are made in the home to press children to learn by rewarding and punishing them for school work. If the trends which Riesman and Whyte have documented are reversed, then they, like the more Marxist-oriented analysts of the 1930's, can add their names to the list of intellectuals who have helped make history by bringing certain salient features of the ongoing society into such strong consciousness that a counterreaction is called forth.

It has not been my intention to deny that major changes have occurred in American society. Many of them have been referred to earlier and many more could be listed. But I would argue that there is no evidence that these changes have basically reversed the pattern of American life which the nineteenth-century foreign travelers saw as uniquely American—equality among diverse strata and a strong orientation towards achievement. It is, of course, difficult to prove this thesis, just as it is hard to demonstrate the opposite. However, my interpretation of the evidence would lead me to concur in the general conclusion of a statistical examination of rates of mental illness over a hundred years, which found no change in such rates over this period and suggested that "Social scientists may well have an exaggerated notion of the extent to which the principal characteristics of American social life two or three generations ago differ from those of today."

D. W. *Brogan*

EDUCATION AND
AMERICAN CHARACTER*

. . . .

From the beginning the school in America has been a democratic
force. I am aware of the social distinctions imported from England
(and from other European countries) in the seventeenth and eighteenth centuries. I am aware of class distinctions at Harvard and of
private tutors in Virginia. But the American school (using the term
in its widest sense) has collaborated with other forces in American
life in making for the kind of equality that I have already discussed
briefly. The school has not set itself against the general trend of
egalitarianism in American life; for some generations past it has—in
its public version, at any rate—been a consciously democratizing
force. This marks the American public school system off from some
other systems giving almost as universal an introduction to elementary schooling. It was not the aim of the Prussian school system
to produce or to aid democracy; its aim was to produce good subjects,
good soldiers. It was the effect rather than the aim of the Scottish
school system to promote political democracy. In France, after the
Revolution, it was impossible—perhaps it still is impossible—to get a
consensus as to what kind of society the public school system has
aimed at promoting. At any rate, it has been impossible to get agreement on the kind of society it *should* aim at promoting.

The American school system has never, that is to say, tried to
thwart the natural development of American society toward a system
of minimal hereditary privilege and a system of maximum opportunity. To make possible the "career open to the talents," to foster
the talents, to increase the opportunities of the average boy and girl,
to give them the tools necessary for the full development and ex-

* D. W. Brogan, *America in the Modern World,* Rutgers University Press, 1960,
pp. 67–75. Reprinted by permission.

Dr. Brogan is Fellow of Peterhouse and Professor of Political Science in the
University of Cambridge.

ploitation of their talents—these were and are the objectives of the American school system. They have been imitated as to aims and copied as to methods in many other countries (for example, in modern England) but America has been the pioneer.

But the American school has been, in the past century and in this one, called on to do more. It has not only been called on to make competent boys and girls; it has also been called on to make good American boys and girls. . . . For much more than a century the American teacher and the American textbook have been creating and fostering helpful myths and thus helping to create and support "a more perfect union." Here, although the detailed aim was different, the American public schools, like the Prussian public schools, were part of the established political order. The orders differed, so did the aims and methods. But this function of the school was common to both systems.

There is no close historical parallel for another function of the American school system—one so important, so dominating, that it is natural that to it much should have been sacrificed and much should continue to be sacrificed even when, as now, the necessity is not so great. That function has been the making of Americans, the induction into the American way of life of the millions of the children of the immigrants who had come to the golden shore with, inevitably, inadequate preparation for a way of life very different from what they had known in Europe. . . .

The children of the newcomers must be taken into the national tradition and it must be made real for them, part of their inheritance by training, by conditioning if not by blood. Of course, the problem was not uniquely American. In all the industrial countries of Europe, with populations drawn from the traditional life of the land, the schools were called on to make possible the adjustment to the modern, literate, mechanized life. Sherlock Holmes saw the London board schools as so many lighthouses, and some of the successes and failures of the American system can be paralleled in Europe.

Nor was the indoctrination of the young into a common political belief and a common habit of political loyalty peculiar to America. It was one of the objects of the educational policy of the first French Republic with its insistence on a uniform language of instruction and the teaching of loyalty to the republic "one and indivisible." That France is now in her fifth republic suggests that this experiment in political education was not an unqualified success. In other European countries the school system was called on to create loyalties that did not come naturally, to make good Prussians out of Poles, good Germans out of Alsatians. In Ireland, so it is credibly reported, the so-called national schools taught the children to sing "I am a happy English child," but there is reason to believe that the political indoctrination of the Irish children was not complete.

In America it was. The patriotism of the children of the immigrants was not in any way inferior to the patriotism of the children of older stocks and the assimilation, through the school system, of the American patriotic tradition was complete. This is a success story and should be noted as such.

An even greater success story was the creation of a tradition in the new states of the Middle and Far West where all were immigrants, immigrants from Europe, immigrants from the East and from the South. The task was great, the need was great, the success was great. . . .

Yet if this was the primary purpose of the school system it was obvious that certain alterations would have to be made in the means, since there was this alteration in the end. In the old traditional school system, largely exported and largely preserved in the East, especially in New England, there was a known, if expanding, body of knowledge that was to be imparted. Once primary school was passed, it was assumed that not all boys and girls would be up to the assimilation of this body of knowledge or would find any use for it if they did assimilate it. That everybody, barring the incurably moronic, should learn the "three R's" was one thing, that everybody should be offered whatever it was that "high school" connotated was another.

Much can be said against some of the innocent but not necessarily harmless illusions involved in the twentieth-century doctrine that no one should be refused as much higher education as he or she was willing to be exposed to. But socially, politically, there was and is a great deal to be said for the ideal if its real justification is allowed for; that justification, as I have suggested, is political, social rather than narrowly "educational." To keep boys and girls at school until eighteen so that they may become sharers in a common, although in some degree artificial, American tradition is a political good and an unmixed good if we do not deceive ourselves as to what we are doing. For remember that a generation ago many of those children, those adolescents who are "wasting their time," would have been on the coal breakers, down the mines, in backbreaking and not necessarily character-building labor on remote and miserable farms. The European observer contemplating an American high school ought to say, if he has any social and historical imagination, that here is a great and humane effort to make citizens and to save children from too-early contact with the necessary brutalities of life.

I shall even do what I have done elsewhere, defend the amount of time spent on games, on playing them, on watching them, on thinking about them. It is a lot of time. I lived for some months opposite a high school in an American city. I was, I must confess, a little astonished by the amount of time that seemed to be spent in standing around waiting for a bus to take teams and cheering squads off to some game or other. I did not, I must confess, think that all this standing and waiting was quite necessary or quite admirable. Yet some of the stress on sport is necessary and is admirable. Not because it builds up the bodies of the boys and girls—I am not sure that it does. At any rate, it does not train them in what is one of the oldest of human skills and is still a very useful one, the art of walking. But sport does unite in a common, deeply felt, and on the whole innocuous loyalty boys and girls (and parents) divided by a lot of barriers. Of course, the success of this unity by sport varies from place to place. It may not work very well on Manhattan Island or in other homes of the blackboard jungle.

Sport is the activity in which American race prejudice, still a national weakness, plays the smallest part. Sport is the easiest means of promotion. Outside the South, what basketball manager will turn down a seven-foot star because he is a Negro? What Harvard man would rather lose to Yale with a team of Lowells and Saltonstalls than win with a team of O'Briens and Konskis? This can be pushed too far. I think it is going too far to die for a college and I think that even star athletes should be required to learn to read and write.

Before I turn to the critical side, I should like to reaffirm my belief in the unifying force of the common high school. Here is the parallel to the Greek city festivals. Who that has seen the return of a victorious basketball team to a middle western town can fail to see the parallel?

> What little town by river or sea-shore
> . . . Is emptied of its folk, this pious morn?

The answer is scores, hundreds; they're off at the game. And if there is no

> . . . heifer lowing at the skies,
> And all her silken flanks with garlands drest?

there is the modern equivalent, the drum majorette.

But the Greeks to whom I have appealed not only preached and practiced what they called "gymnastic," they practiced what they called "music." They prized and rewarded intellectual achievement as they did physical achievement; they even prized it more. And it is the view of the current critics of the American school system that the American school system at all levels, from the primary school right through college, overdoes gymnastic and plays down music. I think the critics are right. I think that the social function of the school is overstressed and that the United States is now rich enough, unified enough, self-critical enough to ask more of the schools than that they should create a national ethos. It is mature enough, or ought to be mature enough, to be ready to ask the schools to lay less stress on making good, loyal Americans and more on making critical, technically competent citizens of a country that can no longer live to itself or be content with meeting its own self-created, historically justified but possibly obsolescent and dangerous standards. Again to harp on my implicit theme, the United States is living in a new, dangerous, unpleasant world and its educational system is in competition, as are all other sections of the American way of life. No one, I think, since Sputnik went into orbit doubts that.

All that I have described was useful, natural, defensible; it still is. The social functions of the school, especially of the high school, are not at an end. But one result of the concentration on that social function was not so much the lowering as the abandonment of standards. What was thought to be "education" in a European secondary school or old New England academy was too narrow for the new world. It was too narrow because it did neglect some useful and new and necessary techniques of the new world. But it was too narrow also because, if the old standards had been insisted on, many, many pupils whom it would have been necessary to exclude from the formal instruction would also have been excluded, to the national loss, from the social molding. So studies had to be found that these pupils could master and possibly use later, which was all right. But these were deemed to be equal with studies that a smaller group could master and use. Typing was as good as trig. This was a practical and tolerable solution a generation ago, a necessary acceptance of facts about American life. But the American school system is no longer concerned with American life, but just with life . . . and death.

That the shock given to American complacency by the Russian triumph was healthy I suppose no one doubts. It was not only an awakening to a serious military danger; it was a firm suggestion to the American people to look at their educational system and to ponder both its defects and what can be done about them. It may be that by waking the American public from its undogmatic slumbers (in most cases it was plain slumber), Sputnik will rank with the shots at Lexington or Fort Sumter. It was certainly seen if not heard around the world.

What are the defects now being brought to the attention of the American parent? They are to some degree the reverse of the attractive medal to which I have called attention. If the main object of the school system is social and political, why should these aims be sacrificed to the mere pursuit of intellectual eminence? One answer is that among the urgent social and political aims of the United States at the present moment is survival in a highly competitive world, and that world cares little for the achievement of internal harmony in the United States and much for the distribution of mere material power. If the present school system is not producing an adequate supply of first-rate scientists and technicians, it is condemned for not doing a job that may be new but is one that must be tackled if the United States is to survive. . . .

Dorothy Thompson

DO AMERICAN EDUCATORS
KNOW WHAT THEY ARE UP TO?*

. . . .

When . . . Russia launched the first and then the second sputnik, a veritable uproar ensued. It was instantly recognized—not only in America but throughout the world—that in scientific achievement Russia had leaped out in front of the United States in precisely the technological field where America had believed herself to be preeminent. The unheralded demonstration that a nation whose population forty years ago was 70 percent illiterate could thus catch up with and surpass the most technologically advanced societies in a

* Reprinted from the *Ladies' Home Journal,* February 1958, pp. 11, 14 ff. (c) 1958 The Curtis Publishing Company, by permission.

specific field, with all the implications of probable military superiority in the field of intercontinental guided missiles, spoke more loudly than all the propaganda "Voices." The achievement was called "a worse blow to America than Pearl Harbor."

In the ensuing reaction and the attempts to explain why we had failed to be the first in the field, charges and countercharges were made in a mood of hysterical exaggeration that did little credit to the American mentality. But the issue of the condition of American education could no longer be avoided. It was right there in the middle of everything—and properly so. College presidents and others pointed out that the American people have been spending more on tobacco and alcohol, or more on new and used cars, or more on recreation than on all forms of education combined, implying that all problems could be solved by a more appropriate apportionment of funds.

But more mature-minded critics also realized that the mere upping of school appropriations and teachers' salaries would not, of itself, answer the question of what American education was up to—and why. The question has been asked, and will go on being asked. Anyone, including this layman, who has followed the educational journals and the writings and speeches of professional educators cannot fail to conclude that there is no clear and comprehensible consensus regarding educational purpose.

The Office of Education in the Federal Government has issued a report on Russian education. Belated as we consider it to be, it is well compiled, precise, and finds no difficulty in correctly defining the purpose of Russian education: to train the child and youth to be an obedient, industrious, enthusiastic and highly competent servant of the state, thoroughly prepared to perform the functions required by a state bent on stepping forward as the premier industrial and military power of the world.

One can vehemently disagree—as this writer does—that this *ought* to be the purpose of education. But Russian education is goal-conscious. Because it is goal-conscious, it is succeeding in realizing its aims.

The Office of Education cannot define the purpose of American education in any concrete terms at all. Its purpose, says the report, is "freedom, peace and the fullest development of the individual." One's mind immediately asks, *Whose freedom? What peace?* Is the individual something in and of himself? How, via education, does one attain this so abstractly defined goal? And is it, in fact, the goal?

Two generations ago, it was not difficult to define the purpose of American primary, secondary and university education. That goal was to create a patriotic, responsible American citizen, an industrious, self-reliant and independent person, equipped with the knowledges and skills essential to making his own way in the world at whatever level of activity his talents permitted, and with a character imbued with the Christian virtues.

Whatever the teaching *methods* left to be desired, the goal was clear and there was consensus regarding the means of reaching it: strict discipline and hard work, stimulated by aspiration, inspiration, and *concrete* and rugged ideas about right and wrong.

Contrary to what most people appear to believe today, this education was *not* brain stuffing. At the higher levels, the great teachers of that epoch taught largely by the ancient Socratic (or dialectic) method, which consisted of a debate between teacher and student, with the purpose of encouraging the student to *think* about the correctness or incorrectness of an answer, and to defend his position. To do so he had to be, of course, in possession of indisputable facts. But he was not encouraged to draw pat and foregone conclusions from them.

Such education, for the intellectually virile and alert, was an extraordinarily *pleasurable* mental exercise. And it was open only to the mentally alert. It created a real elite of brains and virtue as leaders of this democracy.

A defect of this education was that it was practically (though by no means wholly) closed to young men without economic means. Yet the biographies of great Americans record repeated instances of farm boys and poor people's children who worked their way through secondary schools and "academies," studying at night, saving enough to keep them in the university for a year, leaving and returning again, until finally, equipped with a large experience of life, they graduated "with the highest honors."

And if poverty kept out of the universities all too many eager minds, the curricula and standards also kept out the lazy and mediocre offspring of the rich. It was very hard to enter any first-rate university.

A Bachelor of Arts degree from any reputable college was a testimony that its holder had demonstrated his proficiency in at least one ancient and one modern language, in mathematics through higher algebra and trigonometry, was familiar with the great works of English literature, comprehended the fundamentals of physics and chemistry, could give a reasonably coherent account of the history of Western man, and that he could be counted on to behave as a gentleman.

The basis for this was laid in the primary and secondary schools, which were engaged not in developing "the individual"—whatever that may mean—but in producing morally and mentally capable young men and women.

I am not here advocating a complete restoration of curriculum. But it should be obvious that any education must be coherent to a coherent aim, and that its curricula must be such as to cultivate and improve the thinking processes and its standards such as to improve public and private morality and decorum.

Today a B.A. degree from thousands of colleges is no reliable testimony that its holder commands a vocabulary enabling him to read with comprehension the great literary works in his own language, can correctly spell words in common usage, has any familiarity with higher mathematics or the exact sciences, is in possession of any unified body of knowledge whatever, or has ever learned to think logically about anything. Nor is it any testimony of character. It is increasingly impossible even to describe an *educated* man or woman.

The same—and worse—can be said of the holder of a high-school diploma. Dr. Alfred Whitney Griswold, president of Yale, reports in a recent book, *In the University Tradition*, on a student seeking entrance to Yale, that of the twelve junior and senior courses the boy had taken in high school, two were in English, one in American history, and the others were typing, speech, chorus, physical education, journalism, personality problems, and marriage and family— an incoherent mishmash. This youth could not get into Yale, but other "colleges" would, no doubt, receive him. . . .

But it is challengeable whether the development of the *individual* person is even the aim of American primary and secondary education. . . . The "group" idea rules, and the morality of the group is the standard norm. If the sexual standard of the group is loose, then that is "normal" and acceptable, and adolescents who have inhibitions against it are even reprimanded by educational sociologists. . . .

If the standards of the group are rudeness to teachers and parents, sloppiness of dress, resistance to even the most reasonable disciplines, then these are accepted as "normal."

But "groups" do not possess a *character*. They have *characteristics*, or "behavior patterns," which are very different from character. Character is decided by inner will and personal conviction. The pressure of the group (like that of all collectives) is to *conform*—and to conform without reason. Strong characters and independent minds always resist such conformity. It is the "tyranny of the crowd"—the tyranny of the mass—that repeatedly, through history, has ended in the tyranny of one man, or a party, leading the strongest crowd and thereafter imposing by force its own "behavior pattern." And it is rife today in many of our public and even private schools. . . .

. . . If "the group" does not have a character but only character-*istics*, neither does it have a mind. Again, it has a "norm," set by the average, which by a law that appears to regulate all collectivities tends to become subaverage. The mentally and morally superior do not leaven the mass, but are absorbed by it. As in Gresham's Law of currency, bad money drives out good, so does bad behavior drive out decorum.

The mind of the child, furthermore, is put into a strait jacket by the prevailing concept that he must be held with his "age group." Again, an arbitrary or statistically founded "norm" establishes what should be his abilities at seven, nine or twelve, and he is then *cut down* to this level. If, at the age of seven or eight, he is able to read books with a vocabulary of three thousand words or more, he is, in many schools, positively discouraged from doing so—and his parents reprimanded for giving him such books. Writers of school readers and other texts are confronted by "the list"—the age group vocabulary to which they must confine their works. . . .

In the more "modern" schools, children are not encouraged or allowed to skip grades. Striving for good marks is discouraged as "antisocial." The superior child gives his contemporaries "inferiority complexes," they argue, and the desire to excel should not be encouraged.

What are these theorists talking about?

Is the desire to achieve excellence, to be perfect, due only, as they seem to think, to a wish to lord it over one's fellows? It is, in fact, one of the highest human motives. Without this passion for excellence no great book, or work of art, or scientific discovery, or religious insight would ever come to life. And who can best serve and lead this democracy but the *excellent?*

Harold G. Shane

WE CAN BE PROUD
OF OUR SCHOOLS*

. . . .

Despite widespread opinion to the contrary, elementary school age children are learning the fundamentals, the 3 R's, more thoroughly than in 1900. Studies of test scores extending back to 1844 show that each successive generation is learning more subject matter than did past generations. For instance, a top official in one of the largest companies publishing our public school reading and arithmetic tests recently reviewed the test scores made by 230,000 pupils. Even in so brief a period as the past decade there was indisputable evidence of the increased intellectual attainments of children. The average child's reading, mathematics and language usage scores *on the same tests* improved by 12 per cent over a 10 year period. And this despite the fact that a study just completed in New York proved that the average child in a given grade today is *one full year younger* than was the average child of 35 years ago. . . .

Modern education, often given the vague label "progressive" education, has long been accused of debasing our schools academically. Actually, modern educational practices have been maligned by writers who have given any shoddy educational practice the name "progressive."

As schools interpret the term today, so-called "progressive" or modern educational methods are designed to help children learn more than they once did and to make learning have more meaning. For example, certain arithmetical processes today are commonly introduced about a year later than they were in the elementary school of the 1920's. This change was not made to soften the curriculum. Rather it was made in order to help children master content in a few weeks rather than wasting months trying to learn abstract num-

---

ber concepts before they were intellectually mature enough to grasp them.

. . . After 25 years in the field of education I have yet to meet either a teacher or professor of education who believed that "it really isn't important what children learn, just so long as they're happy."

. . . The improving levels of national standardized test scores clearly suggest that the fundamentals, far from being neglected, are now taught more thoroughly than ever. The scores also contradict the statement that "all children are promoted" regardless of whether they have learned the "essentials." Today's high standards of academic achievement patently were not reached by deemphasizing the importance of study. . . .

Do elementary schools, or high schools, for that matter, merit the charge that they are "brain wasting" by neglecting gifted children? A gifted child is one with an intelligence quotient or I.Q. of 140 or above. In an exhaustive study of such brilliant youngsters one of the country's top psychologists found that even some years ago nine-tenths of our gifted children were being identified by their teachers. Far from being neglected, the typical gifted children who were tested were achieving 44 per cent higher test scores than were their less able classmates. That is, gifted fourth grade children had learned approximately as much in four years as the average child learned in eight years of school. All large school systems, and many small ones, have for years made special provision for the intellectually promising boy and girl. There is relatively little brain wasting here considering how limited school funds are.

Further evidence of the fact that mass education has *not* harmed quality education is afforded by a 20 year study of 1470 young men and women of top intellectual promise. Nine out of 10 of this genius-level group went on to college, and two-thirds of the men and one-third of the women completed at least one postgraduate university degree.

But at the same time we cannot afford to be complacent about the educational opportunities of our top-flight students. Rear Admiral H. G. Rickover, the gifted engineer-scientist who created the atomic submarine *Nautilus*, was completely correct when he stated earlier this year that ". . . our schools are not equipped to do justice to the special needs of such pupils." *Truly, the accomplishments of our schools often have been made in spite of limited funds with which to nurture the truly gifted.* If we are not to waste "our most precious natural asset," as Admiral Rickover called the brain power of our genius, the schools must be given additional means to increase their underfinanced programs for the gifted. . . . We have the wealth to do the job, but often have lacked the vision to invest sufficient capital in the "cold war of the classrooms" in an era when our national survival depends on the outcome. . . .

It was stated recently that "the schools have retreated from modern life" because of the way they have deemphasized science and mathematics. . . . As I write, I have before me recent official records from the U.S. Department of Health, Education and Welfare. These reports show, in round numbers, that 400,000 children were taking science and mathematics courses at the turn of the century out of a total population of 75,603,000. Fifty years later, while our population increased by some 100 per cent, the number of high school students enrolled in science had increased by 600 per cent and mathematics class enrollments had grown by 900 per cent.

Bear in mind that this tremendous gain was registered during a period in which nearly all our children had an opportunity to go into high school, not merely the children of the socially or economically privileged. The schools certainly have not "retreated" when today from six to nine times as many of our intellectually competent boys and girls are taking science and mathematics courses as were taking these courses at the century's turn. . . .

It seems fitting to close this review of the reassuring achievements of our public schools with a passing glance at the fuzziest of the criticisms they have received. "The schools have lost their purpose," it has been alleged, because "unessential activities are squeezing out the basic subjects."

Enrollment trends and test scores, previously mentioned, clearly show that relatively more children are taking basic subjects today than in the past, and that the individual child (despite the one year decrease in his age in a given grade) is learning more subject matter than ever before. Obviously, the schools have not defaulted on their academic goals. But are the schools doing more than merely passing along the best in our cultural heritage? Are they preserving and extending moral values? The answer is a resounding Yes, and the evidence is abundant.

The products of our educational system are, with each passing decade, demonstrating our growing maturity as a nation. They are making real the American dream that human beings can live together with dignity and self-respect. . . . The typical product of our educational system may occasionally be misdirected or misinformed, but in the long run he stands for what proves to be right.

. . . We have more often succeeded than failed as a people, and a substantial measure of credit for this success is due to the effectiveness of public education.

Gabriel A. Almond

AMERICAN CHARACTER
AND FOREIGN POLICY*

. . . .

1. GENERAL VALUE ORIENTATION. The characteristic American value orientation would appear to consist of the following interrelated traits.

a. The degree of atomization in the United States is perhaps greater than in any other culture. The American is primarily concerned with "private" values, as distinguished from social-group, political, or religious-moral values. His concern with private, worldly success is his most absorbing aim. . . .

b. The "attachment" of the American to his private values is characterized by an extreme degree of competitiveness. He views himself and his family as in a state of competition with other individuals and families for success and achievement. . . .

c. The American views himself and his family as in a state of competition with other individuals and families for values which are largely "material" in character. What he appears to want are the material evidences of success—money, position, and the consumer-goods of the moment. While the stress is toward money, or what money can buy, the important thing is not the money itself, but the sense of accomplishment or fulfillment which it gives. This sense of accomplishment rests on matching and exceeding the material standard of community and social class; it requires external approval and conformity. . . .

d. There are certain derivative elements of this general value orientation which call for comment. First, intense individualistic competitiveness, in which the primary aim is to get more of what other people want, produces diffuse hostile tension and general ap-

---

* From *The American People and Foreign Policy* by Gabriel A. Almond, copyright 1950, by Harcourt, Brace & World, Inc. Reprinted by permission.
Dr. Almond is Professor of Political Science, Yale University.

prehension and anxiety, which pervades every aspect of the culture including the competing unit itself, the family. The fear of failure and the apprehension over the hostility which is involved in one's relations with other persons produce on the one hand an extraordinary need for affection and reassurance, and on the other, an extraordinary tendency to resort to physiological and spiritual narcosis. . . . Thus an excessive concern with sexuality, an excessive resort to alcohol, and, what is a uniquely American form of narcosis of the soul—the widespread addiction to highly stimulating mass entertainment, the radio, movies, comics, and the like—provide culturally legitimate modes of discharging hostility and allaying anxiety. . . .

2. VALUE EXPECTATIONS. The American is an optimist as to ends and an improviser as to means. The riches of his heritage and the mobility of his social order have produced a generally euphoric tendency, that is, the expectation that one can by effort and good will achieve or approximate one's goals. . . . This belief that "things can be done" is coupled with a faith in common sense and "know-how" with regard to means. The American has a double approach to complex reasoning and theory. He has great respect for systematic thinking and planning in relation to technological and organizational problems. But even this type of intellectualism is brought down to earth by referring to it as "know-how." Know-how implies both the possession of formal technical knowledge and the capacity to improvise and overcome obstacles on the basis of a "feel" for the problem or the situation. In complicated questions of social and public policy there is a genuine distrust of complex and subtle reasoning and a preference for an earthy "common sense." Thus, in these important areas his compulsive optimism, his anti-intellectualism, and his simple rationalism leave the American vulnerable to deflation and pessimism when his expectations are thwarted and when threats and dangers are not effectively warded off by improvisations. This vulnerability is, to be sure, balanced by a certain flexibility and experimentalism, a willingness to try new approaches. If Americans typically avoid the rigidity of dogma in dealing with new problems, they also typically fail to reap the advantages of thoughtful policy-planning. What is involved here is not so much a net loss, but rather the failure to realize the net gain that would result from a greater intellectual discipline.

3. ATTITUDES TOWARD AUTHORITY AND MORALITY. The American tends to "cut authority down to his own size." He has a respect for achievement and a toleration of order-enforcing agencies, but a

distrust of arbitrary or traditional authority. This attitude toward authority also carries over into the field of tradition and custom. Certainly the urban American, and many of the rural ones as well, are not seriously limited by traditional methods of doing things. They are iconoclasts with respect to earlier aspects of culture, and conformists in relation to the most recent value changes. They reject what was done in the past, and they conform to the new things that are being done *now*. But again this iconoclasm is especially noticeable in the sphere of material culture. A greater conservatism obtains in relation to social and political matters. This social and political conservatism is not unique to Americans. What seems to be unique is this combination of mobility of material values and fundamentalism with regard to social and political values.

Similar trends are observable in American attitudes toward moral norms. The norms of Christianity still constitute an important theme in contemporary American culture. Since these moral standards are in obvious and continual rivalry with the competitive ethic, Americans tend to suffer from ambivalence and conflicts in determining what is "proper." . . . Thus, if generous actions, motivated by moral and humanitarian considerations, are accepted without gratitude, are misinterpreted, or are unrequited, a "cynical" rejection of humanitarianism may follow, resulting from the humiliation at having been "played for a sucker." To yield to humanitarian impulses in the "market place" or to moderate one's own demands in the light of "Christian" considerations, to give without the expectation of receiving, to suffer injury without retaliation—these are impulses which have a partial validity; but it is dangerous to give way to them since they dull the edge of competitiveness, confuse and retard the forward course of action.

Mood Versus Policy

Since Americans tend to exhaust their emotional and intellectual energies in private pursuits, the typical approach to problems of public policy is perfunctory. Where public policy impinges directly on their interest, as in questions of local improvements, taxation, or social security policy, they are more likely to develop views and opinions resting on some kind of intellectual structure. But on questions of a more remote nature, such as foreign policy, they tend to react in more undifferentiated ways, with formless and plastic moods which undergo frequent alteration in response to changes in events. The characteristic response to questions of foreign policy is one of indifference. A foreign policy crisis, short of the immediate threat of war, may transform indifference to vague apprehension, to fatalism, to anger; but the reaction is still a mood, a superficial and fluctuating response. To some extent American political apathy is a consequence of the compulsive absorption of energy in private competitiveness. To inform oneself on public issues, to form policies on the basis of careful thought-taking, is hardly a task that is beyond the intellectual competence of a large proportion of the population. The intellectual demands of business life are in some respects as complicated as those of foreign policy. But the American has a powerful cultural incentive to develop policies and strategies relating to his business and professional career, and little incentive, if any, to develop strategies for foreign policy.

The orientation of most Americans toward foreign policy is one of mood, and mood is essentially an unstable phenomenon. But this instability is not arbitrary and unpredictable. American moods are affected by two variables: (1) changes in the domestic and foreign political-economic situation involving the presence or absence of threat in varying degrees, (2) the characterological predispositions of the population. Our knowledge of American character tendencies, meager as it may be, makes it possible to suggest potential movements of opinion and mood which may have significant effects on foreign policy.

1. WITHDRAWAL-INTERVENTION. Given the intense involvement of most Americans with private interests and pursuits, the normal attitude toward a relatively stable world political situation is one of comparative indifference and withdrawal. . . . The existence of this cyclical withdrawal-intervention problem suggests at least two serious dangers for foreign policy decision-making: (1) possible overreactions to threat; (2) possible overreactions to temporary equilibria in world politics. Under ordinary circumstances American emotion and action are directed with considerable pressure in the normal orbits of private competition. However, when threats from abroad become grave and immediate, Americans tend to break out of their private orbits, and tremendous energies become available for foreign policy. Thus, we see the explosions of American energy in World Wars I and II when, after periods of indifference and withdrawal, exceptional feats of swift mobilization were achieved. There is some evidence to suggest that the Russian threat may, if carelessly handled, produce dangerous overreactions. . . .

The danger of overreaction to threat is only one aspect of this withdrawal-intervention tendency of American opinion. Equally serious is the prospect of overreaction to temporary stabilizations in the world crisis. Because of the superficial character of American attitudes toward world politics, American opinion tends to react to the external aspects of situations. A temporary Russian tactical withdrawal may produce strong tendencies toward demobilization and the reassertion of the primacy of private and domestic values. The pull of "privatism" in America creates a strong inclination to self-deception. And while this is less characteristic of the informed and policy-making levels, it undoubtedly plays an important role here as well. . . .

2. MOOD-SIMPLIFICATION. Closely connected with the withdrawal-intervention pattern is a tendency which has to do with characteristic changes in the internal structure of American foreign policy moods. It has already been pointed out that under conditions of political equilibrium American attitudes toward world politics tend to be formless and lacking in intellectual structure. We define policy, as distinguished from mood, as consisting of a relatively stable intellectual structure including (1) explicit assumptions as to the values involved in domestic or international political conflict, (2) explicit evaluations of the relative costs and efficiency of alternative means of maximizing the value position of one's own country or political group. From the point of view of this criterion, American attitudes tend to range from unstructured moods in periods of equilibrium to simplification in periods of crisis. So long as there is no immediate, sharply defined threat, the attitude is vague and indefinite—e.g., apathetic, mildly apprehensive, euphoric, skeptical. When the crisis becomes sharpened American responses become more specific. Here American distrust of intellectualism and subtlety, the faith in "common sense," and the belief in simple answers lead to oversimplifications of the threat and the methods of coping with it.

While these tendencies are more characteristic of the "uninformed general run of the population, they affect policy-makers as well. . . .

3. OPTIMISM-PESSIMISM. . . . During the war and in the period immediately following its termination there was a widely shared belief among Americans and among American policy-makers that the Russian problem could be readily solved by good will and the "man-to-man" approach. The continued thwarting of American overtures and concessions to the Russians now seems to have produced an attitude of hopeless pessimism. Pessimism certainly seems to be justifiable on the basis of the facts, but the negativism which has resulted may possibly constitute a danger if negotiation and bargaining with the Russians in principle is interdicted. The objective

problem would seem to be one of choosing the time, the occasion, and the conditions when negotiation might lead to advantage. . . .

4. TOLERANCE-INTOLERANCE. . . . [The American] tends to take his judgments as to what is right and wrong, proper and improper, from the changing culture as it impinges on him through the various social institutions and media of communication. This makes for a certain flexibility in attitudes toward other cultures and ideologies. But the flexibility is negative rather than positive. That is, the American has moved away from older moral and traditional norms without acquiring new bases of judgment. His toleration of difference therefore is unstable, and there is a substratum of ideological fundamentalism which frequently breaks through the surface and has an important impact on foreign policy. . . .

In general, [an] intolerance of difference is more clearly expressed in periods of normalcy. Thus, even though the possibility appears to be remote, the prospect of a recrudescence of isolationism cannot be excluded. A tactical cessation of Russian pressure might produce just this kind of demobilization and withdrawal reaction and the reassertion of older principles of conduct. This is not to say that such a reaction would be decisive so far as policy is concerned; but it is a prospect which sound policy-planning should anticipate.

5. IDEALISM-CYNICISM. In still another respect American moral predispositions may have consequences for foreign policy. The annoyance and irritation of the peoples of foreign countries over American self-righteousness is, on the whole, a relatively minor source of difficulty. Americans would appear to be happiest when they can cloak an action motivated by self-interest with an aura of New Testament selflessness, when an action which is "good business," or "good security" can be made to "look good" too. Similarly there is resistance among Americans over the straightforward expression of conscience-motivated behavior. What is "good" has to be represented as satisfying the criteria of self-interest. They are happiest when they can allay the Christian conscience at the same time that they satisfy self-interested criteria. In this regard the peoples of foreign countries are well protected, perhaps overprotected, by their own cynicism.

But there are a number of respects in which this moral dualism may produce more serious problems for the policy-maker. There would appear to be a certain cyclical trend in American moral attitudes. . . . The chiliastic faith in the reasonableness of the Russians has now been supplanted by deep resentment over their base ingratitude.

American generosity and humanitarianism is a tentative phenomenon. Along with impulses toward good will and generosity, there is a deep-seated suspicion that smart people don't act that way, that "only suckers are a soft touch." . . .

It would appear to be a reasonable speculation from the foregoing findings that any action involving the giving or loaning of American wealth to foreign peoples, even though it be motivated by calculations of self-interest, activates this fear that "only a sucker is a soft touch." Under conditions of threat, such as those of the present, these doubts and suspicions about "giving things away" have been kept within manageable proportions. But in a period of temporary stabilization when the superficial aspect of the foreign situation encourages withdrawal reactions, these feelings may play a role of some significance.

6. SUPERIORITY-INFERIORITY. In a sense America is a nation of parvenus. A historically unique rate of immigration, social, and geographic mobility has produced a people which has not had an opportunity to "set," to acquire the security and stability which come from familiar ties, associations, rights, and obligations. . . . Being self-made produces a certain buoyancy, a sense of mastery, but it leaves the individual somewhat doubtful as to his social legitimacy. This sense of insecurity and uncertainty may add a strident note to American claims for recognition. This may explain the stereotype of the American abroad, confronted with complex and ancient cultures, taking alcoholic refuge in assertions of American moral, political, and technical virtue. It may also account for a feeling in the United States that American diplomats are no match for the wiliness and cunning of Old World negotiators. In other words, Americans typically overreact in their self-evaluations. They over- and under-estimate their skills and virtues, just as they over- and under-estimate the skills and virtues of other cultures and nations.

It is perhaps this quality among Americans—and among the American elites—which strongly militates against a balanced and empathic appreciation of cultural and national differences so essential to the development of an effective diplomacy. . . .

Either inferiority or superiority feelings in relation to other cultures may have a negative effect on the national interest. Cultural arrogance may alienate other peoples, impair confidence in the United States among actual and potential allies, or aid in some measure in the mobilization of hostile sentiment among neutrals and potential enemies. Cultural subservience, particularly if manifested

by American diplomats and negotiators, may result in real and unnecessary sacrifices of the national interest.

The hypothesis may also be advanced that there is a certain
periodicity of national moods of confidence and lack of confidence.
These have perhaps been associated in the United States with the
fluctuations of the business cycle. One may speculate that not least
among the catastrophic foreign policy consequences of a serious
depression in the United States would be an impairment of national
self-confidence, a sudden welling to the surface of underlying doubt,
which might result in a weakening of foreign policy resolution, a
feeling of being over-extended, a need for contraction, for consolida-
tion, for withdrawal. . . .

1960—A REVISED VIEW[*]

. . . .

Ten years ago, it was necessary to conclude that American mass
opinion in foreign affairs was a "mood" reaction, shifting radically
in response to events. An international crisis produced attention; a
détente produced indifference and relaxation. The Gallup survey's
series of questions on the most important problems confronting the
United States for the period 1935–49 showed gross variations of 20 to
30 percent in response to shifts in the international situation. In the
period since 1948, foreign and defense policies have been cited
regularly with the highest frequency as the most important problems confronting the country. The percentage has varied from the
high 30's to more than 50 per cent. Thus it appears that there has
been a real stabilization in foreign policy awareness and attention,
a broad plateau of appreciation of the continued gravity and salience
of international and security problems. This sustained high level of
perception of foreign policy problems, despite the ups and downs of
foreign policy in the last ten years, suggests a real moderation in the
fluctuation of American moods.

[*] Gabriel A. Almond, *The American People and Foreign Policy* (Frederick A.
Praeger, Inc., 1900), pp. xxii–xxiv. Reprinted by permission.

This should not be construed to mean, however, that the public is well informed about foreign policy problems or has well-structured opinions about policies. Foreign policy still appears to be the area of policy least susceptible of being influenced by either the ordinary person or the opinion leaders. The significance of this finding is that lack of public awareness cannot be viewed as standing in the way of foreign policy decisions by American governmental leaders.

A number of additional points may be made about contemporary opinion on foreign affairs and defense questions. There is a widespread sense of personal and national vulnerability to modern instruments of destruction. People know about blast and fallout—not in their technical details, but enough to appreciate that general war would probably mean catastrophe for the United States in general and for themselves in particular. They also appreciate that the testing of hydrogen weapons has dangers for this and future generations. Nevertheless, a majority of American respondents favor an adequate defense posture, although they tend to define this in terms of the Administration's proposals and moods at any given time.

This potential for responsible support of executive leadership is also reflected in the readiness of the American public to accept higher taxation and other sacrifices in order to sustain a more effective national effort. In the surveys made during the period of the Sputnik shock, it appeared that the public in large majorities was willing to see educational standards tightened; a greater emphasis placed on science, mathematics, and foreign languages; and more money spent on education in general. Questions asked at this time showed almost two-thirds of the respondents as willing to see taxes increased and ready to accept a cut in the American standard of living in order to support a more adequate national effort.

What is overwhelmingly evident, particularly in the surveys since the launching of Sputnik, is the plasticity and impulse toward responsibility in the American foreign policy mood. . . .

8

COMMUNISM AND COEXISTENCE

The year 1955 was filled with Soviet expressions of concern about the potentialities of the H-bomb. . . . they were in an ideological dilemma. They had clung to the Marxist theory that war was inevitable as long as capitalism existed. Capitalism did exist. Therefore there would be war. But war with H-bombs would, or at least might, mean the destruction of everything, themselves included. The theory was thus one of inevitable doom. . . . it was hardly a fitting theory for the exponents of the Brave New Proletarian World. . . . for the first time since 1921, the essential nature of the Soviet theory of coexistence was changed. . . . war was no longer inevitable.

* * *

The unchanging objective of the Communist world enterprise is and has always been a monopoly of world power, and therefore our destruction. This has been the unchanging objective under all circumstances and in all "stages of growth" . . . This truth means

*that the only thing we can do about Communism, if we are un-
willing to surrender, is defeat it. But we of the West have so far
declined to face that cheerless conclusion.*

The first selection of this chapter, an excerpt from a 1959 *Foreign
Affairs* article by Khrushchev, puts his case for peaceful coexistence.
The collapse of the Summit and Khrushchev's tirades at the U.N. in
1960 seem to contrast ominously with his earlier statement. Yet the
Soviet leader persists in his statements that peaceful coexistence is
possible—if the U.S. will co-operate. This is restated in the December
1, 1960, Moscow Manifesto of 81 Communist Parties, which holds
that world war is no longer inevitable.

Can we, in fact, coexist? Can we get along with the Communist
states—competing peacefully, working out more and more areas of
agreement, even co-operating on some things?

Fred Neal argues that this is possible because new factors in the
international scene have now been incorporated into official Communist ideology. Arthur Schlesinger takes a cautious but hopeful
view, based upon his impressions of the internal Russian scene, that
Soviet policies will change in the direction of pluralism. Although
Schlesinger's analysis stems largely from a brief visit to Russia, it
is a feasible (though not inevitable) inference from the scholarly
economic analysis provided by Alec Nove.

On the other hand, the Harvard study of "Communist Ideology
and Foreign Affairs" doubts that the new forces on the Russian scene
are changing the basic drives in the Soviet system and ideology, and
warns that the doctrine of peaceful coexistence is designed to lull us
to sleep. James Burnham's approach is much more caustic than that
of the Harvard paper. He takes specific objection to the Schlesinger
article, grouping him with Rostow and Galbraith as the latest in a
long line of advocates of the mistaken notion that Soviet Communism
has changed. Similarly, other commentators have alleged that the
1960 Moscow Manifesto represents no more than a temporary tactical
shift; that even in that statement of doctrine the Communists declared that "peaceful coexistence of states does not imply renunciation of the class struggle"; and that in his Moscow speech of January
6, 1961, Khrushchev declared that "the policy of peaceful coexistence
is . . . a form of intense struggle between the proletariat and the
aggressive forces of imperialism in the world arena."

Either of these interpretations can be supported with an impressive (though often highly speculative) array of evidence.

Further differences relate to the interpretation of Chinese Communist policies. For the argument about coexistence is not solely among Western leaders, nor only between the West and Russia. The unanimous endorsement of the 1960 Moscow Manifesto came in spite of differences between Russia and China. The Chinese have agreed that a total thermonuclear engagement should be avoided, but they are probably less adamant than the Russians on this point; and they insist that, although world war can be avoided, anti-colonial wars are still desirable and unavoidable. Khrushchev, in turn, does not deny the continued desirability of certain kinds of anti-colonial "wars of liberation." But there is a clear difference of tone between the Russians and the Chinese on these questions. The difference is evident in the following statements:

> The peoples of the socialist states cannot be of two minds as regards the question of war and peace. They think that under present conditions there is no fatal inevitability of war and that disarmament is not only necessary but possible.[1]

> We must stand for and uphold just revolutionary wars, and oppose and stop unjust war . . . The question of whether war can be averted, in our opinion, refers mainly to a world war . . . With imperialism and the exploiting system still in existence, wars [of oppression and liberation] are still unavoidable. The belief that wars of this kind can be avoided is entirely wrong and contrary to fact. Only when the socialist revolution is victorious throughout the world can there be a world free of war, a world without armament; such a world is inconceivable while imperialism exists.[2]

Whether the differences between the Russians and the Chinese are primarily ideological, or reflect simply a power struggle for leadership of the Communist world, or both, is not certain. Although the existence of tension is clear enough, it is difficult to estimate how much of a strain it places upon the Sino-Soviet alliance. Zbigniew Brzezinski thinks that, in spite of the differences, the alliance will hold for some time to come. Robert Scalapino recognizes the factors that hold Russia and China together, but sees increasing signs that the alliance will be severely strained before long.

Scalapino's study carefully reviews the possible policy choices before us in dealing with Communist China, and proposes that we begin to test the possibilities of peaceful coexistence with the Chinese as well as the Russians. He is by no means sure that the Chinese will

---

[1] *Pravda* editorial, June 20, 1960.
[2] Liu Cheng-shen's speech of June 8, 1960.

respond to suggestions leading toward the eventual normalization of relationships, but he thinks we should make the effort.

There are others, of course, who disagree, and who believe that no steps toward negotiation with Communist China should be undertaken until she has proved her desire for peace and her fitness to enter the community of nations. This opposition will doubtless prevent the question of direct recognition from becoming a major issue in American politics for some time to come. However, there is much international pressure for the admission of Communist China to the U.N., and the debate over this will be inevitable early in the decade. Ambassador Wadsworth's statement denouncing attempts to give Taiwan's U.N. seat to the People's Republic of China is included in this chapter. Wadsworth's successor, Adlai Stevenson, has indicated that there is a strong prospect that the objections of the U.S. will, in the course of time, be overridden in the U.N. Even if they are, major problems will remain, and there is little question that the growing strength of Communist China greatly complicates the relationship between the Communist world and the West.

Nikita S. Khrushchev

PEACEFUL COEXISTENCE*

. . . .

From its very inception the Soviet state proclaimed peaceful coexistence as the basic principle of its foreign policy. It was no accident that the very first state act of the Soviet power was the decree on peace, the decree on the cessation of the bloody war.

What, then, is the policy of peaceful coexistence?

In its simplest expression it signifies the repudiation of war as a means of solving controversial issues. However, this does not cover

---

* Reproduced by special permission from *Foreign Affairs*, October 1959, pp. 3–7. Copyright by the Council on Foreign Relations, Inc., New York.

the entire concept of peaceful coexistence. Apart from the commitment to nonaggression, it also presupposes an obligation on the part of all states to desist from violating each other's territorial integrity and sovereignty in any form and under any pretext whatsoever. The principle of peaceful coexistence signifies a renunciation of interference in the internal affairs of other countries with the object of altering their system of government or mode of life or for any other motives. The doctrine of peaceful coexistence also presupposes that political and economic relations between countries are to be based upon complete equality of the parties concerned, and on mutual benefit.

It is often said in the West that peaceful coexistence is nothing else than a tactical method of the socialist states. There is not a grain of truth in such allegations. Our desire for peace and peaceful coexistence is not conditioned by any time-serving or tactical considerations. It springs from the very nature of socialist society in which there are no classes or social groups interested in profiting by war or seizing and enslaving other people's territories. The Soviet Union and the other socialist countries, thanks to their socialist system, have an unlimited home market and for this reason they have no need to pursue an expansionist policy of conquest and an effort to subordinate other countries to their influence.

It is the people who determine the destinies of the socialist states. The socialist states are ruled by the working people themselves, the workers and peasants, the people who themselves create all the material and spiritual values of society. And people of labor cannot want war. For to them war spells grief and tears, death, devastation and misery. Ordinary people have no need for war.

Contrary to what certain propagandists hostile to us say, the coexistence of states with different social systems does not mean that they will only fence themselves off from one another by a high wall and undertake the mutual obligation not to throw stones over the wall or pour dirt upon each other. No! Peaceful coexistence does not mean merely living side by side in the absence of war but with the constantly remaining threat of its breaking out in the future. *Peaceful coexistence can and should develop into peaceful competition for the purpose of satisfying man's needs in the best possible way.*

We say to the leaders of the capitalist states: Let us try out in practice whose system is better, let us compete without war. This is much better than competing in who will produce more arms and who will smash whom. We stand and always will stand for such competition as will help to raise the well-being of the people to a higher level.

The principle of peaceful competition does not at all demand that one or another state abandon the system and ideology adopted by it. It goes without saying that the acceptance of this principle cannot lead to the immediate end of disputes and contradictions which are inevitable between countries adhering to different social systems. But the main thing is ensured: the states which decided to adopt the path of peaceful coexistence repudiate the use of force in any form and agree on a peaceful settlement of possible disputes and conflicts, bearing in mind the mutual interests of the parties concerned. In our age of the H-bomb and atomic techniques this is the main thing of interest to every man. . . .

The Communist Party of the Soviet Union at its Twentieth Congress made it perfectly clear and obvious that the allegations that the Soviet Union intends to overthrow capitalism in other countries by means of "exporting" revolution are absolutely unfounded. I cannot refrain from reminding you of my words at the Twentieth Congress: "It goes without saying that among us Communists there are no adherents of capitalism. But this does not mean that we have interfered or plan to interfere in the internal affairs of countries where capitalism still exists. Romain Rolland was right when he said that 'freedom is not brought in from abroad in baggage trains like Bourbons.' It is ridiculous to think that revolutions are made to order."

We Communists believe that the idea of Communism will ultimately be victorious throughout the world, just as it has been victorious in our country, in China and in many other states. Many readers of *Foreign Affairs* will probably disagree with us. Perhaps they think that the idea of capitalism will ultimately triumph. It is their right to think so. We may argue, we may disagree with one another. *The main thing is to keep to the positions of ideological struggle, without resorting to arms in order to prove that one is right.* The point is that with military techniques what they are today, there are no inaccessible places in the world. Should a world war break out, no country will be able to shut itself off from a crushing blow.

We believe that ultimately that system will be victorious on the globe which will offer the nations greater opportunities for improving their material and spiritual life. It is precisely socialism that creates unprecedentedly great prospects for the inexhaustible creative enthusiasm of the masses, for a genuine flourishing of science and culture, for the realization of man's dream of a happy life, a life without destitute and unemployed people, of a happy childhood and tranquil old age, of the realization of the most audacious and ambitious human projects, of man's right to create in a truly free manner in the interests of the people.

But when we say that in the competition between the two systems, the capitalist and the socialist, our system will win, this does not mean, of course, that we shall achieve victory by interfering in the internal affairs of the capitalist countries. Our confidence in the victory of Communism is of a different kind. It is based on a knowledge of the laws governing the development of society. Just as in its time capitalism, as the more progressive system, took the place of feudalism, so will capitalism be inevitably superseded by Communism—the more progressive and more equitable social system. We are confident of the victory of the socialist system because it is a more progressive system than the capitalist system. Soviet power has been in existence for only a little more than 40 years, and during these years we have gone through two of the worst wars, repulsing the attacks of enemies who attempted to strangle us. Capitalism in the United States has been in existence for more than a century and a half, and the history of the United States has developed in such a way that never once have enemies landed on American territory.

Yet the dynamics of the development of the U.S.S.R. and the U.S.A. are such that the 42-year-old land of the Soviets is already able to challenge the 150-year-old capitalist state to economic competition; and the most farsighted American leaders are admitting that the Soviet Union is fast catching up with the United States and will ultimately outstrip it. Watching the progress of this competition, anyone can judge which is the better system, and we believe that in the long run all the peoples will embark on the path of struggle for the building of socialist societies. . . .

Travelling through the Soviet Union, leading American statesmen and public figures have had full opportunity to convince themselves that there is no hope of sowing strife between the Soviet people and the Communist Party and the Soviet Government, and of influencing them to rebel against Communism. How, then, are we to explain the unceasing attempts to revive the policy of "rolling back" Communism? What do they have in mind? Armed intervention in the internal affairs of the socialist countries? But in the West as well as in the East people are fully aware that under the conditions of modern military technique such actions are fraught with immediate and relentless retaliation.

So we come back to what we started with. In our day there are only two ways: peaceful coexistence or the most destructive war in history. There is no third choice. . . .

COMMUNIST IDEOLOGY
AND FOREIGN AFFAIRS*

. . . .

The rulers of the Soviet Union, Communist China and other Communist regimes constantly proclaim the primary role of Marxist-Leninist ideology as the basis for their policies and decisions. They ascribe to it a unique value as an infallible tool of analysis and guide to action in domestic and international affairs. To any student of Sino-Soviet policy, it is apparent that ideology is by no means the sole determinant of their purposes and courses of action. Their conduct also shows the influence, in various circumstances, of the historic drives of the nations they now control and of strategic and other considerations normally affecting the foreign policy of states.

Indeed, some observers would explain Sino-Soviet policy exclusively in traditional terms of "national interest" and deny that ideology plays any real role today in its direction. Strategic and similar factors, while influencing Soviet and Chinese policy, by no means suffice to explain its thrust and direction. In Sino-Soviet thinking, Communist doctrine directly affects conceptions of the scope and nature of their interests. National interest in traditional terms will hardly explain the worldwide scope of Soviet activities or its preoccupation with revolutionary change throughout the world. . . .

Accordingly, this report reflects the conviction that the Communist creed does play a significant role in shaping the foreign policy of the Soviet Union and China. From this starting point, the first question then is: Which of the Communist tenets are currently relevant to foreign affairs (including relations among the Communist States themselves)?

Communist doctrine embraces, of course, a mass of material de-

---

* *United States Foreign Policy: Ideology and Foreign Affairs, Study No. 10,* prepared by the Center for International Affairs, Harvard University, under the direction of Robert R. Bowie and coordinated by Zbigniew Brzezinski for the Committee on Foreign Relations, United States Senate, 86th Congress, 2nd Session, January 1960, Government Printing Office, Washington, D.C., pp. 13–16, 34–36.

rived from the Marxian scriptures, the glosses of Lenin, Stalin, and others, and many other sources. The successive rulers have repeatedly reshaped the Marxist canon to reflect practical necessities and experience. A vast amount of the inherited theoretical or programmatic doctrine has little or no relation to practical action and is either buried or left for purely scholastic discussion.

There remain, however, a number of concepts and tenets which seem important in molding the orientation of Communist leaders, especially in the realm of foreign affairs:

1. Communist ideology provides a conceptual framework for viewing the world. It looks on history as a continuous conflict in which "progressive" forces contend with "reactionary" forces and defeat them. In the present stage, communism claims to be a superior, a more advanced, form of society. The Communist dictatorship and state ownership and operation of the means of production, it asserts, remove the sources of class conflict and the barriers to efficient use of the productive facilities inherent in capitalist society. Thus the Sino-Soviet bloc, representing the "progressive" forces, is inevitably destined to succeed the "reactionary" system of "capitalism." In short, the basic Communist faith is that capitalism is doomed, that communism is certain to replace it, and that this process must be vigorously abetted.

This does not mean that Khrushchev expects an imminent collapse of the United States, or that he does not know about many of the realities of American life. Doubtless he is aware of the American standard of living, the state of the American economy, and some of the social and economic changes in American life since the great depression. Some of his remarks indicate that he realizes that there is a considerable gap between American reality and the picture painted, for instance, in *Pravda*. Seen through his eyes, however, these facts do not invalidate his conviction that in the long run, capitalism will inevitably decline.

2. In the Communist view, this conflict between the two systems is inherently irreconcilable. It can be resolved only by the ultimate victory of the Communist order. Communist confidence in their ultimate triumph seems to have grown in recent years on the basis of Marxist-Leninist analysis. They now appear convinced that military conflict between communism and capitalism may no longer be necessary for final victory and that the military balance makes capitalism less likely to precipitate such a war as a last resort. Their analysis relies on two processes. First, in the newer nations they count on the struggle for economic growth to lay the basis for Communist takeover. This effort and its effects will disrupt the estab-

lished social order and eventually force these nations to imitate the experience of the Communist States. Second, the Soviet leaders expect the rapid growth of the Soviet Union and the bloc to tip the balance of industrial might in favor of communism by about 1975. Considering industrial development the key to modern power, the Communist leaders believe that this will be a turning point in modern history.

The Communist strategy seems to justify the assumption that they will strive to avoid a total global conflict with the West. An axiom of Communist strategy has been the injunction against risking a direct clash unless certain of Communist superiority. The tactic to be pursued when faced by a superior force is to engage in gradual envelopment and penetration and to destroy the enemy by a process of attrition. To undermine the morale of the superior force, to foster in the opponent an inclination toward ever-increasing compromise, then stage by stage to translate that compromise into capitulation—that is the way to victory whenever lacking the power to impose one's own solution.

The Communists have, however, frequently asserted that certain types of wars are in themselves progressive. Khrushchev reiterated as much immediately after his American trip. If the Soviet leadership should ever conclude that its military and technological superiority would assure victory in a total war without widespread destruction of the home base, it might well be prepared to engage in a so-called progressive war to effect the ultimate collapse of the capitalist world. Khrushchev's boasts and threats are salutary reminders that war as a tool of policy has not been abandoned by the U.S.S.R. However, it seems unlikely that over the next decade the Soviet leaders would be able to reach such a conclusion with any degree of certainty. In such circumstances, Communist strategy is likely to be based on the frequent advice offered both by Lenin, and, in recent times, by Mao Tse-tung, "to avoid a decisive engagement when victory is uncertain and to avoid absolutely a strategic decisive engagement which stakes the destiny of the nation."

3. The Communist Party is the chosen instrument for achieving this millennium. In conformity with Marxist class concepts, moving to the more advanced stage of communism requires the "dictatorship of the proletariat" for its achievement. But the Communist Party represents the proletariat for this purpose. This is one of the key ideas. The party is sanctified as the agent of history and is elevated into an absolute good in its own right. For this reason, each member must be disciplined to accept the party as the spokesman of history and the only true interpreter of the doctrine; and party unity

becomes prima facie evidence of the correctness of its own historical course.

Since the party enjoys the exclusive title to this role, any effort to contest the course or control of the party identifies the individual or group as a class enemy. Thus the doctrine provides the justification for the monopoly of power by the party.

4. Communist ideology makes power central in its analysis of society and history and its own methods and goals. Indeed, the main focus of Communist writings in this century has been on the methods of acquiring and consolidating power. The principal writings of Lenin, Stalin, and Mao Tse-tung as well as Khrushchev's speeches have been preoccupied with the tactics and strategy of political action. By reason of the nature of the doctrine and the party, those reaching the top of the Communist movement are usually driven by an intense urge for political power and dedicated to the use of any and all means to achieve the goals of the party.

5. The creed itself allows for great tactical flexibility. In their practical decisions, the leaders of the party at any time enjoy a wide range of choice, especially since the ultimate goals are both vague and remote. Thus they are able to take account of the strategic and other factors often subsumed under national interest. And the Soviet Union, as the oldest and strongest Communist state, can easily identify its continued progress and security with the interests of the Communist cause as a whole.

These attitudes, plus the initial conspiratorial character of the movement, relieve the leaders from any qualms of conscience regarding the means used. Against non-Communists who oppose the ultimate Communist triumph, any methods are legitimate to achieve the historically inevitable outcome.

6. The ideology contemplates that Communist strategy will vary with the stage and circumstances. Within the Soviet Union, its main function is to justify the continued monopoly of the party and to certify the historical validity of its decisions and actions at home and abroad. Within the bloc, its role is somewhat more complex as an instrument of Soviet direction and control. In non-Communist areas, the movement recruits small numbers of local members with an ideological commitment to provide the hard-core apparatus in each country or area. In its effort to influence and manipulate mass opinion, however, it casts its appeals not in ideological terms but in those best calculated to cater to local discontents or aspirations. Thus at times the policy may appear to run counter to basic tenets of the creed. . . .

. . . According to [one] view, Soviet totalitarianism, the most economically advanced totalitarian society of our age, is now entering upon a new stage of development, the character of which will be determined by the industrialized nature of the Soviet economy. This analysis, partaking somewhat of a materialist determinism, stresses the incompatibilities between totalitarianism and the requirements of a modern, industrial and hence also bureaucratic order. Noting that totalitarianism in the past has seemed largely irrational, it argues that the rationalistic routines of the indispensable managers of the industrial society will necessarily transmit themselves to the totalitarian leadership and gradually effect a fundamental transformation of the system itself. This process, it is argued, will be facilitated by the fact that the totalitarian movement has become highly bureaucratized and therefore shares in many of the operational patterns associated with running the industrial machine. Furthermore, it is argued, the totalitarian movement itself has become increasingly staffed by managerial-bureaucratic elements to whom party membership means no more than an important club association necessary to satisfy career ambitions. The revolutionary torch and the unending question are accordingly displaced by the swivel chair and the punchclock.

But there is no evidence to suggest that "rational" management in itself is incompatible with totalitarianism, which need not be interpreted in terms of irrational terror almost for the sake of terror. Such a "rationalist" system, arising in the context of one-party domination (not to mention international pressures), could be nothing less than a "rationalist" dictatorship, just as total in control as its less predictable and more violent antecedent of the thirties. The institutionalized revolution which still characterizes the existing totalitarianism will inevitably slow down in the future, but by then it will be involved in an economic commitment which also has its own political logic. The totalitarian economy, as many have observed, has been developed in the U.S.S.R. over the last 30 years in keeping with plans oriented to a final (if not precisely defined) goal. It is thus a goal-oriented economy, the goal being communism. That this goal needs more definite formulation is, for our purposes, irrelevant. The important thing is that those in charge of the Soviet society have assumed that economic and social development in all its aspects can be purposefully steered by man in the direction of an ideal solution. This produces consequences, not only economic but also political, quite different from those induced by other economic systems, equally advanced technologically, where, to a larger extent, economic life is self-directive and where ultimate goals, such as plenty and progress, are purposely vague. These goals have less bearing on current decisions than such factors as past experiences, demand, prices, competition and opportunity. In the latter case, a measure of freedom of interplay is inherent. In the goal-oriented economy, all decisions and plans are made, or are rationalized, in terms of the ultimate goal.

The rationalist tomorrow, if it ever comes, will therefore not be an introduction to a democratic form of government, but rather a stage in further totalitarian evolution, accentuating rationalist features present from the start and minimizing some of the irrational outbursts already noted. Such a society, suffering less from internal tensions bred by arbitrary terror and enjoying a greater measure of consumption, might even be a far more effective tool for the promotion of the international goals of its ruling Communist elite. This elite would continue to find in its ideology the justification for power which any self-conscious elite requires. Democracy begins when a ruling elite begins to doubt the absolute righteousness of its rule. Communist ideology, even if gradually eroding as a revolutionary creed, has increasingly become the self-justifying doctrine of the ruling class, and the union of the two requires a continuing conflict with "capitalism."

Insofar as the foreseeable future is concerned, it would be risky to base American policy on the assumption that Soviet totalitarianism is about to erode under the twin impact of urbanization and industrialization. Undeniably, there has been a significant change in the Soviet Union since Stalin's death. The fact that Khrushchev is showing greater sensitivity to popular pressures, particularly with respect to consumption, is slowly beginning to alter the former relationship between the ruler and the ruled. At the same time, however, we must not forget that the wider economic options available to him make his society a more formidable challenger than Stalinist Russia. Khrushchev has been much more successful than Stalin in infusing the Russian society with the will to prevail over the Western World and in associating the Russian people with the goals of his party. As long as the party continues to hold its successful grip on the instruments of power, we can expect it to continue stressing, first, the long-range goals of an ultimate utopia, and, second, the consequent sacrifices necessary to achieve it, though at a diminishing rate of effort. The new push under the slogan of the "extended construction of communism" bears this out and augurs a new phase of revolutionary change for the Soviet Union.

Accordingly, though it is always dangerous to insist rigidly that nothing has changed in Russia (thereby often promoting policies calculated to delay any incipient change), it would be at least equally dangerous to ignore the consideration that during the next decade Soviet policy is likely to remain totalitarian, led by a doctrinaire Communist Party, and dedicated to a radical change of the international order.

Fred Warner Neal

COEXISTENCE AND
THE KREMLIN*

. . . .

During the days of the Bolshevik Revolution and right after, it was doubtful if coexistence—in the sense that it signifies the absence of military conflict with capitalism—was a goal at all. The Russian Communists, dewy-eyed in their naïveté, were firmly convinced that the fall of capitalism was right around the corner, and, not unnaturally, they considered the idea of giving it a push. Particularly when the capitalist powers invaded during the Civil War, military conflict with capitalism was not only a probability; it was a fact—not, to be sure, on Soviet initiative, but the Bolsheviks hopefully thought it could be turned to their advantage.

Soon thereafter, however, first Lenin and then Stalin concluded that capitalist stability was a long-run phenomenon and that coexistence, therefore, was a long-run necessity. But the concept was obviously temporary and uncertain and thus, to the West, neither very reassuring nor very meaningful. . . .

Whether or not the theory of inevitable capitalist hostility was subjected to some reconsideration during World War II—and there is evidence that it may have been—in the Kremlin's eyes the Cold War was caused by capitalist hostility. Consequently, by 1947, at least, Soviet views on coexistence were what they were in 1941. Coexistence was both temporary and dangerous. But it was also necessary, both because of the continued comparative weakness of the USSR and because of the view maintained by Stalin that capitalism was still in a period of long-run stability that would continue until "objective conditions" changed. . . .

* Reprinted with permission from the September 1960 issue of the *Bulletin of the Atomic Scientists,* 935 E. 60th Street, Chicago 37, Illinois.

Dr. Neal is Professor of International Relations and Government, Claremont Graduate School, Claremont, California.

. . . [In 1952] Stalin reiterated Marx's theory that war was an inevitable concomitant of capitalism and added that even if this would be only among capitalist states, it means dangers for the Soviet Union and its allies. They had, therefore, to look to their own devices for protection rather than putting any trust in the idea of long-term coexistence. . . .

It is hard to say what Stalin thought of the atom bomb. Not having it until 1949, it is possible that his publicly stated views about its unimportance were merely dissimulation. However, his public views on the matter did not change after 1949, and it is at least equally possible that the isolated old dictator never appreciated fully the implications of that awful weapon to the extent that many did in the West. However, between the death of Stalin in early 1953 and the 20th Congress in 1956, the Soviet Union—no less than the United States—developed the hydrogen bomb. If the appearance of this instrument of Armageddon laid the groundwork for some ultimate rethinking in the United States, it produced almost immediate re-thinking in the Kremlin. The year 1955 was filled with Soviet expressions of concern about the potentialities of the H-bomb. There was virtually a public, high-level debate in the Soviet Union about whether it was capable of destroying "all civilization," "only capitalism," or "both capitalism and socialism."

Certain it was, in any event, that for the first time the Soviet Communists were faced with something that they were not sure could be controlled by the dialectic, something that threatened them and all Communist development no matter what they did. Particularly, they were in an ideological dilemma. They had clung to the Marxist theory that war was inevitable as long as capitalism existed. Capitalism did exist. Therefore there would be war. But war with H-bombs would, or at least might, mean the destruction of everything, themselves included. The theory was thus one of inevitable doom. Not only was it an ideological cul-de-sac, but it was hardly a fitting theory for the exponents of the Brave New Proletarian World.

It was this matter to which Khrushchev addressed himself at the 20th Party Congress. He reversed both Stalin and Marx and declared that capitalism no longer meant the inevitability of war. The reason he gave was that even though capitalism signified the continuing danger of war, the "peace-loving, socialist forces" in the world were now so strong that they had a chance of being able to prevent it. We know from the Yugoslavs that Khrushchev was also motivated in his new ideological concept by the dangers of the H-bomb to the

Soviet Union. Regardless of his reasoning, however, what counts is the new ideological position: war was no longer inevitable.

Now, for the first time since 1921, the essential nature of the Soviet theory of coexistence was changed. In the sense that coexistence implied the absence of war between the Soviet Union and capitalist powers, no longer was it necessarily only temporary. The theoretical inhibitions that prevented the Soviet Union from thinking of long-term peaceful relations with capitalist powers had been removed.

Implicit in the new theory was also a new interpretation of the concept of capitalist hostility. True, capitalism—as seen by the Kremlin—was on the way out, and Soviet policy might be directed to hastening the final exit. But, despite the return to the pre-1921 view of a "flow tide of revolution," military measures were clearly considered outside the pale. Although the capitalist powers might continue to think of coexistence only as temporary—that is, as a prelude to a military conflict which they themselves would initiate— it was not now out of the question—as it had been formerly—for the Soviet Union to pursue policies calculated to make them change their concept of coexistence as the Soviet leaders had changed theirs.

The new Soviet view of coexistence then received further substance at the 21st Party Congress in 1959, when Khrushchev announced an additional new ideological orientation: the approach to communism. As is well known—to use a favorite Soviet phrase— traditional Marxist theory sees the achievement of communism in three stages—first, the seizure of power by the Communists and the dictatorship of the proletariat; second, the achievement of socialism, with political equality under the proletarian state and all citizens rewarded in accordance with their work; and, finally, communism itself, with the state "withering away," economic plenty, and citizens rewarded according not to their work but to their need. In the Soviet Union, Stalin proclaimed the existence of the socialist stage in 1936. The Communist stage, however, had always been a sort of "pie in the sky by-and-by." They were working for it, but it was in the distant future. Furthermore, previous visions of communism had seen it only on an international basis.

In 1959, however, Khrushchev not only declared that the USSR was on the verge of entering the Communist stage, but he was talking about it only in the Soviet Union. As Stalin had proclaimed "socialism in one country," now his successor was proclaiming "communism in one country," or at least the imminence thereof. Moreover, it was not to be a very utopian utopia. Khrushchev implied that communism would be achieved in the Soviet Union without much more "withering away" of the state than was already indicated in the trend toward decentralization of economic administration and away from the harsher aspects of the police state.

But the important element in Khrushchev's vision of communism was economic plenty. And for all his talk about catching up with and overtaking the United States, he indicated that economic plenty would not mean the same thing in the Soviet Union that it did in the United States. That is, it did not have to be a consumer's cornucopia in the American fashion but simply the satisfaction of essential consumer needs by Soviet standards.

The integral connection between Khrushchev's 1959 pronouncement about the coming of communism and his 1956 pronouncement about war and capitalism is clear. For economic plenty, even by Soviet standards, cannot be achieved unless there is enormously greater production of consumers' goods than indicated by present production possibilities. Soviet capabilities are not such that these possibilities can be altered radically in the foreseeable future unless fewer Soviet resources are devoted to military purposes. Given the present state of the world, with hostile capitalist countries and H-bombs seen lurking behind every launching pad, a major curtailment of resources devoted to defense cannot be risked unless there is some measure of disarmament. Disarmament is not possible without agreements with capitalist countries. And meaningful agreements with capitalist countries are not possible unless Soviet policy thinks—and acts—in terms of *indefinite* coexistence.

There thus emerges, finally, a completely new conception of coexistence. What was for Lenin and Stalin a temporary tactic has become for Khrushchev a basic, strategic doctrine. Both to preserve the Soviet Union and to achieve the Kremlin's clearly stated goals—in the interest of the USSR both as a nation-state and as the center of a world revolutionary movement—"real coexistence" has become a necessity.

It should be said at once that this does not necessarily mean that all Soviet proposals for disarmament are meaningful and not propaganda. The Kremlin is still playing the game initiated by Stalin of trying to break down the American military alliances. But at the same time there is now another goal. This goal is to entice the capitalist nations, in particular the United States, into some kind of disarmament agreement. If all Soviet proposals for disarmament are not necessarily meaningful, neither are they all necessarily only propaganda.

Despite this new position, there are a number of important things the Soviet Union will *not* do in order to achieve its goal of armament reduction and insure coexistence. First and foremost of these, it will under no conditions make any agreements or take any steps deleterious to its hegemony in Eastern Europe. Maintenance of this hegemony continues to be the cardinal plank in Soviet foreign policy. As long as the Soviet Union remains a nation-state, it will have this core interest, and core interests are, by definition, non-negotiable.

Second, the Soviet Union will not abandon its efforts to further communism, especially in the underdeveloped areas, by nonmilitary means. As long as the Soviet Union remains the center of the Communist movement, or even a leading participant in the Communist movement, it cannot abandon its posture of ideological opposition to capitalism or fail to work for communism in such ways as are open to it. The implication of the new concept of coexistence, however, is that such Soviet efforts are less likely to be through covert political subversion—although by no means can one rule this out completely—than through more or less open propaganda and economic maneuvering. There is also implied here Soviet assistance to successful Communist revolutions if and when they occur.

Walter Lippmann has understood Khrushchev to say that the new version of coexistence means that while the Soviet Union may work to bring about communism in underdeveloped areas, the West can do nothing about it. In one way this is correct. Western acceptance of the Soviet view of coexistence would mean no military intervention in the event of revolution. Similarly, however, it means no Soviet military intervention. There is, however, nothing in the concept to indicate that the West could not work against the development of communism by other means. Furthermore, there is at least implied the possibility of Soviet abstention in certain areas—that is, in one sense, spheres of influence in which both American and Soviet core interests would be exempt from each other's attempts at subversion.

Third, the Soviet Union, as long as it remains what it is, cannot give up its Communist dictatorship at home and permit the kind of freedom indulged in in many places in the West. This point has particular relevance in connection with agreements regarding nuclear weapons. Complete and unfettered inspection by foreigners is—at this stage, at least—simply out of the question, both because it would endanger the system and because it ignores the idea of capitalist hostility, which, despite possible new interpretations, continues to color Soviet policies. It is important to note, however, that if this new Soviet view of the world means anything at all, there are perfectly valid reasons—from the Kremlin's point of view—for not permitting complete and unfettered inspection which have nothing whatsoever to do with any intention to violate a testing or disarmament agreement. Indeed, the surprising thing is not that the Russians do not accept full inspection but that they have gone as far as they have in accepting limited inspection.

Now it does no good whatsoever to lecture the Soviet Union about these points . . . The Soviet Union is the Soviet Union, and if Mr. Khrushchev and company have anything to say about it, it will remain such. The West, therefore, is faced with the necessity of either accepting the new Soviet view of coexistence, with all its limitations, or rejecting it. . . .

Arthur Schlesinger, Jr.

INTERNAL CHANGES IN THE SOVIET UNION*

. . . .

Nearly all the changes which have taken place since the death of Stalin have been in what the Western liberal must call the right direction. Despite these changes, the Soviet Union remains a theological society. Khrushchev has not liberalised the régime. What he has done is to begin to normalise it. This is not unimportant: the Soviet citizen is acquiring for the first time a sense of what is normal— what is his "right"—in the way both of personal security and of material comfort, and he is not likely to relinquish these norms willingly short of the threat of war against his country. Still, this is quite a different thing from liberalising Soviet society—from making it less dogmatic and totalitarian, more pragmatic and tolerant.

The heart of Soviet dogmatism is the principle of infallibility,

---

* Arthur Schlesinger, Jr., "Varieties of Communist Experience," *Encounter*, January 1960, pp. 47, 55–57. Reprinted by permission of *Encounter* and *Harper's Magazine*.

Mr. Schlesinger, Professor of History at Harvard University since 1954, is now a Special Assistant to President Kennedy.

applied to leader, to party, and to theory of history. The gains under Khrushchev, far from weakening that principle, may very likely have strengthened it. Thus personal security and consumer goods, by satisfying the urgent demands of the managerial and technical groups, may actually reduce strivings towards intellectual and political liberty and increase political passivity. In the last days of Stalin, Soviet citizens questioned (in the privacy of their minds) the notion that their leadership could do no wrong. But to-day, when leadership is beginning to produce a multitude of pleasurable results, the results themselves—from improving the style of women's shoes to hitting the moon—only verify the infallibility both of the leader and of the ideology behind him. . . .

I have described the Soviet Union as essentially a theological society manned by a collection of true believers. I have suggested that the unquestionable progress in the last half-dozen years towards greater personal security and greater personal comfort may even have strengthened rather than weakened the dogmatic and ideological character of Soviet society. Yet are there no fissures in the Soviet structure? Are there no grounds to substantiate the Polish conviction that "the eventual logic of de-Stalinisation is de-totalitarianisation"?

The most significant remark made to me in the Soviet Union came from one of the wiliest and most experienced of Soviet writers. He said, "In the U.S.S.R., the grandfathers and the grandsons have more in common than either has with the fathers." By this he meant that those who grew up *before* the Revolution and those who grew up *after* the Second World War have a mutual rapport, a common sympathy and understanding, as against those who grew up between the wars.

The older Western assumption had been that the children in a totalitarian society, having been exposed to systematic indoctrination from the cradle, would form the most orthodox, rigid, and hopeless group in that society. One remembers the character of Gletkin in *Darkness at Noon*—the complete Soviet man, steel-willed, fanatical, and indestructible, who took over from the older interrogator and finally broke Rubashov down. As time went on, we supposed, the Soviet Union would consist completely of row after row of Gletkins. Now Koestler's sketch was essentially right for the generation between the wars. The present Soviet élite consists of middle-aged editions of this monolithic Soviet man. But what none of us allowed for is the now evident fact that the sons and daughters of Gletkin are turning against their father. The monolithic style of life bores them, estranges them, leaves them disturbed and rebellious. They are reaching out for beauty and gaiety, for speed and risk, for autonomy, privacy, and self-expression. Instead of the revolution devouring its children, perhaps the children may end by devouring the revolution.

The character of this revolt needs to be defined with precision. It certainly is not a revolt against Communism. Soviet youth to-day are Communists—in somewhat the sense that the youth of Europe and America to-day are Christians. Communism is for them the framework of life and belief. But it does not seem for them, as it did for their fathers, a living and militant faith to which every decision must be sternly referred. Communism controls their day-to-day activity hardly more than Christianity controls the day-to-day activity of Western youth. As against the bleak and sterile dogmatism of their fathers, they—or at least a significant minority among them—appear to be reaching out for concreteness, variety, spontaneity. These rebels accept the political and economic forms of life as permanent. Their own political ideas are confused and sentimental. But they chafe under the moral and aesthetic dogmatism of the all-out Communist ideology. In one way or another, they want to break the mould.

"Young people are curious," Khrushchev himself admitted during his American tour.

> Many of our young people hear about religion, about God, about the saints, about church ceremonies, and they have a curiosity about it. Even if each one of them goes to church only once, they're so numerous that the doors of our churches would never close. The feeling of curiosity is very important.

It is indeed very important, and it is characteristic of Khrushchev as a dictator that he both perceives the mood and concedes its significance. Again and again, one notes the contrast between the complacent certitude of the middle-aged and the open-minded enthusiasm of the young. When an established scholar pompously scolded Alfred Kazin for not having written the right things about Theodore Dreiser, a student approached Kazin after the meeting and said in English, pointing to the older man, "I hope you don't think we are all as illiberal as he is." When Leonard Bernstein and the New York Philharmonic gave Stravinsky's Sacre du Printemps its first Moscow performance in a generation, the stalls (filled with the New Class) were restrained and perfunctory in their response, but the galleries (filled with younger people) gave Stravinsky as well as Bernstein a wild and continuing ovation. At the American Exhibition, young artists clustered with excitement around the abstractions, while Khrushchev, with customary delicacy, said they looked to him as if they had been painted by a little boy urinating in the sand. . . .

The restlessness among the youth represents, I think, a great hope in the Soviet Union for evolution in a pragmatic and pluralistic direction. And, though consumer goods *per se* will work no miracles, one cannot help feeling that the movement towards a consumer society will in the long run begin to erode the dogmatic monolith. There can be no question that Khrushchev has committed his country to the consumer-goods merry-go-round. The critical question is whether the present Soviet capacity to build national power at a high rate through the efficient concentration of talent and resources can survive the transformation into a consumer society—or whether the consumer-goods passion may not upset the system of priorities and sap the single-minded intensity with which the Soviet economy dedicates itself to the building of national power. One detects already a new deference to consumer motives. Two-tone Soviet cars crowd Moscow streets. Television aerials soar over Moscow apartment houses. Russian girls queue up for Italian-style Czech shoes. The director of Moscow television, commenting on the possible exchange of programs between Britain and the Soviet Union, observes (with almost the sense of priorities of an American network official), "Perhaps football matches between the Russian and English teams at Moscow Sports Stadium could be shown. If there were a summit conference that too would be of interest. . . ." In the end, the commitment to the consumer-goods merry-go-round may fix the Soviet Union, as it has already fixed the United States.

All these represent possibilities, not predictions. The Poles keep up their own spirits by pretending that the Polish example is having "great impact on the Soviet Union." One is sorry to report that, in our visit to the Soviet Union, we never heard anybody mention anything going on in Poland. Still, the one thing above all indispensable for the victory of the Polish-Yugoslav tendency is the relaxation of international tensions. The resumption of the cold war would snuff out the inchoate burgeonings in the Soviet Union, jeopardise the incipient liberalism of Poland, and probably freeze the state of affairs in Yugoslavia.

Khrushchev said many disingenuous things in the United States; but almost the least disingenuous was the one for which he was most widely attacked—that is, his speech before the United Nations. Obviously Khrushchev would prefer disarmament on terms which would weaken his side least and the other side most; so, it must be admitted, would we. Yet his desire for a *détente* may well be genuine. It seems to me a grave error to suppose that there is no "real difference" between Stalin's Russia and the Russia of Khrushchev. Stalin *required* international tension: only an overhanging external threat could reconcile his people to his savage interior tyranny. Khrushchev, by diminishing the interior tyranny, diminishes at the same time the need for external crisis. To try to deal with Khrushchev with policies developed in the age of Stalin—which, until very recently, has been the West's idea—appears to me wrong. I would guess that Khrushchev deeply wants a *détente* if only because of his superb confidence that the Communists will win the peaceful competition hands down in every area of human activity. No one in the West should seek a *détente* which would endanger any vital Western interest. But surely one of the strongest arguments for a *détente* is precisely the fact that relaxation might give the forces of pluralism and tolerance a chance to dissolve the ideological dogmatism of Soviet society. . . .

James Burnham

THE CIRCULAR TRAVELS
OF THE PROFESSORS*

. . . .

The Schlesinger-Rostow-Galbraith concept of a Khrushchevian liberalization and *détente*-seeking induced by a growingly consumer-oriented economy falls into place in the long chain of concepts and theories that have served to justify our unwillingness to accept the truth about Communism. The unchanging objective of the Communist world enterprise is and has always been a monopoly of world power, and therefore our destruction. This has been the unchanging objective under all circumstances and in all "stages of growth": in 1903 when the enterprise was founded by a few dozen outcasts with a half-dozen revolvers as armament; in defeat and victory, war and

* James Burnham, "The Circular Travels of The Professors," *Modern Age,* Volume 4, Fall 1960, pp. 385–386. Reprinted by permission.

Mr. Burnham is the author of *The Managerial Revolution, Congress and the American Tradition,* and a number of other works.

peace, Five Year Plans, War Communism, New Economic Policy or Opening of Virgin Lands; under Lenin, Stalin, Malenkov, Khrushchev, Suslov, or Mao.

This truth means that the only thing we can do about Communism, if we are unwilling to surrender, is defeat it. But we of the West have so far declined to face that cheerless conclusion. We therefore invent one theory after another to explain why Communism cannot win, will turn gentle, or will be defeated on our behalf by someone else. In pre-1917 years we explained to ourselves that Communism could not win because Communists were a powerless sect of crackpot fanatics. In 1917 they became patriotic Russian democrats overthrowing reactionary Tsardom. Lenin's New Economic Policy showed them to be reverting to capitalism. Stalin's Socialism in One Country was proof that they had given up world ambitions. With the Popular Front they were transformed into staunch anti-fascist allies. In China there was nothing to worry about, because Chinese Communists were agrarian reformers. After the war, Tito was heaven-sent as he-who-would-do-our-work-for-us: imperial, international Communism would split into a score of rival national Communisms. The Red Army is really Russian, not Communist, and will restrain Communist adventurism. The Sino-Russian conflict absorbs the energies of the Communist bloc, so that there is no excess for external aggression. At each and every moment there is always a theory, usually a choice of theories, to prove that we don't have to meet the challenge of Communism ourselves, because something internal to Communism or someone else or some great impersonal force of History will do it for us.

The idea of Khrushchev the peace-needing, consumer-oriented liberalizer, risen to power in response to an increasingly affluent Russian economy and comfort-minded citizenry, is a postwar egghead link in this continuous chain of excuse and rationalization.

Then, after the weaving of so much fine ideological cloth by our busy trio, Khrushchev the Liberalizer tore it to pitiful shreds in a single morning in Paris last June. Khrushchev, worse luck, doesn't read Professors Schlesinger or Rostow, or even Professor Galbraith. We might be a good deal better off if he did, and we didn't.

Alec Nove

SOVIET GROWTH AND CAPABILITIES*

Growth Prospects, 1959–65 and Thereafter

. . . The Soviet plan for 1959–65 provides for growth of both industrial output and national income at rates much lower than those claimed for the period 1951–58, and lower also than [my] estimates for the actual growth rates in this period. . . .

This, it must be emphasized, is only a slowdown in percentage rate, not in absolute increase. For example, an 8 percent increase in steel output now represents more steel than did a 12 percent increase ten years ago. The Soviet official statisticians are emphasizing this, understandably enough, and they further make the point that the physical increase in the output of most principal commodities now exceeds that of the United States, whereas in past years it was often true that the large increases achieved by the USSR in percentage terms left them as far, or further, behind America in terms of tons. While all this does not make the decline in rates of growth any less real, it must nonetheless be kept in mind, if unjustified complacency is to be avoided. Then, of course, it is true that the "slower" rates laid down by the Soviet planners for 1959–65—8.6 percent per annum for industry, 8 percent for agriculture, and over 7 percent for national income—are very high rates. Can they be achieved?

There is strong evidence for supposing that the special circumstances which have contributed to high growth rates in the past are becoming less effective, and the Soviet planners may not have made sufficient allowance for this. One such factor was the imposition of priorities, the ruthless concentration on the growth-inducing heavy industry. . . . These priorities have been modified, and it seems very doubtful whether they can be changed back again. . . . Other fac-

---

* Alec Nove, *Communist Economic Strategy: Soviet Growth and Capabilities;* Fifth in a series on the Economics of Competitive Coexistence (National Planning Association, Washington, D.C., 1959), pp. 42–47. Reprinted by permission.

Mr. Nove is an authority on Soviet economic affairs.

tors likely to make some slowing down of growth rates inevitable . . . are: the heavy expenditures required for given amounts of raw-materials utilizations and agricultural production; a relative shortage of labor, leading to greater relative reliance on increased productivity; and more limited gains resulting from borrowing Western techniques. Some would add that the growth of the Soviet economy itself renders a slowdown certain, because past tempos were due to some considerable extent to the low starting point and the relative backwardness of the USSR. This, however, is not a conclusive argument. To the extent to which it is relevant, it would seem to be already subsumed among the other factors listed—such as exhaustion of readily accessible materials, or of reserves of underemployed labor.

Against these arguments, several more "favorable" points need to be set. The educational efforts will pay dividends, both in improving the quality of the labor force and in stimulating and facilitating the development of new technique. Soviet planning, with its great opportunities for standardization and assured long runs, may prove very suitable for the development of automation. Automation will also be facilitated by the absence of organized opposition, especially on the part of workers' organization, and by the ideological predisposition of the Soviet leadership to devote resources and capital to its development. The rich natural resources of Siberia, though calling for big initial investments, may eventually pay off handsomely with substantial increases in low-cost output. . . .

What, then, can we expect in the next seven years? Has the seven-year plan, as it stands, allowed sufficiently for the inevitable slowdown? On the whole, the balance of the evidence suggests, but by no means definitely, that the real rate of increase in industrial output may well be below the projected 8.6 percent per annum. The word "real" needs to be emphasized, because the rate officially claimed is very likely considerably to exceed 8.6 percent. . . .

. . . A genuine rate of 8.6 percent per annum should prove difficult to maintain, though 8 percent is by no means excluded. If a "guesstimate" is required, 7–8 percent seems about right. Anything above or below this range looks more unreasonable than anything within it.

In the case of agricultural output, it is necessary to make a much larger reduction in the overoptimistic official plans. The intended rate of about 8 percent per annum is quite unprecedented, even in the years of rapid recovery from Stalin's neglect. The period of diminishing returns has set in, or will very shortly do so; nor can one assume the continuance of the unusually favorable weather conditions of 1958. A rise by 4 percent per annum would be a solid achievement, and certainly seems more likely than the fulfillment of the official plan. Five percent would be remarkable. Anything above this seems practically impossible. Such a rate of progress would be consistent with a rise in national income at a rate gravitating around 6 percent per annum, though here again we can be sure that more will be claimed.

As for the period after 1965, the tendencies towards a slowdown should be counteracted by two factors working the other way: an acceleration in the rate of increase of the labor force, and the drawing of "dividends" from the long-term investment efforts now being made in East Siberia. Therefore there are no economic grounds for expecting any further slowdown in growth in the period 1965–72. Some would even argue for an acceleration during this period, though this is doubtful for political-social reasons.

Progress in the developed satellites is likely to be somewhat slower than this, in China very much faster. It is extremely hazardous to say anything useful about Chinese growth rates at present, in view not only of the remarkable (and often incredible) statistical claims and the drastic nature of social changes still in progress. But, if public order is maintained, it does seem as if the pace of Soviet development is likely to be surpassed by a wide margin.

Clearly, such progress would constitute a formidable challenge. The official aim of reaching the present industrial output of the United States by 1965 seems outside the bounds of practical possibility, the more so as the USSR is not (as is claimed) already past the half-way mark. However, even the achievement by that date of three quarters of the present American level would be serious enough, and such an achievement is all too likely. This, of course, would still leave America well ahead, to an extent dependent on American growth. It would also mean that "overtaking America" either per capita or in absolute terms by 1970, in industrial production, is not a practicable aim. On the other hand, agricultural production in the USSR is already over two-thirds of America's and may well surpass it by 1965, the more so as the problem in the United States is the restriction rather than the stimulation of farm output. In any event, the relative growth in the economic might of the Soviet bloc will be impressive, even while it will not reach the absolute and relative levels described in the more optimistic passages of the campaign speeches of the Soviet leaders.

The Standard of Life

How far will Soviet growth affect living standards? Clearly, part of the potential appeal of the Soviet system would reside in its ability to demonstrate the achievement of more prosperity for the citizens. It does not follow that even a spectacular increase in the national product and in industrial production must lead to higher living standards. Thus in the early period of Soviet industrialization there was a rise in national income and a very big increase in aggregate industrial production, accompanied by a drastic fall in the standard of living of both workers and peasants. Even today, while Soviet national income is many times higher than in 1928, the purchasing power of the average wage has increased relatively little. . . .

We must expect a genuine increase in the standard of life in those countries of the Soviet bloc which have already passed through the stages of "primitive accumulation," and the plans of the USSR and of the major European satellites all show a marked preoccupation with improvements in the way of life of their citizens. It would indeed be very foolish of us to hold the crude propaganda-poster view that the leadership is merely a collection of power-hungry thugs who totally neglect the citizens. To admit that the Communist chiefs are interested in welfare does not, of course, imply any kind of moral approbation. More than one dictator has taken much trouble to clothe, feed, and pay his peoples and, indeed, this is usually best from his point of view. Farmers have been known to feed their animals well, too, without wishing to give them votes. We should accept as a fact that an effort is being made markedly to improve the low living standards of the USSR and of such countries as East Germany, Czechoslovakia, and Poland. Khrushchev's seven-year plan theses show that he is very conscious of the political value of more welfare. The effort seems to be quite real.

The extent of the real improvement must depend on a number of factors. One is progress of agriculture, to which extensive reference has already been made. Another depends on the determination with which the promised campaigns to improve housing and industrial consumers' goods production are carried through. At present it does appear as if a fairly high priority is being given to these sectors. But there remains another and more serious difficulty, connected with the nature of the system itself. Neither in theory nor in practice is the system adapted to the satisfaction of consumers' wants. While certainly able, if appropriate decisions are taken, to increase production of cotton cloth, toothbrushes or frying pans, the system responds clumsily—if it responds at all—to the ever-changing pattern of demand. The Marxist theory of value fails to recognize the role of demand, and the price system fails to "transmit" to the producers the requirements of the consumers—except in the unhelpful sense that a useless good has no value and a totally unsalable article is not worth producing.

The outlawing of private trading and strict limitations on private services have not been replaced by effective state-organized action. In this field the profit motive is singularly hard to replace. In so far as local authorities are responsible for welfare, the fact that they are not truly elected deprives the population of an effective means of pressure upon their "representatives." These weaknesses do not seem curable within the existing political and economic system. Yet, above a certain level, increases in living standards involve not so much the consumption of more basic products but, more precisely, improvements in quality, finer adjustments to what people really prefer, and the provision of more services. Here the advanced countries of the West are several generations ahead of the USSR.

There is really no prospect whatever of the USSR overtaking the West in the field of living standards. Over time, of course, the lag should diminish gradually. Developed countries like Czechoslovakia already compare very favorably with such a poor "Western" country as Italy. China, on the other hand, may be pressing down her very modest living standards in the effort to build a great industry in the shortest time. The USSR, with gradual improvements in the appalling housing conditions, genuinely impressive social services and increased variety in the shops, will be able to make a better impression on visitors from the poorer countries of the world, and the impression will be the greater because these countries believe that Russia was once as poor as they are now, and that she has lifted herself up by her own bootstraps. This belief is politically significant.

Robert A. Scalapino

COMMUNIST CHINA AND U.S. POLICY*

. . . .

Communist China is very likely to emerge as one of the major world powers of the late 20th century. The future of China hinges upon many imponderables, of course, but almost all signs point to the rapid increase of state power—economic, military, and political— under the Communists. The vast manpower and resources of China are being mobilized as fully as possible for this purpose. Primary targets include such fields as iron and steel, and heavy industry in general. In view of their accomplishments to date, there is good reason to believe that in their priority areas, the Communists will obtain notable results. The Chinese industrial revolution will certainly be uneven, but it may be one of the most rapid the world has seen.

A portion of this rising economic power will be channeled into military uses. In some respects, the Chinese Communists have been primitive in military tactics and weapons; Mao's greatest "Marxist" innovation, that of "surround the cities," was itself a sign of that primitivism, a peasant army supplied in part with homemade small arms. Yet in this field, as in others, the Communists are likely to skip many stages of military evolution. The atomic age for Communist China is probably not far distant. Meanwhile, Communist forces may already have obtained their first missiles from the Soviet Union. Communist China has a long way to go before it can be considered a first-class military power; although its army is the largest in the Asian-African world, its air and naval power is relatively weak, and

---

* *United States Foreign Policy: Asia, Study No. 5*, prepared by Robert A. Scalapino for Conlon Associates Ltd., for the Committee on Foreign Relations, United States Senate, 86th Congress, 1st Session, November 1959, Government Printing Office, Washington, D.C., pp. 131–135, 145–155.

Dr. Scalapino is Professor of Political Science at the University of California, Berkeley.

its modernization campaign has just begun. This is a field, however, where the leaders will certainly be dedicated to advancement, and where even a few years may make a substantial difference.

While it may be en route to major power status, Communist China will continue to be dependent upon the Soviet Union. At this stage, both Soviet economic aid and the Soviet military shield are essential. And this dependence, while gradually lessening, will probably exist for a very considerable time. It is very probable, however, that Chinese insistence upon equality in their alliance with Russia will come well in advance of their real attainment of that status. The shifting power balance between these two states and its effect upon their relations are clearly of crucial importance to the entire world.

The growth of state power in Communist China is not likely to be accompanied by an equal growth in living standards. The common man will live, but he will not live well. Priorities will remain with producer, not consumer goods. And unless the Government undertakes a crash program of birth control, populational increases will eat deeply into productive gains. The odds are strongly that the coming decade for the average Chinese will be one of unremitting toil and sacrifice for the glory of China and the hope of better things to come.

This could be a serious weakness for the Communist state. Certainly, it will put a premium upon the augmenting and skillful manipulation of political power. Perhaps Communist man lives less by bread than other man. He lives also by pageantry, propaganda, and persuasion, all encased in the coercive armor of Communist power. In China, moreover, these energy-producing substances are given in the form of heavy nationalist injections. Patriotism and socialism have been blended. Three revolutions, the nationalist, the industrial, and the Communist, have been mixed together. In the years ahead, the Chinese Communists seem likely to wield their persuasive-coercive techniques so as to keep mass material needs and demands at the minimum required for productivity and social order. In no other manner can they produce industrialization of the type and on the time schedule they demand.

Consequently, the chances are remote that any basic political "liberalism" will evolve in Communist China in the near future. Yet Chinese totalitarianism will have its own unique forms, and a certain dynamism that cannot be ignored. The bloody era is over, at least temporarily, and now heads are being shaped, not chopped. The effort at present and in the future will be to create so perfect an organizational man that coercion in its crude forms will be outmoded,

except for "bandits" and "backward people misguided by reactionaries" like the Tibetans.

The implications of these developments to the world cannot be
over-emphasized. To some extent, Communist China may have an
appeal to certain countries and individuals as a model, a nation
moving from the depths of backwardness toward modernity in giant
strides. Its programs and techniques are likely to receive attention
similar to that long given the methods of Japan and the Soviet Union.
But the influence of China as a model will be strictly limited. This
country cannot really become an ideal to most of the late-developing
peoples of the world. The harshness of life and the continuing poverty of its people will prevent that. Moreover, admiration, even when
present, will be increasingly mixed with apprehension, especially
among those societies that border China. Progress and poverty, the
rapid growth of state power in Communist China, coupled with low
mass living standards, present dangers to Asia and the world. The
power of Communist China will increasingly demand recognition.
And the dangers that this power poses to the non-Communist world
will increasingly demand the closer cooperation of free nations if the
threat is to be met effectively.

Chinese Communist Foreign Policy

. . . The Sino-Soviet alliance is currently based upon vital mutual
interests outweighing such negative factors as may exist. It will not
be ruptured over trivial issues, and it will probably endure for a
considerable period. However, Sino-Soviet mutual interests are likely
to be reduced with the passage of time, and strains in this alliance
be increased.

Chinese Communist leaders have repeatedly acknowledged a
great ideological and material debt to the Soviet Union, and that
debt is very real. An assessment of the Sino-Soviet alliance, therefore,
should first pay homage to its strengths, in terms of the advantages
accruing to the major parties. . . .

Yet the long-term solidarity between the U.S.S.R. and Communist
China is by no means assured. Their relationship is becoming increasingly complex. Even at this point, there have been suggestions
of hard bargaining, uneasiness, and disappointments. Whatever the
precise nature of current relations, the Sino-Soviet alliance faces the
following hazards:

(a) Increasing competition between two expanding societies, dynamic, nationalist, and with marked cultural differences despite some
common ideological bond. Notwithstanding their gratitude (and this

may be mainly at the elitist level), the Chinese regard the Russians as foreigners. From most indications, relations have been more businesslike than fraternal. Chinese nationalism everywhere is ascendant. Enormous pride is shown in the capacity to move from dependence upon Russian aid to independence from it. The symbols used to identify Chinese communism and progress are increasingly indigenous ones. Even the venerable dragon has found a respectable place in the new China. And Mao Tse-tung is proudly heralded as foremost among modern expounders of Marxist theory and champion of Communist practice.

Meanwhile, for the first time in history, a true boundary is being established along the vast Sino-Soviet frontier. Chinese and Russian power will soon confront each other on a greatly expanded basis. Men and machines are moving into areas that were once arid, empty expanses or cold, hostile forests. Can the old Sino-Russian border disputes and rivalries for spheres of influence be permanently set aside in the face of these developments?

(b) Differences in practice lead to differences in theory, a thorny problem to rationalize in an ideological empire that appeals to supreme authority and aspires to "supreme truth." For communism, this is an age of pragmatism, yet the inner compulsion for ideological conformity remains. There can be different routes to communism, accommodations to diverse cultures, and different timings of development, but there can be no national communism, say the leaders. However, do not differences in culture, in problems, in experience and revolutionary stages produce important differences in the practices from which theory must flow? In certain respects, Chinese communism differs significantly (and consciously) from the Russian model. This creates a problem similar to that of the Western medieval church—how to prevent doctrinal heresy and schism in a period of practical diversity and flux.

(c) Given the enormous interaction between Russian and Chinese societies at every level, mutual influence upon the internal politics of the other party is probably unavoidable. Sino-Soviet relations may be sufficiently important to create key internal issues around which policies, factions, and even national leadership could conceivably revolve. That such issues would always be resolved in favor of a strengthened alliance seems dubious.

(d) The coordination of policy toward the non-Communist world, particularly the United States, must also pose a problem to the Sino-Soviet alliance, a problem that will not become lighter as Chinese power grows.

Some of the factors discussed above may materialize slowly or not at all. It is possible that they can be handled without a disruption of the alliance. Western allies have worked out many complex problems. Yet, increased strain upon Sino-Soviet relations due to some combination of these factors is very possible, particularly if general world conditions encourage it. . . .

U.S. Policy Toward China

Perhaps there are three general lines of approach to an American China policy, although there are interconnections among these lines and innumerable variations within them.

(1) CONTAINMENT THROUGH ISOLATION—ONE APPROACH TO COMMUNIST CHINA. At present, U.S. policy is strongly committed to the maximum isolation of Communist China, and the full recognition of the National Government on Taiwan as the Government of China. Toward the Communists, our policy is composed of political non-recognition, economic embargo, and opposition to almost all forms of interaction between the free world and mainland China.

This policy is defended upon numerous grounds and the following major themes can be set forth:

(a) The recognition of Communist China in any degree or form is not in the national interest of the United States because that Government has shown implacable hostility to us, is guilty of grossly immoral actions, is dedicated to the establishment of world communism, and has given no indication of being willing to fulfill its international obligations.

(b) Communist China stands condemned as an aggressor by the United Nations, and any recognition or admission to the United Nations would seriously damage the meaning and effectiveness of that body. Moreover, it would result in the weakening or destruction of the Republic of China to which we are committed.

(c) We cannot see clearly into the future at this time. It is always possible that Communist China will collapse or that some colossal upheaval will take place. We can afford to wait.

(d) If we were to shift our China policy, it would be taken as a sign of weakness or capitulation by many of the free peoples of the world, and particularly the weak nations of Asia which look to our firmness for support. By our unyielding stand, we have bolstered the Asian will to resist.

(e) There is some basis for treating the Soviet Union differently from Communist China. There are signs indicating that the Soviet Union for various reasons may be interested in an accommodation with the United States, but Communist China is in an entirely different era and mood.

Collectively, this is a formidable argument. The validity or partial validity of some of these points can scarcely be challenged. Yet there remain a number of questions concerning a policy of containment through isolation that must be raised.

(a) The moral issue has its well-known complexities. If our decisions respecting relations with foreign governments were to be based upon moral judgments rather than the world as it is, we could not possibly conduct meaningful foreign policy, let alone attempt to lead the "free world" (which contains some peoples unfree and some governments immoral). We have long since discovered that we cannot impose our standards and values upon the world. We do believe that the success of our foreign policy is in the general interests of morality, but success depends upon proper tactics. And these tactics might involve trying to bring a government that we consider immoral into some framework of negotiations, agreements, or international organization where more varied pressures could be exerted upon it. . . .

The questions of international obligations and the drive for world communism are of course legitimate, but they are not to be answered fully by citing Lenin, Mao, or Khrushchev. Non-Communist states may be pardoned for having doubts as to whether the Communists will now rely upon peaceful competition, as Mr. Khrushchev avers, although the Communists seem to have increasing confidence that this will suffice. Our defenses must be strong to help them hold to that viewpoint but we should offer better incentives as well. In the final analysis, communism will choose its tactics in accordance with the circumstances. Mao and the Chinese Communists in particular are past masters at the practice of pragmatic communism. We should be aware that U.S. policy does influence and affect Communist tactics, just as their policies influence ours. And it is the short-range tactics of communism rather than its long-range goal that must concern us most. Like every messianic movement the world has ever known, this one is likely to fall short of its goal and be changed many times in the course of pursuing it.

(b) The arguments against the admission of Communist China in the United Nations are familiar and have some merit, especially for the United States. Communist China was labeled an aggressor by a majority of the nations in the United Nations, and no treaty settling the Korean war has ever been signed, although Chinese troops, it should be noted, have been withdrawn from North Korea. There are further questions concerning the increased prestige that would go to

Communist China, what would happen to Taiwan, and whether Communist China in the United Nations would not act as a disruptive force.

These issues can only be weighed and assessed against the realities of the current world scene. Irrespective of the noble sentiments expressed in the Charter, the United Nations cannot in fact be considered a league of the pure. It is in practice a prominent international forum in which cases are put before the world, an area of contact for the purposes both of talking and negotiating over vital issues, and a valuable instrument for advancing technical, nonpolitical causes relating to world health and well-being. These are all considerations suggesting the importance of universal membership. . . .

The prestige of Communist China would be enhanced if it were admitted to the United Nations and granted a permanent Security Council seat. In fact, however, its prestige and power are not essentially dependent upon United Nations admission. If its power has steadily grown, it is the product of developments within China and the Moscow-Peiping alliance, developments that seem very likely to continue. United Nations membership in the final analysis neither adds nor detracts much from a prestige or power that must be indigenously developed, as the case of Nationalist China well illustrates.

Certainly the admission of Communist China would be a heavy blow at the Nationalist Government, or should one say the confirmation of a blow that has long since been struck? The main question is how long the fiction can be maintained that the Nationalist Government is the Government of China. Perhaps this situation can continue for some time, particularly if the United States exerts its full influence and if Communist China misbehaves. As the last few years have shown, however, there is a very clear danger of loss by steady attrition on this issue. A government having effective control over only 10 million people cannot indefinitely hold a "major power" position in the name of the 660 million Chinese.

(c) Communist China may collapse, but this is in the category of extremely remote possibilities that cannot weigh heavily in American thinking or policy on Asia. It is much more logical to make out a general case for a "let the dust settle" policy: to argue that both Chinese Communist domestic and foreign affairs are in flux, especially her relations with the rest of Asia, and that in this respect the trends are currently favorable to us; furthermore, that time is needed for Taiwan to adjust to its future, and premature action would be unwise.

There is considerable merit in this argument and also considerable danger. Events are moving rapidly in Asia and this is likely to be true for the indefinite future. The dust will not settle in our lifetime. We cannot continue indefinitely with policies that are not in tune with developing realities, and it will be extremely difficult under the circumstances to time policy adjustments in Asia accurately from the standpoint of our maximum advantage. Some changes now taking place are generally favorable to us; others are not. In the latter category is the rapidly developing state power of Communist China, and the general strength of the Sino-Soviet bloc. It is very questionable as to how long we can hold this power in check with a policy of containment through isolation.

(d) One of the most complex and difficult factors to assess in contemplating alternative China policies is that of the probable Asian responses. How tenaciously must we hold to our present policy lest we be considered a shifting, unreliable ally? Is it correct that the uncommitted nations of Asia are moving to our side, and approve, at least privately, of our current position on Communist China?

As is well known, non-Communist Asia is deeply divided on the China issue, as on most other matters. Thus attitudes and policies depend upon the particular category to which the Asian state belongs. First, there are our small Asian allies. These can be placed in two categories: the Republics of China, Korea, and Vietnam; and the Philippines and Thailand. The first three governments, drawing upon their own experience, believe that coexistence is impossible, consider that this is an era of war to the death, and argue that all policies should be fashioned accordingly. . . . Our other small allies, the Philippines and Thailand, . . . favor an isolation policy toward Communist China. . . .

. . . But the non-Communist "big three" in Asia—India, Indonesia, and Japan—all have reservations about current American policy, and all prefer to follow different lines of approach. Thus the statement that "Asia expects firmness and will regard change as capitulation" must be questioned.

(e) One of the basic issues confronting U.S. policy is what should be the relation between our policies toward the U.S.S.R. and Communist China. Two interesting theses have been advanced in recent years:

(i) To isolate Communist China as completely as possible and to press it into the arms of the U.S.S.R. are the best ways to heighten internal tensions and produce friction in the Sino-Soviet alliance. This thesis seems doubtful. Aid to China has not been an enormous strain upon the Soviet Union, and it has paid rich dividends. The

Chinese Communists may well have felt that the terms were too stiff, but it was the United States that sought to prevent them from bidding elsewhere. And may not Russia find it an advantage to serve as Communist China's spokesman in the international scene? It would seem logical to argue that the more independent Communist China becomes from Russia, the greater the possibility of competition and rivalry. . . .

(ii) The U.S.S.R. may be in a position and mood to make serious negotiations feasible, but Communist China is in a Stalinist phase, rigid and implacable, and negotiations are pointless. This thesis may have validity. But there are certain arguments to be advanced against it. The Soviet Union appears to be in a more negotiable mood with respect to the United States than Communist China, but this has not been thoroughly tested with respect to either Communist state. It is possible that both ends of the Sino-Soviet alliance, despite their substantial differences in stage of development and power, are in approximately the same position with respect to negotiating: a desire for peace but an unwillingness to make any basic concessions that are considered to affect their national interests. Further, it is possible that this rough equality of position is due to the fact that Communist China has a Russian military shield behind it, and extensive treaty guarantees from the Soviet Union. This appears to be an era when the Communist world, like its non-Communist counterpart, coordinates foreign policy more closely than domestic policy, at least insofar as the Sino-Soviet section is concerned. There is definite evidence that the Russians clear international issues, especially those affecting Asia, with Communist China. Thus, in one sense, Communist China is already involved in major power negotiations, without bearing any direct responsibility for such secret positions as it may take.

It is questionable whether the Soviet Union is prepared to take any position in opposition to the interests or wishes of Communist China. There is, moreover, another troublesome problem in connection with the thesis that we cannot and should not negotiate with Chinese, but only with Russian Communists. If there is an element of independence between these two in the field of foreign policy, do we not court miscalculation on the part of the Chinese Communists? And is it not miscalculation that provides the gravest chance of conflict in this atomic age? Despite the services of the Indians, this problem was apparent at the time of Chinese Communist entry into the Korean war; the channels of communication between the United States and Communist China were not adequate.

The major issues relating to China policy having now been set forth, two possible alternatives to our current position can be presented in more succinct fashion.

(2) NORMALIZATION OF RELATIONS—A SECOND APPROACH TO COMMUNIST CHINA. This policy would encompass the recognition of Communist China by the United States, support for its seating in the United Nations, and general treatment equal to that which the United States accords to the Soviet Union.

This policy is supported upon the following grounds:

(a) In accordance with established international practice to which U.S. policy has usually adhered, the recognition of Communist China would not signify approval of the regime, but rather its existence as a de facto government, having control over some 660 million people. . . .

(b) Normalization of relations, if successful, would give us greater access to the Chinese people, from whom we are now almost completely cut off. It would thus make possible some kind of informational and cultural relations program in which we could not possibly lose, and which might provide certain pressures upon the Communist leaders to deemphasize hate and fear of the United States. Moreover, it would provide us with direct communications in terms of official channels, thereby reducing the threat of miscalculation on both sides.

(c) The primary function of the United Nations today is as an international forum whereby issues can be debated and nations called to account before the world; as an instrumentality for the mediation of disputes through its technical staff; and as a valuable organization for a multitude of nonpolitical purposes of a social, educational, or research nature. As long as the government controlling one-half of the people of Asia is outside the United Nations, that organization will be seriously handicapped in terms of the above functions. . . .

(d) If we are to have a strong policy in Asia, it must be one attuned to the realities of that area and one that interacts with the national interests of the major non-Communist Asian nations. . . .

Taken together, these points constitute an extremely impressive challenge to the policy of containment through isolation. There are two ways in which this policy might be questioned, of course: first, in terms of some of its premises or facts; second, in terms of its sense of timing and procedure. Arguments of the first type have already been raised earlier in this report. . . .

The second set of questions regarding this approach relates basically to matters of technique. Even if one accepts many of its premises as valid, this policy as stated may be deficient in its sense of staging, timing, and development, thereby lacking sufficient leverage or bargaining opportunities for our position and facing many political hazards. In these respects, the second approach may have some of the weaknesses of inflexibility and unrealism for which it criticizes the present policy.

The third alternative represents the basic recommendation of this report, and is supported, in our opinion, by its findings.

(3) EXPLORATION AND NEGOTIATION—A THIRD APPROACH TO COMMU-NIST CHINA.

This policy would be multifaceted and would have three basic objectives:

(a) To test the willingness of Communist China to coexist with us.

(b) To seek an expanded policy that would retain certain firm commitments, but also present a more dynamic, flexible, and positive tone.

(c) Through the actions, to make possible a greater degree of collective agreement on the China issue among the major nations of the free world, and hence provide a firmer basis for collective action if and when necessary. This policy contains the following proposals, based upon a sequence of stages:

1. Stage one:

a. An offer for the mutual exchange of journalists with Communist China; if this program is successfully inaugurated, to be followed by proposals for the exchange of scholars and commercial representatives.

b. Permission for some prominent individual or group not in the national executive branch of the Government to go to Communist China and conduct such informal discussions with the leaders as are possible.

c. The launching of informal, private discussions between the United States and our European allies, Japan, and some of the leading "neutrals," particularly India, Burma, and Indonesia, to solicit ideas and some cooperative thinking about the problem of China.

This first stage would seek to test the position of Communist China and its interest in improving relations with the United States. It would also test the position of our allies and some of the "neutrals," indicating our possible interest in a more positive, flexible policy, and one in which they might assume some joint responsibility. If the results of these actions showed some promise, the next stage should be undertaken.

2. Stage two:

a. Abandonment of CHINCOM restrictions and permission for trade on the same basis as that with the U.S.S.R.

b. Informal discussion with our allies and "neutrals" on the following four-point program: admission of Communist China to the

United Nations; recognition of the Republic of Taiwan; the seating of this Republic in the Assembly; the enlargement of the Security Council to include India and Japan as permanent members, as well as China.

c. Simultaneous discussions with our small allies pledging full and continued support to all of our treaty obligations.

d. Simultaneous special discussions with the National Government on Taiwan, looking toward the following agreement:

1. The United States would continue to honor its existing obligations to Taiwan and the Pescadores. It would underwrite the defense of the Republic of Taiwan, and would support an expanded economic-technical assistance program.
2. The military forces of Taiwan would be withdrawn from the offshore islands, together with those civilians desiring to leave.
3. The United States would endeavor to help in the resettlement of any mainland refugees who wished to leave Taiwan following the establishment of the Republic of Taiwan.

e. If feasible, the United States would negotiate a treaty of commerce with Communist China, and if successful, this would be followed by de facto recognition.

Under any conditions, this would be a complex and difficult stage. It is obviously unrealistic to consider the above proposals as more than general suggestions of the directions in which we should move and the positions that we should hold. Both improvisation and basic changes might be required. Moreover, the precise timing of this policy in each of its phases would have to be determined with respect to the international scene. . . .

The four-point program raises a number of difficulties which should be admitted. It would be acceptable at present neither to the Communists nor to the Nationalists. Either might refuse to sit in the United Nations if the other were present under any designation. Communist China is likely to hold to its claim on Taiwan tenaciously. It might also be impossible to get Taiwan into the United Nations, even if the government of that time were willing to sit, due to a Russian veto. Various techniques should be explored, including that of treating Taiwan membership in the Assembly as a matter of the continuing membership of a government already recognized, but given a changed designation. . . .

The program suggested above forms the only basis for any possible agreement among major elements within the free world. It also accords with the existing facts. There is a separation between mainland China and Taiwan at present and two separate governments are operating. The United States, moreover, takes cognizance of these facts, having tried to persuade the Nationalists to abandon any idea of returning to the mainland by force, and having guaranteed the military defense of Taiwan. There are no legal obstacles; the status of Taiwan has not been fixed by international pact, although admittedly we did promise during World War II that it should belong to China. The Taiwanese people themselves have given considerable indication of wishing to remain separate from the mainland, and could be tested by plebiscite if this were agreed.

The broad program suggested above does not contemplate a world without problems or without fear. It assumes that our military defenses will have to be strong, and that we will need a bold, dynamic program of international economic cooperation with non-Communist nations, especially in the Asian-African world. And, clearly, this program is not without its risks and difficulties of execution. But among the alternatives that confront us, it deserves serious consideration as the best long-range policy to serve American national interests.

Zbigniew Brzezinski

PATTERN AND LIMITS
OF THE SINO-SOVIET DISPUTE*

There can no longer be any doubt that in the course of recent months a significant and sharp disagreement has developed between Moscow and Peking. The essence of the argument concerns the question of methods to be used by the Communist camp in its struggle for a world-wide victory. More specifically, the following issues have generated particular heat: 1) the problem of war in the

---

* From "Pattern and Limits of the Sino-Soviet Dispute," *Problems of Communism*, Vol. IX, No. 5, Sept.–Oct. 1960, pp. 1–7.

Dr. Brzezinski is Associate Professor of Public Law and Government at the Russian Institute, Columbia University.

period prior to a complete Communist victory; 2) the matter of peaceful coexistence and the related problems of how to capitalize on the anti-colonial struggle; 3) the issue of disarmament and the sharing of nuclear weapons;[1] 4) the stages of the domestic construction of communism. The Sino-Soviet dialogue evokes echoes of the violent disagreement in 1909 within the Bolshevik movement between Lenin and A. A. Bogdanov and his supporters. The latter rejected the view that a phase of "organic development" was transitionally at hand, and they charged Lenin and his group with drifting in the Menshevik direction, with abandoning the revolutionary struggle which, according to the Bogdanovites, was "more essential . . . than ever before."

The very existence of Sino-Soviet differences has far-reaching implications for the future of the Communist bloc. Even if the dialogue initially began over matters of method, the argument inevitably has become an ideological one, given the close relationship between theory and practice, between ideology and power, in the Communist system. . . .

The disagreement between the Soviet Union and China is one between two members of an international revolutionary and ideologically-oriented movement, or more precisely between two ruling national parties of that movement. One has been the recognized leader of the international movement and heads the most powerful state within the complex of nations controlled by the movement; the other gained power through its own efforts, is still physically much weaker, but already commands great prestige because of its potential power (and in our age consciousness of the future affects the present to an unprecedented degree); it also postulates more radical conceptions.

The argument between them appears to be taking place within the framework of certain mutually recognized limits. By limits is meant a measure of common agreement despite conflict. In the Second World War, such limits between the Allies and the Nazis

---

[1] In a militant speech Liu Chang-sheng, vice-president of the Chinese trade unions, has hinted strongly that only by sharing its nuclear weapons with the other Communist states can the Soviet Union exert pressure on the West to accept a nuclear ban: "We hold that the utmost efforts must be made to reach agreements on the banning of nuclear weapons and to prevent the outbreak of a nuclear war in the world. Soviet mastery of nuclear weapons has now deprived US imperialism of its monopoly of such weapons. The Soviet Union and the other socialist countries should continue to develop their lead in the sphere of atomic energy and, at the same time, the people throughout the world should wage a more extensive struggle against imperialism and against nuclear weapons. Only in these circumstances can such agreement be reached." (Radio Peking, June 8, 1960.)

were very few: perhaps the best example involves mutual acceptance of certain norms for the treatment of POW's. In the Korean War, such limits were more extensive and involved mutual abstinence from measures which might expand the war. The cold war between the US and the USSR was limited by a mutual desire not to detonate the bomb lest both perish. It is axiomatic that the more extensive the limits, the more contained the conflict. The more conscious of these limits the parties involved in the conflict, the more inhibited their behavior.

In the case of the Sino-Soviet disagreement, the limits would appear to be these:

1). There is no *conscious* effort on the part of the weaker unit to displace the major party as the leader of the camp. There *is* an effort to get Moscow to adopt a different point of view. However, if this should succeed, the nature of leadership in the camp would change. For this reason, the stakes for Moscow are extremely high, even though the Chinese proclaim that what is involved is merely an effort (in Liu Chang-sheng's words, see fn. 1) to clarify "some problems involving basic principles" concerning "the question of war and peace." The Chinese have, therefore, sought to reassure the Soviets by reiterating, over and over again, their allegiance to the principle of Soviet leadership. However, the more open the disagreement becomes, the greater the difficulty in obtaining a change in the Soviet position without affecting Soviet leadership. 2). Both parties are *very conscious* of the fact that their unity is a decisive factor of strength in relation to the non-Communist world, which both of them (but perhaps not to the same degree) interpret as hostile. The importance of unity has been stressed and restressed by both in the course of the dialogue, with both placing special emphasis on the November 1957 declaration of unity issued by all bloc parties. Both have used this theme in part in an effort to buttress their particular arguments but also in part as a mutual reassurance. Chou En-lai made it very clear recently that the Chinese consider unity "the surest guarantee" of eventual victory, that only by "relying on this great unity" could communism triumph.

3). Unlike the situation of 1948 with respect to Yugoslavia when the Soviets erroneously calculated that an open condemnation would result in Tito's fall, Moscow presumably realizes that Mao Tse-tung's leadership is firm; similarly, the Chinese probably entertain fewer illusions concerning the stability of Khrushchev's regime than do many Western commentators. As a result, both regimes realize that in one way or another they will have to deal with each other. . . .

. . . The emerging pattern is one of an impasse between the two partners, an essentially dynamic situation involving continuing maneuvers on both sides to test each other's commitment to its position and the extent of its willingness to risk an open condemnation by the other. Yet neither, given their ideology, is quite willing to precipitate an open clash by being the first to make an implicit condemnation.

Formal unity is thus likely to be preserved, at least until such time as the more radical partner can feel that unity, which it now describes as the necessary prerequisite for victory, is no longer needed. A repetition of the Yugoslav situation of 1948 is therefore improbable. Nonetheless, the divergence between the two is likely to persist, and in effect it already amounts to a denial of the homogeneity of the Communist camp. Under the cloak of formal unity, the differences between the Soviets and the Chinese are more acute and more substantive than those which led to the Soviet-Yugoslav split, and they already have been articulated to a greater extent.

However, the mutual recognition of limits helps to preserve formal unity, and mutual hostility towards the common enemy is likely to draw the regimes closer together in any moment of international tension. For this reason, there is no point in expecting a split between them, as in the 1948 Yugoslav case. The situation is unprecedented and we ought to search for a formulation which best describes it. Perhaps a contradictory term like *divergent unity* might be helpful, and preferable to more traditional notions of either "a split" or "an alliance." The Chinese-Soviet relationship is in many ways much closer than the traditional alliance: both regimes are rooted in a movement viewed as part of an historical process whose course they understand, and whose outcome they can predict; they share the same long-range aspirations and the same enemies; they are striving to reconstruct their societies on basically similar lines; they use similar operational concepts and organizational devices. At the same time, however, their commitment to a basic ideology can generate intense conflicts of interpretation precisely because both adhere to that ideology.

The foregoing reasoning suggests that no simple projection of the present dialogue can be made. While the impasse between the two parties is likely to continue, the allegiance of other parties to Moscow may help to restrain the Chinese by underscoring their isolation within the camp. This, by itself, however, suggests a greater interdependence in the bloc between the leader and the led, and a greater accommodation of interests. The future could even see an adjustment of perspectives between the Soviets and the Chinese, particularly if Soviet foreign policy should be crowned with major successes. The Chinese, like Bogdanov, may then conclude that nothing succeeds like success and get in step with the marching company. Furthermore, the death of either Khrushchev or Mao Tse-tung might contribute to the elimination of the element of personal animus which presumably has already crept into the relationship. In any prolonged succession struggle, the other party might even be tempted to make its position unequivocal in order to ensure the success of a faction more sympathetic to its views.

However, even if that did happen, the situation of divergent unity would probably persist, given the relative independence of each regime and the resulting absence of clearcut subordination. A crisis between them could come about if international communism, toeing Soviet prescriptions, fails to score successes sufficiently impressive to satisfy the impatient in the camp. At such a point, much would depend on the ability of the Soviet regime to shift gears and to adopt a forceful and militant revolutionary line. To assume that the passage of time would not make this easier is only a speculative guess: on the other hand, any Western failure to maintain its own political, economic or military development would certainly facilitate a change in the Soviet posture.

Looking at the Communist camp alone, its long-range problem is the absence of a recognized ideological arbiter. It was Lenin's ability to combine ideological creativity with political skill that finally drove the more extreme Bogdanov back into the Bolshevik ranks. It was the unity of ideology and autonomous state power that made Stalinism into a homogeneous system. But without a common power center jealously protecting certain universal ideological imperatives, Marxism-Leninism has already shown itself to be inadequate in providing unity for international communism. Differing perspectives and differing interests, still defined within the framework of the ideology, can lead to differing prescriptions for action and in turn undermine unity.

It is to be remembered, however, that these processes take place within an ideologically-oriented system that is highly hostile to the outside world. A situation of divergent unity can endure for a long time, with many ebbs and flows. Naive and persistent talk about a Sino-Soviet split is not only senseless but may well have the effect of drawing the regimes closer together. One does not promote a heresy in a church to which one does not belong.

James J. Wadsworth

COMMUNIST CHINA AND THE U.N.*

. . . .

The truth about the Chinese Communists is clear. No amount of distortion, hoping, or wishful thinking is going to alter it. Their record in international affairs is a long chronicle of violent aggression. They have an addiction to force as a rooted principle and a fanatical hostility toward those whom they cannot control. And these characteristics are, I submit, repugnant to the United Nations and decisively disqualify them to sit in this organization.

Now, Mr. President, a number of speakers have cited the so-called "principle of universality" as if it were an accepted legal principle which should lead the United Nations General Assembly to consider the change which has been suggested here. But this idea of universality is not supported by the charter. I ask the members to reread article 4. This does not provide that membership in the United Nations is open to all states, regardless of their qualifications. On the contrary, it lays down the requirements that members shall be peace-loving, shall accept the obligations of the charter, and shall, in the judgment of the organization, be able and willing—let me stress that last word—willing to carry out these obligations. So that those who advocate admitting this regime on the basis of universality apparently ignore the fact that the charter lays down certain criteria for judging states which seek admission. And the rules of procedure of the General Assembly repeat these criteria, specifically requiring the Assembly to consider whether an applicant is a peace-loving state. By this criterion Communist China utterly fails to qualify. How different is this regime from those of the new members which we have admitted this year!

We have heard some speakers who apparently would like the

---

* Statements by James J. Wadsworth, from the *Department of State Bulletin,* Vol. XLIII, No. 1114, October 31, 1960, pp. 686–687.

Mr. Wadsworth has served in the State Department for many years. He was U.S. Ambassador to the U.N. during the latter part of 1960.

United Nations to say to the people of Peiping: "You don't qualify, but because you are so big we will ignore the criteria and let you in." I suggest that such an approach is bad law, bad sense, and bad for the organization.

Then other speakers seem to want us to say: "Your behavior is bad and for that you don't qualify, but we will let you in and perhaps we can reform you." Not only does the charter give no ground for this view; experience gives still less. In fact, it is clear that the Chinese Communists would consider their being seated in the United Nations as a complete vindication of their belligerent policies. And they, as well as a large proportion of the world, would consider that they had shot their way into their seats in this hall.

Now there are some who allege that the Chinese Communist regime represents the will and aspirations of the people of China. . . . Now, that the Peiping regime *controls* the people of the mainland no one will deny; it is regrettable but true. But they cannot be said to represent them.

The head of the Soviet delegation [Nikita S. Khrushchev] cited the establishment of diplomatic relations between Communist China and a number of the United Nations member states. Leaving aside the Soviet bloc members, I think we ought to realize that only one-quarter of the non-Communist membership of the United Nations has relations with Peiping. To my mind this is not a very large figure to boast about, considering the other claims which are made for this regime.

Again Mr. Khrushchev, and also some of his colleagues, made much of a supposed attempt by the United States to push through a "two-China" concept. There is no such attempt, and there never was. This is one of the very few topics on which there is complete agreement between the Government of the Republic of China and the Chinese Communist regime; and since both have maintained emphatic opposition to this concept, Mr. Khrushchev's charge is, on the face of it, absurd.

Mr. President, the issue is not "two Chinas" or "one China." It is the behavior of the China which seeks admission now in place of the China which has been sitting here so honorably since the inception of this organization. It is the history of this regime, who alone among the world's divided countries—China, Korea, Viet-Nam, and Germany—claim the right to reunify their country by war. . . .

9

NUCLEAR STRATEGY
AND
DISARMAMENT

The prevailing opinion is that general nuclear war, if it does not destroy the world, will certainly destroy the participants [and is therefore suicide] . . . Just what is meant by "suicide" deserves careful attention. There is little question that some extreme level of damage would warrant our use of the word. Retaliation that would inflict 150 million or more fatalities to either the Soviet Union or the United States would certainly qualify. Would 50 million, or 20 million, or 1 million? These . . . might at first glance seem equivalent to total destruction. But most people on reflection would agree that they are not. In the mid-1960's, 50 million fatalities in the United States would mean 150 million survivors.

* * *

There is no need to enter the guessing game as to whether one-third or two-thirds of the population of the two opponents and what proportion of the neutral world (depending on how the wind blows) will be destroyed. This is a guessing game that verges on madness

. . . The increasing split between intellect and affect, which is so characteristic of our Western development in the last centuries, has reached its dangerous, schizoid peak in the calm and allegedly rational way in which we can discuss possible world destruction as a result of our own action.

In Chapter Eight we saw that, although there are conflicting interpretations of Soviet foreign policy, fairly general agreement exists that the Russians do not want a thermonuclear war. Communist theory has taken account of the fact that the explosive power of the new weapons is measured not in tons of TNT equivalent, as in most of World War II, nor even in thousands of tons (kilotons), as in the case of Hiroshima and Nagasaki, but in millions of tons (megatons). The Russians know that each Polaris nuclear submarine carries more explosive force in its sixteen missiles than all of the bombs exploded by both sides in World War II, including the A-bombs on Japan. They have taken official cognizance of the dangers which the new military technology holds for them as well as for us.

Nonetheless, the key U.S. foreign-policy assumption is still that the Russians will continue to push for their national and ideological objectives; and that behind their policy is the implied sanction of force, including thermonuclear force, of which they have at least as much as we. In short, the present Administration believes that the Russians are prepared to take risks which could lead to all-out war, even though they would prefer to avoid one.

This leads to our military policy of deterrence. First, there is the thermonuclear deterrent against a direct attack on our territory. This is based upon our power to cause enemies terrible damage by retaliating on their cities and bases if they should hit ours. As Henry Rowen shows in this chapter, we have to ensure that our power to retaliate would survive their first blow on our airfields and missile sites. So we have some bombers in the air at all times; we "harden" our missile bases by putting them underground beneath layers of concrete; and we have other missiles moving around at the bottom of the ocean in nuclear submarines (current plans call for putting twenty-nine of these into operation, with a missile range extended from its present 1,500 miles to 2,500 miles).

The threat of "massive retaliation" might effectively discourage a direct H-bomb attack on our territory. But is it an effective deterrent against a small-scale, local aggression in some part of the Middle East or Asia? Clearly not. Hence, the Kennedy Administration has stepped up the development of tactical forces equipped to fight "limited" wars. Edward Teller believes that our troops need "tactical" atomic weapons for this purpose, but this view is not the dominant one today; for, as the Mershon study cited here argues, it would be difficult to prevent any kind of atomic war from "escalating" to thermonuclear dimensions. Even Henry Kissinger, who was arguing for a tactical atomic capacity as recently as 1957, has now changed his mind, and believes that our limited-war emphasis should be on non-nuclear weapons (known as "conventional" weapons in the curious military jargon of our time).

For Herman Kahn the strategic policy outlined above is inadequate. He argues that the deterrence policy will not deter the Russians from a very serious kind of threat to our position—the threat to launch a major attack on our principal allies. The Russians, he says, have no reason to believe that if they strike directly in Europe, for example, we will hit the Soviet Union with H-bombs. They cannot believe this for two reasons.

In the first place, we assure them repeatedly that ours is a policy of retaliation, of the "second strike." (Teller insists upon this in his article.) This could be interpreted by them as a statement that we will never be the first to introduce thermonuclear weapons into a direct U.S.-Soviet conflict, thus giving them a free hand in Europe.[1] To prevent this, we must have a "Credible First Strike Capability."

But, Kahn goes on to say, our first-strike capability will not be credible as long as we have practically no civil defense program. For this means that our civilian population is offered as hostage to our strategy. Yet, according to Kahn, Rowen, and Teller, a large-scale civil defense program would make it possible for the greater part of our population to survive a major H-bomb attack, and we would even be able to rebuild our economy within a decade. By this reasoning, civil defense becomes an integral part of our strategic doctrine, compelling the Russians to believe that against certain kinds of provocations we would be ready to face up to the necessity of thermonuclear war.

Such a war, Kahn says, would be terrible. But, if we take the necessary precautions, it would not be the end of civilization, nor even of the United States. We must be ready to "think about the unthinkable," build our civil defenses, even talk about the eventuality of our

---

[1] Actually, the Kennedy Administration, while insisting that its policy is a second-strike one, nonetheless appears to have maintained a thermonuclear guarantee to the NATO powers. Doubts by the Europeans that we would ever fulfill this guarantee have led to demands for their own thermonuclear force, either separately or under NATO auspices.

striking first. Only then can we prevent the spread of Communism, reduce the danger of thermonuclear war, and survive even if there is such a war.

There are many who argue that a major civil defense program undertaken on a crash basis would itself be a provocative act; and Harrison Brown warns of the dangers to our values and way of life which he thinks such a program would entail.[2]

Throughout the sixties controversy will no doubt continue over whether a true "balance of terror" exists, or whether there is a "missile gap" which has unbalanced the situation in favor of one side or the other. The one indisputable fact in the situation will be the extraordinary peril resulting from the existence of massive stockpiles of thermonuclear weapons. The Mershon study excerpted in this chapter sets forth in terrifying detail the many facets of this peril, and Harrison Brown and James Real comment on some of its implications. Kahn has calculated that if the present trends are allowed to continue unchecked, thermonuclear war is almost inevitable well before the end of the century.

How can the present trends be checked? Some critics argue that world government is the only solution. But world government will not be in existence in the sixties, so that is no answer to the immediate problem. The case for unilateral disarmament is made here by Erich Fromm; he concedes, however, that it is unlikely to be accepted by either the U.S. or the U.S.S.R.

Mutually agreed disarmament on a substantial scale seems almost as unlikely as the unilateral kind. It is true that Khrushchev has proposed a plan for total disarmament. It is also true that total disarmament could be a great boon economically to the Soviets. But, given the present level of international tension, we can hardly expect that the ultimate sanction of force will be given up by any of the major powers.

Is there nothing to be done, then, except drift toward the holocaust? There is still one hopeful prospect—arms control. Robert Bowie here explains this concept, which is based upon the fact that both sides do not want a direct thermonuclear clash, and therefore have

---

[2] Brown is not against all civil defense programs. He thinks that as long as thermonuclear weapons exist—which will be the case for a long time to come—some steps have to be taken to provide for the preservation of life and the recovery of the country after a possible attack. However, he thinks that the measures taken should be modest in scale, and spread over a long period of time, so that they do not in themselves increase tensions.

a mutual interest in such matters as reducing the danger of war by accident or miscalculation, slowing down the further diffusion of nuclear weapons, and so on. This might or might not include some measure of disarmament at this stage; but the emphasis is on keeping tensions under control, and preventing the situation from getting out of hand. It demands constant discussion between the powers over the entire range of foreign affairs and military policy. It proceeds by small agreements, each carefully examined and tested by experience.

It demands, in other words, the political and diplomatic skills of negotiation, bargaining, and conciliation. The skills of politics will meet their severest test of the decade in this area of arms control. If they fail there, any success in dealing with the other issues of the sixties will be tenuous indeed.

Henry Rowen

DETERRING DIRECT ATTACK
ON THE UNITED STATES*

. . . .

The keystone of U.S. military policy has come to be the deterrence of direct nuclear attack against the United States through the threat of nuclear retaliation against the aggressor. The centrality of this objective scarcely needs explanation. We must attain it even in situations of the greatest international tension, situations in which the enemy's temptation to strike might be very great. Moreover, the task of assuring retaliation following a direct nuclear attack is much more

---

* Henry Rowen, *Study Paper No. 18: National Security and the American Economy in the 1960's,* prepared for Joint Economic Committee, 86th Congress, 2nd Session, January 1960, Government Printing Office, Washington, D.C., pp. 9–12, 29–32.

Mr. Rowen has written extensively on military, political, and economic affairs.

difficult than is often believed. It is not automatic. We must have a strategic nuclear force which is prepared to survive a well-designed and well-executed surprise nuclear assault, and which can retaliate effectively. . . .

The objective of keeping nuclear weapons from landing on the United States has presented us with a dual problem: We must be prepared to retaliate after a well-designed and well-executed surprise attack, and we must operate our forces in a way which does not inadvertently trigger the very war we are trying to deter. We want to look formidable, but there could be risks in looking too threatening, especially if there were some weak links in our system of retaliation. And we want to avoid the unauthorized or accidental launching of weapons against Russia. Avoiding inadvertent war requires regard to safeguards which put an additional burden on our ability to retaliate against deliberate attack.

Deterring an attack against the continental United States through the threat of retaliation is the primary mission of our long-range bomber and missile forces. Over the next several years, this means primarily the medium-range B-47 bomber, the longer range B-52 equipped with its Hound Dog air-launched missiles, and Atlas and Titan intercontinental ballistic missiles of the Strategic Air Command, and the Navy's Polaris submarine missile force. Beyond that, there are the Minuteman ICBM and possibly an air-carried ballistic missile. No longer is this objective assigned to any considerable extent to overseas land-based forces. With the growth of Soviet nuclear delivery capabilities, it became increasingly clear that our overseas forces stationed close to the sources of Russian striking power could not be counted on to withstand an all-out nuclear assault. This fact, which has important implications for nations planning on creating their own strategic forces, became evident well before the advent of Russian ballistic missiles and has greatly influenced the development by this country of intercontinental range and sea-mobile nuclear delivery capabilities. This is not to say that overseas-based forces have no contribution to make to general war. They may be able to help significantly in limiting damage if deterrence fails, to contribute to a U.S. strike in response to an attack on an ally, or to penalize the aggressor if his attack were poorly executed by disrupting some part of it. However, our bedrock capability for deterring an attack on the United States must in the future reside largely in our strategic airpower (including the Navy's ballistic missile forces).

The other force contributing significantly to this objective has been our continental air defense system. It helps to protect our retaliatory force primarily by trying to give it warning of attack. It does this by providing warning barriers to detect enemy vehicles en route, and by providing active defenses designed to shoot down some part of the attacking force. If the enemy were to offset our active defenses by sending more vehicles, this larger enemy attack would become easier to detect in preparation for launch or on the way. And apart from its warning contribution, active defenses help to protect non-ready bombers and missiles and those command and communication functions that are essential to carrying out the task of retaliation.

It is becoming widely recognized that we face in the immediate future the crucial task of assuring that our strategic power can retaliate with high confidence in the face of growing Soviet offensive and defensive capabilities, and to do this while keeping the risks of accidents and unauthorized actions low.

Much of this current concern is currently being focused on the possibility of a near-term weakness of our strategic force—symbolized by the "missile gap." The concept of the "gap" is primarily concerned with one aspect of the problem of retaliation, the vulnerability of our forces to a ballistic missile attack. In fact, we should be concerned over the growing Soviet ballistic missile force, for ballistic missiles are a remarkably efficient and formidable surprise attack weapon. The great and predictable speed simplifies the aggressor's problem of coordinating a world wide attack on widely separated bases; this speed also makes totally ineffective all existing active defenses; its combined accuracy and warhead yield may assure the destruction of the soft elements on bomber and missile bases: bombers, missiles, above-ground buildings, and crews. Some of our responses to this and other challenges have been announced: the "fail safe" or "positive control" method of launching bombers on the basis of ambiguous information on enemy movements, the sheltering of our first generation Atlas and Titan intercontinental ballistic missiles, plans for keeping some bombers in the air with bombs at all times, the procurement of the Polaris submarine missile system which promises the combination of mobility and concealment. Later systems will include the dispersed and sheltered and possibly rail-mobile Minuteman ICBM, an air-launched ballistic missile, and more advanced models of Polaris.

These actions, while crucial, deal only with one of the obstacles to retaliation. Other actions are underway to offset the others: for example, to assure that our forces can be more certainly controlled in war by providing protected command and communications systems, and a better ability to penetrate enemy defenses. An advancing

Soviet technology and weapons capability forces us continually to adopt new and expensive methods of operating existing equipment and to procure radically new systems. It is not well understood that the job of preserving a deterrent force is a complex and continuing one, and that it calls for frequent and often expensive changes in our military posture. . . .

The prevailing opinion is that general nuclear war, if it does not destroy the world, will certainly destroy the participants. The list of those who have held this view is a long and distinguished one. Some believe that for this reason general nuclear war has been effectively abolished, while others believe that deliberate war has been eliminated and worry only about the chance of an unintended or "accidental" war. They all hold that rational governments would never deliberately choose nuclear war, that it will not be especially difficult to deter a general war. They also do not distinguish levels of damage —damage would be total. [War thus becomes mutual suicide.]

Just what is meant by "suicide" deserves careful attention. There is little question that some extreme level of damage would warrant our use of the word. Retaliation that would inflict 150 million or more fatalities to either the Soviet Union or the United States would certainly qualify. Would 50 million, or 20 million, or 1 million? These would be disasters so far beyond our experience that they might at first glance seem equivalent to total destruction. But most people on reflection would agree that they are not. In the mid-1960's, 50 million fatalities in the United States would mean 150 million survivors. And probably a substantial economic base would survive as well. In addition to grave economic loss, the Soviet Union suffered well over 20 million fatalities during World War II. Judging by the recovery of the Soviet Union since World War II, one cannot say that level of damage was fatal. This does not mean that this experience was one that the Russians would care to repeat. Far from it. It does mean, however, that we must be careful to distinguish between those levels of damage that are a disaster and those that are lethal to a country. This distinction has important implications for our defense policies.

What intensities of attack would produce these different levels of damage? An attack delivering roughly 4,000 megatons could inflict damage in the lethal range if not moderated by civil defense. (The delivery of this weight of attack might require the launching of a much greater weight, and for the side striking second, the possession of even greater forces.) It would probably kill about 120 million people from blast and fallout if they failed to take much advantage of the shielding provided by existing buildings, and at the present public level of understanding of how to behave if we are attacked, this seems to be a reasonable assumption. A very much smaller attack than this could do great, if not necessarily lethal, damage; 50 high-yield bombs totaling about 500 megatons delivered on our largest cities might cause about 30 million fatalities if the populations had not evacuated or sheltered. A larger attack could kill practically our entire population.

The vulnerability of the Soviet Union population to a large attack is roughly comparable to that of the United States. Assuming again that there is no civil defense—a much more dubious assumption with regard to Russia—the damage from, say, a 4,000-megaton attack would be comparable to that in the United States. However, damage from a 50-city attack would be substantially less, for Russian industry and urban population is less concentrated than ours.

What level of attack might be expected? It is essential to distinguish between the situation of the aggressor and that of the defender. The aggressor has the advantage of attacking with an undamaged force and possibly by surprise. If his attack were to destroy a large proportion of the defender's force and possibly disrupt the remainder, and if his active defenses were to exact further attrition of the surviving force, then the actual weight of attack delivered by the defender might be small. And much of it might be delivered against the wrong targets. The weight of attack against civil targets might be significantly less than the smaller of the attacks illustrated. Finally, the effect of the defender's delivered attack would depend very much on the aggressor's use of civil defenses. The aggressor can use civil defense to especially good advantage for, in addition to planning on receiving a reduced weight of attack, his population may be able to evacuate cities and seek fallout shelter well before most of the defender's retaliatory attack arrives. It is somewhat disquieting in this connection to observe that the Soviet Union has been carrying out an extensive civil defense training program in which all adults are supposed to have received over 20 hours of instruction.

The risk to the defender's civil society is much greater. It is threatened initially by the aggressor's undamaged strategic force. The aggressor could inflict lethal damage especially if the defender had little civil defense. However, this does not mean that he would necessarily want to do so or that his attack would be unconstrained. If he wished to take his enemy by surprise and if he wished to retain forces in being, his initial strike might have to be quite limited in size. And it would have to be sent largely against the defender's military forces if damage were to be reduced to his own cities and remaining military forces. The weight of attack sent directly at the defender's population centers might be only a small part of the total, and the aggressor might choose not to attack population directly at all. Where military forces and populations are close together, a purely military attack against an unprepared population would almost certainly do great civilian damage.

Even for the defender, population damage could be drastically reduced over a wide range of attacks by civil defense. Relatively cheap measures (well under a billion dollars a year) could make a big difference. The difference between having an unprepared population and one trained to use available structures as fallout shelter, equipped with radiation meters, provided with emergency food supplies, and trained in decontamination techniques, could reduce fatalities by perhaps 50 million. With special fallout shelters it might be possible to reduce fatalities from a large attack by perhaps a comparable amount in addition. Beyond this, we might build blast shelters, arrange for the evacuation of the population of cities to rural shelter areas in a crisis, plan on the use of nonurban industry and adopt other measures to promote postwar recovery. A large scale program of civil defense might be as large as $5 to $10 billion or more a year, a tremendous amount compared with present civil defense expenditures but not, it should be noted, compared to our defense budget nor even to the amount we are now spending on our general war objectives.

Even allowing for civil defense preparation, the long-term radiation effects discussed above would be greatly intensified in any heavily attacked country if ground bursts were used. The survivors of the war might average a long-term radiation dose of 200 or 300 roentgens, and many would receive much more. This is 50 to 100 times as much as they would get from natural sources. It would increase the proportion of seriously defective children born from about 4 percent to about 5 percent of the total, and the resulting concentration of strontium 90 in bones would produce a large increase in the incidence of leukemia and cancer. The lives of the survivors might be shortened by an average of 5 to 10 years. And there would be other serious medical and environmental problems as well.

In spite of such unprecedented problems, this does not mean that economic recovery is impossible even following a heavy attack. If a large population were to survive through protective measures, with the economic resources surviving outside of major cities, and with careful preattack planning to help us get through the initial period of disruption, recovery would seem to be possible. About one-third of the population of the United States and about half of the manufacturing capital of the United States is located in our 50 largest metropolitan areas. This is much of the United States, and most people think of the survival of the United States in terms of what might happen to these metropolitan areas. Conversely, two-thirds of the population and about half of the manufacturing industry of the country lie outside of these areas. (The comparable figures for the Soviet Union are about four-fifths of the population and six-tenths of manufacturing industry outside of the 50 largest cities.) Half of our population and one-third of manufacturing are outside of the 150 largest urban areas. According to one informed optimistic estimate it might even be possible to restore something like the pre-war consumption standard for the survivors in 10 years or so after an attack which had destroyed our 50 largest metropolitan areas.

In sum: (1) An attack delivered on the 50 largest cities of the United States, in the absence of civil defenses, and if the population of these cities were to be found there at the time of the attack, would kill perhaps 30 to 40 million people. (2) This damage, while indeed catastrophic, would not be lethal—the Nation could in time recover, especially if plans for getting through the initial period of disruption had been made. (3) If the population of these cities were to be evacuated and sheltered they would be much less vulnerable, but an attack on the cities would still do great material damage. (4) A larger attack of, say, several thousand megatons, could kill over half of an unprotected population mostly from radioactive fallout (damage almost as great would result from a purely military attack against air-bases). (5) This scale of attack need not be lethal if modest civil defense preparations (fallout protection and recovery) have been made; though larger attacks are possible so are larger civil defense programs. (6) The vulnerability of the Soviet Union to a given weight of attack delivered on target is somewhat lower than that of the United States but roughly of the same order of magnitude. However, the combination of a civil defense program combined with the threat that the Soviet Union might strike first could give that country an advantage we would do well not to depreciate. . . .

Edward Teller

DETERRENCE, TESTING,
AND LIMITED WAR*

. . . .

There is one important and straightforward step which we can take to increase stability and decrease the probability of a third climactic world war.

We must develop a second-strike force. We must be in possession of retaliatory weapons which no Russian attack can wipe out. In possession of such a second-strike force, we can confidently say to the Russians, "We shall never start an all-out nuclear war but if you attack America with nuclear explosives you can be quite sure that you will suffer the full force of a similar attack."

A second-strike force will make it unnecessary that we unleash our nuclear might on the basis of suspicion, however well founded. I am firmly convinced that the Russians are not eager to have an all-out conflict in which they, too, would suffer heavily. They would surely lose all their industry of which they are proud and on which they base their hopes for world domination.

We are actually on the way to develop a second-strike force. We are using our industrial potential and our ingenuity to disperse our retaliatory force in such a manner that no attack, however swift and ferocious, can possibly wipe it out. But this development will cost many billions of dollars and even so it may not be sufficient.

With continued nuclear testing we could reduce to one-half or one-third the weight of our retaliatory bombs. Lighter bombs can be carried by smaller missiles. Smaller missiles are less expensive. They can be handled by fewer people on smaller and more secure bases. They can be made safer against destruction by shock from an enemy bomb. They can be dispersed and hidden more easily, or

---

* Edward Teller, from "Policy for Peace," copyright, 1960, by *The Houston Post.* Reprinted by permission.

Dr. Teller is currently Professor of Physics at the University of California, Berkeley.

better still, they can be made very mobile. If their position can be easily changed every day over a road network, the aggressor will have a virtually impossible task in finding them. . . .

Some bombs in our second-strike force should have large yields. But it does not necessarily follow that in order to construct these large bombs we need to perform tests with very large explosives. Most of the needed information can be obtained with the help of experiments of moderate size. At any rate, explosions small or large can be carried out underground or in space and need not contaminate our atmosphere.

We must not lose sight of our main objective. This is to make sure that no nuclear attack will destroy our country. The best assurance we can have is to make it quite clear to Russia that an attack on us would be both expensive and useless. Retaliation by our second-strike force would make an attack most expensive for an aggressor. By building up our passive defenses we would make sure that our nation can survive even if our enemies unleash the most destructive bombs against us. Too little has been done about simple common-sense passive defense, which is defense indeed in the strictest sense of the word. We could be prepared with proper shelters, effective organization and selected stockpiles of materials needed for reconstruction. Thus we could insure our survival and our speedy recuperation. . . .

The idea of massive retaliation should be abandoned and the expression stricken from our international vocabulary. We must never repay a smaller insult with bigger injury. Such an act would not be in accord with our deepest moral convictions. It introduces into our world an intolerable element of instability. And it is not even a practical proposition. For years we had a monopoly of nuclear weapons. During these years communism spread over Eastern Europe and China. We did not use nuclear weapons to confine the communist empire in its earlier boundaries. Massive retaliation was not used. I believe that few people wanted to see it used. I certainly did not.

But today we are facing a different situation. Our monopoly is gone. If we were ever to use massive retaliation as a response to a limited Russian conflict we can be sure that Russian nuclear weapons will reach our country in considerable numbers. Under these conditions it is practically certain that we shall not unleash all-out war except in the very last emergency.

We know this and the Russians know it. Thus the threat of massive retaliation will not deter the Russians from attacking our allies. Surely we cannot be satisfied with our national defense unless it provides a possibility of aiding our allies and shielding the free people of the world without resorting to all-out war. We must find ways to stop limited aggression. . . .

The Russians are masters of the salami technique. After the war, Hungary elected a democratic government but the Russians controlled the police. They did not advance any radical claims. They demanded small changes. Slice by thin slice, they whittled away at the independence of Hungary. This is what the Hungarians call the salami technique. Now there is nothing left of the salami.

We must be prepared to resist Russian aggression. Small conquests will be in the long run as dangerous as big ones. But if we want to preserve the peace we must be particularly careful that a small conflict should not turn into a big conflagration. It is therefore necessary that we should be able to accept every Russian challenge on the same scale at which it is offered. We must be thoroughly prepared for a limited war. This is not easy. The Russians can choose the time and place of the next crisis. They will be ready and prepared with massive forces. We will be thousands of miles away. Nevertheless we can be successful in defending the country attacked if two conditions are satisfied. We must be able to employ the most modern and mobile weapons. And the country which is invaded must be determined to defend its own freedom.

Within hours after the invasion, we could air-drop commando groups over the invaded country. There may be no more than five to 50 men in a group. These groups could carry nuclear weapons which would enable them to complete their mission even when faced with massed enemy power. Their mission will be to prevent the invader from concentrating his forces. In the face of nuclear weapons the aggressor will have to disperse his own men. But the dispersed forces can be attacked successfully by people who are determined to defend their homes.

The power of native resistance has been demonstrated in recent years in the greatly differing examples of Hungary and Algeria. Only the full concentrated armament of a great power can conquer a determined people. With our tactical nuclear weapons we can stop the Russian steam-roller. The rest must be accomplished by the population of the invaded country. In this manner, nuclear arms could be used strictly for defense. And such defense would not leave the country in ruins. It would do less damage than conventional warfare. . . .

Nuclear weapons have been pictured as instruments of all-out destruction. This need not be so. In a limited war there will be no purpose in bombing cities. The cities will not serve in a short and mobile war as centers of production or links in the transportation system. On the battlefield itself, one could and should use nuclear weapons of appropriate size. One does not need to overhit any target.

But is it possible to keep a nuclear war limited? The Russians have said no. Should we believe them? It is to the interest of the Russians that we abstain from using nuclear weapons. In the absence of such weapons their salami tactics will work.

There are three ways in which a war might be limited. One can limit the weapons. One can limit the territory. And one can limit the aims. No limitation on weapons will work and no limitation on weapons should be attempted. We should use appropriate weapons and use them with discrimination without doing unnecessary damage to the innocent bystander. Nuclear weapons can be so used. It is possible to limit the territory and the aims of a war. This is the usual historical way in which wars have been limited. If an aggression has occurred, we can declare what we consider the theater and the purpose of the war. As long as the Russians will not enlarge the conflict, neither will we.

A limited war will not grow into an all-out nuclear conflict unless the Russians choose to attack us in America. If we are prepared with a reliable second-strike force, the Russians certainly will not start an all-out war.

A solid capability for limited warfare is desperately needed and should be developed. Today we do not possess such a capability. . . . We have started to develop tactical nuclear weapons. But we are at the very beginning of such a development. We could and we should use additional nuclear experiments to develop these weapons. All of these experiments could be carried out at a power less than and sometimes much less than 1,000 tons TNT equivalent. No conceivable technical inspection system could detect such tests. If we continued our test moratorium and the Russians developed such weapons, the results would be disastrous.

Herman Kahn

A FIRST STRIKE CAPABILITY*

. . . A Credible First Strike Capability may seem to many Americans like a possibility for the Soviets—but not for us. One sees many statements to the effect that "We will never strike first." In the context in which the remark is usually made (a "dastardly" surprise attack out of the blue against an unprepared enemy), this position is undoubtedly correct. Such a capability would not be worth much to the U.S. However, we have many treaties and other obligations. There is the obligation to come to the aid of NATO nations if they are attacked. It is generally supposed that this aid includes the use of our SAC against the Soviet heartland, even if the Soviets attack Europe *but not the United States*. From a technical point of view this means that in this instance *we* would strike *first!* The agonizing decision to start an all-out thermonuclear war would be ours. Surely there is a serious question whether we would live up to our treaty obligations under such circumstances.

That this doubt is plausible can be seen in the response of Christian Herter to a question by Senator Morse on the occasion of the hearings on his nomination: "I cannot conceive of any President involving us in an all-out nuclear war unless the facts showed clearly we are in danger of all-out devastation ourselves, *or that actual moves have been made toward devastating ourselves.*"

A thermonuclear balance of terror is equivalent to the signing of a nonaggression treaty which states that neither the Soviets nor the Americans will initiate an all-out attack, no matter how provoking the other side may become. Sometimes people do not understand the full implications of this figurative nonaggression treaty. Let me illustrate what it can mean if we accept absolutely the notion that there is no provocation that would cause us to strike the Soviets other than

---

*Herman Kahn, *On Thermonuclear War*, pp. 27–32. Copyright (c) 1960 by Princeton University Press. Reprinted by permission.

Mr. Kahn is a member of the Senior Staff at the Rand Corporation, Santa Monica, California.

an immediately impending or an actual Soviet attack on the United States. Imagine that the Soviets have taken a very drastic action against our allies in Europe. Let the action be as extreme or shocking as the reader's imagination permits. Suppose, for example, that the Soviets have dropped bombs on London, Berlin, Rome, Paris, and Bonn, *but have made no detectable preparations for attacking the United States, and our retaliatory force looks good enough to deter them from such an attack.* As far as we can tell they have done this horrible deed simply to demonstrate their strength and resolve. Suppose also that there is a device which restrains the President of the United States from acting for about twenty-four hours. It is probably true that if the President were not restrained he would order an attack on the [U.S.S.R.]. . . . However, we have assumed the existence of a 24-hour device which forces him to stop and think and make his decision in cold blood. The President would presumably call together his advisors during this time. Most of the advisors would probably urge strongly that the U.S. fulfill its obligations by striking the Soviet Union. Now let us further suppose that the President is also told by his advisors that even though we will kill almost every Russian *civilian,* we will not be able to destroy all of the Soviet strategic forces, and that these surviving Soviet forces will (by radiation or strontium-90 or something else) kill every American in their retaliatory blow—all 180 million of us.

Is it not difficult to believe that under these hypothetical circumstances any President of the United States would initiate a thermonuclear war by all-out retaliation against the Soviets with the Strategic Air Command? Few would contend that there is any plausible public policy which would justify ending life for everyone. It should be clear that our retaliation would not restore Europe; we could only succeed in further destroying it either as a by-product of our actions or because the surviving Soviet forces would subsequently destroy Europe as well as the United States. I am not saying that the United States would stand idly by. We would clearly declare war on the Soviets. We would make all kinds of *limited* military moves. We would go into a crash mobilization on at least the hundred-billion-dollars-a-year level. But there is one thing that we almost certainly would not do: We would not launch an all-out attack on Soviet cities.

There were two important caveats in the situation described: 180 million Americans would be killed, and the President would have twenty-four hours to think about his response. Let us consider these in turn. If 180 million dead is too high a price to pay for punishing the Soviets for their aggression, what price would we be willing to pay? This is a hard and unpleasant question. I have discussed this question with many Americans, and after about fifteen minutes of discussion their estimates of an acceptable price generally fall between 10 and 60 million, clustering toward the upper number. (Their first reaction, incidentally, is usually that the U.S. would *never* be deterred from living up to its obligations by fear of a Soviet counterblow—an attitude that invariably disappears after some minutes of reflection.) The way one seems to arrive at the upper limit of 60 million is rather interesting. He takes one-third of a country's population, in other words somewhat less than half. No American that I have spoken to who was at all serious about the matter believed that any U.S. action, limited or unlimited, would be justified—no matter what our commitments were—if more than half of our population would be killed in retaliation.

The 24-hour delay is a more subtle device. It is the equivalent of asking, "Can the Soviets force the President to act in cold blood and full knowledge, rather than in the immediate anger of the moment?" This depends not only on the time he has to learn and ponder the effects that would flow from his actions, . . . but also on how deeply and seriously the President and his advisors have thought about the problem in advance. This latter, in turn, would depend on whether there had been any tense situations or crises which forced the President and the people to face the concept that war is something which can happen, rather than something that is reliably deterred by some declaratory policy that never need be acted upon. (The effects of the war are usually considered irrelevant to one's declaratory policy, since it is assumed that the declarations will deter the war.) . . .

. . . Credibility [of a First Strike Capability] does not involve the question "Do we or the Soviets have the capability to hurt the other side on a first strike?" It is well known that this capability exists and in all likelihood will continue to exist. Credibility depends on being willing to accept the other side's retaliatory blow. It depends on the harm *he* can do, not on the harm *we* can do. It depends as much on *air defense* and *civil defense* as on *air offense*. It depends on *will* as well as *capability*. It depends on the *provocation* and on the *state of our mind* when the provocation occurs. One should also note that being able to use a Credible First Strike Capability to influence Soviet or European behavior depends not only on our will, but also on Soviet and European estimates of our will. Serious problems may be created for us if either of them does not believe in our willingness to attack under certain kinds of provocation. . . .

ACCIDENTAL WAR:
SOME DANGERS IN THE 1960's*

Our aim in this paper is to consider the possibility that a major accidental war may occur at some time in the next 10 years. "Accidental war" as we use it here is equivalent to "war by miscalculation," and "unintentional war." A formal definition is not required; the question of transcendent practical interest is the likelihood that a large-scale nuclear war between East and West may, through some combination of circumstances, come about without the intention of either side to launch such a war. We limit our consideration to the next 10 years because this now seems to be the critical time period and because predictions further into the future become too speculative. . . .

A—Defense Systems Accidents

Accidents of this type are almost entirely a consequence of modern weapons and their associated technology. Our concern is with the possibility that at some time in the 1960's a large nuclear attack might be launched as a result of a technical mishap or a simple human mistake. . . .

Accidents may occur at any point in the processes of 1) information gathering, 2) information evaluation and decision-making, and 3) the launching or near-launching of weapons carriers. Warning of an attack in progress will come from radar systems and, as developments progress in the 1960's, from the Ballistic Missile Early Warning System (BMEWS) and the Midas early warning satellite. Warning of an impending attack will come largely through intelligence activities. In principle, and as far as possible in practice, the ultimate responsibility for information evaluation and decision-making rests with the President. A great deal of auxiliary machinery exists to ad-

---

* *Accidental War: Some Dangers in the 1960's,* prepared under the guidance of John B. Phelps, by a research seminar in The Mershon National Security Program, The Ohio State University, Columbus, Ohio, June 28, 1960, pp. 1–19. Reprinted by permission.

vise him and in some cases to save time in implementing decisions he may reach. Some time-saving, more or less precautionary, steps, such as the launching of bombers under "positive control," may be taken on the authority of lesser commanders. Retaliatory forces in the 1960's will almost certainly consist of manned bombers with a rapidly growing proportion of first and then second and third generation missiles.

It is of interest to consider some of the incidents which have occurred in the U.S. strategic machinery to date and some kinds of possible accidents which might be hypothesized. . . . Precautionary measures have been taken in SAC as a result of ambiguous warnings on many occasions. Nuclear weapons have been involved in about 10 major accidents but there have been no nuclear explosions. One operational ICBM blew up on its launching pad. Anti-aircraft missiles have misfired several times and have been accidentally launched at least twice. False radar warnings, including an apparent flight of bombers moving over the Atlantic at 2000 mph, have occurred frequently. There have been many test alerts of U.S. retaliatory machinery. On the communist side of the fence very little is known, but Premier Khrushchev is reliably reported to have told Vice President Nixon about an erratic Soviet missile which was destroyed by a signal from the ground as it headed toward Alaska.

Many kinds of possible systems accidents have been suggested, sometimes, we believe, without much technical basis in fact. Neither a flock of geese nor a shower of meteors is likely now to trigger U.S. retaliation with manned bombers.

Similar dangers are certainly increased, however, as we move more firmly into the missile age and warning times become shorter, particularly if our retaliatory forces are vulnerable. The technical development of our over-all machinery of retaliation in the next decade presents some major problems with respect to safety and the avoidance of potentially dangerous accidents. More sensitive radars are more likely to give spurious signals. Faster reaction times will require less human decision-making and a greater dependence on automation. Computers may be required to discriminate reliably between missiles and meteors in a few minutes at most. Increasingly reliable unjammable and rapid means of communication must be built. It is clear that the President has already been obliged to delegate, in fact if not in principle, some of his ultimate authority to order the use of nuclear weapons, first for defensive purposes, and second for retaliation. He will be forced to delegate more. The present "positive control" of airborne SAC bombers has no parallel in ballistic missiles.

Operational missile warheads are not armed until ready for firing, but the missiles do not have effective "destruct" systems which would allow them to be destroyed in flight.

Communist and Western defense systems may be expected to follow the same very general course of development, although technical emphases and operational systems will differ. There is strong evidence, from air safety records for instance, to suggest that communist systems will be somewhat less sophisticated insofar as technical safeguards against accidents are concerned. There is also a question about how much responsibility is delegated to communist commanders. Thus Premier Khrushchev recently implied that Marshal Malinovsky or others could order an attack on U-2 bases.

B—Accidental Nuclear Explosions

. . . The chances are of the order of one in 100 that a U.S. nuclear weapon will explode at some time in the next 10 years. This extremely approximate estimate is for essentially mechanical malfunctions only; we make no attempt to quantify the various possibilities of human error. Nor do we have any basis for quantitative speculation on the likelihood of explosion of the nuclear weapons of other countries. Probably the communist nations, including China, are and will be less safety conscious than the U.S., and the spread of nuclear weapons to more countries in the next decade certainly compounds the problem.

There will probably be, in all the nuclear countries, great pressure for the development of lighter, smaller and more novel weapon designs. Provision must be made for arming weapons by remote control. Various technical compromises between military reliability and safety will have to be made. For these reasons, experience with manned bomber-carried weapons to date is not an infallible guide to the future. Considering all these factors, we are led to the very general conclusion that the accidental explosion of one or more nuclear weapons in the next 10 years is not improbable.

Would an accidental nuclear explosion start a war? Possibly, but probably not, unless it occurred in a time of extreme tension as discussed below. Or unless it happened to destroy an important city or military target or there were reasons to believe that it was really an enemy weapon. An accidental explosion probably would not result in the full design energy yield of the weapon and it might therefore be relatively less destructive. Several accidental explosions in a short time period could have serious consequences, but the probability of these happening coincidentally is infinitesimal. In sum, it appears that accidental nuclear explosions are among the least likely direct causes of accidental war.

C—Human Aberrations

The carefully planned and elaborate safety devices built into U.S. weapons systems are designed to minimize the probability of serious accidents resulting from human error or inadvertence. What about the possibility that a person, in some position of responsibility in a man-machine system and suffering from some form of mental aberration, could intentionally bring about a significant act of war? Our concern here includes not only persons with formal responsibility, such as missile or aircraft commanders, but also persons of any rank or status who might be capable of causing serious mischief.

History furnishes numerous examples of failures and incompetence among military commanders—there are a few clear cases of military misadventures undertaken wtihout authorization. But because mental illness has only very recently been recognized as a distinct medical problem, the historical data are of limited value. And modern weapons have enormously multiplied the capacity for mischief that may rest, at least temporarily, with an individual. . . .

On a statistical basis and over a period of years, the probability of a few breakdowns in positions of great responsibility is high. Some efforts have been made to build safeguards against human aberration into weapons systems. Thus Air Force regulations require that the signal to an airborne bomber to proceed to its target must be verified by the officer members of the crew. A further measure of control is exercised over the refuelling plane if one is required and, in extreme cases, an errant bomber can be destroyed by other planes in its flight if this is possible. It is also known, for instance, that present plans for the Polaris weapons system provide for verification of the command to launch missiles by several members of the crew. Undoubtedly other safeguards in U.S. weapons systems exist but have not been made public. There inevitably remain, however, situations in which individuals, such as the pilot of a nuclear armed fighter-bomber, are largely free of safeguards. There are a few people in very special positions—Francis Powers is an example—who are subject to a minimum of restraints. It should be noted that the possibilities for trouble-making by an aberrant individual are by no means limited to the delivery of nuclear weapons. Thus a U-2 ground crewman, for instance, would have been in a position to sabotage Powers' flight.

Essentially no data are available on human breakdowns and safeguards to minimize their consequences in the communist armed forces. There are probably fewer specific allowances made for mental illnesses than in the Western nations. The distribution and regulation of critical responsibilities among individuals may be similar in practice although quite different in principle. Reports from defectors to the West indicate that communist pilots, for instance, are under relatively strict orders to shoot down their errant comrades.

The dangers of accidental war resulting from some form of human aberration in the next 10 years are nearly impossible to quantify. But the range of possibilities is very large and, at least in comparison with technical accidents, safeguards are harder to devise.

D—Unintended Spread of Limited Wars

The unintended spread of less-than-general, limited war into a general war including a massive nuclear exchange is viewed by many observers as the most likely origin of an accidental war in the next decade. The reason for this belief doubtless arises from the near certainty of the occurrence of military conflicts between the two opposing world power blocs, and thus, to a greater or lesser extent, between the major nuclear powers.

One of the prominent uncertainties in an analysis of possible future wars is the role of nuclear weapons. These weapons are probably historically unique in that, while they are completely untried (except as destroyers of cities) in warfare, the professional military planners, apparently somewhat more on the American side than on the Russian, are becoming more and more dependent on them in future strategies for limited as well as general war.

This is particularly important in Europe where NATO is essentially committed to meeting any kind of attack with U.S. nuclear weapons. This fact, together with the Russians' apparent lack of acceptance of the idea of a nuclear limited war and the destruction such a war would cause throughout Europe, makes very unlikely a limited war in Europe without a simultaneous U.S.–U.S.S.R. nuclear exchange. Indeed, any kind of armed conflict on a major scale in Europe which is not rapidly brought under control would probably trigger a general nuclear war.

In Asia and the Middle East, however, limited wars are more likely to stay limited as they have in the recent past. In these areas wars are more likely to be fought by "proxies" rather than by the great powers themselves. We will probably continue to see struggles between satellites and client states of the two power blocs, revolutions involving strong support of the rebels by a neighboring state, and violent internal rebellions. In most of these cases the major nuclear powers will only be involved to the extent of providing the material means to maintain the conflict and, possibly, specialized manpower such as pilots and submariners. Occasionally a major power may be involved directly on one side or the other as the U.S. was in Korea, but the conflict would probably remain limited if the other major power stayed out. In general, the use of proxies will assist in keeping a conflict limited, since they will not usually possess the means, particularly nuclear weapons, of spreading the conflict. But this argument may be less valid in the later sixties.

We can pick out several factors which will help to determine whether a limited conflict will spread. It is essential that communications be kept open between the combatants, or at least between their great power supporters, so that no action by one side will be interpreted by the other as requiring an expansion of the conflict. The costs of the struggle must not be allowed to get so high for either side—in terms of geography, military losses, physical destruction, political and economic factors, etc.—that it would be impossible to negotiate some kind of settlement rather than face an expansion of the war. This will require some changes in the traditional goals or end points of wars—"unconditional surrender," "punishment of the aggressor," etc.—as well as some modification of the traditional military doctrine of attempting primarily to destroy the enemy military forces. It will also be helpful to end or at least stabilize, in terms of geography and force, the military portions of the struggle as soon as possible (preferably before they begin).

It is well to note carefully the difficulties the use of nuclear weapons adds to keeping a conflict limited. The distinction between the use and non-use of such arms is qualitatively clearer and surer than that between various weapon yields and/or targets—the main criterion of "limitation" sometimes postulated by proponents of a nuclear limited war strategy. In addition, their great destructiveness and the lack of knowledge of their over-all effects in war adds to the uncertainties attached to any use of nuclear weapons. Finally, the use of nuclear weapons by one side in a limited war would doubtless require the other side to do likewise. This would, in turn, probably bring the two major nuclear powers more actively into the struggle, with the consequent increased likelihood of the war spreading.

If one of the major nuclear powers does become involved in a limited war, it may or may not have the means for fighting the war with conventional forces. A "starving" of conventional capabilities may thus tend to force the use of nuclear weapons, with all their hazards, in a limited war.

Our discussion has tacitly assumed the current distribution of nuclear weapons among nations. As these weapons become more widely diffused the problems of limitation of war become correspondingly great, since more nations will have the means of spreading the conflict and/or bringing in the major powers. This problem is especially disturbing with respect to Communist China, since the Chinese rulers are on record as believing that a general nuclear war would be less disastrous for China than for its enemies.

E—Catalytic War

The danger of catalytic war results very largely from the spread of nuclear weapons to a larger number of countries. It is possible that a small nuclear power could, in the right circumstances, launch a successful, unidentified, sneak attack on one or more of the major powers and thus precipitate a massive nuclear exchange between them. Viewed in the context of the historical behavior of nations, the likelihood that a nation would be strongly motivated to undertake such an attack seems small. Concealment of the source of the attack would be, at least in many cases, difficult.

A kind of general war catalyst which could become significant as more countries acquire nuclear weapons is that in which one of the small power participants in a limited war deliberately undertakes to cause a spreading of the conflict, by either an initial use of nuclear weapons or by their use in a deliberately provocative way. Red China seems to represent a particular danger.

F—Diplomatic and Military Miscalculations

East-West tensions have fluctuated in the years since World War II, but there has been a trend for periods of tension to occur more frequently during the last five to ten years. In a time of tension in the next decade, nuclear war could result from intelligence blunders or miscalculated high-level decisions. . . .

Taiwan and West Berlin have been scenes of crisis in the past and are likely to be in the future. If the United States came to the Nationalists' aid again in defense of the Offshore Islands, chances of war would probably be greater than they were in 1954 and 1958, as China grows stronger and especially when she develops her own nuclear weapons. Defense of the islands, and even of Formosa, will become militarily difficult against even short-range missiles with nuclear warheads. Similarly, in Germany, if control of the access routes to West Berlin are turned over to East Germany as Russia threatens, some form of limited war could well result, and with the West committed to the use of nuclear weapons the situation would be dangerous. Attack on a Western airlift into Berlin might also mean expanded war. Because leaders on both sides of the Iron Curtain seem to recognize the danger of any war in Europe and because Russia does and will continue to have control over East Germany, the danger here will probably be less than that in the Taiwan Straits when China develops her own weapons.

The recent U-2 incident shows how a state of tension can arise suddenly during a period of relative calm. Soviet threats of retaliation against U-2 bases if further flights are attempted and U.S. slowness in announcing that the flights had been stopped set up an atmosphere of threat and counter threat.

In each of these postwar crisis situations either the U.S. or the U.S.S.R. threatened some kind of forceful action and each took some kind of measures to carry out, or react against, the threat. In each crisis forces were more or less poised for action, and a miscalculation or accident could have touched off a war. . . .

In the preceding section we have briefly discussed several types of accidents which *could* lead to war in the next 10 years. Whether any of these accidents, by themselves or in combination, *would* lead to war depends very much on the state of tension or "readiness" for war which exists when the accident happens. . . .

. . . It is very doubtful that either popular or official outrage would lead to a real demand for nuclear war. It is possible, however, that public demands for "firmness" or "action" might greatly increase the danger of war in times of tension. . . .

. . . It seems prudent to assume that there will be, in the 1960's as in the last 15 years, occasional peaks of tension. At these times accidents, of whatever nature, are most likely to lead to war.

The greatest danger, in a time of tension, is that normally insignificant events or accidents may set in motion on both sides a series of events leading to disaster. We might have a kind of self-generating accidental war. Predictions tend to be conjectures. But in a time of moderate tension, let us say, a small war occurs—there have been many of these in the postwar years. A major power which considers its interest threatened decides to intervene on a limited scale and does so. Its intervention is met by warnings and threats from the other side. One side, and probably then the other, places its forces on some level of alert. Intelligence-gathering processes are under great strain. National leaders are watching events with anxiety. One side places its forces in a higher state of readiness and the other, predictably, follows suit. The danger at this point is enormously heightened by any pressure to launch a pre-emptive attack. The situation is tense and conspicuously unstable. Any spark—a false radar warning, an accidental overflight, a failure in communications—could trigger an accidental war.

The critical point in this cycle of events is reached not when one side becomes convinced that the other side is about to attack, *but when either side concludes that the situation has deteriorated to a state where war is inevitable.* This kind of critical point is even harder to specify or to determine in advance; clearly the side which perceives the "inevitability" of war first has the advantage. All this offers the possibility of shortening drastically and tragically the time period over which the strategic guessing game is played.

Occasional attempts have been made to discuss the U.S. strategic deterrent in relation to a "retaliatory threshold": a level of provocation below which strategic retaliation would not be launched. Certainly, both the Western and the communist nations, in evident recognition of the dangers, tolerate incidents which might in former times have led to war. Overflights, accidental or deliberate, occur; planes are occasionally shot down; radio broadcasts are jammed; abductions occur; insults and threats are traded; and so on. Some lesser overt acts of war would probably also be tolerated, depending on the circumstances. But because of the extremely wide variety of possible provocations the significance of an unambiguously defined retaliatory threshold is doubtful. Moreover, a threshold, if it were to reduce the danger of accidental war, would have to be known to the enemy, and this contradicts the long-standing military principle that it is desirable to keep the enemy guessing. . . .

G—Conclusions

We believe that a number of steps to reduce the danger of accidental war are feasible at the present time. Some of these steps will require formal or informal agreement among nations. Others, which have apparently received little serious consideration, can be taken unilaterally by the United States with no significant loss of military security. Unilateral steps include:

a) Official recognition of the danger of accidental war and a publicly declared intention to seek ways to reduce the danger.

b) Recognition, in practice, that the traditional military principle which aims at keeping the enemy guessing at one's intentions may be dangerously out of date in the nuclear-missile age.

c) In the military sphere, still greater emphasis on relatively invulnerable strategic forces and a flexible non-nuclear capability.

d) Communication to possible enemies of the manifestly non-aggressive character of U.S. military plans and preparations. More information on weapons system safety measures can be released without compromising security. Military training operations, including practice alerts and SAC flights, can be conducted in a conspicuously non-aggressive manner. U.S. strategic doctrine can be made to stress exclusively, in word and deed, a second-strike capability. Imaginative study of this communication problem might reveal many helpful measures. Reciprocation of some of these unilateral measures by a potential enemy could yield very significant gains in the stability of the deterrent balance.

Multilateral measures on which U.S. initiative is needed include:

a) Clearer recognition and study of the accidental war problem as an important area of arms control negotiations. A variety of small but collectively very significant safeguards against accidental war might be more susceptible of negotiation at this time than, say, a nuclear test ban.

b) Special study of the possibility of providing very fast and reliable communication between top national leaders on each side to help head off any crisis before it leads to disaster. A number of ingenious safeguards against deception could be built into this "assurance system."

Harrison Brown and James Real

THE ARMS RACE[*]

. . . .

There are few people in America today who care to be identified with a belligerent militaristic policy which is likely to lead to war. It is generally recognized that the time is past when talk of "preven-

[*] Harrison Brown and James Real, *Community of Fear*, Center for the Study of Democratic Institutions, Santa Barbara, 1960, pp. 31–39.

Dr. Brown is Professor of Geochemistry, California Institute of Technology. Mr. Real is a publicist and a consultant to the Center for the Study of Democratic Institutions.

tive" war could be rationalized. Yet the war machine gathers strength, and serious consideration of its diminution or dismantling is rare and often timid. Aside from the difficulties involved in the *Realpolitik* of the international situation, there are domestic forces, largely unspoken, that commit us more absolutely each day to the path away from effective arms control—not to speak of actual disarmament.

There are many knowledgeable persons who believe that under no circumstances should research and development on new weapons systems be stopped. There would always be the fear that the potential enemy might develop a greatly superior system of offense or defense which would give him a considerable advantage. The only way of minimizing the danger of such a threat is to maintain a diversity of research and development covering all major aspects of military technology. Since individual nations cannot justify stopping development programs on weapons systems, it is clear that the tug-of-war in this area is likely to continue—that new offensive systems will continue to replace old ones and that these in turn will necessitate new defensive systems. As the research and development continue, there will be new breakthroughs which will make possible still newer systems and render older ones obsolete.

Persons who insist upon perpetuating the military research and development race have an impressive argument when they point to the development of the thermonuclear bomb. Following World War II, strong forces in our government, particularly in the scientific community, discouraged the establishment of a research and development program aimed at producing megaton weapons. Many factors were involved in this attitude—some of them practical, others emotional and moral. There were others, however, who believed just as strongly that our lack of effort in this direction could be suicidal. What if the Russians were to develop such weapons first? Would they hesitate to make use of their new-found strategic advantage?

The pro-hydrogen bomb forces eventually won out, and a vigorous program was established, which was successful in a spectacularly short time. The Russians, of course, established their own program, which was also successful.

Today the proponents of maintaining extremely strong programs in the development of weapons systems can point to much more than the hydrogen bomb as justification for their views. The rapidly increasing deterrent gap has resulted in large measure from our not financing missile development adequately. The Polaris development, had it come earlier, would have done much to relieve the situation.

Thus, no matter what is possible it must be pursued. Can gigaton (a billion tons of TNT) bombs be built? We must do the work and see. Can climate over the Soviet Union be altered? We must experiment. Can the earth be burned, broken, kept from rotating? Can all life be eliminated? Can we make the oceans boil? All of these questions must be considered. If we don't consider them, the Russians might, and if successful they would have us at a disadvantage. . . .

If the arms race continues, as it probably will, its future pattern seems clear in broad outline. As a result of the emergence of the current tremendous capabilities for killing and destroying, programs will be started aimed at the evacuation of cities, the construction of fallout shelters in regions outside the major metropolitan areas, and the construction of limited underground shelters. Increased offensive capabilities will then emerge which will to some extent neutralize these efforts. Larger bombs will be compressed into sufficiently small packages to be carried by ICBM's. Very large bombs (about 1,000 megatons) will be built which, when exploded at an altitude of about 300 miles, could sear six Western states.

The new developments will cause people to burrow more deeply into the ground. Factories will be built in caves, as will apartment houses and stores. Eventually most human life will be underground, confronted by arsenals capable of destroying all life over the land areas of the earth. Deep under the ground people will be relatively safe—at least until such time as we learn how to make explosives capable of pulverizing the earth to great depths.

The arms race and the associated uprooting of established institutions will outstrip by far the spiral of upheaval described by Wang Chi during the war which preceded the T'ang dynasty:

> *"These days, continually fuddled with drink*
> *I fail to satisfy the appetites of the soul.*
> *But seeing men all behaving like drunkards,*
> *How can I alone remain sober?"*

The Soviet Union has apparently, in the last few years, instituted a civilian defense program of substantial magnitude. It is probable that within the next two or three years the United States will embark on a crash shelter program for a large proportion of its citizens and some of its industry. Once the shelter program is underway, it will constitute a significant retreat from the idea of the obsolescence of war.

Once the people are convinced that they can survive the present state of the art of killing, a broad and significant new habit pattern will have been introduced and accepted, one grotesquely different from any we have known for thousands of years—that of adjusting ourselves to the idea of living in holes. From that time onward it will be simple to adjust ourselves to living in *deeper* holes.

Tens of thousands of years ago our Mousterian and Aurignacian ancestors lived in caves. The vast knowledge which we have accumulated during the intervening millennia will have brought us full cycle. The epic of man's journey upward into the light will have ended. . . .

Erich Fromm

THE CASE FOR UNILATERAL DISARMAMENT*

. . . .

Even though the broader concept of complete—rather than graduated—unilateral disarmament is . . . not a practical possibility in the near future, as far as the United States and the USSR are concerned, I believe it worthwhile to present the arguments for this position. . . . Thinking through the arguments for a radical—even though practically unacceptable—position contributes to breaking through the thought barrier which prevents us now from getting out of the dangerous circle of seeking peace by means of threat and counterthreat. . . .

The proposal for complete unilateral disarmament has been advocated from a religious, moral or pacifist position by such men as Victor Gollancz, Lewis Mumford, and some Quakers. It has also been supported by men like Bertrand Russell, Stephen King-Hall,

* Erich Fromm, "The Case for Unilateral Disarmament," from *Daedalus*, Vol. 89, pp. 1016–1020, copyright © 1960 by The American Academy of Arts and Sciences. Reprinted by permission of Harcourt, Brace & World, Inc.

Professor Fromm is on the staff of the Psychology Department of Michigan State University, and Professor of Psychoanalysis at the National Autonomous University of Mexico.

and C. W. Mills, who are not opposed to the use of force under all or any circumstances, yet who are uncompromisingly opposed both to thermonuclear war and to all and any preparation for it. This writer finds himself somewhat between the position of the strict pacifists and men like Bertrand Russell and Stephen King-Hall.

The difference between these two groups, however, is not as fundamental as it may seem. They are united by their critical attitude toward the irrational aspects of international politics and by their deep reverence for life. They share the conviction of the oneness of the human race and faith in the spiritual and intellectual potentialities of man. They follow the dictates of their conscience in refusing to have any "part in making millions of women and children and noncombatants hostages for the behavior of their own governments." Whether they think in theistic terms or in those of non-theistic humanism (in the sense of the philosophic continuum from Stoic to eighteenth-century Enlightenment philosophy), they all are rooted in the same spiritual tradition and are unwilling to compromise with its principles. They are united by their uncompromising opposition to any kind of idolatry, including the idolatry of the state. While their opposition to the Soviet system is rooted precisely in this attitude against idolatry, they are critical of idolatry whenever it appears in the Western world whether it is in the name of God or of democracy.

While there is no proponent of unilateral disarmament who does not believe that the individual must be willing to give his life for the sake of his supreme values, if such an ultimate necessity arises, they are all equally convinced that to risk the life of the human race, or even the results of its best efforts in the last five thousand years, is immoral and irresponsible. As warfare becomes at once more senseless and more devastating, the convergence between religious pacifist, humanist, and pragmatic opponents to nuclear armament grows.

From the standpoint of the proponents of unilateral disarmament, to continue the armament race is catastrophic, *whether the deterrent works or not*. In the first place, they have little faith that the deterrent will prevent the outbreak of a thermonuclear war. They believe that the results of a thermonuclear war would be such that in the very "best" case they completely belie the idea that we ought to fight such a war in order to save our democratic way of life. There is no need to enter the guessing game as to whether one-third or two-thirds of the population of the two opponents and what proportion of the neutral world (depending on how the wind blows) will be destroyed. This is a guessing game that verges on madness; for to consider the possibility of the destruction of 30%, 60%, or 90% of one's own and the enemy's population as an acceptable (although, of course, most undesirable) result of one's policy is indeed approaching pathology. The increasing split between intellect and affect, which is so characteristic of our Western development in the last centuries, has reached its dangerous, schizoid peak in the calm and allegedly rational way in which we can discuss possible world destruction as a result of our own action. It does not take much imagination to visualize that sudden destruction and the threat of slow death to a large part of the American population, or the Russian population, or large parts of the world, will create such a panic, fury, and despair as could only be compared with the mass psychosis resulting from the Black Death in the Middle Ages. The traumatic effects of such a catastrophe would lead to a new form of primitive barbarism, to the resurgence of the most archaic elements, which are still potentialities in every man and of which we have had ample evidence in the terror systems of Hitler and Stalin. It would sound most unlikely to many students of human nature and psychopathology that human beings could cherish freedom, respect for life or love after having witnessed and participated in the unlimited cruelty of man against man which thermonuclear war would mean. It is a psychological fact that acts of brutality have a brutalizing effect on the participants and lead to more brutality. . . .

What is the likely future of the social character of man in a bilateral or multilateral armed world, where, no matter how complex the problems or how full the satisfactions of any particular society, the biggest and most pervasive reality in any man's life is the poised missile, the humming data processor connected to it, the waiting radiation counters and seismographs, the over-all technocratic perfection (overlying the nagging but impotent fear of its imperfection) of the mechanism of holocaust? To live for any length of time under the constant threat of destruction creates certain psychological effects in most human beings—fright, hostility, callousness, a hardening of the heart, and a resulting indifference to all the values we cherish. Such conditions will transform us into barbarians—though barbarians equipped with the most complicated machines. If we are serious in claiming that our aim is to preserve freedom (that is, to prevent the subordination of the individual under an all-powerful state), we must admit that this freedom will be lost, whether the deterrent works or does not work.

Aside from these psychological facts, the continuation of the arms race constitutes a particular threat to Western culture. In the process of conquering nature, producing and consuming have become

Western man's main preoccupation—the goal of his life. We have transformed means into ends. We manufacture machines which are like men, and we produce men who are like machines. In his work, the individual is managed as a part of a production team. During his leisure time, he is manipulated as a consumer who likes what he is told to like and yet has the illusion that he follows his own taste. In centering his life around the production of things, man himself is in danger of becoming a thing, worshiping the idols of the production machine and the state while he is under the illusion of worshiping God. "Things are in the saddle and ride mankind," as Emerson has put it. Circumstances which we created have consolidated themselves into powers which rule over us. The technical and bureaucratic system we have built tells us what to do, it decides for us. We may not be in danger of becoming slaves, but we are in danger of becoming robots, and the human values of our tradition are threatened—integrity, individuality, responsibility, reason, and love. Talking about these values more and more becomes an empty ritual.

This trend toward a world of impotent men directed by virile machines (both in the United States and in the Soviet Union)—brought about by technological and demographic factors, and by the increasing centralization and bureaucracy in big corporations and government—will reach the point of no return if we continue the arms race. Dangerous as our present situation is, we still have a chance to put man back into the saddle, to effect a renaissance of the spiritual values of the great humanistic tradition. Unless such a renaissance occurs, unless we can achieve a radical revitalization of the spirit on which our culture is founded, we shall lose the vitality necessary for survival and we shall decay, just as many other great powers have decayed in history. The real threat to our existence is not Communist ideology, it is not even the Communist military power—it is the hollowness of our beliefs, the fact that freedom, individuality, and faith have become empty formulas, that God has become an idol, that our vitality is sapped because we have no vision except that of having more of the same. It seems that a great deal of the hatred of Communism is, in the last analysis, based on a deep disbelief in the spiritual values of democracy. Hence, instead of experiencing love of what we are *for*, we experience hate of what we are *against*. If we continue to live in fear of extinction and to plan mass destruction of others, the last chance for a revival of our humanist-spiritual tradition will be lost. . . .

Robert R. Bowie

BASIC REQUIREMENTS OF ARMS CONTROL*

The concept of "arms control" includes any agreement among several powers to regulate some aspect of their military capability or potential. The arrangement may apply to the location, amount, readiness, or types of military forces, weapons, or facilities. Whatever their scope or terms, however, all plans for arms control have one common feature: they presuppose some form of cooperation or joint action among the several participants regarding their military programs. Is such cooperation feasible between major powers whose national purposes are in basic conflict? Concretely, is there any basis for such arrangements between the USSR and the United States? If so, what are the conditions and limits of reliable arms control?

Definition of the Problem

Many are convinced that agreements for arms control with the Soviet Union are not possible or in the national interest of the United States. In general their view derives from some or all of the following propositions:

(1) Military forces are only the reflection of political hostility. They are not the source or origin of tensions and conflicts among nations. Consequently, it is futile to try to regulate or reduce military forces separately from their underlying political causes. When basic hostility is resolved, reduction in arms will follow automatically as the nations feel themselves more secure and less threatened. To

---

* Robert R. Bowie, "Basic Requirements of Arms Control," from *Daedalus*, Vol. 89, pp. 708–710, 713–716, copyright © 1960 by the American Academy of Arts and Sciences. Reprinted by permission of Harcourt, Brace & World, Inc.

Dr. Bowie is Director of the Center for International Affairs and Dillon Professor of International Relations at Harvard University. From 1953 to 1957 he was Assistant Secretary of State for Policy Planning.

attempt control of military forces before removing the political sources of friction or threat is to put the cart before the horse.

(2) The purposes of the Sino-Soviet bloc are fundamentally hostile to the non-Communist nations. In the Communist view the conflict between their "system" and any other is irreconcilable and will be resolved only by the ultimate victory of the Communist order. Its leaders believe that Communism is destined to triumph throughout the world, and they intend to advance their cause by the vigorous use of all feasible means. Apparently, the Communist ideology no longer considers a global military showdown inevitable under present conditions. But the Communist leaders still define "wars of libera- tion" as "progressive," and have not abandoned the use of force (as in Hungary) or threats (as in Berlin) when either serves their interests.

(3) The Communists would not make or carry out any arms agree- ment in good faith. Any means are legitimate in seeking to promote Communist advance. Treaties are only instruments for pursuing their basic aims and will be violated or evaded as suits their interests. In 1939–1940, the Soviet Union overran and divided Poland and absorbed Esthonia, Lithuania, and Latvia, in flagrant violation of nonaggression treaties with each of these nations. Soviet disregard for commitments regarding Eastern Europe, and of its Potsdam obligations regarding Germany, is too well-known to need laboring.

It would be rash indeed to disregard these lessons in devising and analyzing any arms-control proposals. The grounds for distrusting the Soviet Union and its purposes should make even the optimistic cautious. The record of broken agreements should warn us not to rely on Soviet promises or good faith as the basis for arms-control measures. And the only safe course is to accept at face value the constant Communist assertions of their basic hostility to our social order.

But, this does not dispose of the problem. One could also cite many agreements which the Soviets have carried out. The crucial point is to understand what kinds of arrangements they can be ex- pected to comply with and why. The safest premise is this: in break- ing or keeping agreements, the Soviets *can be trusted* to pursue their own interests as they see them. Hence, measures for arms control should be reliable if they can be so devised that compliance will be more in the Soviet interest than evasion or violation.

Distrust is not, of course, limited to one side. The Soviets, re- flecting Communist ideology, are deeply suspicious of the "capitalist" nations and of their "ruling circles," which are seen as ruthless and unscrupulous in maintaining and improving their power and position.

Within this conception, however, they are expected to pursue their interests. . . .

Basic of Common Interests

At the threshold is the question: How can the Soviet Union and the United States have parallel or common interests in measures to control armaments if their basic purposes are antagonistic?

The answer lies essentially in the changing nature of war, especially general war. Until recently, large-scale military force could be used as an effective instrument for the pursuit of political aims. An aggressor might hope to win and to benefit from his victim's defeat. Conversely, potential victims could normally assure their own security by confronting the possible aggressor with sufficient opposing strength, either alone or with allies, to deter attack or defend themselves if it occurred. The resulting balance might preserve peace for extended periods under favorable conditions.

The development of modern weapons has changed the situation radically. As always, threat has produced deterrent which has largely succeeded thus far in preventing large-scale war. But the military balance remains unstable, entailing substantial risks and burdens. More important, these conditions jeopardize both sides. The loss of one need not be the gain of the other. If large-scale war meant mutual destruction, it would not advance the political interests of either side; both would be better served, *despite basic political hostility,* by preventing its occurrence. Thus, military instruments, while still related to political conflict, have taken on a life of their own and have become a separate source of tension and danger. . . .

Balancing of Restrictions

One serious obstacle to arms control arises from the difficulty of equating the impact of specific restrictions or other terms on the several parties. The task of assessing the effect of any acceptable change in military forces or armaments on the absolute and relative capability of the parties is extremely complex.

Since the armed forces of each nation rely on their own special "mix" of armaments and men, any restriction of a particular weapon has different impacts on each of them. In the 1930's enormous amounts of energy and time were devoted without success to efforts to equate different kinds and numbers of conventional weapons. Nuclear weapons and missiles have, if anything, made this task even harder because of the wide range of uncertainty regarding their effects on offense and defense and the relations between nuclear and conventional capabilities. Moreover, with dynamic-weapons technology, each side is likely to be ahead in developing specific fields, and therefore will appraise the prospects and significance of newer weapons in quite different terms. Especially under these conditions, military experts on each side almost inevitably tend to overestimate the harm to their capability from any proposed restriction and to discount its effects on the potential enemy. Hence, the greater the uncertainty regarding the value and equivalence of weapons and forces, the more likely is the conservative bias on both sides to block agreement on any material change.

A second obstacle arises from differing appraisals by the United States and USSR of the value and costs of inspection inherent in the divergence between a "closed" and an "open" society. Effective inspection is more vital for the United States than for the USSR. . . .

The Soviets undoubtedly look on their secrecy as a military asset. In allowing it to be pierced by inspection, they consider they are making a separate, or additional, sacrifice of their military potential. Hence, they will assess the cost of reciprocal inspection (particularly, if intensive) as high, especially as compared to its value for them. The United States will certainly not estimate the burden as nearly so great, though it might appear more onerous (at least for private activities) if negotiations ever got down to practical details.

The consequence is that, in striking a balance between costs and value of inspection, the United States will inevitably favor more intensive and thorough systems and methods than the USSR. In this respect their interests tend to diverge materially and to obstruct agreement on a common system.

Their interests may diverge in another respect. A system which succeeded in neutralizing the all-out deterrent could have ancillary consequences differing according to the purposes of the two sides. For the Soviets, widespread confidence in the system might make it more difficult to utilize the fear of war for attaining political advantages. For the United States, one result might be to narrow the value of the all-out deterrent in inhibiting aggression in peripheral areas. Today, lack of certainty about its use may deter rash Soviet action, especially where the stakes are small compared to the price of a mistaken judgment. Some forms of arms control, by more effectively neutralizing the strategic capabilities, could erode this effect in the less vital areas. Finally, the prospect of rapid technological change complicates the creation of an acceptable system. Where radical innovation has become usual, a nation may hesitate to tie its hands too tightly when the future is so uncertain.

Limits of Inspection

Inspection (used here to mean any method of obtaining or verifying evidence) has come to be the cornerstone of arms control. Indeed, it is often said that inspection must be "foolproof." If, in fact, 100 per cent certainty were required in the inspection system, virtually no arms control would be feasible. In practice, no technique depending on human skills and judgment can be infallible. This truism is especially applicable in a field where actual experience is so lacking. Moreover, the Soviet Union (certainly) and the United States (probably) would not agree to inspection of the scope and intensity which would be necessary to attain the highest feasible reliability.

But infallibility is not the proper criterion. Inspection should be viewed as a technique for reinforcing and maintaining the self-interest of the parties in the continued effective operation of the system. The restrictions and the related inspection should be considered as a system of deterrence. Their combined aim should be to create *risks* of detection which a rational participant would not consider worth running. He need not believe that the inspection techniques are certain to discover the violation: he need only be convinced that the odds of discovery are too high to make the attempt worthwhile in the light of the possible benefits and costs. Of course, the reliability of the inspection process is still a vital factor in determining the extent of feasible arms control. But it can not be judged in isolation. It is intimately related to the nature of the restriction and remedies included in the system, and to the interest of the parties in its continued operation. . . .

Conclusion

. . . Within the limits discussed, there is room for substantial measures to stabilize the deterrent and to make initial modest reductions. Moreover, experience with inspection, and the application of imagination and invention to developing its techniques, could broaden the area for further measures. In particular, by cooperation through such means, the major opponents might be able to work out ways of maintaining the strategic deterrent at lower levels of resources and expenditures, especially if newer generations of missiles create the possibility of relatively invulnerable defensive capability. If their role comes to be recognized as one of essentially mutual neutralization, more modest levels might be adequate within an operating arms-control system. Moreover, in such a context, a reduction in the levels of conventional forces is within the realm of feasibility and could serve to lower the general level of defense expenditures below what otherwise might prevail.

These prospects fall well short of total disarmament. But realism seems to require recognition of the fact that such a state can be approached, if at all, only under conditions which permit international enforcement to operate effectively. In particular, it appears to call for an international agency with adequate authority and coercive means to punish and constrain a violator of the system. And that presupposes such fundamental changes in the political sphere as would pose a different range of problems within a new context. Such changes, if they occur, will depend on a wide range of policies and actions, involving many fields besides arms control. Limited progress in arms control to stabilize the situation will help in providing the time for such other actions to produce results.

10

THE EMERGENT NATIONS

The world in which we live is a world divided not merely into two camps—ours and that of the Communists—it is also a world divided into other camps, such as the traditional and the modern, the rich and the poor, the hungry and the satiated, the illiterate and the educated, the free and the oppressed. Potentially the most tremendous social force in the world of the 1960's will be the people who know they no longer have to be hungry and poor, who want education and freedom, who want bicycles, refrigerators, movies, and radios, who want to see the city, who want what science and technology have made possible in the West, and who want it now.

The great power struggle of recent years, which was the focus of the past two chapters, has been pretty much a matter of East versus West. The sixties could see the beginning of a new alignment—North versus South. For most of the well-established, highly developed countries of the world are in the Northern Hemisphere; whereas the Southern Hemisphere contains the newly independent nations,[1] most of which are desperately poor. Unless something is done about it, the economic gap between the rich and the poor nations will grow even wider in the next decade; and since the poor are no longer content with their poverty, this widening gap portends disaster.

As C. P. Snow has observed, the gap is essentially between those nations which have been through a number of successive scientific revolutions, and those which have not. This is the substance of the Stanford Research Institute study, which opens the readings for this chapter. As is pointed out elsewhere in the Stanford study, the problem of the underdeveloped countries is made especially acute by their extraordinary increases in population, and it is suggested that "a possible approach would be for the U.S. government to study (with the governments of other nations, through the United Nations or bilaterally) the possibility of providing research funds to certain foreign agencies and laboratories (for example, in Japan and India) for the large-scale human testing of [birth-control] devices . . ."[2]

Of course, birth-control proposals evoke one of the many controversies which surround this whole question of our relationship with the underdeveloped countries. Already most of these controversies, which will be debated throughout the sixties, are taking shape.

The broad liberal-conservative confrontation involves the extent to which we should ask specific commitments in return for our aid to the underdeveloped countries. On the one hand, we have those who say that we shall have to spend more; that our aid should build economic rather than military strength; that we should not be perturbed by the fact that countries receiving our aid might nonetheless be neutralist in their foreign policy, socialist in their economic organization, and non-democratic in the formative stages of their political institutions. Various aspects of this approach are presented here by Triska and Koch, Walter Lippmann, Melville Herskovits, and Kwame Nkrumah.

On the other side, Senators Hickenlooper and Goldwater clearly favor a more limited financial commitment, and demand that this

---

[1] Eighteen new nations were admitted to the U.N. in 1960 alone.

[2] *United States Foreign Policy: Possible Nonmilitary Developments and Their Potential Impact on Foreign Policy Problems of the United States, Study No. 2;* prepared by the Stanford Research Institute, under the direction of Dr. Eugene Staley and Mr. Guy Benveniste for the Committee on Foreign Relations, United States Senate, 86th Congress, 1st Session, September 1959, Government Printing Office, Washington, D.C., pp. 41–45.

commitment be tied to a *quid pro quo* in the power struggle against Communism.

However, the complexities of this problem cannot be contained within the limits of a conservative-liberal debate. George Kennan does not subscribe to the Hickenlooper-Goldwater cold-war approach to the problem. Still, his attitude on foreign aid is a very cautious one, and he does not see how we can relieve underdeveloped countries from dealing with the major part of their problems themselves.

The M.I.T. Center study is much more positive than Kennan in its advocacy of aid, and it calls for an increase in the U.S. contribution of between $1.5 billion and $2 billion a year. This study reflects the analysis of W. W. Rostow, in his *Stages of Economic Growth*,[3] which reveals that we are dealing not with one type of situation but with many different countries—each with its own complex of economics, politics, sociology, and psychology, and each at a different level of development. The selection by anthropologist Dorothy Lee underscores the extraordinary delicacy with which the more advanced countries must approach the problems of peoples at a much lower level of development if change is to be effected without total disruption of a culture. This places a heavy responsibility on the members of the Peace Corps, and on the personnel of all of our technical-aid programs. *The Ugly American* may be an exaggerated picture of events, but it is not entirely without substance; we cannot afford that kind of representation in the future.[4]

Beyond all this there is Gunner Myrdal's point that trade, no less than aid, will be the real test of our intentions.

The Kennedy Administration is committed, at least in general terms, to a major effort to help alleviate the problems of the underdeveloped nations of Asia, Africa, and Latin America. More spending has been proposed—although there will be a much greater emphasis on long-term loans than on outright grants, and other affluent countries will be expected to increase their contributions. There will be less stress on military aid, more on economic. Greater attention will have to be given to the problem of ensuring that aid designed to relieve poverty and hunger accomplishes its purpose, instead of becoming a source of supply for black-market speculation. Neutralism will be an acceptable foreign policy on the part of recipients of our aid. We shall experiment with such devices as the Peace Corps—though on a

---

[3] Rostow was a member of the group which prepared the M.I.T. Center report.

[4] On the other hand, Russian technicians do not always make friends wherever they go.

limited scale at the outset, for the dangers inherent in a large-scale operation inspired only by benevolence and enthusiasm are apparent.

There is no doubt that our Administrations of the sixties, whatever their political complexion, will treat the problem of our relationship with the emerging nations as a matter of the gravest importance and urgency. Whether we are guided by selfish national interest, or by moral considerations, or by a happy conjunction of both, we shall be compelled to act. Dynamism and enthusiasm will be needed, for this is an extraordinary opportunity to ally ourselves with the aspirations of the hitherto dispossessed and unprivileged peoples of the world.

But enthusiasm, this chapter shows, will not be enough. We must recognize that most of the job will have to be handled by the new nations themselves. And, in the contribution that we make, we shall have to display sensitivity, intelligence, and wisdom in a degree never before demanded of us.

Stanford Research Institute

SCIENCE AND UNDERDEVELOPED COUNTRIES*

It is the policy of the United States . . . to aid the efforts of the peoples of economically underdeveloped areas to develop their resources and improve their working and living conditions by encouraging the exchange of technical knowledge and skills and the flow of investment capital . . . [for] . . . raising standards of living, creating new sources of wealth, increasing productivity and expanding purchasing power.

---

* *United States Foreign Policy: Possible Nonmilitary Developments and Their Potential Impact on Foreign Policy Problems of the United States, Study No. 2,* prepared by the Stanford Research Institute, under the direction of Dr. Eugene Staley and Mr. Guy Benveniste for the Committee on Foreign Relations, United States Senate, 86th Congress, 1st Session, September 1959, Government Printing Office, Washington, D.C., pp. 41–45.

This policy was formally declared by Congress and the President in the Act for International Development of 1950 and has been repeatedly reaffirmed.

The problem of economic and social development is widely regarded as second in international importance only to the problem of peace and security itself, and success or failure in relation to it will have a considerable influence on the chances of maintaining peace and security. The problem is one which scientific developments have had a substantial part in creating, and one which further scientific developments may help to meet.

The very wide gap between the level of material well-being of the economically advanced countries and the grinding poverty of the economically underdeveloped countries reflects the uneven diffusion of modern science and technology over the world.

A good index of the extent to which a society has been able to take advantage of the productive power inherent in modern science and technology is its use of inanimate forms of energy. . . . It has been estimated that an average man working 48 hours a week for a year exerts an amount of physical energy roughly equivalent to 150 kilowatt-hours of electricity. In the United States, the consumption of energy from inanimate sources represents approximately 84 times this amount for each man, woman, and child. In effect, each American has 84 synthetic slaves working for him. The average person in India has only one such slave, in Turkey four, in Ethiopia one-tenth of a slave.

Not only is there a tremendous gap in living levels between underdeveloped and highly developed countries, but the gap seems to be widening rather than narrowing. According to the statistical services of the United Nations, rates of economic progress in the highly developed countries continue to be more rapid, on the whole, than in the underdeveloped countries, though some of the latter are now successfully accelerating their economic growth trends.

Another sobering thought is that, despite all the vaunted progress of modern times, there are probably more poverty-stricken people in the world today than there were 50 or 100 years ago. This is because economic advancement has been slow or nonexistent in most of the underdeveloped countries, while their populations have been growing. Thus today two-thirds of the people of the world live in countries usually classified as underdeveloped. . . .

Of course, poverty and the lack of opportunity for self-development that it implies have been the lot of ordinary people in most of these countries for centuries. Poverty is not new. But there is a new factor. This is the awareness of poverty, the realization that it is not the inevitable lot of man, and the determination to do something about it.

This new awareness, often referred to as the revolution of rising expectations, has come about largely as an indirect consequence of modern science and technology. First, the wealth-producing capacity of science and technology was demonstrated in the more developed countries, proving that dire poverty for the masses is not inevitable. Second, the greatly improved means of world travel and communication brought this demonstration to the attention of increasing numbers of people in the less developed countries.

The result has been a social movement imperceptibly started in colonial days by the contacts of soldiers, administrators, traders, and missionaries and rapidly accelerated by the increase in communications and education, by the social upheavals of two World Wars, and by the winning of independence in many former colonies. This vast movement can be characterized as a quest for change in man's affairs by large sectors of the world population who previously had lived within static social patterns. This accelerated transition and transformation causes many strains and pressures throughout the social organism; dealing with these strains and pressures often requires the utmost wisdom.

The world in which we live is a world divided not merely into two camps—ours and that of the Communists—it is also a world divided into other camps, such as the traditional and the modern, the rich and the poor, the hungry and the satiated, the illiterate and the educated, the free and the oppressed. Potentially the most tremendous social force in the world of the 1960's will be the people who know they no longer have to be hungry and poor, who want education and freedom, who want bicycles, refrigerators, movies, and radios, who want to see the city, who want what science and technology have made possible in the West, and who want it now. This force, this revolution in expectations, may prove to be the principal modern impact of science on man—the impact on his ways of thought and on his values. . . .

Some of the scientific advances of the next decade will make the development problem still more urgent. Further improvements can be expected in facilities for international communication. These will tend to speed up and intensify the worldwide flow of information and ideas, by way of travel, letters, books and periodicals, films, radio, television, and tape recordings or other means of reproducing sounds and sights. Within underdeveloped countries, communication will also improve as a result of the further spread of existing technical means like roads, newspapers, movies, and the radio. There may be new developments such as much less expensive radio or possibly even television, receivers for use in every village of Asia and Africa, or new methods of education making use of electronic devices or other technical aids together with better understanding of the psychology and of the needs of diverse cultures. In consequence, the revolution of rising expectations will be accelerated and demands for development will become still more insistent.

If attempts to speed up development meet with frustration, or if it appears that the Communist countries, such as Communist China, are much more successful in bringing about development than the non-Communist countries, the world political repercussions could be serious indeed. . . .

One of the most important issues of the next decades will be: Can the gap between rich nations and poor nations, no longer tolerable in a world of close communication and interdependence, be progressively narrowed by constructive, evolutionary means which level upward rather than downward?

If the answer is negative, the alternative might be a series of revolutionary struggles in which poor nations would become alined against rich ones in struggles that would probably involve the Communist and the Western Power blocs and make nuclear war more likely. In a world of widening gaps between poor and rich nations, the discontents of the poor would eagerly be played upon by skilled political forces dedicated to the overthrow of freedoms we value highly. No purely military strategy could cope with such a combined economic-political-military threat.

Can economic and social development be speeded up enough to bring real improvement and hope to poorer nations and to rescue the world from the threat of a calamitous political drift? . . .

Some encouragement can be taken from the fact that the Western nations have successfully met a similar issue internally during the last hundred years, with substantial help from scientific developments.

A hundred years ago the social issues that had arisen in the wake of the industrial revolution led Marx and Engels to forecast in "The Communist Manifesto" that capitalist societies would more and more split "into two great hostile camps"—in one the rich owners of capital, in the other the poor workers or proletariat. The rich would grow fewer and richer, the poor more numerous and more miserable. This polarization of society would lead to proletarian revolution.

The reality, however, has been quite different from the forecast. Within the economically advanced countries, instead of the rich growing richer and the poor poorer, an outstanding social fact has been the rise of broad, middle-income groups. No proletarian revolutions of the type Marx foresaw have occurred in the advanced capitalist countries, and only in underdeveloped countries have Communist revolutionaries been able to seize power.

What defeated Marx's confident forecast about the inevitable course of events within the industrially advanced countries? There were many factors, including the effects of representative government in bringing reforms through the ballot box, reforms which often tended toward more even distribution of wealth. But certainly one of the most important factors of all was the enormous increase in wealth-producing capacity which came from the progress of science and technology in the last half of the 19th century and the first half of the 20th century. This made it possible in the economically advanced countries to achieve a very substantial rise in income levels for the masses.

Can science and technology similarly contribute today to the solution of the problem of poor countries versus rich countries by raising the productive capacities and the incomes of all, but especially of the poor countries? No one will doubt that the answer is yes, given the necessary social and political decisions to make effective use of the potentials of science and technology. Social and political decisions, not science and technology in themselves, may be the controlling factors. . . .

Jan Triska and Howard E. Koch, Jr.

THE ASIAN-AFRICAN COALITION*

. . . .

The political independence of the Asian-African countries was an outcome of a fervent nationalism originally introduced by the European colonial powers in their own terms. In the process, native nationalism acquired anti-European tendencies and became a forceful, intolerant, ceaseless counterattack. It has graduated into an anti-colonial, anti-imperialist, and anti-Western feeling of profound content. With political awakening came an awareness of grave economic and social deficiencies, which, if not remedied, could negate the positive achievement of national emancipation. . . .

So long as European controls remained, politically and economically these countries lived for the convenience of Europe. Coincidentally, institutions were imposed involving partial self-government, which the inhabitants accepted. These functioned well, at least superficially, as long as the crucial matters remained in the hands of the colonial powers. With independence, these half-absorbed institutions only imperfectly constructed upon the bedrock of indigenous traditions and institutions served poorly in an hour of need. Economically underdeveloped and endowed with all the maladies associated with a low standard of life, the Asian-African countries faced similar if not identical problems of catching up with modern agricultural and industrial development.

Socialism has been accepted by a large proportion of the native intelligentsia as the only adequate solution to the pressing problems of economic and social reconstruction. To achieve the optimum of

---

*Jan Triska and Howard E. Koch, Jr., "Asian-African Coalition and International Organization: Third Force or Collective Impotence?," *The Review of Politics,* Vol. 21, No. 2, April 1959, University of Notre Dame, Indiana, pp. 426–432. Reprinted by permission.

Jan F. Triska is Assistant Professor of Government at Cornell University, and Co-Director of the Soviet Treaty Project, Stanford University.

Howard E. Koch, Jr., is Senior Researcher with the Conflict Studies Project, Stanford University.

productive efficiency, formal emphasis has been placed on the social control of economic resources and their utilization. The concept of a planned economy has been commonly, and naturally, equated with the national aspirations of the underdeveloped countries. In Burma, for example, the principle was included as a provision of the Constitution of 1948.

This is not to suggest that Western philosophy and democratic concepts are rejected out of hand, but rather that an effort is being made to synthesize socialism and democracy with indigenous customs and thought (with due tribute paid to local conservatism)—to discover and apply that which appears to be applicable, and to reject the rest. Although capitalism has fallen into discredit, communism on the Soviet model, because of its oppressive features, has not succeeded in taking its place. . . .

. . . Prime Minister Nehru has observed:

> "There is much talk in communism of the contradictions of capitalist society, and there is truth in that analysis. But we see the growing contradictions within the rigid framework of communism itself. Its suppression of individual freedom brings about powerful reactions. Its contempt for what might be called the moral and spiritual side of life not only ignores something that is basic in man but also deprives human behavior of standards and values. Its unfortunate association with violence encourages a certain evil tendency in human beings."[1]

What appears to be in vogue today is a new synthesis of a purified and up-dated Marx the economist—as reinterpreted by contemporary Western thinkers—and a modification of the techniques of economic development in general and forced industrialization in particular of Soviet Russia and of Communist China. The robust development of China's economy within nine years under a brand new interpretation of Marxism is rapidly becoming the strongest inducement to the Asian-African nations to follow a similar path. But, says Nehru, socialism must be divorced from politics; it must not become "a way of life but a certain scientific approach to social and economic problems." It must not interfere with democracy, but both socialism and democracy must become means leading to the end, "the ideal of the welfare state."[2]

But events in Pakistan, Burma, Iraq, Thailand, Sudan, and, to

---

[1] Nehru's letter circulated confidentially among his friends and was later reprinted in the *Journal of the Indian Congress Party*. Reprinted in *The New York Times Magazine*, September 7, 1958, p. 13.

[2] *Ibid.*, pp. 110–111.

some extent, Indonesia suggest that for the underdeveloped countries of Asia and Africa, democracy may be a luxury they cannot afford, a contradiction in terms, an illusion. Each has attempted to make its way within the framework of parliamentary democracy, only to abandon the experiment in favor of a less free but more efficient military dictatorship or some form of authoritarian regime. A fear has been gaining ground in Asia that the party system of the Western constitutional democracies, while excellent in some environments, cannot provide the controls necessary for a progressive national life. This concern has been reinforced in many countries by the spectacle of parliamentary instability and irresponsibility against a background of severe social and economic disorder. And, in the process, socialism in its varied forms, within the framework of a more controlled political environment, is becoming the universally acknowledged "means" rather than a free economy subject only to the moderate controls of democratic society. Throughout much of Asia and Africa, it would be difficult to find an intellectual who did not consider himself a socialist or a party which did not espouse socialist economic doctrine regardless of its place on the political spectrum.

Apart from what socialist doctrine offers in an economic sense, it has a very definite appeal in that it represents a break with the past, a severing of connections with the capitalist exploitation of days gone by. Thus, Asian and African nationalism has come to have an economic appendage. . . .

Although some Asian and African states, such as the SEATO and Baghdad Pact adherents, have accepted alignment with the West there was a strong sentiment throughout the Asian-African world against taking sides in any power conflict with which its countries were not immediately concerned. Close involvement with either the East or the West suggested the ultimate subordination of their national interests to the overriding requirements of the two conflicting power groups. As prospective allies, neither of the great power blocs appeared in a particularly good light.

The deterioration of Soviet relations with the West, in the years preceding the explosion of June, 1950, forced the relatively defenseless states, particularly those in Asia, carefully to consider their position with respect to the major contenders. Nehru urged a policy of neutrality upon the statesmen of Asia and Africa and suggested that if such a policy gained wide adherence, an open conflict might be avoided. Although this was an attractive stratagem, it did not at once acquire the following necessary to make it effective.

By 1950, with the intensification of the cold war to the point of actual fighting and with the appearance of a functioning Asian-African voting bloc in the United Nations, the policy of non-involvement presented new possibilities. While all of the Asian and African countries could by no means be considered neutralist, the influence of those countries advocating the policy was sufficiently strong—and the policy itself, in a period of mounting tensions, sufficiently attractive and promising—to invite the support prerequisite to its becoming a dynamic element in international relations.

Essentially, the first norm of neutralism, that of non-involvement in military pacts or alliances, was a "negative" principle. With the advent of the Korean crisis, it was extended to non-participation in armed conflicts. As the Korean affair proved, the principle had corollaries: non-extension of hostilities, pacific settlement and mediation, and collective measures for the maintenance of collective security (with some reservations). The second norm of neutralism was "positive": the maintenance of friendly relations with all states. Burma has maintained relations with Israel and the Arab states simultaneously, and with Japan, at whose hands it suffered severely during the Second World War. And the neutralist segment of the Asian-African bloc has endeavored to maintain friendly ties, although occasionally strained, with both East and West.

Neutralist statesmen have resented the tendency, particularly prevalent in the Western states, especially in the United States, to examine their policy exclusively in its negative context. They deny that their position implies a withdrawal into isolation, or that it suggests a lack of convictions, a self-centered indifference to the moral and immoral, and a denial of responsibility in the community of nations. Nehru, neutralist *par excellence,* commented in a radio address during his visit to the United States: "We have chosen the path of non-alinement in any military or like pact or alliance. Non-alinement does not mean passivity of mind or action, lack of faith or conviction. It does not mean submission to what we consider evil."[3]

The uncommitted Asian-African states accepted neutrality as a long-range policy based on positive thought, responsible action, and constructive propositions for reducing world tension; a policy which might go so far as to offer potential leadership to those who would press in its name for solution of the most painful international problems, for mediation, for bridging the gap between the East and the West which might otherwise remain open and could lead to a world cataclysm.

In this way, the policy of neutrality of the Asian-African leaders

---

[3] United States Department of State Bulletin, XXXVI (January 14, 1957), 50.

has traveled full circle. From the simplest, least imaginative, most natural, and least resisted policy at home, neutrality became a foreign policy *par excellence*. In domestic politics there is less popular resistance to a foreign policy which offers great leeway and only broad limitations, and is pragmatic, reliable, and without surprises. Since it is potentially a policy of collective strength based on individual political and military weakness, it is singularly attractive to all but radicals. In the context of contemporary power politics, the policy of neutrality can also be viewed as a technique of modern isolationism most suited to survival in the present interdependent world.

To statesmen in both the United States and the Soviet Union, neutralism has proved a source of frustration. United States policy has been directed toward the political conversion of uncommitted countries. While some of them have been willing to accept the aid that accompanies conversion, few have been willing to accept the creed, with all of its implications. As a matter of fact some members of the bloc, notably the neutralist countries, regard United States policy in Asia as an arm of its anti-Soviet policy and, consequently, opportunistic and uninterested in Asia as such.

At first glance, Moscow appears to have fared much better than Washington in [the] open rivalry for the friendship of the Asian-African nations. By its formally consistent, enthusiastic, and vocal advocacy of neutralism it has ridden high on the emotional waves of anti-imperialism; in doing so, it has not found it difficult to discover in every conceivable issue an occasion to revive the deep-seated local prejudices of colonial yesterday. Soviet merchants—eager to please and stressing the equality of the consumer with the seller—have traveled the length and breadth of the Asian-African countries promoting wares at fairs and local festivities. . . . Soviet trade conditions have been most acceptable—low rate of interest, long-term credits, reasonable prices—and all commodities offered in trade by the contracting parties were *a priori* acceptable. Soviet economy—just as the economies of its satellites, which have carried out a considerable part of this Soviet economic offensive—has had many possibilities of streamlining and adapting its functions to political circumstances. Thus, the Soviet government has employed entirely different trade standards in its dealings with the Asian-African nations from those with the Western countries (where hard, businesslike bargains have been a Soviet specialty). All kinds of cultural, promotional and friendship meetings and conferences have been held in the Soviet Union, usually on the territory of the Soviet ethnic groups and nationalities related to the Asian-African nations, more often than not sponsored by the Soviet Committee for Solidarity with Asian and African Countries. Soviet technicians, assistants, engineers, and advisors have ranged the Asian-African countries in increasing numbers and are often reported doing more than technical advising (for example in Yemen and Iraq). At present, the Soviet Union appears to be successful in stirring up the Kurdish national movement, the Moslem people living in Turkey, Iraq, Iran, the United Arab Republic, and the Soviet Union. Clearly, the political impact of this activity would seem to be more than proportional to the energy, initiative and money spent.

And yet, when studied more closely, the results of the renewed Soviet drive in Asia and Africa become less clear-cut. First, the principal Soviet weapon has been trade, not aid (economic or military) or culture or revolutionary activities. The trade, however, has been more important as propaganda than as trade. . . .

Second, as far as Soviet foreign aid to the Asian-African nations is concerned, the sums involved have been quite modest. . . . Actual Soviet deliveries have remained far behind their promises of aid and have been not outright grants or gifts but rather loans and barter arrangements. Of course, magnitude is not the only consideration; viewed from the well-managed propaganda viewpoint of the Soviet Union, the impact—both in the Asian-African countries and in the West—has been considerable. The future of Soviet economic aid to underdeveloped Asia and Africa, if judged merely from the point of view of growing Soviet economic capabilities, is wide open.

Third, Communist China, now in its tenth year, has emerged on the international scene as a new source of economic aid to Asian-African countries, from Yemen to Cambodia. . . .

Fourth, objections have been registered against the Soviet Union's participation in Asian-African meetings and conferences on the grounds that it is neither an Asian nor an African power. . . .

If the Soviet Union has made its very considerable investment in Asia-Africa with the intention of realizing some political return, perhaps the primary obstacle to its policy is the apparent determination of the neutralist countries to remain neutral. The principal objective of the Asian and African countries, that of strengthening their independent status, has changed very little. Soviet economic, technical, cultural, political, and ideological assistance is welcome so long as it is consistent with that objective. Western assistance is accepted on the same terms. Domestic interference on the part of either is not knowingly tolerated. In this respect, the position of the uncommitted countries, if maintained, is a barrier as formidable to the Soviet Union as it has been to American policy-makers. . . .

Kwame Nkrumah

INDEPENDENCE FOR AFRICA*

. . . .

The great tide of history flows, and as it flows it carries to the shores of reality the stubborn facts of life and men's relations one with another. One cardinal fact of our time is the momentous impact of Africa's awakening upon the modern world. The flowing tide of African nationalism sweeps everything before it and constitutes a challenge to the colonial powers to make just restitution for the years of injustice and crime committed against our continent.

But Africa does not seek vengeance. It is against her very nature to harbour malice. Over 200 millions of our people cry out with one voice of tremendous power—and what do we say? We do not ask for death for our oppressors; we do not pronounce wishes of ill-fate for our slave-masters; we make an assertion of a just and positive demand; our voice booms across the oceans and mountains, over the hills and valleys, in the desert places and through the vast expanse of mankind's habitation, and it calls out for the freedom of Africa; Africa wants her freedom; Africa must be free. It is a simple call, but it is also a signal, a red light of warning to those who would tend to ignore it.

For years and years, Africa has been the foot-stool of colonialism and imperialism, exploitation and degradation. From the North to the South, from East to the West, her sons languished in the chains of slavery and humiliation, and Africa's exploiters and self appointed controllers of her destiny strode across our land with incredible inhumanity—without mercy, without shame, and without honour. But those days are gone, and gone forever, and now I, an African, stand before the General Assembly of the United Nations and speak with the voice of peace and freedom, proclaiming to the world the dawn of a new era. . . .

---

* Official Records, United Nations General Assembly, 869th Plenary Meeting, 15th Session, 23 September 1960.
Mr. Nkrumah is President of the Republic of Ghana.

I look upon the United Nations as the only organization that holds out any hope for the future of mankind. Cast your eyes across Africa: the colonialists and imperialists are still there. In this twentieth century of enlightenment, some nations still extol the vain glories of colonialism and imperialism. As long as a single foot of African soil remains under foreign domination, the world will know no peace. The United Nations must therefore face its responsibilities, and ask those who would bury their heads like the proverbial ostrich in their imperialistic sands, to pull their heads out and look at the blazing African sun now travelling across the sky of Africa's redemption. The United Nations must call upon all nations that have colonies in Africa to grant complete independence to the territories still under their control. In my view possession of colonies is now quite incompatible with membership in the United Nations. This is a new day in Africa, and as I speak now, thirteen new African nations have taken their seats this year in the General Assembly as independent sovereign states. The readiness of any people to assume responsibility for governing themselves can be determined only by themselves. I and the Government of Ghana, and I am sure the Governments and peoples of independent African States, share the joy of welcoming our sister States into the family of the United Nations. There are now twenty-two of us in this Assembly and there are yet more to come.

I would suggest that when the Charter of the United Nations comes to be revised, a permanent seat for an African nation should be created on the Security Council, in view not only of the growing number of African Members of the United Nations, but also of the increasing importance of the African continent in world affairs. This suggestion applies equally to Asia and to the Middle East. . . .

The problem of Africa, looked at as a whole, is a wide and diversified one. But its true solution lies in the application of one principle, namely, the right of a people to rule themselves. No compromise can affect this cardinal and fundamental principle, and the idea that when a handful of settlers acquire a living space on our continent the indigenous inhabitants must lose this right, is not only a serious travesty of justice but also a woeful contradiction of the very dictates of history.

Out of a total African population of over 230 million people, some 3 percent are of non-African origin. To suppose that such a small minority could in any other continent produce acute political difficulties would be unthinkable. Yet such is the subconscious feeling of certain European settlers in Africa that to them the paramount issue in Africa is not the welfare of the 97 percent but rather the entrenchment of the rights of the 3 percent, of these European settler minorities in Africa.

To these minority settlers a solution seems impossible unless what they describe as "justice" is done to the foreign 3 percent. Justice, they say, must be done to this group irrespective of whether it means that injustice continues to be done to the remaining inhabitants. I believe that a reasonable solution can be found to the African problem which would not prejudice the minorities on the continent. No effective solution, however, can be found if political thinking in regard to a solution begins with the rights of the 3 percent and considers the rights of the 97 percent only within the framework which is acceptable to the rest.

The world must begin at last to look at African problems in the light of the needs of the African people and not only of the needs of minority settlers. Colonialism, imperialism and racialism are doomed in Africa, and the sooner the colonial Powers recognize this fact the better it will be for them and the world. . . .

. . . It is essential that we on the African continent take positive steps to isolate ourselves as far as is possible from the effects of nuclear warfare. One of the first and most practical steps which could be taken in this regard is to prevent any State having nuclear weapons from possessing military bases on the African continent.

This is one of the main reasons why the Government of Ghana believes that no African State should enter into an alliance of a military nature with any outside Power. Any such alliance not only involves the State concerned in the risk of being drawn into nuclear warfare; it also endangers the security of the neighbouring African States.

"Fall-out" is no respecter of frontiers, and a declaration of neutrality cannot save the people of any African State from nuclear poisoning once atomic war is introduced into the African continent. A military alliance with any atomic Power is therefore, in the view of the Government of Ghana, a threat to the security of Africa and world peace. . . .

U.S. POLICY AND AFRICA*

. . . .

SENATOR HICKENLOOPER. . . . The African problem is recognized by everybody as a very difficult one. I have the impression at times that these various African nations want our help but they do not want to call it help. They claim great independence of thought and spirit and yet they are constantly wanting assistance. What is their attitude and how does that square with independence of action, and so on?

MR. HERSKOVITS. May I call your attention to what I said at the end of my statement about using the phrase "economic cooperation" instead of "economic aid"? All over the world today, new nations are as sensitive as we were in the early days of our own independence about anything that seems to imply dominance by an outside power. I feel that one of the reasons they come to us is because they trust us.

SENATOR HICKENLOOPER. Well, they say they do not.

MR. HERSKOVITS. Some of that is for home consumption. I am sure we all understand how that works.

SENATOR HICKENLOOPER. Well, I think they had better change their tune a little bit and say something for our consumption if they are wanting our assistance.

MR. HERSKOVITS. It seems that we are going to have to exercise a certain measure of understanding of the way in which human psychology works. Here are people who have been thinking, not in terms of world problems, but almost exclusively in terms of getting out from under colonial rule and what they have been deprived of because of the colonial status under which they have lived. Now they want some of the things that they see other nations have.

I do not know to what you particularly refer, and, of course, no

---

* *United States Foreign Policy.* Hearings Before the Committee on Foreign Relations, Part 1, Africa, 86th Congress, 2nd Session, January, February, and March, 1960, Government Printing Office, Washington, D.C., pp. 116–120.

Dr. Melville J. Herskovits is Director of Northwestern University's Program of African Studies.

Senator Bourke Hickenlooper is U.S. Senator from Iowa.

one has come to me asking for aid, but when I have discussed such matters with African leaders I have found that what they are saying is, "We want to be considered as much as any other country when these programs are set up."

. . .

SENATOR HICKENLOOPER. There are a number of highly capable and, in my opinion, highly intelligent leaders in each of these countries. I have met a number of them, and they seem very dedicated people, at least at the outset. When I say "at the outset," I mean one never knows what power will do to a leader as time goes on. Many leaders who start out with great dedication and high ideals become rather oppressive later on. But the ones I have met, I am convinced have great dedication and a very high competence. They have a great mass of people in those countries who are really quite primitive.

Their governments are composed of a small cadre of leaders. The great mass of people, whether it is because of colonialism or whatever, have just not experienced the responsibilities of self-government. What is going to happen in the next few years with this type of government? Will there be a trend toward more dictatorship in those countries? Is there a capability within the peoples of the countries at the moment—based on experience, let us say, because I think capability is there whether experience is there or not—to exert the basic rights of individuals or will they follow their leaders right into a dictatorship or some type of autocratic government? . . .

SENATOR HICKENLOOPER. Do not misunderstand me, I am not a believer in attempting to impress our system on some other group. I am not so sure our system would be best for certain other peoples who have different backgrounds, traditions, and history. However, I think there are certain basic rights that ought to run through different social systems.

I am no authority on Africa. I have been over Africa, the length and breadth of the continent, as a matter of fact, but only for a short time. I have had the impression that in a number of these African countries, they have had . . . a very high, complex, and traditional system of government, of justice, of human relations, and of property rights that had worked very well for a long time. The difficulty was that some of their forms did not quite coincide with the colonial powers' idea of what justice was. I have the impression that the colonial powers went in and tried to superimpose a certain concept of justice on an age-old system that had worked very well, and all they did was confuse these people. Now they are in a state of confusion as to what is right and what is wrong. I think that has been especially noticeable in the Kikuyu tribe in Kenya which had really a very complex and highly organized system of government but which has now been utterly confused to a point that they do not know what they are doing. They do not know what is right and wrong. They are going to have to have some reorientation, some readjustment of their concepts. Either they must go back to their older forms or try to learn about the new ones.

MR. HERSKOVITS. Senator, you have put your finger on what, so far as I am concerned, is the basic problem in Africa, the degree to which there is retention of the old in the face of requirements of the new; I am not worried about the readjustment that must take place. I do not think the Africans have become as confused as it seems on the surface, so that they will not be able to work out an amalgam between the various elements that have gone into their experience. All people do this; as far as we know, it has been happening as long as there have been human societies, and I see no reason to suppose the Africans, after a time where there will be undoubted periods of adjustment, will not work this out.

. . .

SENATOR HICKENLOOPER. Without doubt they will eventually work out a system under their own responsibility which probably will fit their particular needs better than any other system will fit it. But I am concerned about the immediate future, and the possibilities of totalitarian influence coming into Africa, the invasion of Communist ideas, the blandishments and the glittering promises of communism, in order to get a foothold there and to saddle their doctrines on these people as opposed to what we think should be an orientation toward a free system of individuality and responsibility.

I think in this transitional period there is a great danger of this because people in confusion sometimes follow the leader who talks the loudest and makes the greatest promises. Although things may, perhaps, work out all right in future generations, it is the present that is our problem.

MR. HERSKOVITS. As I said, I am not too disturbed on that score. If there is any one thing that African leaders with whom I have discussed this problem have said, it is, "We do not want to exchange one form of domination for another."

SENATOR HICKENLOOPER. Well, have they not done that?

MR. HERSKOVITS. No. Where?

SENATOR HICKENLOOPER. Well, as a matter of fact, there are a number of these African leaders now who are virtual dictators.

MR. HERSKOVITS. Do you mean dictators in the sense of being Communist dictators? I do not quite understand.

SENATOR HICKENLOOPER. I mean dictators in the sense that some of these leaders, who have recently come into power, have used various devices and means to suppress opposition.

MR. HERSKOVITS. There is this possibility. But I have not seen it yet. For example, there is still an official opposition in Ghana.

SENATOR HICKENLOOPER. It has to be a little careful.

MR. HERSKOVITS. When I listened to Dr. Danquah on Mr. Huntley's television program from Ghana, he did not seem very careful to me. And he is still talking.

SENATOR HICKENLOOPER. I do not know. I am just asking.

MR. HERSKOVITS. Frankly, I think it is a bit dangerous to think of African matters in terms of European patterns expressed in European words. You may very likely have something that looks to us like totalitarianism, and yet will have great popular support; and I mean real and not imposed popular support. Thus there is no question about the fact that [the] Convention People's Party, the ruling party in Ghana, has very great popular support.

Now, they are doing some things that people accustomed to systems like our own, who have been brought up to believe in the values of such systems, do not like. . . .

SENATOR HICKENLOOPER. That gets down to the question of how far we should go in supporting and encouraging the development of systems which are inimical to what we believe to be a basic system of governmental and political conduct.

MR. HERSKOVITS. My fundamental position is that this is not anything we can do much about, unless it be in terms of giving or refusing loans. The principle of noninterference is particularly important here where we are dealing with young nations. They are going to have to work out their own destinies, and all we can do, it seems to me, is to watch the process with understanding and sympathy. As long as they stay inside their own borders, we must help them to develop the kind of economic and educational structure that seems to me is the best insurance against the kind of happening that you are afraid of.

SENATOR HICKENLOOPER. I am not by any means suggesting that we attempt to force any particular form of government on these people.

However, there is a question of how far we should go to furnish financial contributions to countries which would seem to use that money to further systems of government which do not promote individual responsibility and individual dignity, and so on. It is a question of what we should do in regard to countries which seem to have a tendency to promote totalitarianism in their government and permit rule by a few at the top.

MR. HERSKOVITS. Well, my feeling is very simply, that as long as they pursue a policy of nonalinement—and I think nonalinement for most Africans means being friendly with the West—their posture as regards the international situation does not bother me very much.

SENATOR HICKENLOOPER. It has been my experience that nonalinement, so far [as] the African and some of the Asian nations are concerned, means alinement with Communist nations, especially in voting in the United Nations.

We see the new nations with a greater tendency year by year to vote against the nations of the West. Maybe it is colonialism that they did not like, but it poses a very serious question. . . .

MR. HERSKOVITS. If I may, I would like to refer to page 74 of my report, where I analyze some figures on U.S. votes in the United Nations on major issues of colonialism on the basis of tabulations that were furnished me by the Department of State. There I compared the vote of the United States with two anticolonial countries, India and Liberia, and two of the colonial countries, United Kingdom and France, and with the U.S.S.R.

The U.S.S.R. was in agreement with Liberia on 62.5 percent of the issues as against our 52.5; with India 65 percent as against our 60 percent. I would not have expected so little disparity. I certainly would have thought, and I gather you, sir, would also have thought, the comparative figures would have been quite different. It is striking, from this point of view, to see how often we voted with the anticolonial powers on colonial issues. What interests me is the fact that we have not made the most of this in our public relations.

SENATOR HICKENLOOPER. I do not want to prolong this questioning at the moment, but the important thing is not a statistical overall total in voting, because there are a lot of bread-and-butter votes that go on in the United Nations. You add those up and the percentage is very impressive, and there are a number of practically unanimous votes in the United Nations. The important thing is the key votes on important issues which we consider to be fundamental. It is on these key issues where it is important for these nations to side with us.

You take statistical reports on how many times we voted the same way as another country and that is not necessarily the criterion. It is how many times country X and the United States saw eye to eye on fundamental issues. . . .

Hon. Barry Goldwater

WE MUST BE SURE THAT FOREIGN AID GOES ONLY TO OUR FRIENDS*

. . . .

Another aspect of our policy is the foreign aid program. To it, in the last 14 years, we have committed more than $80 billion worth of American treasure—in grants, loans, materiel, and technical advice. I will not develop here what every thinking American knows about this gargantuan expenditure—that it has had dire consequences, not only for the American taxpayer, but for the American economy; that it has been characterized by waste and extravagance both overseas and in the agencies that administer it; and that it has created a vast reservoir of anti-Americanism among proud peoples who, however irrationally, resent dependence on a foreign dole. I would rather put the question, Has the foreign aid program, for all of its drawbacks, made a compensating contribution toward winning the cold war?

This test, let me say parenthetically, is the only one under which the foreign aid program can be justified. It cannot, that is to say, be defended as a charity. The American Government does not have the

---

* From "The State of Our Nation"—speech delivered by United States Senator Barry Goldwater before the Senate, March 15, 1960.

Senator Goldwater, from the state of Arizona, is author of *Conscience of a Conservative*.

right, much less the obligation, to try to promote the economic and social welfare of foreign peoples. Of course, all of us are interested in combating poverty and disease wherever it exists. But the Constitution does not empower our Government to undertake that job in foreign countries, no matter how worth while it might be. Therefore, except as it can be shown to promote America's national interests, the foreign aid program is unconstitutional.

It can be argued, but not proved, that American aid helped prevent Western Europe from going Communist after the Second World War. It is true, for example, that the Communist Parties in France and Italy were somewhat weaker after economic recovery than before it. But it does not follow that recovery caused the reduction in Communist strength, or that American aid caused the recovery. It is also true, let us remember, that West Germany recovered economically at a far faster rate than France or Italy, and received comparatively little American aid.

It also can be argued that American military aid has made the difference between friendly countries having the power to fight off or discourage Communist aggression, and not having that power. Here, however, we must distinguish between friendly countries that were not able to build their own military forces, and those that were. Greece, Turkey, Free China, South Korea, and South Vietnam needed our help. Other countries—England and France, for example —were able to maintain military forces with their own resources. For many years now, our allies in Western Europe have devoted smaller portions of their national budgets to military forces than we have. The result is that the American people, in the name of military aid, have been giving an economic handout to these nations; we have permitted them to transfer to their domestic economy funds which, in justice, should have been used in the common defense effort.

Now let us note a significant fact. In each of the situations we have mentioned so far—situations where some evidence exists that foreign aid has promoted American interests—there is a common denominator: In every case, the recipient government was already committed to our side. We may have made these nations, on balance, stronger and more constant allies, although even that is debatable. But we did not cause them to alter their basic political commitments. This brings us to the rest of the foreign aid program, and to the great fallacy that I see underlying it.

Increasingly, our foreign aid goes, not to our friends, but to professed neutrals—and even to professed enemies. We furnish this aid under the theory that we can buy the allegiance of foreign peoples— or at least can discourage them from going Communist—by making them economically prosperous. This has been called the stomach

theory of communism, and it implies that a man's politics are determined by the amount of food in his belly.

Mr. President, everything we have learned from experience and
from our observation of the nature of man refutes this theory. A
man's politics are, primarily, the product of his mind. Material wealth
can help him further his political goals, but it will not change them.
It is thus the height of folly to try to promote anti-communism by
giving money to governments that are not anti-Communist, but that
are, indeed, far more inclined to the Soviet-type society than to a
free one. And let us remember that the foreign policies of many of
the allegedly neutral nations that receive our aid are not neutral at
all. Is Sukarno's Indonesia neutral when it encourages Red Chinese
aggression, or Nehru's India when it censures the Western effort to
recover Suez but refuses to censure the Soviet invasion of Hungary,
or Nasser's United Arab Republic which equips its armed forces with
Communist weapons and Communist personnel? Is American aid
likely to make these nations less pro-Communist? Has it, Mr. President?

But let us, for the moment, concede the validity of the stomach
theory, and ask a further question: Is our foreign aid program the
kind that will bring prosperity to underdeveloped countries? We
Americans believe—and we can cite 150 years of experience to support the belief—that the way to build a strong economy is to encourage the free play of economic forces: free capital, free labor, a
free market. Yet every one of the "neutral" countries we are aiding is
committed to a system of state socialism. Our present policy of government-to-government aid strengthens socialism in those countries.
We are not only perpetuating the inefficiency and waste that always
attend government-controlled economies; but by strengthening the
hand of those governments we are making it more difficult for free
enterprise to take hold. For this reason alone, Mr. President, we
should eliminate all government-to-government capital assistance,
and should encourage the substitution of American private investment.

Our present foreign aid program, in sum, is not only ill administered, but it is also ill conceived. It has not, in the majority of cases,
made the free world stronger; it has made America weaker; and it
has created in minds the world over an image of a nation that puts
prime reliance, not on spiritual and human values, but on the material things that are the stock in trade of Communist propaganda.

In the future, if our methods are to be in tune with our true
objectives, we will confine foreign aid to military assistance for the
nations that need it and that are committed to a common goal of
defeating world communism. . . .

Walter Lippmann

MR. K. AT THE U.N.*

. . . Outside of Western Europe and North America there has very recently and very suddenly been a dramatic expansion of Soviet influence. At the General Assembly of the U.N. 15 new African nations are about to be admitted, and by the end of this year there will probably be still more. In the main, the Soviet Union has the inside track in dealing with these new nations. Moreover, it has broken into the Western Hemisphere. Inside the U.N. the influence of the Soviet Union, which for years was in a tiny minority, has increased greatly, and Mr. Khrushchev will be in New York to make the most of it.

Our own influence has declined seriously. In the first General Assembly after the end of World War II the American nations, which then voted together, had 43 percent of the votes. This was a base on which to build an easy majority with the Western Europeans and in itself it was quite sufficient to exercise a veto. Now, the American states—even apart from Cuba's defection—are less than a quarter of the total.

* * *

In the General Assembly, as in the world which it represents, a preponderant majority of the countries are very poor, have a primitive economy, and are highly discontented with their condition. The great masses of the people are illiterate, and the country is fortunate if it has even a small class of educated men and trained civil servants. There is no mystery as to why the Soviet Union and even the Chinese have the inside track. They do not stand for democracy, which is impossible in most of these countries, or for free and private enterprise, which is also impossible. They stand for dictatorships using

* Walter Lippman, "Mr. K. at the U.N.," from Mr. Lippmann's column, *Today and Tomorrow*, © 1960, New York Herald Tribune, Inc. Reprinted with permission.

Mr. Lippmann, as an author and newsman, has contributed to American political and foreign-affairs thought for more than half a century.

technicians. The handful of educated leaders in the backward countries, and also in countries not so backward, can imagine themselves following the Soviet pattern. But they cannot imagine themselves following the political pattern of Eisenhower and Nixon and Kennedy and Johnson, of General Motors and U.S. Steel.

All this poses for us the grave problem of how, despite the Soviet initial advantage, the Western powers can exert enough influence to maintain their vital interests. Anyone, in my opinion, is a fool who thinks that there is an obvious and easy solution to this problem. What is certain is that the solution, if there is one, will not be found by thrashing around wildly, looking for scapegoats and trying to find someone in the foreign service to blame for the fact that Castro and Lumumba exist.

* * *

It is clear enough, I think, that on the whole and increasingly we shall have to deal through international institutions in Asia, Africa, and the Americas. Throughout these vast territories there is underway an historic revolution against poverty and against social and political inferiority to the Western white man. We cannot act successfully when we act alone, because we are unable to divest ourselves of the suspicion that we are the great counter-revolutionary power. Within international institutions, the U.N., the O.A.S., the World Bank and the like, we can have a certain immunity, and can have influence because we have so much to contribute.

The first item, then, in a solution of the problem of our relationship with the more or less revolutionary countries of Asia, Africa, and America, is to turn from unilateral action to action through the international institutions.

* * *

The second item is, I believe, to take the leadership of the highly developed countries in persuading them to accept the principle that it is the duty of the haves to finance the have-nots in order that they may break the vicious circle of their backwardness. It is highly important, in my view, that this should be done as a duty and not as a favor or as charity.

The duty of the haves to the have-nots is a new and great idea, often advanced by individuals but never as yet adopted by governments. It is the kind of idea which might, which could, restore to us and to our Western allies the initiative which we no longer possess.

George F. Kennan

DOUBTS ABOUT ECONOMIC AID*

. . . .

The demands frequently made upon us by the independent countries in part of the world seem to me to run something like this: "We," they say, "are determined to have economic development and to have it at once. For us, this is an overriding aim, an absolute requirement; and we are not much concerned about the method by which it is achieved. You in the West owe it to us to let us have your assistance and to give it to us promptly, effectively, and without conditions; otherwise we will take it from the Russians, whose experience and methods we suspect anyway to be more relevant to our problems." In response to this approach, a great many people in my own country have come to take it for granted that there is some direct relationship between programs of economic aid on the one hand and political attitudes on the other—between the amount of money we are willing to devote to economic assistance in any given year and the amount of progress we may expect to make in overcoming these troublesome states of mind I have been talking about.

This thesis, as well as the reaction to it at home, seems to me to be questionable at every point. I find myself thrown off at the very start by this absolute value attached to rapid economic development. Why all the urgency? It can well be argued that the pace of change is no less important than its nature, and that great damage can be done by altering too rapidly the sociological and cultural structure of any society, even where these alterations may be desirable in themselves. In many instances one would also like to know how this economic progress is to be related to the staggering population

---

* From *Russia, The Atom and the West* by George F. Kennan, pp. 73–77. Copyright © 1957, 1958 by George F. Kennan. Reprinted by permission of Harper & Brothers.

Dr. Kennan was a professor in the School of Historical Studies at the Institute for Advanced Study in Princeton when he delivered the Reith Lectures, which were published as *Russia, The Atom and the West*. He is now U.S. Ambassador to Yugoslavia.

growth with which it is associated. Finally, many of us in America have seen too much of the incidental effects of industrialization and urbanization to be convinced that these things are absolute answers to problems anywhere, or that they could be worth *any* sacrifice to obtain. For these reasons I cannot fully share the basic enthusiasm on which this whole thesis is founded.

I must also reject the suggestion that our generation in the West has some sort of a cosmic guilt or obligation vis-à-vis the under-developed parts of the world. The fact that certain portions of the globe were developed sooner than others is one for which I, as an American of this day, cannot accept the faintest moral responsibility; nor do I see that it was particularly the fault of my American ancestors. I cannot even see that the phenomenon of colonialism was one which could be regarded as having given rise to any such state of obligation. The establishment of the colonial relationship did not represent a moral action on somebody's part; it represented a natural and inevitable response to certain demands and stimuli of the age. It was simply a stage of history. It generally took place with the agreement and connivance of people at the colonial end as well as in the mother country. Nor were the benefits derived from this relationship in any way one-sided. The Marxists claim, of course, that colonialism invariably represented a massive and cruel exploitation of the colonial peoples. I am sure that honest study would reveal this thesis to be quite fallacious. Advantages, injuries and sacrifices were incurred on both sides. Today these things are largely bygones. We will do no good by scratching around to discover whose descendants owe the most to the descendants of the other. If we are to help each other in this world, we must start with a clean slate.

I can well understand that there are instances in which it will be desirable for us from time to time to support schemes of economic development which are soundly conceived and which give promise, over the long run, of yielding greater stability and a new hopefulness for the countries concerned. I trust that we will not let such demands go unanswered when they arise. There is no fonder hope in the American breast, my own included, than that the experience we have had in developing a continent will prove relevant and helpful to others. Every American would like to see us take a useful part in solving problems of economic development elsewhere in the world. But action of this sort can be useful only if it proceeds on a sound psychological basis. If there is a general impression in the recipient countries that this aid represents the paying of some sort of a debt from us to them, then the extension of it can only sow confusion. The same is true if it is going to be interpreted as a sign of weakness on our part or of a fear that others might go over to the Communists, or if it is going to be widely attacked in the recipient countries as evidence of what the Communists have taught people to refer to as "imperialism," by which they seem to mean some sort of intricate and concealed foreign domination, the exact workings of which are never very clearly explained.

Unless such reactions can be ruled out, programs of economic aid are apt to do more harm than good, psychologically; and it ought properly to be the obligation of the recipient governments and not of ourselves to see that these misinterpretations do not occur. To those who come to us with requests for aid one would like to say: "You tell us first how you propose to assure that if we give you this aid it will not be interpreted among your people as a sign of weakness or fear on our part, or of a desire to dominate you."

These are not the only psychological dangers of foreign aid. There is the basic fact that any form of benevolence, if prolonged for any length of time (even in personal life this is true), comes to be taken for granted as a right and its withdrawal resented as an injury. There is the fact that any program of economic development represents a change in the terms of competition within a country and brings injury to some parties while it benefits the others. It is hard to give aid to any other country economically without its having an effect on internal political realities there—without its redounding to the benefit of one political party and the disadvantage of another.

All these considerations incline me to feel that, desirable as programs of foreign aid may sometimes be from the long-term standpoint, their immediate psychological effects are apt to be at best mixed and uncertain. For this reason, foreign aid, as a general practice, cannot be regarded as a very promising device for combating, over the short term, the psychological handicaps under which Western statesmanship now rests in Asia and Africa.

Finally, I do not think for a moment that the Soviet Union really presents the alternative people seem to think it represents to a decent relationship with the West. Moscow has its contribution to make to what should be a common task of all the highly industrialized countries; and there is no reason why this contribution should not be welcomed wherever it can be really helpful. But Moscow is not exactly the bottomless horn of plenty it is often held to be; and it is rather a pity that it has never been required to respond all at once to the many expectations directed to it. We ourselves should be the last, one would think, to wish to spare it this test. The results might be both healthy and instructive.

What, then, is there to be done about these feelings of people in

Asia and Africa? Very little, I am afraid, over the short term, except to relax, to keep our composure, to refuse to be frightened by the Communism alternative, to refrain from doing the things that make matters worse, and to let things come to rest, as in the end they must, on the sense of self-interest of the peoples concerned. . . .

THREE STAGES OF GROWTH*

. . . .

By grouping the underdeveloped areas according to the strategic problems which must be solved before they can move forward into the next phase of the modernization process, we can identify three rough and necessarily somewhat arbitrary categories.

Societies in category A are still close to the traditional stage. While a new political awareness is apparent, especially in societies with a colonial past, only small numbers of the elite have any clear perception of what is required for progress toward modernization. Literacy and popular participation in the national life are low, and the economy has been modernized only to a limited degree. The basic problems to be overcome if modernization is to proceed include the training of men capable of conducting modern economic and political activity; the development of modern institutions; the creation of an agricultural framework capable of generating increases in agricultural productivity; the buildup of a modern transport network, sources of power, and other minimum social overhead capital requirements; and the development of natural resources so as to earn necessary foreign exchange. These are the characteristic problems to be solved in most of Africa south of the Sahara, in the more backward parts of the Middle East, and in certain Latin American countries.

---

* *United States Foreign Policy: Economic, Social, and Political Change in the Underdeveloped Countries and Its Implications for United States Policy, Study No. 12;* prepared by the Center for International Studies, Massachusetts Institute of Technology, under the direction of Max F. Millikan, for the Committee on Foreign Relations, United States Senate, 86th Congress, 2nd Session, March 1960, Government Printing Office, Washington, D.C., pp. 2–8.

The nations in category B have already gone some distance toward creating a minimum quantum of modern men and of social overhead capital. Institutions of centralized government exist. The men in power are committed in principle to modernization, and isolated parts of a modernization program have been begun but are not yet effectively related to each other. The leaders of these countries usually have not sufficiently articulated the complex of goals toward which the nation should be striving and lack a sufficiently realistic understanding of the effort and energy required to make progress toward them. The problem is in part to focus the energy and talents of the leadership on the tasks of modernization, in part to provide constructive opportunities for men throughout the society to participate effectively in programs relating to their interests and welfare. It is at this stage that systematic programing becomes important, not only to insure some degree of balance among increasingly interrelated efforts, but also to provide a symbolic national framework within which each man and group can find the relation of his own special effort to a common national purpose. Egypt, Iran, Iraq, Pakistan, Burma, and Indonesia are representative countries in this group.

The nations in category C are committed to attempt a takeoff into self-sustained growth and have developed the necessary human resources and social overhead to make this possible. They have well-considered programs for simultaneous advance on many related fronts, but they require capital from abroad in substantial amounts to supplement their domestic resources. They have not yet accumulated all the basic physical, human, and institutional resources required for modernization; and there persists the dual problem of maintaining operational unity around modernization in a national program and decentralizing participation in the program to wider and wider groups. But there is already enough momentum in these processes to carry forward if the whole effort is not hobbled and brought to a halt by an inability to mobilize the necessary resources from abroad. India is the prime example of a country at this stage of its evolution. . . .

Economic Policy

Economic policy is peculiarly important, not so much because the economic dimension of modernization will determine its outcome but because American economic aid is a possible and mutually accepted way of affecting the alternatives open to transitional societies and of affecting the contours of a society as a whole. Observations on four aspects of American economic foreign policy follow.

Technical assistance.—Although technical assistance programs will not require budget allocations as large as those for capital expenditure and loan programs, their potential influence in shaping the evolution of transitional societies, especially societies in the early stages of transition, may well be decisive. The central tasks of technical assistance programs are to bring the knowledge and skills available in developed countries to bear on the problems of modernization and to develop to the fullest the human resources of the recipient country. They should offer opportunities for as many groups in the society as possible to participate in the modernization process and lead whenever possible to the building of permanent institutions performing the functions for which assistance was initially given. If properly administered and staffed, these programs can convey an image of American purposes and modes of operation which will encourage continuing future cooperation.

Allocation of capital.—If American capital assistance is to have maximum leverage in encouraging the underdeveloped countries to follow a course consistent with American interests, it must have the following characteristics:

1. The economic criteria which determine U.S. capital assistance must be clear and unambiguous; and we must be firmer than we have frequently been in the past in the application of those criteria.

2. The offer of capital on terms requiring the recipient to meet conditions for its productive use must be held out consistently over long enough periods of time to permit the incentive effects to work. Such a result cannot be expected from programs which are assured no more than 1 or 2 years of life.

3. The amounts offered must be large enough and the terms flexible enough to persuade the recipient that the game is worth the candle. This means that we must invest substantially larger resources in our economic development programs than we have done in the past. Our rough estimates suggest that a reasonable American share of an effective world development effort might involve from $1.5 to $2 billion more U.S. public investment in development annually than we have been making.

4. The kinds of capital we offer and the purposes for which we encourage it to be used must be sufficiently varied so that the lack of capital will not inhibit the growth of any important sector of the economy dependent on foreign exchange. If, for example, the use of foreign assistance is limited to social overhead or big industrial projects, there may well develop in other sectors bottlenecks which will

lead first to economic stagnation and then to political and psychological frustration.

5. For political as well as economic reasons the leadership in underdeveloped countries should be encouraged to formulate their development goals in national terms. At an appropriate stage in the transition they should be urged to work out and discuss widely in their countries coordinated programs or plans which will underline the relationship of individual and local effort in particular sectors to national purposes and objectives.

6. In order that recipients of aid may free themselves from dependence on extraordinary external assistance as rapidly as possible, they should be encouraged to relate their own economic development to the growth of the international economy.

Assistance to land reform.— . . . The United States should strongly support land reform programs. It should assist governments engaged in such programs by offering to provide capital and technical assistance and food surpluses to cushion any temporary decline in food deliveries resulting from agricultural reorganization.

International organization of aid.—To coordinate the efforts of the increasing number of national and international agencies offering economic assistance is an urgent task. In our view, however, to attempt to lump the existing agencies together in a single international organization to administer aid would be neither a feasible nor a desirable solution. The resources granted to such an international pool of capital would in all likelihood not be sufficient to make a serious dent on the development problem. Each donor nation, moreover, will have a strong tendency to retain control over the administration of its assistance funds through its own national agencies. The problem of coordination can best be solved not by creating a new aid-administering organization but by developing appropriate means of coordinating the operations of the various national and international agencies now in existence. Such coordination could be furthered by enlarging regional programs of cooperation; by creating an effective organization of lenders within the free world as well as a forum where lenders and borrowers can get together periodically; and by developing the consortium technique as a method for bringing the maximum resources of the international community to bear on the development problems of each country.

The Focus of Policy at Different Stages of the Transition

We have placed in category A most of the new nations in Africa south of the Sahara and north of the Union as well as some of the less developed countries in the Middle East and Latin America. A dominant concern of American policy toward these countries should be to design our diplomacy, our information programs, and our economic assistance efforts so as to communicate our deep concern with the modernization of their societies. Our programs should be directed specifically toward such objectives as helping to carry out systematic surveys of needs and available resources; developing programs of technical and administrative training and of basic education, particularly in the rural areas; helping to create the schools, technical institutes, financial agencies, agricultural extension services, and other institutions necessary for modernization; and supplying capital for essential utilities such as transport, communication, power, and irrigation. Serious thought should be given to the possibility of taking steps to discourage large-scale militarization in Africa and thus create a unique opportunity for the new African countries to pass through the modernization process without incurring the costs of large military establishments. The United States might take the initiative for an international convention, possibly under United Nations auspices, guaranteeing African states against aggression and prohibiting deliveries to them of any arms except those needed to maintain internal order.

In the nations considered under category B—such as Egypt, Iran, Iraq, Pakistan, Burma, and Indonesia—a good many of the separate preconditions for growth are being established but the relationship between individual effort and national development goals is not sufficiently or widely enough understood to provide the motive force for takeoff. In these areas American programs should continue to include the elements listed for category A nations, but the main purpose of American policy should be to help focus the attention and energies of the existing leadership groups and of all the diverse rural and urban elements of the society on the constructive tasks of modernization. The major bottlenecks to progress are a lack of unified purpose among those in power and a failure on their part to agree on what is required if local resources, human and material, are to be mobilized to achieve the goals of modernization already symbolically accepted. The role that the United States can play in helping to crystallize a consensus on development priorities is necessarily limited, but if we are clear what we are trying to do we can utilize our diplomatic posture, our technical assistance, our criteria for supplying capital, our policies with respect to land reform, and our military assistance in ways which will encourage the necessary attitudes.

The nations in category C have achieved many of the technical conditions for takeoff and they are more or less firmly committed to an accelerated drive to modernization. The essential American and free world task in such countries—India, Brazil, the Philippines, Taiwan—is to assure that foreign exchange is not a bottleneck during the takeoff period.

Since India is not only the largest free world nation, containing some 40 percent of the total population of the underdeveloped areas, but is also the foremost example of a non-Communist state engaged in the takeoff process, Indian needs will bulk large in American lending policy. First, the free world nations must provide sufficient aid for India so that a shortage of foreign exchange does not prevent further growth; over the third 5-year-plan period, something above $1 billion a year in loans and grants must be provided from all sources. Second, American food and fiber surpluses should be used on a large scale both to cover the possibility of bad harvests and to give the Indian Government confidence to increase employment and domestic purchasing power without excessive worry about the inflationary consequences of such a program. Third, the United States should use its influence to the maximum to assist the Indians in mounting an accelerated program designed to diffuse high productivity agricultural techniques to the peasantry. Fourth, the free world assistance program to India during its takeoff should be designed so as to encourage India to take advantage of the energies latent in the private sector while fully supporting essential public enterprises. Lastly, ways must be found to meet the foreign exchange requirements of small-scale enterprise, which has exhibited surprisingly vigorous growth in recent years.

In the coming decade India may experience either a decisive break-through into modernization under democratic auspices and in association with the West or a critical failure which would damage, perhaps irretrievably, the prestige of democracy in India, if not in all of Asia. Given the relatively modest sums involved for both the United States and Western Europe and the enormous common costs of failure, this is an occasion for boldness and generosity.

Dorothy Lee

THE CULTURAL CURTAIN*

Programs of induced change are being initiated with increasing concern for the requirements of organization and planning, as well as for the technical training and selection of workers. Yet, throughout the years, their success or failure cannot be explained solely on the basis of these factors. Proposed changes which were clearly necessary and beneficial have often been summarily rejected by the people concerned, or have met with apathy and indifference. Programs have been launched successfully only to fail in the long run. Worse than this, the change itself has sometimes been readily accepted, but has brought unpremeditated results in its wake—destruction of the fabric of the society, loss of the meaning of life, and other unimaginable hardships. . . .

In such cases, the factor which has been overlooked, the factor which has made for difficulties of communication, is that of culture. Perhaps a proposed program runs completely counter to the religious tenets of a people. For example, it is reported that the Girl Scout manuals which were recently sent from the United States to a school in Indonesia were thrown away unused. The people to whom they were sent are Mohammedans, and they explained that as Moslems they found it abominable to have human beings equated with bears, beavers, and wolves, and to have girls urged to name themselves after animals. Sometimes no account is taken of social groupings. In this country, when Navahos were resettled on irrigated farmland, the arrangements went counter to their established groupings. They were established as individual families of parents and children, far from their relatives, despite the fact that they had been used to working their fields co-operatively in larger units, along extended

* Dorothy Lee, "The Cultural Curtain," *The Annals of The American Academy of Political and Social Science,* Vol. 323, May 1959, pp. 121–128. Reprinted by permission.

Dr. Lee has been on the staff of the Merrill-Palmer School since 1953. She taught anthropology at Vassar College from 1940 to 1953.

kinship lines. For these and similar reasons, the project did not prosper.

Most of all, we have often been unaware of the importance of the totality of a way of life. Students of culture are coming to realize that any practice or concept is linked to, as well as supports, many other practices and beliefs which eventually constitute the whole cultural framework; and that it has a special function within this framework. A person from a different culture often finds it difficult to discover or recognize this function; it is easy to see the trait as merely a queer custom. So, in our ignorance, we have tampered with one trait, not realizing that thus we were actually tampering with the whole.

Until recent years, changes were introduced, whenever they appeared obviously necessary or desirable, by traders, missionaries, or colonial governments in a piecemeal or even haphazard fashion. Though some such changes were introduced through the rapacity of traders or the exigencies of colonization, many stemmed from humanitarian motives, and were clearly indicated at least in the eyes of the Western agents.

It was clear to workers in South Africa, for example, that when infants nursed until they were two or more they exhausted their mothers physically and interfered with their work. Bottle feeding was introduced. Soon the mothers were even more exhausted, because they began to bear children every year. The taboo on intercourse during lactation no longer worked to space their children at intervals of three or four years. Again, it was clear to colonial governments and missionaries that infanticide and head-hunting, as well as the poor sanitation attending childbirth, were evils to be eradicated. Yet they never considered the results of such an eradication and were unprepared for the enormous increase in population in areas where population and food resources had previously been kept in balance. The consequence of their humanitarianism was overcrowding, malnutrition, and a sentence of emigration for people deeply attached to their homeland.

What went wrong here? The change had obviously been effectively introduced; it had been accepted by the people, or at any rate it had not been rejected. In fact, it had probably been welcomed. But this was not enough. The agents literally had not known what they were doing. They knew nothing of the cultural framework of the society with which they were dealing, and they tampered in ignorance with one of its sustaining parts. They knew nothing of the ecological relationship with the habitat which the culture helped maintain. This is not to say that, knowing this, they would have refrained from acting to save lives and abolish fear; but rather that they would have taken account of the function of the traits which they were changing or displacing, and then would have acted accordingly. . . .

To balance such unfortunate occurrences, we have many cases where change has been introduced with happy results, by agents who have had knowledge and understanding of the culture of the group with which they were dealing. Such is the work of the British Health Centre in Natal, which was established in 1940. These workers studied the ramifications of the entire culture, as well as the history of the Zulu group with which they were dealing. According to the report written in 1953, the comprehensive health program they proposed to institute suggested the introduction of change in three areas: in food habits, in the treatment of tuberculosis, and in practices which led to erosion. The first of these was definitely successful; the second only partially so; and the third was not attempted because investigation showed that if it could have been effectively introduced, it would have taken away from the people practices which were of great value to them.

The first undertaking was of a kind which is usually very difficult to carry out. The effect of malnutrition is not directly demonstrable; it is difficult to explain to people why a change in their food habits is necessary. Why interfere with them? What harm do they do? An attempt to change them usually meets, in addition, obstacles stemming from the emotional and symbolic significance of food. Among the Zulu, general resistance stemmed from their close tie to their ancestors. This, they said, had been the diet of the ancestors; it was the sanctioned diet. The ancestors, who were concerned with the daily affairs of the people, would be angered if the diet was changed. The team, however, armed with history, showed the people that the diet had in fact been richer and more varied in ancestral times, before the coming of the Whites.

There were additional difficulties when it came to the attempt to increase the consumption of milk, particularly among women of childbearing age. These came from a taboo protecting the cattle, which represented perhaps the greatest value to the Zulu. Women, in any reproductive capacity, while pregnant or lactating or lochial or while menstruating, were dangerous to the cattle, and should therefore avoid all contact with them; to consume milk was to come into such contact. To prevent all possibility of error, girls after pubescence were forbidden milk at all times. In addition, people could consume the milk only of the right cattle; these were the cattle owned by the head of the household to whose kinship group they belonged. This meant that, if they were away from the appropriate cattle, they could not include milk in their diet.

The team of workers recognized and respected the strength of the religious beliefs that supported these customs. They did not attempt to tamper with them. Instead, they hit upon a simple solution. They introduced powdered milk. Though the nature of this was known, it could not be associated, either symbolically or emotionally, with cattle.

In their attack on tuberculosis, the team of workers again met resistance. For people who found deep satisfaction in eating out of a common dish and living in close contact with friends and relatives, the concept of isolation was thoroughly unacceptable. To go to a hospital a hundred miles away, to be long ill away from all loved ones, to face the probability of dying away from home and the protection of the ancestors, was a terrifying prospect. Besides, the Zulu had no reason to doubt the efficacy of their curative methods. These stemmed logically from a set of premises which the Western workers could not prove to be wrong, although they knew them to be so. Through a consistent effort at understanding and responding to the cultural roots of the resistance, the workers finally did make some progress in changing methods of treatment. However, they had to abandon their plan to enlighten the people as to how tuberculosis was spread because, to these Zulu, any disease associated with labored breathing or pains in the chest was due to the machinations of an ill-wisher. Therefore to tell a father that his daughter had brought tuberculosis into the family would be to accuse her of being an evil witch. If they had insisted on keeping their Western plan of a "good" attack on tuberculosis, they would have endangered their entire tuberculosis program.

When the team came to consider the question of erosion, they found out that the pressing need was for the reduction of the herds of cattle. Yet the meaning of life for the Zulu man was bound up with the lives of his cattle. He saw in them the link between himself and his ancestors. With them he validated his marriages, and created and strengthened all affinal bonds. He knew and loved each one of his cattle, each detail of their personal appearance and each idiosyncrasy. To ask these people to reduce their herds would have been tantamount to asking them to destroy a loved family member or the strength of their social bonds, or to give up an important part of the value of life. So the team abandoned this part of their program, at least temporarily; they wisely decided to refrain from destroying value. In fact, the people's values would probably have defeated all attempts to institute voluntary reduction of herds. . . .

Many of us in Western society assume that progress is good and is naturally recognized as such by all. But in many other societies progress is not a goal, nor a desired good beckoning to action. We can possibly introduce change to these people as the eradication of ills, but not in the name of the "bigger and better," or even of the new. We have assumed that, if people had a higher income, they would spend it in the interests of what is in our own view a higher standard of living; we have found to our confusion that this is not necessarily so. From the Middle East, from the Far East, from Africa come reports that when the price of agricultural products or the level of wages is raised, people work less since they can maintain their known and tried way of life with less effort. We have learned that people have to be helped to recognize their wants and aspirations. And beyond this, we have helped them to see that it is possible to achieve what they want, to translate their dreams into plans. Occasionally, we have interfered to the extent of creating aspirations where none seemed to be present.

The obstacles presented by cultural differences have often been overcome. Many cases such as that of the comprehensive health program among the Zulu, carefully and reflectively undertaken, have been reported in recent years. Planned change is also being brought about by people working in their own countries who know the culture they are dealing with, its symbolism, its values, and its pattern of perception. So Ibn Saud quoted the Koran over the radio and the telephone when inaugurating these systems, Chinese Communists reinterpreted Confucianism in support of Communist ethics, and Japanese architects used their understanding of native notions of space and family relations to achieve the miracle of housing families in a net space of 380 feet square. In this country, we are studying profitably the introduction of these changes. To this, and to our increasing awareness of the factor of culture in experience and communication, we can add what we already have as our heritage—an understanding of the technology we are introducing within the cultural framework of which it is a part.

Gunnar Myrdal

NOT ONLY AID*

. . . .

If the rich nations made a determined move to shape their general economic policies more in the interests of the underdeveloped ones, this would be of a vastly greater consequence to the economic development of those countries than any aid which they could ever hope to get. If instead the rich countries persist in carrying on their ordinary business with the underdeveloped world on the principle of narrow economic nationalism and adjustments to the wishes of short-sighted vested interests at home, even generous aid becomes nothing more than a palliative.

One explanation of this emphasis on aid is undoubtedly charitable feelings. There is in America a basic sentiment of generosity toward those who are less fortunate—a sympathy for, and solidarity with, the underdog. This has its roots in America's singular material and spiritual history. I believe that important elements of American behavior in external and internal relations would be misunderstood if this trait were not recognized. The concern for the down-and-out is, unfortunately, not so strong among the other nations in that one-sixth of the non-Soviet world which is well off and economically progressive. A measure of the practical consequence of this is the fact that, directly and indirectly, the United States is probably paying close to ninety per cent of the capital grant aid and technical assistance in various forms which are actually given at present to the poorer majority of mankind. But this same generous America often turns out to be niggardly and selfish in its ordinary commercial and financial policies and practices, as in various degrees do all the other rich countries.

---

* Gunnar Myrdal, *Beyond The Welfare State.* Copyright 1960 by Yale University Press, pp. 239–241.

Gunnar Myrdal, the distinguished Swedish economist, has been Professor of Political Economy and Financial Science at the University of Stockholm since 1933 and now serves as Research Director for Asian Study, The Twentieth Century Fund.

These attitudes and behavior patterns are reflected in the public discussion in America of the country's international responsibilities. Good and public-minded Americans in the great liberal tradition, whether they happen to vote the Republican or Democratic ticket, are continuously pleading for more generous American aid to the underdeveloped countries, and for aid without political strings. These Americans persistently put forward the perfectly valid argument that the basic justification for aid is simply that the peoples of underdeveloped countries become healthier, happier, and economically more progressive, and that they thus will have a better chance to become freer and stronger as independent nations. Yet, in contrast to the energy and courage displayed in holding up to the nation its duty to give more aid to underdeveloped countries, and to give it more wisely, stands the shy halfheartedness—even among the nation's intellectual leaders—in facing the need to break down the heavy barriers of nationalistic policy measures which dominate America's foreign economic relations. The situation is not very different in the other rich countries, except that they are less willing to give aid, though they might now be becoming more willing.

To understand this disparity of attitudes, we have again to focus our attention on the fact that the Western countries are all democratic Welfare States. They are rich, and even considerably larger amounts of aid would not substantially lower their own living levels. The idea of assuring the needy an allowance in cash has an immediate appeal, and it fits into the type of thinking which is basic to their own national social security schemes. But even more important is the fact that aid in cash does not upset the complex system of public policies, which form the substance of the national Welfare State, and does not adversely affect any special interest group. Basically, the greater willingness to give cash aid than to change commercial and other policies is another international implication of the Welfare State in the rich countries. . . .

In a better integrated world the rich countries should, in the common interest, largely abstain from putting up barriers to foreign trade and, in particular, should open their markets to the underdeveloped countries. . . . As industrial development gets under way in underdeveloped countries, outlets should be given them for industrial exports as well. At the same time, it should be admitted that the underdeveloped countries cannot themselves follow this principle without compromising, perhaps seriously, their ambitions for planning economic development. The rich countries, and in particular the United States, have often acted upon the opposite "double standard morality," insisting upon following a protectionist policy on their own behalf, while preaching the virtues of free trade to the underdeveloped world.

Their commercial policies are to an astonishing extent dominated not only by such special group interests as can be understood to have a considerable weight—like, for instance, those of the textile industry and its workers in Great Britain and elsewhere . . . —but also by interests which are clearly petty. That the oil industry can move the State Department in Washington around is remarkable, but not surprising. But that, in an underdeveloped country in South East Asia, the American organization for technical assistance does not dare to help the country develop its fishing industry, because it would upset a few American exporters of canned fish, is perhaps shocking to the uninitiated. . . .

EPILOGUE

Cornelius P. Cotter

A few decades ago social philosophers were preoccupied with defining the good society and charting courses to it. Today we find them speculating upon the survival prospects of Western Civilization and, indeed, of human society. A few decades ago we looked exuberantly toward government as an agency for achieving the good life for all Americans and for the rest of the world, toward which we cast an avuncular eye. Today we scrutinize the evidence, accumulated by successive twentieth-century dictatorships, that government can also be employed as a terrifyingly effective machine for rendering the life of man "nasty, brutish, and short"—to employ the words used by Thomas Hobbes to describe life in a hypothetical state of nature.

The gap between the utopian novels of Edward Bellamy and H. G. Wells, and the foreboding expositions of the society of the future which are to be found in Huxley's *Brave New World* and Orwell's *1984*, is a measure of the progressive disenchantment which man has experienced during the first five decades of the century. Bellamy, it may be recalled, like H. G. Wells, described a society of the future in which man was master of his natural environment, of his technology, and of his passions. Contrast this to the uses to which science, technology, and education are put in the societies described by Huxley and Orwell, not to mention the more popular current novels which open or close with melodramatic depictions of scattered population remnants struggling to escape the inevitable aftereffects of hydrogen-bombing.

Pessimists say we have failed to exploit our opportunities to press science and technology into the service of man and have instead hinged them to the service of war, mass hatred, and idle foppery. The symbols of twentieth-century achievements, we are told, will be the mushroom cloud and the tailfin. While children go hungry abroad—and indeed in some depressed areas at home—surplus agricultural commodities spill out of gorged storage bins and burden ships in the reserve fleet to their Plimsoll lines. While medical research suffers shortages of funds, a sybaritic people lavish funds upon the pursuit of momentary pleasure. While our religious heritage and the objective facts of life would seem to dictate that we should seek harmony and understanding with others, we crudely indulge prejudices at home and inefficiently prepare for war abroad. This is an age, we are told, which could tempt Jeremiah back to life.

Regardless of the accuracy of these perceptions, it can with certainty be said that the twentieth century is a hyperbolic age. In it we have had not war but world war, not poverty but mass unemployment, not economic setbacks but great depressions. It is also an age in which we aspire to full employment, to the eradication of disease, to the prolongation of human life, to the exploration of space, to the defeat of poverty and hunger, and to the proliferation of education and the opportunities associated with it. Radical advances have been made in the field of medicine and in the enlargement of educational opportunities in this nation and in the world at large. A fantastic rise in the standard of living and in the material aspirations of human beings has occurred. The development of mass communications and transportation has bound the world together more tightly than in any previous human era. The expansion of leisure time provides the opportunity, if not the certainty, of human fulfillment of a kind available only to the select few in earlier societies.

Yet a great difference exists between the possibilities for further perfecting ourselves and our society, and the realities of the world in which we live. No amount of scientific and technological discoveries can relieve us of the burden of thinking through certain basic moral and ethical questions in the same manner that mankind has had to think and rethink them in past generations. We must know why we wish leisure time. We must examine the consistency between varying alternative uses of leisure time and the maintenance of a way of government which depends in large part upon voluntary leisure-time public service. We must determine why we wish to be free, and, perhaps even more important, we must decide how much freedom we are willing to surrender to government in order to preserve our independence from the domination of other nations. Nearly a century ago, faced with the problem of measuring freedom against threats to national survival, a Supreme Court justice said, "It could well be said that a country preserved at the sacrifice of all the cardinal principles of liberty is not worth the cost of preservation." Today the requirements of national survival encourage a flexible approach to these cardinal principles. Yet, beyond a certain point, flexibility of principle becomes a denial of principle, and the pressures and dangers of the sixties will provide a crucial test of our ability to adhere to the democratic political theory which we profess.

INDEX OF AUTHORS